More praise for *The Search for the Panchen Lama*

"[An] informative new book on China's repression of Tibet. . . . A compelling and disturbing account of a little-understood continuing political struggle, one that pits the vast material advantage of China over the moral and spiritual authority of the Dalai Lama. When Ms. Hilton comes to the latest battle over the Panchen Lama, her narrative has the grip of a political thriller. . . . [This] valuable account serves the purpose not of sanctifying the Tibetans but of telling the truth at a time when the might of China has gone into an effort to falsify it."—Richard Bernstein, *New York Times*

"A superb account of the Panchen Lama's selection and kidnapping."
—Jonathan Mirsky, *New York Review of Books*

"Invaluable insights into the history and religious traditions of Tibet. Westerners know little about the Panchen Lama, the Dalai Lama's counterpart, a gap Hilton adroitly fills with her groundbreaking account of the roles the two highest lamas played in Tibet in the past and how the Panchen Lama came to be a pawn of the Chinese. . . . Hilton's exacting and compassionate exposé will safeguard what is known of the truth."
—*Booklist*, starred review

"Brimming with political intrigue, [the book] is colored with amusing anecdotes about the oddities of Tibetan life and with the poignancy of a people whose land has been torn apart. . . . Irrespective of its larger implications, *The Search for the Panchen Lama* is a great story."
—Seth Faison, *Los Angeles Times Book Review*

"Hilton excels as a storyteller. . . . [The] book will serve as an excellent guidebook for Western readers to understand the Tibet that, for so long, has been reduced to what a reporter called 'caricatural simplicities by Hollywood.' "
—Wen Huang, *Chicago Tribune*

"Excellent and artfully written. . . . [Hilton's] wonderfully detailed writing illustrates the spiritual and political contours of these events. . . . [She] reports the story of the quest with great skill."
—*Publishers Weekly*, starred review

P9-DFS-315

From the British reviews:

"A fantastic adventure story and intrigue. . . . If you want a crash course in Tibetan history and affairs in addition to a rattling good story, this is the book."   —*The Spectator*

"Excellent . . . a cool and intelligent explanation of the political intricacies surrounding the Panchen Lama that finds a compelling climax in the search for the tenth Panchen Lama's reincarnation."   —*The Observer*

"The story of the intrigues through which both the Tibetans and the Chinese sought to influence this choice is enthralling. Hilton's skill and careful research give an authoritative account of an unfolding tragedy."
                                        —*Times Literary Supplement*

"It is unlikely that Ms. Hilton's book can be bettered. It is meticulously researched, and written with a strong eye for humour." —*The Economist*

"Hilton tells this intriguing and fateful story, vital to the destiny of Tibet, without false sentiment. She thus makes her case—the case of anyone who opposes what a brutal Communist regime has done to Tibet—all the more damning."   —*Sunday Telegraph*

✤

The Search for the
Panchen Lama

ISABEL HILTON

✤

W. W. NORTON & COMPANY

New York • London

Copyright © 1999 by Isabel Hilton
First American edition 2000
First published as a Norton paperback 2001

All rights reserved
Printed in the United States of America

For information about permission to reproduce selections from this book, write to
Permissions, W. W. Norton & Company, Inc., 500 Fifth Avenue, New York, NY 10110

The text of this book is composed in 11.5/14.5 Monotype Sabon
Manufacturing by Haddon Craftsmen, Inc.

Library of Congress Cataloging-in-Publication Data
Hilton, Isabel.
The search for the Panchen Lama / Isabel Hilton.—1st American ed.
p. cm.
Includes bibliographical references and index.
ISBN 0-393-04969-8
1. Rgyal-Mtshan-nor-bu, Panchen Lama XI, 1990 2. Bstan-'dzin-rgya-mtshao,
Dalai Lama XIV, 1935– 3. Panchen lamas—Biography. 4. Buddhism and politics—
China—Tibet.

BQ7945.R597 S47 2000
294.3'923'092—dc21
[B]   00-028016
ISBN 0-393-32167-3 pbk.

W. W. Norton & Company, Inc., 500 Fifth Avenue, New York, N.Y. 10110
www.wwnorton.com

W. W. Norton & Company Ltd., Castle House, 75/76 Wells Street, London W1T 3QT

1 2 3 4 5 6 7 8 9 0

To the political prisoners of Tibet

Contents

�

List of Illustrations

✳

PICTURE ACKNOWLEDGEMENTS

Grateful acknowledgement is made to the following for permission
to reproduce black and white photographs:

No. 1: Virginia Crompton; no. 2: © Sarah Lock/Tibet Images; nos.
3, 4, 5, 6, 7, 8, 9, 10, 12, 13, 15: Department of Information and
International Relations, Dharamsala; no. 11: © CORBIS/Abbie
Enock, Travel Ink; nos. 14, 16, 20, 21: Isabel Hilton; nos. 17, 19:
Tibet Information Network; no. 18: © Stone Routes/Tibet Images

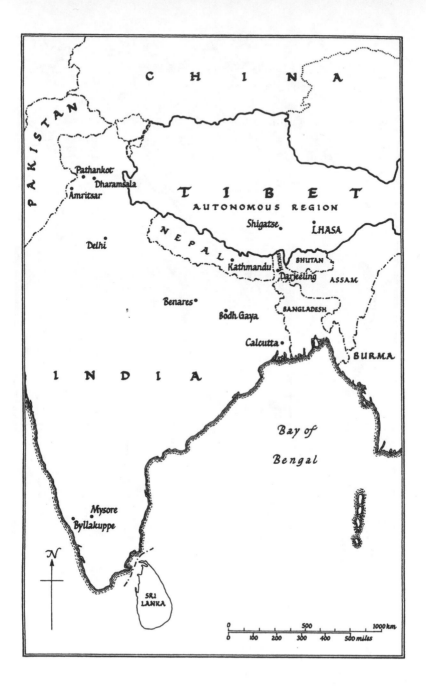

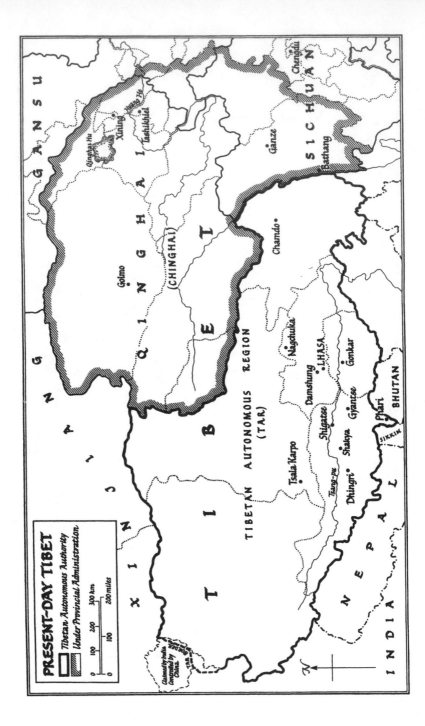

PRESENT-DAY TIBET

☐ Tibetan Autonomous Authority
▨ Under Provincial Administration

0 100 200 300 km.
0   100   200 miles

GANSU

QINGHAI

Qinghai Hu

Xining

Tsaring Tso

Tashilobi

(CHINGHAI)

Golmo

XINJIANG

SICHUAN

Chengdu

Ganze

Bathang

Chamdo •

TIBET

TIBETAN AUTONOMOUS REGION (T.A.R.)

Naghuka •

Damshung

Tsala Karpo •

Shigatse

LHASA •

Gomkar

Gjantse

Shakya •

Phari

Dhingri •

Tsang-Pw

SIKKIM

BHUTAN

NEPAL

INDIA

Claimed by India
Controlled by China

Acknowledgements

✢

There are many people who have made substantial contributions to this book, through their encouragement and support, advice and information. The project would not have got under way without the enthusiasm and encouragement of Anne McDermid, then of Curtis Brown, and Clare Alexander, then of Viking Penguin, both of whom were quick to see the point and eager to see it done. Michael Wills, then of Juniper Films, staked much of his time and money to back a long and difficult documentary project on the same subject. I am grateful to him and to many of his former staff at Juniper, in particular Charlotte More-Gordon.

Without the co-operation of His Holiness, the Dalai Lama, of course, the story could not have been told at all. His Holiness was patient and accommodating and submitted uncomplainingly, even at what were sometimes difficult and delicate moments, to repeated interrogations on his actions and motives, reactions and predictions. Such access to his side of the story was a privilege for the author, for which I am more than grateful. The staff in the private office in Dharamsala, notably Tsering Tashi and Tenzin Geyche, were unstinting with their time and assistance. Not only did they squeeze spaces out of the Dalai Lama's diary where there were none, but they helped with contacts, advice and expertise. To both of them I owe a large debt.

Without the assistance of such accomplished Tibetan interpreters as Tendar-la, of the Department of Information and Foreign Relations, who not only translated but was always ready with new suggestions and advice, many of the interviews that form the raw material of this account would have been impossible. I am grateful to him, and to the department for lending me his services.

In Dharamsala, too, I was lucky to have the assistance of Francisca van Holthoon, who helped with language and advice, and of Jane Perkins, whose enthusiasm for Tibet and knowledge of the workings of the exile community were invaluable. I am grateful, too, to the founders of the Amnye Machen Institute, Jamyang Norbu, Tashi Tsering and Lhasang Tsering, for their insight and analysis.

Sonam Topgyal, now first minister in the exile government, gave generously of his time, as did Amchok Rinpoche, Khamtroul Rinpoche and the medium of the state oracle. All three offered patient explanations of procedures that were, to me, esoteric.

What began as a chance remark over a dinner table in India turned into many long journeys. In the course of those trips, I shared many unforgettable moments with some of the protagonists of this story. I remember with particular affection and gratitude the open and welcoming monks of Tashilhunpo monastery in southern India and the generosity of spirit they showed towards this stranger.

I am also greatly indebted to Jasper Becker, of the *South China Morning Post* in Beijing, who opened up many paths for others to follow, both for his hospitality and for his valuable professional advice. In Delhi, Jan and Tim McGirk's warm welcome and kind hospitality when I fetched up, with embarrassing frequency, on their doorstep was invariably a source of delight.

Professor Jamphel Gyatso, of the Academy of Social Science in Beijing, whose knowledge of the life and work of the tenth Panchen Lama is unparalleled, was unfailingly courteous and helpful, as were others in the Institute of Tibetology in Beijing. Christine Chu gave me many insights into Tibetan religious life and practice. In Hong Kong, I am particularly grateful to Nancy Nash, not only for helping me but for making me laugh as much as she did. There are many scholars and travellers without whose legacy my own understanding of the many issues that I encountered on this journey could not have grown – the work of John Snelling, Charles Bell, Hugh Richardson and C. R. Bawden are essential to anyone setting out. But I could not have grasped the complexities of contemporary Tibet without the advice and assistance of Robbie Barnett, then of the Tibet Information Network, whose experience and knowledge of Tibet is matched only by his liberality with both. Without his generous help, this project would have been infinitely more difficult and my debt to him is more than I can repay.

Both Antony Harwood, of Gillon Aitken Associates and Andrew Kidd of Viking Penguin inherited this book from predecessors.

They took up their respective burdens gracefully and have carried them with patience and consideration. I would like to thank Andrew Kidd for his close and expert attention to the text and for the many improvements to it that he effected. Those flaws that remain are my own.

Neal, Alexander and Iona Ascherson have all suffered – first by my frequent absences and then by the neglect that goes with chewed pencils and torn-up pages. Despite these abuses, they have been uncomplaining and kind to me throughout.

Finally, there are others, especially in Tibet, whom I cannot thank by name, though they gave me invaluable assistance at great risk to themselves. Without their courage, parts of this story would not have taken place, let alone been told. I will always be grateful, not only for what they entrusted to me, but for the example they gave of devotion to the truth and of determination to defend it.

Chapter One

✲

Choekyi Gyaltsen, more widely known as the tenth incarnation of the Panchen Lama, died on a freezing night in January 1989 in his own monastery of Tashilhunpo, in Tibet. The death, when it came, was curiously unexpected for those who loved him. He had been taken for dead before, during the long dark years of imprisonment, but then he had returned, reborn almost, and this sudden, second death seemed the more cruel for being the death of hopes revived.

This far-away event did not go entirely unnoticed in the West: it made the news on British television, a ninety-second death notice tucked away in the segment to which obscure foreign events are confined. The newspapers gave it some attention, too: judicious obituaries described how the tenth Panchen Lama had stayed behind in Tibet when the Dalai Lama had fled, thirty years before, and recorded his early collaboration with the Chinese. They told of his redemption from the shame of that collaboration through his official disgrace in the Cultural Revolution and his return, in the final decade of his life, as a public figure and occasional critic of the regime. Then events moved on. The death of the Panchen Lama slipped away into that undifferentiated fog of recent, curious but forgettable news items.

For me, too, it was an event that had passed, another landmark in the erosion of the old Tibet, a further small step towards the absorption of that singular land into the uniformity of China. It was not until five years later that the significance of the Panchen's death was to come home to me: in Tibetan Buddhism nobody simply dies – and especially not such a figure as the Panchen Lama, second only to the Dalai Lama in his religious status. Death in this belief system is merely a passage to another life. The tenth Panchen Lama was dead; the task, for his followers and co-believers, was to find the eleventh incarnation. At the time, early in 1989, I had no idea that this was to become an issue which, a few years later, would convulse the Tibetan world and absorb many of my own waking hours. It began, for me, the first time I met the Dalai Lama.

In 1994 I made the first of what were to be many journeys to Dharamsala in northern India, and home of the Tibetan government in exile. I was going to interview the Dalai Lama for a documentary film. With the director, Jonathan Lewis, I flew to Delhi, took a rattling overnight train to Pathankot, then a taxi for a further four and half hours, winding north along deep river valleys into the foothills of the Himalayas. It was February and bitterly cold.

This was my first encounter with Tibet in exile: as our taxi climbed the vertiginous, twisting roads that led to the hilltop on which Dharamsala perched, India seemed to fall away. The Indian men, women and children who had thronged the streets for most of the journey gave way to flocks of young Tibetan monks in maroon robes and old men in *chubas*, to old ladies in long skirts and striped aprons, walking slowly, feeding beads through their fingers as they said their rosaries. On a rock at a bend in the road 'Free Tibet' had been painted in English and Tibetan.

The muddy streets that form McLeod Ganj, the mountain village at the commercial heart of the exiled Tibetan community's home, were lined with shops selling Tibetan trinkets, souvenirs, jewellery, books and religious pictures. In the centre of the village there was a small temple with heavy wooden prayer wheels that creak and squeak as they are turned by the faithful, sending the devotions inscribed on them to heaven. Among the crowds on the streets there drifted groups of foreigners: backpackers, volunteers, tourists and the occasional Western Buddhist monks and nuns, lumpy and incongruous with their shaven heads, maroon robes and Doc Marten boots.

We stayed in a large and recently erected Indian hotel that clung tenuously to the side of the mountain. It had already acquired a weary air: the corridors looked as though they had been sprayed with light machine-gun fire, the bathrooms sprang a score of leaks whenever a tap was turned on, and the gloomy dining room offered an implausible range of dishes, supplied, as I later learned, from the grubby food stalls in the market.

The hotel's one indisputable asset was a wide balcony that hung over the valley. We sat in the brilliant winter sunshine and watched the light reflecting on the golden roofs of the compound that housed the main temple. Above it lay the Dalai Lama's residence, a modest enough building set in a luxuriant garden. Monkeys played around the hotel and clattered over the flat roof of the dining room as we ate. At night, the temperature plummeted and I shivered between grey sheets and thin, damp blankets.

The next day we paid a formal call on one of the Dalai Lama's private secretaries, Kelsang Gyaltsen, a sophisticated man in his early forties, fluent in English and German. He wanted to talk through our interview with his boss, arranged for the following day. 'His Holiness is very open,' he told us. 'You can ask him anything.' We enquired about protocol. There was none, he said.

In a way that was true. The Dalai Lama's life in exile, I discovered, is a curious *mélange* of archaic court ritual, modern security and impoverished informality. For his followers, he is a Buddha in human form, a religious figure who commands almost unquestioning devotion. It is the dream of devout Tibetans to see him at least once in their lifetime, and thousands have made the difficult and dangerous pilgrimage from inside Tibet.

He is also the latest, and perhaps the last, of the theocratic kings of Tibet, fourteenth in a line which began, in theory, with the first to be named as Dalai Lama, Sonam Gyatso, but in fact with the Great fifth Dalai Lama, who after being aided to victory in the Tibetan civil war of the seventeenth century by a Mongol prince, Gushri Khan, established the Gelugpa, his sect, as the ruling strand of Buddhism in Tibet. The present Dalai Lama still commands the court protocol due to a ruling theocrat: his immediate entourage approach him with lowered heads, their eyes cast down in the Presence. He is surrounded by security men, both Indian and Tibetan, who protect him from the bad or the mad. (It is not just in exile that the life of a dalai lama has become vulnerable: after the Great Fifth, six dalai lamas in succession died suspiciously early.)

But, unlike his predecessors, this Dalai Lama is also an international star, a role he has achieved through a combination of a bewitching personality, moral force and a willingness to accept the Western predilection for the exotic with good-humoured tolerance.

In exile, the Tibetans have re-created what they could of the life they valued. There are versions of the main monasteries; there is a government in exile that is headed by the Dalai Lama but is, at his insistence, elected, and supported by a voluntary tax on the community. A library in Dharamsala contains such manuscripts as have been saved, smuggled out or reprinted, schools continue to offer education in English and Tibetan to children from exile families and from families inside Tibet. There is a cultural troupe that preserves the songs and dances of the homeland and a propaganda department that collects and circulates information from inside Tibet. It appears, at first glance, a success story, a tribute to the resilience and deeply rooted culture of the Tibetans. But many contend that it is more fragile than it looks and depends, to a degree that worries many, on the charisma and force of will of the present Dalai Lama.

Two days after our arrival we drove the short distance to the palace compound to meet him. Once inside the heavily guarded gates we climbed the steep hill to the audience room, a long, low bungalow with deep verandas set out with pots of geraniums in bloom. We waited in a large anteroom, heated – barely – by a fat black pot-bellied stove whose smokestack described a crazy series of turns before it found its exit. The room was festooned with the souvenirs of public life: glass cases displayed the accumulation of tributes, keys to cities and small towns around the world, ceremonial certificates with peace institutes.

We were joined by a thin, spare, bespectacled man in his forties, wearing a brown *chuba*. Tenzin Geyche, another of the Dalai Lama's private secretaries, is descended from one of Tibet's old aristocratic families. He crossed to the stove and held out a hand tinged with blue. 'It's so cold,' he complained.

As I was to discover, Tenzin Geyche has worked so long with the Dalai Lama that he has developed an uncanny ability to ventriloquize: he sits, leaning forward, prompting respectfully as his boss searches for words in what he calls his 'broken English'.

'His Holiness is ready,' he said.

The audience room was large and decorated with vivid religious paintings. A door opened at the far end and the Dalai Lama appeared, walking briskly. 'You must be the BBC,' he said.

'And you must be the Dalai Lama,' replied Jonathan.

The Dalai Lama laughed as though it was the funniest thing he had ever heard. 'Yes,' he said. 'Yes, I am the Dalai Lama,' and he launched into another storm of chuckles.

He sat in an armchair and fixed me with an enquiring smile.

The Dalai Lama is not the easiest man to interview, though certainly one of the most charming. There are no restrictions on what can be asked, but there is no doubt who is in control and the answers can be elliptical. There are those in his community who believe that his famous laugh is his best weapon. 'Be careful,' I had been warned by one Tibetan intellectual. 'He uses that laugh when he doesn't want to say anything.'

I could never quite decide whether or not this was true. It is certainly an unanswerable laugh: the first signs of it are rarely absent – the corners of his mouth turn naturally upwards, the eyes are generally alive with good humour. It's as though the laugh is being contained, by force, but waiting for a moment's inattention to escape. When it does, it takes him over – it comes from the belly, his shoulders heave, his head goes back, the eyes narrow, and he rocks in his chair until it passes. It is a great full stop of a laugh, putting an end to any further pursuit of the line of enquiry, deflecting impertinence or hostility, changing the subject, disarming the questioner.

There is one matter about which he rarely laughs: on the subject of the Chinese occupation of Tibet one encounters a different Dalai Lama – the holy man turned statesman who is driven to secure a future for his country. He himself is both the key to that future and the obstacle. As long as he is alive he is the focus of the exiles' dream of return, a dream he says he shares. For Tibetans inside Tibet he is the memory of another life, one religious light that has not gone out and which has, miraculously, escaped the Chinese to become a symbol of freedom. So strong still is the allegiance he commands it is hardly imaginable that he could ever return to Tibet. When, in a brief period of thaw in relations in the late seventies and early eighties, the Dalai Lama sent three personal delegations to Tibet, the news of their arrival generated a wave of emotion so powerful they were mobbed by thousands of Tibetans desperate to see, hear and touch the people who represented the Dalai Lama. The Chinese were appalled.

The interview concluded, the attendants produced *khatas* (ceremonial white scarves), and photographs were taken. We said good-bye to the Dalai Lama, neither of us expecting to see him again, and left, delighted by the encounter with a man whose presence had proved more than equal to his reputation.

That evening we dined with Jane Perkins, an Englishwoman who had settled in Dharamsala more than ten years earlier, at the Hotel Tibet, the hub of social activity for passing Western trade. The hotel is the chief exhibition room for what the Dalai Lama's brother, Tenzin Choegyal, later described as the 'Shangri-La syndrome' – Westerners who are seeking answers to a variety of personal questions by means of the Tibetan cause. At one table three Tibetans listened politely as an American man loudly lectured them on the finer points of Buddhism; at another three middle-aged women exchanged accounts of their emotions on seeing the Dalai Lama at a public audience; in the bar a less spiritual group could be heard warming up on the hotel's vividly coloured cocktails.

Jane, Jonathan and I talked late into the evening about the Tibetan question. One issue that had convulsed at least part of the Tibetan community in the previous months and was still the cause of sporadic outbreaks of violence was a bitter dispute about recognition of the head of the Kagyupa sect of Tibetan Buddhism. Three hundred years before the Gelugpa gained the ascendancy, the Kagyupa had been the ruling sect. Their late leader, the sixteenth Karmapa, had fled Tibet and established himself in a monastery in exile in Sikkim. The sect had many Western followers and was rich and successful in exile, so when the sixteenth Karmapa died, it was, perhaps, inevitable that there should be a dispute about the identity of his reincarnation.

As the conversation turned to the continuing importance of reincarnate lamas, I asked Jane about the fate of the Panchen Lama.

'He died,' Jane reminded me, 'in 1989.'

'And his reincarnation?' I asked.

'He hasn't been found yet,' she said. It was five years, almost to the day, she pointed out, since the death of the Panchen Lama. Immediately I was full of curiosity. Who was looking for the reincarnation? Were the Chinese interested? What had happened to the practice of identifying important religious reincarnates after the Chinese occupation? Could the child be found in exile? Did the Panchen Lama still count or had the last incarnation's chequered history discredited the line? Jane answered as best she could: yes, it was an important issue, and yes, by now, under normal circumstances, the child would have been found. Everyone was concerned about it, she said, but whatever was happening was happening in secret.

Some reincarnates had been found in the exile community – some had even been non-Tibetan children – and some had been found in Tibet since the liberalization of the late seventies had restored a limited religious freedom and a cautious revival of traditional beliefs. A few had even been smuggled out: the latest boy, the little Nechung Rinpoche, had been brought out of Tibet only a few months previously and was living in Dharamsala. As we talked I became gripped by the idea of a search that had to surmount the daunting political barrier of Chinese hostility to the Dalai Lama and the formidable physical obstacle of the Himalayas to find a boy who would, in old Tibet, have grown up to be one of the most powerful figures in the land.

Over the next few days I asked everyone I met about the Panchen Lama. It was clear that the question of the Panchen Lama's reincarnation was one of the key problems facing the Dalai Lama's government, a matter of the keenest religious and political importance inside and outside Tibet. A great deal depended on its outcome. It was Tibetan tradition that the Panchen Lama and the Dalai Lama maintained a close spiritual relationship, the Panchen Lama as the reincarnation of Avalokiteshvara, the Buddha of Boundless Light, and the Dalai Lama as the earthly representation of the Chenrezig, the Buddha of Compassion. As the highest *bodhisattvas* in the Gelugpa sect, successive reincarnations had acted as tutor and disciple to each other, and after the death of one tradition held that the other would play a key role in identifying his reincarnation. In religious terms, then, the Dalai Lama had a responsibility to find the young reincarnation of the Panchen Lama, and when the time came, the child he identified would be expected to recognize the reincarnation of the Dalai Lama. On this simple fact hung the huge importance of the issue: in old Tibet the discovery of the reincarnation of the Dalai Lama was not only a religious matter – the boy would be brought up as an object of religious veneration, and also as king.

The Dalai Lama no longer served as Tibet's secular ruler, but his role as the continuing focus of Tibetan identity and culture was almost more crucial. In the Tibet of former times, with its vast religious establishment, the search for the Dalai Lama was often

riddled with political manœuvring; the candidates often died young
– poisoned, many believe, by those with an interest in perpetuating
the reigns of the regents who ruled until a Dalai Lama came of
age.

These periods of regency could be dangerous times for Tibet,
with competing interests vying for power and the lack of a single
political authority. But the death of one or even successive dalai
lamas had not constituted a threat to an entire culture: at the very
least, the powerful religious establishment would always ensure
that the search began for another. Today, such cohesion as the
exile community had maintained – and the most important shared
belief with Tibetans in Tibet – depended on the person of the Dalai
Lama. In exile, shorn of his temporal power, his symbolic value
had grown. If there were to be a successor to the Dalai Lama, then
the young Panchen Lama was a vital link in the chain that would
lead to the recognition of his reincarnation.

In the days that followed I discovered what I could about this
esoteric issue and the complexities of the religious and political
beliefs in which it was framed. It was the beginning of what was
to be a long, often frustrating journey into a world thick with
spirits and demons, with political intrigue and hidden history.

I had little idea, either, of the structures and beliefs of Tibetan
religion, or even what precisely was meant by reincarnation. I
spoke no Tibetan and found the names so difficult I had to write
them down, laboriously, before they slipped away. The story of
a human tragedy I could grasp: other people's tragedies are a
journalist's work. The politics and history of Tibet could be understood. But other people's religious beliefs were a challenge of a
different order, and one that had to be tackled. I decided to visit
the medium of the state oracle.

I found him in a small, corner room in the Nechung monastery.
He gave me his card. 'The Venerable Thupten Ngodub,' it read,
'Medium of the state oracle of Tibet'. There was a phone number,
too. Thupten Ngodub was a young monk with a face of almost
theatrical calm and a soft, deep voice. As well as being the medium
of the state oracle, he was celebrated as a cartoonist: his Mickey
Mouse was particularly famous. 'In order to avoid any misunder-
standing,' he said by way of prelude, 'I want to explain that at the
moment, in this conversation, I am just an ordinary human being.'

8

At other times Thupten Ngodub is the means by which the principal protector divinity of the Tibetan government, Pehar Gyalpo, communicates with the Dalai Lama. When the medium goes into a trance of possession, even the Dalai Lama listens. Thupten Ngodub confirmed that the oracle had been consulted over the reincarnation of the Panchen Lama, but precisely what the oracle had said, he was unable to tell me.

'I have no recollection of what has happened after I come out of a trance,' he said. 'The process of finding the Panchen Rinpoche has begun, but I am not sure what steps have been taken, though His Holiness has said that reincarnation has taken place. The Chinese are trying to find him, too, but the Chinese are not serious about this matter. They want to use it for their own benefit. It is our custom for the Dalai Lama to make the final decision.'

'But what if the Panchen Lama is reborn inside Tibet? How will the Dalai Lama find him and what will happen to him?' I asked.

'If the rebirth has taken place in Tibet,' said the medium, 'we would want him to be brought here. I believe that it won't take place in China because the Chinese tortured the last incarnation. High lamas have the ability to choose where to be reborn. That is my personal opinion, of course.'

I said goodbye to the medium and walked out into the golden light of the late afternoon. The sun was hanging low over the plains below and the red paint and gilt of the monastery's temple was glowing in the last moments of the day. A flock of parrots swooped noisily over my head and landed in a tree.

I walked slowly back through the compound, past the two-storey building that houses the offices of the government in exile. Small painted nameplates announced the offices of state: Ministry of Religion and Culture, Home Ministry, Security Office, the National Assembly.

It was a tiny, threadbare operation. The doors opened off a simple veranda, and inside the offices were cluttered and ill-equipped: it could have been any small business in the Third World. Opposite rose the more imposing building that houses the Kashag, the cabinet, and the meeting place of the national assembly. There was a trace of incense in the evening air and the sounds of daily life rose from the cramped living quarters that huddled against the hill below: pots and pans banging, voices, the cries of children and a thin fragment of music from a two-string violin. I could hear the tinny sound of Indian music coming from a loudspeaker in the Kotwali bazaar, two miles down the valley, and the lights of the Indian settlements had begun to twinkle yellow in the gathering dusk.

In Dharamsala it is easy to become immersed in this little Tibet, to forget the fragility of this community, perched on its hillside above the immense hubbub of India and backed against the formidable mountains that mask the ferocious power of the Chinese state beyond. In that twilight it seemed peaceful, but also pathetic – a tiny group of exiles, nursing fading memories of home and searching for one small boy in the vastness of a land they could visit only under the suspicious gaze of the conqueror. The Chinese had troops and an imposing security apparatus. They could control almost every aspect of religious and private life in Tibet. The exiles had dreams, protector deities and faith. It hardly seemed an equal contest.

As I sought further clues about the Panchen Lama, I began to learn more about this little community and the private tragedies and stresses that ran through it. Every week brings a trickle of new arrivals from Tibet, men, women and children who have crossed some of the world's highest mountain passes to reach their goal: to be near the Dalai Lama. They bring, on the whole, few skills and are a headache for a government in exile which has few funds of its own. The established exile community is not always friendly.

In the forty years since the exodus of 1959 new generations have grown up in India and, as always happens, each generation must define itself afresh. They grow up with the memories of their parents and grandparents, with the official ambition of the Tibetan exiles to reclaim their homeland. They are brought up to respect their traditions. But the Tibet of those traditions has gone for ever. The new generations speak a motley collection of languages – their native Tibetan, the English of their education, the Hindi of their home in exile. They are more Westernized than any previous generation; most have never seen Tibet and probably would find it hard to live there if they were given the opportunity.

The recent arrivals, on the other hand, have borne the brunt of the Chinese occupation. They are mostly poorly educated, speaking only Tibetan and perhaps rudimentary Chinese. Many can barely read or write. They have abandoned everything and risked their lives to get to India, animated by a desire to see the Dalai Lama and to put themselves at his service. But the truth is that they face a difficult life in exile.

On the last day of my visit the monks of several exile monasteries were holding a *puja*, a prayer ceremony for the long life of the Dalai Lama: he was entering his sixtieth year, which in the Tibetan reckoning is a time of danger. The large prayer hall, high up in the compound, was filled with monks, seated cross-legged in rows, heads shaven, tea bowls laid out in front of them. A throne set with cushions draped in yellow silk awaited the Dalai Lama. To one side of it, the dignitaries of the state and the church: several government ministers, the medium of the oracle and the abbots of various monasteries.

Outside, in the bright sunshine, the fragrance of the tall pines that clothe the slopes of the mountain mingled with the stronger smell of incense and the pungent scent of burning butter from the lamps in the hall. A powerful deep note from a pair of long horns sounded the arrival of the Dalai Lama, who came quickly up the steps, preceded, incongruously, by an Indian army officer carrying a sub-machine-gun.

The Dalai Lama grinned and hurried inside, slipping off his shoes to climb the dais, where he sat, beaming and swaying gently to and fro as the sonorous chanting of the monks filled the hall. Beyond the central hall a shabby group of pilgrims sat: their dark brown faces and worn clothes marked them as devout visitors from Tibet, people for whom, until now, the Dalai Lama had been a remote, if precious memory. For those who had stayed behind in Tibet, the most important figure in the Buddhist faith had been the Panchen Lama.

Over the previous few days everyone I had talked to had told me that the search for the Panchen Lama was a critical issue, but nobody could tell me much about the process now in train. There were rumours and theories, but it soon became clear that only the Dalai Lama had the authority and the knowledge to speak about it. If the story was to be followed, it could only be followed with his permission and co-operation. As the ceremony wore on, I watched him, rocking gently back and forth on his throne, sometimes chanting, sometimes apparently lost in his own thoughts. Would he agree to admit an outsider to this most sensitive of issues? The ceremony over, I left a letter with the private office and prepared to take the winding road back down from Dharamsala to the dust and noise of India. A few hours later, as I fended off a swarm of beggars and lepers on the grimy station platform at Pathankot, Dharamsala seemed like a dream.

Months went by as I waited in London for a response. From time to time I tried to telephone. Eventually, I wrote again, setting out why I felt it important that the story be told. Four months after my visit, word came back from India. The Dalai Lama had agreed. It was five and a half years since the death of the tenth Panchen Lama. It was time for his successor to be found.

Chapter Two

✡

Many Tibetan intellectuals feel that Westerners view their country as a kind of religious Disneyland, a place of pure spirit unsullied by greed or personal ambition and untainted by politics. Indeed, Tibet has proved a powerful myth in the Western imagination: it was difficult to access at a time when the West was expanding eastwards in the eighteenth and nineteenth centuries, and its remoteness bred this romantic – and inappropriate – idea, later known as Shangri-La. Lhasa became a trophy city for Western adventurers and Tibetan Buddhism a kind of spiritual playground for Western whimsy.

The reality, of course, is different. As in medieval Europe, much of the strength of religion in Tibet came from its close association not with some kind of idealistic notion of commonality but with power. The physical emblem of that power is the great brooding mass of the Potala Palace, built in the seventeenth century by the founder of the state authority of the Gelugpa sect, the Great Fifth Dalai Lama.

Even today, the Potala is a heart-stopping sight. I had my own first glimpse of it through the dirty windows of a rattling bus one freezing February afternoon in 1995. I was not in the best of humours. I had read the early travellers' tales of Tibet, the adventures of those men and women who had forced their way across high mountain passes and endured months of hardship to reach the holy city. I had found the modern route to Shangri-La in some ways more straightforward, but altogether less romantic.

Lhasa is still not the easiest place to get to, though the obstacles are no longer primarily geographical but political. There are two main approaches for the foreign traveller – one by air, through the Chinese city of Chengdu, a route easily strangled when the Chinese authorities want to keep out present-day intruders, and one by land, from the unprepossessing town of Golmud, in the Chinese province of Qinghai. That route, the Qinghai–Tibet highway, follows an old caravan trail down through Nagchu. It takes between thirty and fifty hours, provided the bus does not break down.

In the summer months there is also an air route from Nepal, available only to those who have had the foresight to obtain a visa in advance, since the Chinese embassy in Kathmandu declines to issue visas to individual travellers. It is also possible to travel by road from the Nepalese border through Shigatse, Tibet's second city, to the capital. But when I first visited Lhasa, it was winter. The flight from Kathmandu was not in operation, the road from Nepal was blocked by snow and the route through Nagchu extremely doubtful. That left the air bridge from Chengdu.

I could see no objection to the route, for I had long wanted to visit Chengdu. When I lived in China, in the early seventies, Chengdu, like most cities, was closed to foreigners. Stranded as I was then in Beijing, remote Sichuan, the most populous Chinese province in the far west of the country, had a certain romance. Like Lhasa, Chengdu was an inaccessible city of dreams. But when I finally landed there, in 1995, I found, to my disappointment, that it was disappearing fast. The city was in the grip of the redevelopment fever that had been consuming China since Deng Xiaoping's pronouncement, in 1979, that getting rich was within the new rules of Communism. Chengdu was a noisy building-site.

My hotel, picked at random from a guidebook, turned out to be a vast and elderly building that was being ripped apart and refurbished. Half transformed, it seemed to embody the distracted condition of China itself, scrambling to discard the past in the desperate rush to modernity and the prosperity it promised to bring. The foyer boasted a doorman in a scarlet tailcoat and an outsized top hat that rested, comically, on top of his ears, pushing them outwards in a parody of the Mad Hatter. Half the hotel was still furnished with the dirty maroon carpets and heavy leather armchairs, each sporting a stained antimacassar, which were the relics of old socialist chic. In the dusty, cavernous ballroom smartly dressed young prostitutes, decked out in miniskirts and bright make-up, whiled away the afternoons, waiting for customers. Raucous groups of young men in baggy suits occupied other tables, talking loudly into mobile telephones and steadily filling the large ashtrays and spittoons. They were the new money-making élite.

Elsewhere, teams of workmen were busy renovating, painting

over the dreary décor with five-star gloss. In the Bank of China exchange bureau on the ground floor, two lavishly made-up clerks cheated their customers with brazen insolence. When challenged, they affected astonished contempt that any hotel guest could be so small-minded as to count their money.

There was a new business centre, equipped with fax and telex machines, open twenty-four hours a day, but the gleaming machines were connected to the same creaking infrastructure that had frustrated communications for decades. The lines were unreliable and sending a fax could take hours. Outside, in the car park, a Lincoln Continental had settled on deflated tyres. It had once been black but now had taken on the colour of the city's dust. The doors were sealed with strips of paper on which was written 'Seized by order of the People's Court'. I asked the telex operator about the car one day. 'What car?' he said, gazing firmly past it.

In the dark recesses of the west wing of the hotel was a bureau of the state-run China International Travel Service. CITS held the key to onward travel to Tibet. The government of the People's Republic of China is unable to impose a separate visa requirement for Tibet because it claims Tibet as an integral part of China. Other methods, then, have to be devised to prevent foreigners from reaching Lhasa when their presence is deemed undesirable. The most common is to put extraordinary difficulties in the way of anyone who tries to buy a ticket for the flight to Lhasa.

The manager of the CITS office was a man in his thirties who sat smoking behind a dark brown counter, bare except for a very large Nescafé jar, now half full of tea leaves, which he topped up from time to time with water from a battered Thermos flask. He wore a loose suit and was treated with nervous respect by his two female assistants.

'Lhasa?' he said. 'No problem.' A week-long tour could be organized, but I would need not one but two guides, to be paid for in advance, and the daily programme of cultural sites and shopping would be determined before departure and could not be varied. He named a price which would have financed at least six weeks of normal travel.

Even as I declined I knew that, had I agreed, a ticket would have appeared, as if by magic, the next day. Since I *had* declined, the flights might remain 'full' for weeks. My only alternative would be the new breed of independent travel agents who cared little for official policy and would gladly, for a price, furnish a ticket. I also knew that such operators led a precarious life and were frequently raided by the security authorities, who were reluctant to see independent operators undermine their scope for extortion.

The manager of the CITS office rapidly lost interest when I declined the guides, the all-inclusive tours, the limousine service from the airport and Lhasa's most expensive hotel. I was too poor, I said. I just wanted an air ticket. He shrugged disdainfully. The flights, he said, were booked up, but if I cared to wait until a group was going, perhaps he could do something. He returned to his jar of cold tea and I stayed put.

I had nothing but time. I hoped that the irritation of my presence would eventually goad him into action. He ignored me for an hour, then, as his lunch break approached, he sighed theatrically and reached for the telephone.

'No limousine. She says she can't afford it,' he shouted into the phone.

I waited for what I thought must be the inevitable refusal. But on the other end, in Lhasa, it was decided, apparently, that for that low-season week at least, even a poor tourist was better than none at all. Permission was granted. The ticket would be available that afternoon for the following day's flight.

The next morning the airport was fog-bound. The corridors were thronged with stranded travellers who sat staring at the grey murk beyond the smeared windows. If it did not lift by noon, the flight would be cancelled. It did not lift. I returned, dispirited, to my drab hotel. The next day dawned equally foggy. As I waited at the airport that morning I noticed a young man with a large camera picking his way through the waiting passengers, who were seated on their assorted bundles like so many displaced persons. Carefully, he lowered himself to a squatting position and pointed his camera at me. I looked at him and raised my own camera at him. He lowered his lens and grinned, sheepishly. He was smartly dressed and, I realized, had no luggage.

Embarrassed, he crossed the corridor and knelt down beside me. 'I hope you don't mind,' he said. 'I work for the South-West Airlines in-flight magazine. Are you going to Lhasa? What is your name?'

In all my years of travelling in China, I had never seen an

in-flight magazine on any domestic flight. I stared at him. 'I don't understand,' I replied.

He shrugged and retreated. Ten minutes later, out of the corner of my eye, I noticed him again, once more trying to take my picture.

On the third day the airport reopened. Hardly daring to believe it, I boarded the flight for Lhasa. The plane took off and circled slowly towards the west. As we climbed the grey city fell away and we broke through the cloud cover to the brilliant blue above. We flew over billowing banks of cotton wool for nearly an hour, then the white mass began to be pierced by jagged snow-covered peaks – the mountains of Tibet. They sparkled in the luminous clarity of the air. I surveyed my fellow passengers: a handful of military men and several prosperous-looking Han Chinese. Three rows behind me, a Tibetan man stared silently out of the window. The flight was otherwise empty. There was, of course, no in-flight magazine, but there was an in-flight propaganda video. It showed brightly costumed ethnic minorities singing of the joys of belonging to the great Chinese family. My Tibetan travelling companion gazed at it, expressionlessly.

On descent I looked out for the city but saw nothing but a forbidding mountain landscape. The airport was three hours from the town. We disembarked to a freezing baggage hall. I walked slowly, conscious already that the thin air made every step an effort. A sick headache had set in, and by the time the luggage made its grudging appearance the dank cold had already begun to penetrate my layers of clothing. I picked out my rucksack. It was covered in a thick layer of what were unmistakably – and inexplicably – chicken droppings. Outside the airport a rickety bus was filling up with passengers. I handed my noxious luggage over to the driver and settled on to an unyielding seat. With a grinding of gears the bus lurched off. The sun was warm, but in the deep mauve shadows the cold was paralysing. We ground on in silence, along a route that at one point detoured through a huge cement works. On the outskirts of Lhasa my heart began to sink as we bowled along a wide street lined with the gimcrack buildings that were all too reminiscent of the Chinese cities inland. Was this the legendary capital of Tibet?

But then the Potala came into view. It seemed to grow from the living rock, its huge bulk appearing, by some architectural sleight of hand, to float above the city, its colours vivid in the thin clear air, its façade alive with the fluttering of the curtains that decorate its thousands of windows. It was architecture as theatre, an assertion of spiritual and temporal power, still managing to impose its authority on a city it once dominated but which was now despoiled by the symbols and tastes of another power.

The Potala was built by the Great Fifth Dalai Lama, the first of the Gelugpa hierarchs to assume secular power. His accession as king of Tibet in the seventeenth century had brought a measure of peace to a country riven for more than a hundred years by sectarian warfare. It marked the foundation of the Tibetan state in the form that was to persist until the Chinese invasion of 1950.

The Great Fifth's Tibet was one of the most inhospitable, inaccessible and spectacularly beautiful lands on earth. It spread across some eight hundred thousand square miles of terrain from present-day Sikkim and Bhutan, Nepal and India in the south to the deserts of Xinjiang, the home of the Uighurs and the Kazakhs, in the north. To the north-east, the people were scattered across the land the Tibetans call Amdo, now divided between the Chinese provinces of Qinghai and Gansu, and his influence went further still, into the great steppes of Mongolia. To the south-east, the people lived in the grasslands and lush valleys of Kham, now given to the Chinese provinces of Sichuan and Yunnan. Most of this vast territory lies above 15,000 feet. It includes the world's highest mountain – Chomolongma to the Tibetans, Mount Everest to Westerners – and is the source of all Asia's great rivers.

Tibet was well protected in every direction. To the south, the Himalayas formed an intimidating boundary, and to the west, the Pamirs divided Tibet from the peoples of Turkestan; to the north, the great Kunlun mountains and the dreadful wastes of the Taklamakan desert formed another barrier, and to the east, the mountain ranges of Amnye Machen protected Tibet from the predatory might of China. In the days of the Great Fifth, it was a sparsely populated land but not, for all that, a poverty-stricken one. Life was hard and often short in the thin air and savage climate but the country had riches of its own: the Chinese still call it *Xizang*, or Western treasure-house.

Despite the later myth of Shangri-La, Tibet was neither an isolated nor a peaceful country. From the steppes to the north two great military empires arose: that of the Mongolians, who in the thirteenth and fourteenth centuries were to conquer territories that stretched from China to distant Europe; and, in the seventeenth century, that of the Manchu, who achieved a moment of tribal unity that gave birth to another, less extensive conquest. Both were to shape the destiny of Tibet.

The Tibetans were a power themselves in the Central Asia of the eighth century, under their king, Trisong Detsen, who dominated Turkestan and Nepal and harried and attacked western China. In 763 he even sacked the great Tang dynasty capital, Chang-an. When her military might faded Tibet was to become another kind of power, an empire of religious and spiritual influence so formidable that in the eighteenth century the Manchu emperor of China felt it appropriate to step down from his throne to receive the visiting Great Fifth Dalai Lama in person.

The key to this ascendancy was Buddhism, a philosophy which had originally been elaborated in India by the young prince Gautama, more than two millennia before the Great Fifth Dalai Lama set his architects to work. It had gone through many evolutions since the prince first revealed his theory of the path to enlightenment in the park at Benares. From that first teaching to a group of sceptical ascetics it had grown and spread.

The first Buddhist missionaries arrived in China in the first century AD, travelling along the northern trade routes. The traces of their passage can be found in decorated shrines on a route from north-west India to Kizil, Kucha and Bazaklik, near Turfan, in Xinjiang to Dunhuang in Gansu. Under the Northern Wei dynasty (386–535) it became, for the first time, a mass faith. But it was in Tibet that Buddhism was to strike its deepest roots.

The faith made its first tentative appearance there in the fifth century but did not take a firm hold until two hundred years later, when a diplomatic marriage between a Tibetan warrior and a pious Chinese princess created the conditions for the first age of Buddhism in Tibet. The warrior was Srongtsen Gampo, who established overlordship of the other chieftains of central Tibet and went on to subdue Upper Burma. He was troublesome to western China, too, and the Tang emperor Taizong was forced to propitiate him with the gift of a princess of the imperial house.

Chinese poetry contains many laments penned by unfortunate

princesses condemned, for diplomatic reasons, to a miserable life among barbarians, dreaming in their bleak steppe tents of the cosmopolitan comforts of the capital. Princess Wen-Ch'eng, though, seems to have been made of sterner stuff. She arrived in Tibet with the essentials of her native civilization – silks and brocades, paper, writing brushes and musical instruments – packed in her luggage. She also brought her faith, and found that she shared her Buddhist beliefs with another of the king's wives, Princess Bhrikuti Devi, the daughter of the king of Nepal.[1] Between them, they converted the energetic young king.

Srongtsen Gampo was not a man to do things by halves. As with Napoleon in another age in Europe, he combined an enthusiasm for military affairs with a passion for civic organization: he introduced a criminal code and laid down moral precepts by which he expected his people to live. He chose Lhasa as his capital and, on the top of the highest hill, he began to build the structure that would be expanded by the fifth Dalai Lama a thousand years later to become the Potala Palace.

But it was Srongtsen Gampo's enthusiasm for propagating Buddhism that ensured him a permanent place among the Tibetan saints: he is still revered as an incarnation of Chenrezig, the Buddha of Compassion. He sent envoys to build chapels in northern China and invited monks from China, Nepal and India to come to Tibet to begin the work of translating the Buddhist scriptures into Tibetan.[2] He established the Buddhist priesthood and instructed his people: 'Return good for good. Do not fight with gentle people. Read the scriptures and understand them.'[3]

This first golden age of Buddhism was ended in the second half of the ninth century by the reign of Langdarma, who hated Buddhism and set about destroying it in the name of Tibet's native religion, Bon. In the three short years of his reign, Langdarma disbanded the monasteries, burned the scriptures and persecuted the monks until one pious monk, unable to endure any longer the destruction of his faith, stabbed Langdarma to death.

It was a well-planned assassination. The monk escaped by turning his cloak and riding his horse through the river, washing off the black dye with which he had disguised it. He spent the rest of his life in a cave, expiating the sin of taking a life. His crime earned him an honoured place in Tibetan Buddhist ritual – the Black Hat

Dance,[4] an annual celebration of the assassination. Langdarma was dead, but the damage was done, and Buddhism had to wait until the extraordinary rise of the Mongols for its next powerful patron.

In 1264 Kublai Khan, the grandson of Genghis, became the first emperor of the Mongol dynasty in China. He adopted Buddhism as his personal faith and favoured not the Chinese but the Tibetan form, with its elements of Tantrism and traces of Bon. His conversion was more than a personal or, for that matter, a spiritual decision: with Buddhism as his private faith, he also saw that it could be tactically useful in taming the troublesome Tibetans.

Genghis Khan had conquered Tibet, and the dynastic history records the assimilation of the Tibetan army under the command of the Mongolian prince Auluchi, but most of Tibet proper was beyond the direct control of the Yuan dynasty bureaucracy. Kublai Khan therefore tried to domesticate the Tibetans through religion. He invited Sakya Pandita of the Sakya monastery to the Mongolian court and, in 1270, offered control of Tibet to Sakya Pandita's nephew in an arrangement that confirmed Mongolian patronage of the Sakya sect.

When their powerful Mongol patrons fell in China, the Sakya sect was overthrown in Tibet by a secular king. They were to lose their spiritual predominance, too, and the challenge to it came from a monk named Lobsang Drakpa.

Lobsang Drakpa was born in 1357 at Tsongkha, the 'land of onions'; thus the name by which he is remembered – Tsongkhapa. He became a monk but grew disillusioned with the lax living of the Kagyupa and Sakyapa sects who, in Tsongkhapa's eyes, had become degenerate and unspiritual. His response was to found a new sect, the Gelugpa, the fourth major sect of Tibetan Buddhism and the one that was finally to predominate in the struggle for political power.

In 1392, when Tsongkhapa was thirty-six, he took his first thirteen disciples. He taught them his precepts of discipline, austerity, abstinence and celibacy and encouraged them to master the philosophical texts of Buddhism before they ventured into the esoteric mysteries. His disciples were well trained. They went on to found all the great monasteries that eventually became the backbone of the Gelugpa state.

Buddhism's erstwhile patrons, the Mongols, the brilliance of their Chinese empire shattered, had been driven north-eastwards and had fragmented into rival groups. A hundred years later another Mongol prince, Altan Khan (1543–83), was to play a part in Tibet's destiny.

Altan Khan was a western Mongol who was converted to Buddhism by two Buddhist lamas whom he had won as part of his booty after a battle. At the time Altan Khan was at the apogee of his power: he had neutralized his enemies, the Oirat Mongols, and established a relationship of respect, if not equality, with China. The Mongols had all but forgotten their ancestors' interest in Buddhism, but Altan Khan was receptive to new ideas. Three years after Altan Khan's conversion to Buddhism, his nephew, Setsen Khungtaiji, suggested to him that he could consolidate his spiritual destiny by inviting an eminent holy man to establish a 'special relationship' with him, much as the emperor Kublai had done centuries before with the lama Phagpa-lha.[5]

The monk he proposed was a Tibetan by the name of Sonam Gyatso, the son of a minor aristocrat in the Tibetan province of Ü who was a celebrated Buddhist teacher and the leader of Tsong-khapa's Gelugpa sect. In 1576 Altan Khan sent a mission to Tibet to invite Sonam Gyatso to Qinghai. The monk duly reached Qinghai in May 1578, after a seven-month journey from the Drepung monastery, near Lhasa.

The two men met in the Yanghua temple and sealed a pact that was to bring important benefits to each. Integral to their agreement was a central doctrine of Tibetan Buddhism, which supplied the key to legitimizing their respective religious and political powers. The doctrine was that of reincarnation.

In Western philosophical and religious traditions, the notion of reincarnation has retreated to the eccentric fringe. But the idea of successive lives has a long history and was, at one time, more widely espoused in European thought. Plato and Pythagoras both believed in it and spread the idea through their teachings. The Nestorians, part of a Neoplatonic revival in the fifth century, believed and taught it to Muhammad. The ancient Jewish sects, the Pharisees and the Sadducees, held that the spiritual powers of holy men had been honed through successive rebirths.[6] The Zoroastrians also believed in it, and Julius Caesar records it as a belief of the Celts: 'They wish to inculcate this as one of their leading tenets, that souls do not become extinct, but pass after death from one body to another, and they think that men by this tenet are in a great degree excited to valour, the fear of death being disregarded.'[7]

Most religions at some time paid attention or gave some credence to a concept that was to take such firm hold in Tibetan Buddhism: that sentient beings must return to earthly life many times, caught in a cycle of death and rebirth, until they reach a spiritual plane that releases them from the sufferings of the world.

In Eastern thought the belief in reincarnation remains both widespread and deeply held. Gautama's teachings, from which the beliefs of the Tibetan schools of Buddhism derived, began with the idea of the Brahma, the metaphysical absolute from which all things come and to which all return. In Hindu philosophy the true self of every human being is identical with Brahma and the goal of the spiritual quest is the revelation of that self. It is a long, hard road and demands many rebirths before an individual is freed from the cravings that bind him to the material world. In Buddhist belief all sentient beings, including animals and insects, are part of this cycle.

Most sentient beings are reborn into the world through their failure to overcome their attachment to it. But the rebirth in the world of a highly realized spiritual being is a voluntary act, an act of sacrifice undertaken to help others along the path to enlightenment. As successive generations developed and added to the teachings of the Buddha, there grew up in Tibet a practice that remains peculiar to the Tibetan schools: the search for and identification of reincarnated individuals.

The search has a spiritual justification. A highly realized being who is prepared to postpone nirvana to return to earth in the service of all sentient beings is clearly worth locating. But the importance of the doctrine in Tibetan society was, to put it no more strongly, highly reinforced by the development of Buddhism as a central social and political force. Monasteries – and the men who led them – held wealth and power. The selection and training of those men was more than a purely spiritual matter.

As the monastic network expanded rapidly in the tenth century, Tibet's monasteries became wealthy and powerful. The reputation of a monastery, and therefore the flow of donations it received, rested on the renown of its leading teachers. When such a teacher died, the question of succession naturally arose. Most of the Tibetan sects, by now, were nominally celibate. The question was, then, how to legitimize the successor of a respected teacher.

The Sakya sect, who had ruled Tibet under Mongol patronage, had adopted a system of inheritance from uncle to nephew. Another major sect, the Karma Kagyupa, invented the system that was to become central to Tibetan political and religious life. After the death of the leader of the Karma Kagyupa in 1283, his disciples decreed that their master had been reincarnated in the person of an infant boy, Rangjung Dorje, whom they duly recognized as their second ruling lama.[8] The practice gradually spread to other sects. When the Gelugpa sect was founded by Tsongkhapa more than a hundred years later they, too, adopted it.

Tsongkhapa's last disciple, Gedun Drub, became one of the Gelugpa's most important spiritual and political leaders. He founded the monastery of Tashilhunpo in Shigatse, in which, nearly a thousand years later, the drama of the eleventh Panchen Lama was to be played out. When Gedun Drub died, his reincarnation was recognized first in Gedun Gyatso and, on his death, in the infant Sonam Gyatso, the man who now sat in the Yanghua temple with Altan Khan, laying the foundations of a new politico-religious power structure.

For Altan Khan, who dreamed of a revival of the glory his people had enjoyed under Genghis Khan, legitimacy lay in demonstrating a linear connection with the legendary Mongol emperor, which would boost his own claim to leadership. Sonam Gyatso was already a respected spiritual master and teacher, legitimized from childhood by his recognition as the third reincarnation of a line of Gelugpa masters.

Both men emerged from the meeting strengthened by reciprocal endorsement and by some judicious backdating: Altan Khan bestowed on Sonam Gyatso the title of 'Ocean of Wisdom', or Dalai Lama. Sonam Gyatso applied his new title retroactively to his two previous incarnations, numbering himself the third Dalai Lama. In honour, perhaps, of his new Mongol patron, Sonam Gyatso also proclaimed himself the reincarnation of Phagpa-lha, Kublai Khan's spiritual adviser and a key player in the earlier version of this politico-spiritual alliance.

Altan Khan, for his part, received the title of 'King of the Turning Wheel and Wisdom', and to seal the bargain, the newly entitled Dalai Lama recognized Altan Khan as the reincarnation of Kublai Khan himself. Altan Khan thus established a direct link to Kublai's grandfather, the great Genghis Khan, which allowed him to present himself as the heir to the Mongol empire.[9]

The meeting is recorded as a moment of great piety on all sides, but the political benefits were also clear. Altan Khan had gained an association with a religion that was growing in prestige across Central Asia. Sonam Gyatso had the support of a powerful prince on whom he could rely for patronage and help in spreading the faith.[10]

Altan Khan now protected Sonam Gyatso's efforts to convert the Mongols to Buddhism, and under his patronage the Buddhist church developed as a state within a state in Mongolia, distributing titles and accumulating enormous wealth. The relationship did not go unnoticed in Beijing, where Altan Khan was regarded as a troublesome barbarian. When in 1578 the emperor Shenzhong heard of the pact between Altan Khan and Sonam Gyatso, he asked the Tibetan to persuade his patron to stop raiding Chinese territory. Sonam Gyatso induced Altan Khan to withdraw his forces to Mongolia, a lesson in the political uses of spiritual authority the Chinese were not to forget.

But while Sonam Gyatso had been scoring his success in Mongolia, the Gelugpa had been faring less well in their native Tibet. After the overthrow of the Sakya, sectarian rivalries had grown, and in 1605, in a period of political turbulence, Tsangba Khan, the king of the province of Tsang, installed the tenth Karmapa, a Kagyupa lama, on the throne and declared war on the rival Gelugpa sect.[11]

Over the next few years, Tsangba Khan killed hundreds of Gelugpa monks and sacked the Gelugpa monasteries of Drepung and Sera. When Sonam Gyatso's successor, the fourth Dalai Lama, died, Tsangba tried to deprive the Gelugpa of future leadership by prohibiting the search for his successor. It was only when he fell seriously ill and began to believe that he had been cursed by the late Dalai Lama that a prominent Gelugpa lama, Lobsang Choekyi, was able to persuade Tsangba to permit the search for the fourth Dalai Lama in return for the restoration of his health. Shortly afterwards, Lobsang Gyatso was found and Tsangba Khan's health was, indeed, restored. The child was destined to become the greatest of Tibet's theocratic monarchs, the Great Fifth Dalai Lama.

Lobsang Gyatso was born in 1617 in what is now Lhokha in the province of U, the son of a small serf-holder and village chief. He was identified at the age of six by Lobsang Choekyi, the astute cleric who had cured Tsangba Khan of his illness, and brought to Drepung monastery to be educated. Lobsang Choekyi himself became the child's religious tutor, and the bond which developed between them was to shape Tibetan politics for more than two hundred years.

In gratitude to his mentor the young Dalai Lama bestowed on Lobsang Choekyi the title of Panchen Lama, or 'Wise Teacher', and in 1637, Lobsang Choekyi initiated the fifth Dalai Lama into full monkhood. The Dalai Lama was twenty; the Panchen Lama was sixty-three. It was the Panchen Lama who was to guide his young pupil through the critical next steps in the consolidation of Gelugpa power.

The Gelugpa's situation remained precarious. Tsangba Khan was now dead, but in 1631 his son had inherited both his father's throne and his dislike of the Gelugpa. The sect clearly needed a new protector and, as luck or – more likely – good judgement on the part of the Panchen Lama would have it, one was to appear.

Gushri Khan was the leader of one of the four major tribes of the Oirat Mongols. They were a nomadic people whose grazing lands ran through the Urumchi region of modern Xinjiang and the lands north and south of the Tianshan mountains. Like other Mongol nobles before him Gushri Khan sought to raise his own status through an alliance with prominent Buddhist teachers. In 1635 he travelled to Tibet disguised as a pilgrim to seek religious instruction from the Gelugpa's most famous teacher, the Panchen Lama.

He presented the Panchen Lama with 2,000 ounces of silver and pledged to be his religious devotee, but the visit had another purpose. In the mosaic of rival Mongol tribes which had emerged after the breakdown of the Yuan dynasty, competing princelings were supporting different Buddhist sects. Gushri Khan's rival, the king of Qinghai, Chogthu Khan, was a patron of the Karmapa and an ally of the Gelugpa's enemy, Tsangba Khan. Gushri Khan was in search of a religious cause, and the Panchen Lama needed a military patron for the Gelugpa.

A relationship was cemented that was to transform the fortunes of all involved. Five years later Gushri Khan had defeated his and the Gelugpa's enemies, the tenth Karmapa was deposed and the fifth Dalai Lama was on the throne of Tibet. Gushri Khan's powerful patronage established the Gelugpa as Tibet's dominant sect, and despite some sporadic resistance, it remained so until the flight of the fourteenth Dalai Lama into exile in India in 1959.

Secure at last from persecution, the fifth Dalai Lama turned his attention to the trappings of power. The Potala was, at the time, a relatively modest building that housed the first shrine of King Srongtsen Gampo. Armed with the confiscated treasures of Tsangba Khan and even the timbers of Tsangba's palace in Shigatse, the fifth Dalai Lama set about expanding it into the vast and extraordinary structure it is today.

The government the fifth Dalai Lama established was to remain the template of the Tibetan state until the Chinese occupation in 1950 shattered Tibet's political structures. It consisted of the Kashag, with one lay and three religious ministers, a lay bureaucracy staffed by members of the aristocracy and a religious bureaucracy staffed by monk officials recruited from the major monasteries. The aristocracy, estimated at some two hundred families,[12] lived off large landholdings worked by serfs, who were entitled to receive seed and to work their own land. Each aristocratic family was obliged to provide one of its number for government service.

The pillars of the government were the three main Gelugpa monasteries – Sera, three miles north of Lhasa, Ganden, twenty miles to the east, and the Dalai Lama's home monastery, Drepung, five and a half miles north-west. Each was a vast medieval university which housed thousands of monks and had authority over hundreds of smaller subordinate monasteries. Their revenues were secured by manorial estates.

Each monastery was composed of several colleges, or *dratsang*, the unit to which the individual monk owed his primary allegiance. Each college in turn had several residences, which usually recruited monks by their place of origin. Beneath the umbrella of the monastery, these semi-autonomous sub-units guarded their own traditions and, on occasion, fought with each other.

The fifth Dalai Lama was at the top of the secular and religious trees, though not, formally at least, the head of his own religious order. That honour was the preserve of the Ganden Tripa, the head of the Ganden Phodrang[13] of Drepung monastery. The system was nominally hierarchical; the Dalai Lama was a highly revered figure, but obedience to his will was by no means guaranteed. The monasteries, and the colleges within them, were frequently in dispute.

The monasteries, as in medieval Europe, were a source of medical relief for the poor and the only place where a boy from a modest background could both receive an education and gain a foothold in the power structure. Through entering religious life, any boy of ability in this otherwise rigid and stratified society had a chance of rising to a high position in a monastery or in the government bureaucracy.

There was, of course, one other way on to this ladder of power, which was, theoretically, open to any male child, no matter how miserable his background. The belief in reincarnation and the practices that grew from this belief were peculiar to Tibet and opened up the most powerful positions in this elaborate theocracy – those of the Panchen Lama and the Dalai Lama – to the humblest of citizens. It also had the effect of entwining the most deeply held spiritual beliefs with the crude struggle for secular power. In the 1990s, three hundred and fifty years after the establishment of the Gelugpa state, this was to remain true. The search for the reincarnation of the tenth Panchen Lama became a story not just of spiritual belief and personal heroism but of politics at the highest level.

Chapter Three

✶

I set about exploring Lhasa. I had taken up residence in the Holiday Inn, a grandiose hotel built to accommodate the small but important tourist trade the Chinese hoped would provide a steady income for their troubled administration in Tibet. It was all but closed in that non-tourist season, and the heating had been turned off. I bargained heavily for a room. The irritated manager had his revenge: he gave me one on the sunless side of the building, where the temperature never rose to a level that was even tolerable.

In the restaurant a handful of staff huddled round a single heater. A blanket of chill enveloped the spacious lobby with its gleaming polished floor. The front desk was generally abandoned: the staff spent their days hidden in a small back office. If they were summoned to the desk they arrived in a cloud of warm air that surged out as they opened the back-office door, only to dissipate in the lobby's penetrating chill.

Outside, the daylight hours offered a fierce sun that shone in a startlingly clear blue sky. The hotel was near the old summer palace of the dalai lamas, the Norbulingka. The present Dalai Lama describes his joy when the moment came to abandon the gloomy rooms of the Potala for a summer in Norbulingka, then a place of theatrical festivals and celebration. It was shelled by the Chinese in 1959 as the people rallied to its gates to defend their Dalai Lama from what they thought was a planned kidnap attempt. Now it is shorn of its ritual importance as the Dalai Lama's residence. It is abandoned to the secular attention of tourists.

The Norbulingka once lay in the country, and the Dalai Lama's procession at the change of seasons was an occasion for outdoor celebration. Now the Chinese suburbs have crept up and surrounded it. Dreary compounds of small apartment blocks built behind high protective walls have filled in the rural spaces, and the main roads are lined with single-storey karaoke bars. As I walked into town the Chinese girls who work in these bars, opened for the benefit largely of the substantial Chinese army garrison, were sitting on low stools, taking the sun.

The Chinese say they are modernizing Lhasa, and they are certainly demolishing the traditional city at frightening speed. In place of the simple whitewashed buildings of Tibetan tradition are modern buildings of the finest karaoke kitsch. As I approached the Potala I saw that the little village of Shol that had lain at its feet was gone. In its place was a vast dusty building site in which Tibetan men and women were chipping stone blocks into smaller fragments. They were working, I learned, on what was to be a huge plaza, to be opened to mark the thirtieth anniversary of Chinese administration in Tibet. It would contain a small funfair, at the foot of the Potala itself.

Beyond the Potala, I eventually reached Lhasa's most sacred temple, the Jokhang. It once lay at the centre of a grid of narrow streets. The Chinese have cleared many of them, and now it opens on to a large square that is more easily patrolled by the security forces. On the other three sides of the Jokhang the streets remain, thronged at this, the pilgrimage season, by visiting nomads browsing the market stalls. The nomads are easy to spot: their faces are burnt dark by the fierce mountain sun, and the women are festooned with coral, silver and turquoise jewellery. They walk with a rapid stride, their long dusty skirts swaying to the rhythm of their gait.

In front of the Jokhang a group of pilgrims were performing prostrations on flagstone worn smooth and polished by generations of devotees. It was nearly the Tibetan New Year, a holy time, but also a time of political tension. I walked back towards the Potala. A Tibetan gatekeeper sat in a warm hut. 'It's closed,' he said. 'Come back tomorrow morning.' The next morning it was still closed, and the day after that. On the fourth day, I began to lose patience, but the gatekeeper was sympathetic.

'You have to talk to the authorities,' he explained apologetically.

He pointed to a telephone. He silently dialled a number and handed me the receiver from which a voice was shouting '*Wei!* *Wei*', the customary Chinese telephone greeting. I rallied my most commanding Chinese manner and barked back. Why, I demanded, was the palace not open at the hours displayed on the noticeboard? It was an outrage, I protested, when tourists wanted to visit. The voice said something could be done, but there would be an extra charge.

I took it as permission to proceed and began slowly to climb the long stone staircase that zigzagged up the side of the building. As I approached the top an elderly face appeared over the parapet above. 'Psst!' it said. 'Dalai Lama? Dalai Lama picture?' I shook my head and the face disappeared.

The voice on the telephone turned out to belong to a Tibetan in his thirties. He was a man of medium height but powerful build. A spreading belly strained against his green army uniform. A gun hung from his belt and the metal tips of his large black boots struck sparks from the paving stones. He played with a huge ring of keys as he regarded me with an expression that did not convey warmth. 'Where is your Chinese guide?' he demanded. 'The one who was on the telephone?'

'I don't have a guide,' I said. He shrugged and beckoned me in. He hustled me across the courtyard and pointed to a surprised young man in civilian clothes. 'He'll show you round,' he said. 'Hurry up.' He hustled me along, with my new guide, throwing open doors, pushing us into room after room, then, as soon as we were in, hustling us out again. Tsongkhapa's shrine, the great throne room, the cramped apartments of the Dalai Lama right on the roof, all passed by me at breakneck speed. In twenty minutes we were back where we began. 'Sixty yuan,' he said. I handed over the money.

'And the extra charge of sixty yuan,' he demanded.

'That's too much,' I replied. His face darkened and he locked the last door. 'The Potala's closed,' he said.

I made my way back down the steps. At the bottom the gatekeeper was talking to an elderly Tibetan nun. She was dressed in a dusty brown gown and her face was streaked with dirt. She carried a small cloth bag and a rosary.

'Did you see it?' the gatekeeper enquired as I passed. 'What did you think?'

'It's magnificent,' I said, 'but empty.' He smiled. The nun's eyes were filled with tears.

'They won't let her in,' he explained. 'Just foreigners now.'

I walked back to the hotel, picking my way through the wreckage of the village of Shöl. On a nearby hill a radio mast marked the spot once occupied by the ancient school of medicine, destroyed since the Chinese occupation, as were nearly 90 per cent of Tibet's temples. Pious Tibetans have rebuilt many of them now, but Lhasa is still being destroyed by new projects: the mass migration of ethnic Chinese from the overcrowded provinces of China and the government's modernization plan, which threatens to erase the old city, leaving only a token reminder of its past. When the projects have been completed the Potala palace will be marooned in a Chinese metropolis.

The impact of the Chinese administration on Tibet has been devastating, but the influence has not been all one-way. In their efforts to subdue Tibet, the Chinese Communist Party, like the emperors before them, has found itself forced to adopt some unusual methods.

In 1990 the Politburo of the Chinese Communist Party issued a new set of rules. The impulse to order and control was nothing unusual, but the subject of their deliberations was so far removed from any topic of which Karl Marx would have approved that it must rank as one of the most bizarre moments in the history of twentieth-century Communism. For the 'rules' set out the Party's guidelines on the subject of reincarnation.

Over the months that followed they were to be revised and refined many times as the self-confessed Marxist, materialist atheists of the Chinese Politburo wrestled with the challenge of submitting to a set of bureaucratic regulations a selection process that had its origins in medieval religious beliefs. For, arcane though it must have seemed to them, the procedure still, in the late twentieth century, had the potential to destabilize an entire political system. In the four centuries that had passed since Altan Khan bestowed the title of Dalai Lama on Sonam Gyatso, the practice of identifying important reincarnates had become a fundamental feature of Tibetan political and religious life.

Trulkus, or reincarnate lamas, were vital to the economic well-being of the monasteries: as superior spiritual beings, they attracted followers and donations, and the prestige of an important *trulku* reflected well on his peers. Within the monastery, a *trulku* headed his own household or *labrang* – a miniature court which held the accumulated property of successive reincarnations. The wealth of an individual *trulku* derived largely from donations, though if a *trulku* came to hold a high political position his *labrang* could be expected to benefit correspondingly. It was usually the senior figures of a *trulku's labrang* who would take on the task of finding the next reincarnation on the death of the master.

A *trulku*, of course, enjoyed high status, benefiting as he did from the prestige of his previous incarnations, but he also had onerous responsibilities. He would be expected to support his monastery with large donations from his household funds at every stage of his education. At each rite of passage in his religious life he was obliged to treat the entire monastery, which could run to several thousand monks, to tea and rice, if not a gift of cash. The funding for these expenses had to be raised from his own personal following. It was therefore important to a monastery to be able to attract as many *trulkus* as it could. This, in turn, led to a tendency for new lineages to be created: on the death of a well-known teacher it would be decided to search for his reincarnation, and a new lineage would be established.

The most important quest, of course, was the search for the reincarnation of the Dalai Lama. The system had supreme spiritual validation, but it also had a measure of political merit. The elevation of the entire family of each Dalai Lama to the nobility made some contribution, at least, to the renovation of the ruling class. To look for a gifted child in infancy and train him for the job was not a bad way of choosing a ruler.

But it had its problems, too. The consequences of the choice were obviously important, and the nominally spiritual process subject to political pressures. It was also true that the children chosen did not always turn out quite as expected.

The successor to the Great Fifth was a case in point. When the Great Fifth died, in 1682, at the advanced age of sixty-eight, the political forces around Tibet had changed. Gushri Khan was dead and the Manchus had conquered China. Tibet was still protected by the Mongols of the region of Kokonor lake who were loyal to the Dalai Lama.

At the time of the death of the Great Fifth, his chief minister, Sangye Gyatso, was administering Tibet's temporal affairs. He is described as having been a man of great ability and learning, a noted scholar of history, medicine and astrology. He was also a man with an extraordinary will, which he did not always use to straightforward ends. At the moment of the Great Fifth's death, the building of the Potala palace was not complete. Since the men who laboured on it did so out of devotion to the Dalai Lama, Sangye Gyatso feared the great work would be abandoned if the death of the Dalai Lama were to be discovered. He decided, therefore, to conceal it.

Sangye Gyatso managed to keep the secret for some thirteen years, not only from the people of Tibet but also from the Mongol chiefs and the Manchu emperor. He announced that the Dalai Lama was in a spiritual retreat so deep that he could not be disturbed. When visitors came, Sangye affected to consult the great man, only to return with the message that the master's meditation could not be interrupted. As the Tibetan scholar K. Dhondup wrote:

Rituals signifying the Dalai Lama's meditation were performed daily. Meals were taken into the antechamber as usual. The Dalai Lama's seal was used on all official transactions. On important occasions, the Dalai Lama's ceremonial gown was placed on the throne in the audience hall and all officials followed the routine as though the Dalai Lama was physically present.[1]

If the visitor was important, an elderly monk with a slight physical resemblance to the deceased was employed as a stand-in.

However, as the Dalai Lama was dead, Sangye Gyatso knew that somewhere there was a child in whom the Great Fifth had chosen to reincarnate. How was he to be found without the secret of the Dalai Lama's death being discovered, and, once found, what was to be done with him?

The resourceful regent sent out search parties, on the pretext of looking for a different reincarnation, and in 1685, three years after the death of the fifth Dalai Lama, Sangye Gyatso identified a two-year-old child, Tsangyang Gyatso, as the reincarnation. The child and his mother were confined under virtual house arrest for twelve years. In 1697 Sangye Gyatso belatedly despatched a messenger to inform the Manchu emperor of the Dalai Lama's death, and later that year announced the news in Tibet, along with the claim that the sixth Dalai Lama had been found. The new incarnation was, by now, a tall and handsome young man. He was duly enthroned and handed over to the teachers who were to begin the rigorous and somewhat delayed religious education that his role demanded.

Unfortunately, in his long confinement, Tsangyang Gyatso had developed his own ideas of how he wished to live his life. He preferred riding and archery to religious texts and the delights of the young women of the taverns in the village of Shöl, just below the Potala, to the rigours of abstinence and celibacy. When he reached the age of twenty, he refused to take his monk's vows, and despite the repeated appeals of Sangye Gyatso and the massed ranks of the senior clergy, he would not be persuaded.

The stalemate was broken when Tibet was invaded by disillusioned Mongol forces. Sangye Gyatso was summarily executed, and the sixth Dalai Lama sent under heavy guard to Peking. He never arrived.

Few episodes of death and reincarnation were as strangely handled or had such serious consequences as the death of the fifth and recognition of the sixth dalai lamas. The process, however, was always vulnerable to manipulation, and even when it went smoothly there was necessarily a time-lag between the death of one dalai lama and the birth and maturity of his successor during which the government of Tibet tended to be weak and fractious.

A large number of dalai lamas failed to reach their majority and the suspicion lingers that they were poisoned by those who thought Tibet better ruled – or more malleable – under a regency. Only four dalai lamas were to play an important role in the government of their country: Sonam Gyatso, the first to bear the title but, because of the backdating, numbered the third Dalai Lama; the fifth, who became the first Gelugpa ruler; the thirteenth; and the present Dalai Lama, the fourteenth.

Despite its drawbacks, the practice of finding reincarnates continued at all levels in Tibet until the aftermath of the revolt against the Chinese in 1959. Under the Chinese, the monasteries were largely disbanded and the search for reincarnate lamas banned as feudal superstition. But among those who fled Tibet and began to re-create their religious institutions in exile, it continued. As access to the population inside Tibet became more difficult, *trulkus* began to be recognized in the exile community, and as the new monasteries struggled to establish themselves, the *trulkus* were, once again, key components of monastic success.

The stakes became, if anything, higher in exile. Exile brought Tibetan Buddhism into contact with Western converts who were willing to finance their new faith on a scale impossible for the struggling Tibetan community to contemplate, and in the successful monasteries, the process was, once again, subject to conflict.

When I first visited Dharamsala, in 1994, one such conflict had already been raging for several years: the dispute about the reincarnation of the sixteenth Karmapa. The Karmapa is the direct spiritual descendant of the early Kagyupa ruler of Tibet who, under the patronage of the warlord, Tsangba Khan, was the bitter enemy of the rising power of the Gelugpa in the seventeenth century. The Kagyupa lost their state power but remained an important sect in Tibet.

After the uprising of 1959 the sixteenth Karmapa fled Tibet and established a monastery in exile in Rumtek in Sikkim. The Kagyupa was perhaps the most successful sect in exile, and over the years attracted a large following of Western devotees. By the time of the sixteenth Karmapa's death in 1981, they had become one of the wealthiest and best established of the exile Tibetan Buddhist orders. The search for his reincarnation officially began the day after the sixteenth Karmapa's cremation.

According to the Kagyupa tradition, this ought to have been a fairly straightforward affair, since the Karmapa have had the helpful custom of leaving written or oral instructions on where they plan to be reborn. The new incarnation offers further assistance to search parties by revealing himself through extraordinary deeds.

The system has worked fairly well for more than eight centuries, but on this most recent occasion, the Karmapa's instructions did not come to light. Four regents were entrusted with the management of the Karmapa's considerable assets until the new incarnation could be found. But as time went by, the sect began to be torn with rumour and strife.

Then, in March 1992, one of the regents, Situ Rinpoche, made a dramatic announcement: the late Karmapa's instructions had, miraculously, been found inside an amulet that the Karmapa had given to him in 1981. Situ Rinpoche had worn it faithfully since receiving it from the master but had not looked inside until 1990.

Only then, after accidentally wetting it in the bath, did he notice that it contained the missing instructions. Situ Rinpoche's explanation might have had a better reception had it not also contained the admission that the four regents had collectively forged an earlier letter. When, a month later, one of them died unexpectedly in a car crash, the affair took an ugly turn.

During the funeral rites for the dead regent, the surviving regents were closely questioned by impatient followers, who had waited, by then, twelve years for the reappearance of their master. Their stories contradicted each other, and the Karmapa's followers began to divide into factions.

Situ Rinpoche now claimed that a child from eastern Tibet was unquestionably the Karmapa lama. The child, he said, was on his way to Tsurphu monastery. His Holiness, the Dalai Lama, he added, contacted by telephone in Rio de Janeiro where he was attending the Earth Summit, had given his blessing.

In the uproar that followed, Situ tried to argue the child's case. The birth, he said, had been accompanied by miraculous portents – the sound of trumpets and conches had been heard for two hours in the sky, and when the boy had set out for his monastery from his home in eastern Tibet, three suns appeared in the heavens. Situ's fellow regent, Shamar Rinpoche, remained unconvinced. As the rituals for the dead regent continued in Rumtek monastery, rioting broke out between the rival factions.

The child himself was installed under conditions of high security in Tsurphu monastery and was officially approved by the Chinese government as the reincarnation of the Karmapa. The tone of the official press coverage of this unusual event gave rise to suspicion that the boy was expected to grow up a loyal citizen of socialism. It did nothing to further his claim with the dissenting faction.

Despite many attempts at mediation, this dispute continues and a rival candidate has now been produced. Meanwhile, the young Karmapa in Tibet receives the homage of the faithful and is paraded, from time to time, by the Chinese government as evidence of its enlightened religious policies.

It would be tempting to blame events like the Karmapa controversy solely on the disruption to Tibetan life of the Chinese occupation. Certainly that has been an important factor. But even in old Tibet the process was too important, and too esoteric, to be entirely free from conflict. Exile had added to the problem of locating and identifying *trulkus* and of ensuring that they receive the education and training that will allow them to grow up as the holy men their followers expect them to be.

Birth as a reincarnate holy man is not enough: a *trulku* is born with potential, but if he does not receive a spiritual education, he will not fulfil it. A rigorous life of discipline and religious study is required if the child is to develop the spiritual accomplishments of his predecessors. This is not easy, even for the *trulkus* who are discovered in exile.

Ideally, a *trulku* should be kept apart, allowed to play only with other reincarnates and with the attentions of devotees kept under strict control. But in the West it has proved difficult to keep *trulkus* from the corrosive effects of material civilization. In the struggle to raise funds to help support the monasteries the *trulkus*, with their powerful emotional appeal, are an important asset. But a fund-raising tour of California and the attractions of the sophisticated toys and video games showered on them by Western followers can create headaches for the child's religious tutor. Problem teenage *trulkus* are not unknown.

In Tibet itself there are different problems. For decades after the occupation the recognition of *trulkus* was forbidden. The monasteries were disbanded and the teachers who would have transmitted the tradition to the young reincarnates were dead, scattered or in exile. But in 1979 Chinese policy changed. Limited recognition of *trulkus* is now permitted, as long as it remains under official control.

For the exile community this presents further problems: it is only in exile, they believe, that a child can receive a spiritual education uncontaminated by political ideology. Besides, the presence of a *trulku* among his devotees is a valued part of religious life. The exiles who want to find a reincarnate face the double hurdle of locating a child who may have been born in Tibet and of trying to ensure his proper care and education.

In Dharamsala in 1994 I went to find a monk who had become something of a local hero for the role he had played in such a search. The Nechung monastery occupies a peaceful corner of the hillside just beyond the government compound. Its abbot is Thupten Ngodub, the medium of the state oracle who had encouraged me to pursue the story of the Panchen Lama on my first visit. He had also told me about Dorje, the Nechung monk who had, a short time before, succeeded in smuggling out of Tibet the child who had been recognized as the reincarnation of the Nechung Lama.

I found Dorje in the monastery, in a small room furnished with a bed, an altar and the paraphernalia which I learned to associate with Buddhist monks – a radio, a cassette recorder, a few books, a roll of lavatory paper. There was a low table covered with a red towel on which were laid out a green highlighter and a rosary. Dorje was chatting on a mobile phone when I arrived and I sat, not without effort, cross-legged on the floor, while he finished. Outside a group of monks were chopping meat for *momos*, Tibetan dumplings. The sounds of their laughter and conversation drifted in through the curtained door.

The Nechung Lama, Dorje explained, had come into exile in 1960 and worked as a language teacher first in Delhi, then in Hawaii. When he fell ill in 1980 he moved back to Dharamsala, where he died in 1983, leaving only the death-bed instruction that the Dalai Lama would be the ultimate arbiter of his reincarnation. After four years of fruitless searching, the monastery was told by the oracle to consult the Dalai Lama. He, in turn, told them the child would be born in Tibet.

In 1987 Dorje went to Tibet. 'My instructions were to look for a special child. There are many special children in Tibet – some are born with letters on their tongue. But these days their parents don't make it widely known if that happens. I was supposed to get them all together and pick one, but I failed,' he said.

Given the scale of the task, I did not find his failure surprising, the less so when he told me that his mission was secret. I wondered what pretext he could possibly have used to gather the children together.

Dorje had been instructed to visit the sacred lake of Lhamo Latso, at Choekhorgyal, some ninety miles south-east of Lhasa. Lhamo Latso lies at a height of around 9,000 feet in the mountains of Gyatsa county in Lhokha, a brilliant azure jewel set in a ring of grey mountains. The elevation and the surrounding peaks combine to give it a highly changeable climate, and the continuous passage of cloud and wind creates a constantly moving pattern on the surface of the waters. On that surface visions appear to those who seek them in the right frame of mind.

In the case of a reincarnation the visions contain clues, which must be interpreted and understood. It is advanced religious work, and only respected spiritual masters are trusted with it. The lake is one of the first ports of call for any search party looking for a reincarnation. But when Dorje visited it, the weather was bad, and though he saw a vision of a house and some scenery, there was no clue as to where he should search.

After three months he returned to Dharamsala for more consultations with the Dalai Lama and the oracle. This time the Dalai Lama gave more precise directions, and the oracle was asked to supply the names of the birthplace and the parents. This, Dorje said, he did.

'The second time it was easy. I had the exact place and all I had to do was look for the child. I began asking people and collecting names. In fact, I came up with seven names and returned to Dharamsala.' The oracle and the Dalai Lama both endorsed the first name on the list.

Dorje was sent back to Tibet. 'I had to examine the child. I was looking for some unique characteristic,' he said. 'I interviewed the parents, and the mother started telling me about her dreams. The child had dreams, too: he dreamed that the Chinese were chasing him and his mother said that he was always very scared of soldiers.

'I believe that was because of Rinpoche's escape in 1960,' he said, 'when he collected all the sacred things from the monastery and escaped into India. That was what was making the child afraid. I became convinced I had found him.'

The parents agreed to let the boy go to India. 'They had no idea that their son was a *trulku*, but they were very religious. In normal circumstances they wouldn't have agreed to part with their child, but they knew that he would be near His Holiness, so they agreed. I chose an auspicious day for his departure and I found them holding a ceremony. The child was ready to come with me, and we set off for the border with Nepal.'

Dorje disguised himself as a layman, but the boy had no papers. They came out, prosaically enough, on a tourist bus, with the child concealed under a towel and a Swiss tourist's rucksack carefully arranged on top of him.

'I think the fact that he wasn't caught was another sign that he is special,' said Dorje.

'What would have happened to him if you hadn't found him?' I asked.

Dorje shrugged. 'If a child isn't found, then he is in great difficulty. He is the reincarnation of a previous lama, but he hasn't been trained to handle it. Some go insane, some die in accidents, and some just die without ever being recognized. The importance of finding the boys young is that you have to train them – it takes fifteen years. That's why it's so important that the Panchen Lama be found and brought out – he has to study under a great master and it has to be His Holiness. In the monasteries in Tibet the monks have to spend their time doing farm work and building work: they hardly have time to study. The Chinese want to find this precious child to use him against the Tibetans in exile. Look what is happening to the Karmapa. He talks of being loyal to the great motherland – if he was free he wouldn't talk like that.'

We strolled out along the monastery veranda. Suddenly Dorje gave a yelp of pleasure: a boy in monk's robes was looking at us from the stairwell. Dorje lunged at him and enveloped him in a great bear-hug. 'Meet Nechung Rinpoche,' he said. 'He speaks English. Say something,' he said to the boy. Nechung Rinpoche grinned and slipped out of his grasp, his flip-flop sandals slapping on the hard floor of the veranda as he sprinted out of reach in a flutter of maroon robes.

As I left the Nechung monastery I reflected on Dorje's story. The means he had used to find the Nechung Lama's reincarnation were sanctioned by tradition – the consultation of the oracle and the higher spiritual authority of the Dalai Lama. In old Tibet it is unlikely that a monk would have carried the responsibility for the search and the testing alone. Given the importance of reincarnate lamas, it is not surprising that an elaborate set of practices should have developed to help the search parties identify them.

Though the child was not presumed to retain the body of knowledge mastered in his former existence, he was expected to have some memory, albeit fragmentary, of his past life. The child's utterances would be trawled for signs of this. And when it came to the tests, the successful candidates were often said to have recognized at least one member of the household of the previous incarnation and to be able to identify objects that he had owned in his past life. If a child was proclaimed the reincarnation, of course, then supporting evidence would probably be found in the dreams of those close to him and the birth would have been marked by miraculous portents.

Perhaps the most comprehensively documented search in Western writings on Tibetan Buddhism is the search for the present Dalai Lama. It was, by his own account, a singularly uncontested event. It began as the body of the deceased Dalai Lama rested in state in his summer palace, the Norbulingka. The head, it was observed, turned towards the north-east, and on the wooden pillar on the north-east side of the shrine on which the body rested, a curious star-shaped fungus grew. The state oracles and learned lamas were consulted, and the likely direction was confirmed when curious cloud formations were seen, also to the north-east.

The regent had a particularly fruitful visit to the sacred lake the following year: he saw a vision of the three Tibetan letters, *Ah*, *Ka* and *Ma*, followed by a picture of a monastery with a jade-green and gold roof and a house with turquoise tiles. Search parties located the house the following year.

The monastery in the regent's vision was the famous monastery of Kumbum, in Amdo, and the village of Takster yielded a house which matched the description and in which a boy had been born two years previously. The search party arrived in disguise, but the child went to sit on the lap of a monk who was wearing around his neck a rosary that had belonged to the thirteenth Dalai Lama. The child asked for the rosary and the lama replied that he could have it if he could guess who his visitor was. The boy replied, correctly, that he was from Sera monastery and gave the names both of the lama and of his servant. The next morning, when the party prepared to leave, the child wanted to go with them.

A larger party was sent, bearing a series of objects that had belonged to the previous incarnation. The child identified all of them correctly. The rest of the puzzle was fitted into place: the letter *Ka*, they concluded, signified Kumbum, the letter *Ah*, Amdo. Alternatively *Ka Ma* might have meant the local monastery of Karma Rolpai Dorje.

So overwhelming was the sum of the evidence the search party was convinced they had found the child. The only subsequent problem, which was overcome, was the ruinous ransom exacted by a Chinese Muslim warlord, Ma Bufang, who controlled the province.

Once installed in his dark and chilly living quarters high up in the Potala, the young Dalai Lama delighted his tutors and servants by his apparent familiarity with the life of the palace. I once asked the Dalai Lama if he remembered anything of his previous incarnations. He laughed.

'Not really,' he said. 'Sometimes a feeling. Nothing important.'

The authenticity of the fourteenth Dalai Lama was never challenged, and he grew up to be a leader worthy of the office. But the Karmapa controversy was evidence of the explosive potential inherent in the search for reincarnate lamas. The process is a heady mixture of religious belief, esoteric mystery and real material interests. The higher the stakes, the greater the likelihood of trouble. In the search for the Panchen Lama, the stakes were enormous.

Chapter Four

✶

After word came through in the summer of 1994 that the Dalai Lama had approved my following the selection process of the eleventh Panchen Lama as closely as time and distance permitted, I in turn agreed that confidences entrusted would not be betrayed. Discretion, until the process was complete, was clearly vital. Later, it was to become painfully obvious how vital.

That summer things appeared to have reached a temporary stalemate, which afforded me time to explore the background in greater detail. Both sides – Dharamsala and Beijing – were presenting the search for the reincarnation of the Panchen Lama as a spiritual matter. Each side accused the other of politicizing the issue. Both sides were being, in part at least, disingenuous.

For Beijing, the definition of the search as spiritual enabled the government to pretend that it was not meddling, that the whole affair was in the hands of the religious establishment properly responsible for it. In Dharamsala, where claims to spiritual authority were stronger, the insistence that the search was a purely religious matter was also a means of asserting the Dalai Lama's final authority in the identification of the child.

Both sides invoked history to support their case and for both the person of the eleventh Panchen Lama, whoever he turned out to be, was only the latest manifestation in a long tradition. The ownership of that tradition, the right to define the process and determine its outcome, was a critical factor of legitimacy for both the Dalai Lama and the Chinese government.

Overhanging all the arguments was the memory of the tenth Panchen Lama, whose face looked benevolently down at me from a dozen postcard stalls in Dharamsala and whose death in 1989 had precipitated this slow-burning crisis. The argument over his life and the role that he had played still raged, and both sides claimed him as their own. As I began to put together the pieces of the puzzle that formed that tragic, ambiguous life, I discovered that the intertwining of politics and the role of the Panchen Lama stretched back to the very beginning of the Gelugpa state.

Officially, there is no connection; but just as the role of the Dalai Lama can be defined in many ways, so the Panchen Lama – and his complex spiritual, personal and political relationship with the Dalai Lama – has reflected through successive reincarnations the wider politics of his time. Devotees of the Panchen Lama insist that, of the two, the Panchen Lama is spiritually superior. Followers of the Dalai Lama insist that from the day the fifth Dalai Lama became the head of the theocratic state, the Panchen Lama's role was defined as non-political. The Panchen, being an aspect of the Buddha, ought to operate only in the realm of pure thought and, in religious terms, is untrue to his nature if he deals in temporal affairs. The Dalai Lama is an aspect of the Bodhisattva, the active reflex, and is free to operate in the world.[1] That, at least, was the theory, but other forces and other powers were to have their say as history played itself out.

Even at the beginning, the case that the Panchen Lama was a non-political being would have been hard to argue with any conviction. The first man to hold the title was a consummate political operator and, if anyone deserved to be called a kingmaker, it was he. Lobsang Choekyi was born in Drugya Bewa village, west of Shigatse, in 1570, or, in the poetic style of the Tibetan calendar, on the fifteenth day of the fourth month of the Iron Horse Year of the tenth Tibetan calendrical cycle. At the time the monks of Bengom monastery were searching for the reincarnation of their abbot and a search party passed through Lobsang Choekyi's village in 1575. The child aroused their interest and one of the party stayed behind to observe him.[2]

At the age of thirteen Lobsang Choekyi entered the monastery, where he took his vows and demonstrated such precocious learning that he was enthroned as the abbot the next year. The title appears to have been a formality, since the young abbot did not administer the monastery. He was soon to leave it to pursue his studies, first in the then still minor monastery of Tashilhunpo, later in the most prestigious of the big three monastic universities, Ganden, founded by Tsongkhapa. In 1598, by which time he was concurrently abbot of two monasteries, he was also invited to be abbot of Tashilhunpo. He accepted only at the repeated insistence of the monks.

It was not a particularly attractive job: Tashilhunpo was a small monastery with a money problem so severe the monks barely had enough to eat. Lobsang Choekyi proved himself a resourceful administrator and, having ordered a series of giant cooking utensils to be cast, he secured the funds to fill them by persuading the local landowners to donate enough land to Tashilhunpo to guarantee the monastery's income. He built a tantric college, which meant that the monks could complete their monastic education without having to go to Lhasa, and from its modest beginnings Tashilhunpo rose under his administration to be one of the great monasteries of Tibet.

On the peak of a towering hill opposite Tashilhunpo rose the massive walls of Shigatse *dzong*, the huge fortress of Tsangba Khan, the warlord champion of the Karmapa and the Gelugpa's enemy. Lobsang Choekyi was still in his post when Tsangba Khan began his persecution of the Gelugpa sect. By 1605 the Gelugpa monasteries were under attack and the fourth Dalai Lama was dead.

As a renowned scholar and important Gelugpa hierarch, Lobsang Choekyi had known the late Dalai Lama intimately. It was he who had administered the young reincarnate's first vows when he had arrived from Mongolia and become his tutor and friend, eventually, in 1614, ordaining him into full monkhood. Perhaps when the Dalai Lama suddenly died in December 1616, at the untimely age of twenty-eight, Lobsang Choekyi shared the general suspicion that Tsangba Khan had murdered him.

It was he who cured Tsangba Khan of his illness and extracted from him in return the promise that the search for the child who was to become the Great Fifth be allowed to continue without interference, and undertook the young Dalai Lama's training and initiation once he had been found. It was also he who invited Gushri Khan to help establish the Gelugpa as the dominant sect of Tibet.

He cultivated relations with the rising power of the Manchu, who were shortly to conquer China's decaying Ming dynasty. Even in his extreme old age he was called upon by the Dalai Lama to use his diplomatic skills in a lingering religious conflict with the king of Bhutan. He was a consummate political operator and a formidable religious figure.

Tashilhunpo eventually housed 5,000 monks in the main monastery and a further 4,000 in its subsidiary monasteries, supported by sixteen manorial estates. Lobsang Choekyi himself is credited with the recruitment of 150,000 disciples, of whom 50,000 took vows to be lay Buddhists, 100,000 took initial vows and 50,000 were finally ordained.[3]

Lobsang Choekyi was the first to be known as Panchen Lama, the title given by the young fifth Dalai Lama to the man who was both his spiritual and political mentor. The title was retrospectively applied to three previous incarnations of the abbots of Tashilhunpo, however, therefore he come to be numbered the fourth Panchen Lama.[4]

The relationship between the Great Fifth Dalai Lama and the Panchen Lama was fundamental to the successful establishment of the Gelugpa theocracy, and the two men became the twin pillars of the Gelugpa hierarchy. From then on, through successive incarnations, each would play a role in the recognition and education of the reincarnation of the other, when their respective ages permitted. Their places in the theological firmament were defined: the panchen lamas' prestige derived both from their illustrious lineage and their scholastic achievements; to dalai lamas belonged the exercise of state power.

In this respect, the arrangements established by the fifth Dalai Lama and the fourth Panchen Lama are clear in their intent. But even the power of the Dalai Lama, and of the central government of Tibet, had its limits. Geographically its boundaries were fuzzy, so over large areas of Tibet the voice of government was so faint as to be all but inaudible. There were also practical limitations: although the government had powers of life and death over its subjects, important decisions were often challenged, and the collective power of the monasteries was also a force to be reckoned with.

Perhaps because they had no formal political role, the panchen lamas tended to escape the untimely death that was to afflict so many dalai lamas. The fourth Panchen Lama died at ninety-two, an age that is remarkable at any time and in any place, but which in seventeenth-century Tibet must be counted as little short of miraculous. His body was placed in the great Maitreya chapel of his own monastery, and forty monks chanted sutras for fourteen days for his early reincarnation. A gold stupa was built for the preservation of his body and a hall crowned with a golden roof built to house it.[5]

There it was to lie for just over three hundred years, an object of devotion for the faithful, until the fourth Panchen Lama, too, became a victim of the Chinese occupation of Tibet. The stupa was broken open and his bones were scattered, an act of desecration that his successor, the tenth Panchen Lama, vowed to erase. In 1989 he succeeded, but it was to be his final act.

In Tibetan politics, as elsewhere, there is often a considerable gap between the ideal and the real. In the ideal version of Tibetan history the Dalai Lama is the wise leader of the nation and his relationship with the Panchen Lama is warm and mutually enriching. In fact, after the death of Lobsang Choekyi, the relationship between the panchen and the dalai lamas was never as close or harmonious again. Not until the ninth Panchen Lama and the thirteenth Dalai Lama was the relationship between the two patriarchs to be as significant as that between the fifth Dalai Lama and the fourth Panchen Lama. But whereas the early relationship was important for its closeness, the later was catastrophic for its discord.

The fourth Panchen Lama had used his talents in defence of his religious order, but the fruits of his energies were to prove a complicated legacy for Tibet. The title of Panchen Lama had been created for him, and in the now rich and powerful Tashilhunpo monastery he left behind a base that was to grow into an important focus of power in the region of Tsang, historically a rival of the Lhasa province of Ü. It can hardly have been the intention of a man who spent his whole life advancing the interests of the Gelugpa that he create an institution that would, eventually, challenge the authority of the Dalai Lama.

The experience of exile creates many myths, and the past becomes a battleground in which the contemporary struggle for legitimacy is fought anew. For the Chinese government, the legitimacy of the occupation of Tibet rests on a number of factors of which two are central: the claims that, historically, Tibet was 'always' a part of China, and that the Tibetan system of government was one of feudal serfdom in which the Dalai Lama was a political despot, shored up by a serf-owning religious establishment.

The exile interpretation of history is that Tibet was never subject to the political control of Beijing. The relationship between the Dalai Lama and the Qing emperors was one of priest to patron: the Qing emperors acknowledged the spiritual superiority of the Dalai Lama and, in return, offered protection to his rule in Tibet. In the exile memory Tibet's political past was one of harmony and prosperity, that of a people living content within a deeply religious culture, offering voluntary allegiance to their spiritual leader.

Both versions of events contain elements of mythology and each is reinforced by the demands of contemporary disputes. In exile, the figure of the Dalai Lama has assumed a dominance far greater than was true in Tibet before the Chinese invasion. In old Tibet, although the Dalai Lama was nominally head of state, even his religious supremacy was not total. In exile he has been acknowledged as the leader, or at least the spokesman, of all sects of Tibetan Buddhism in a way that was not the case in Tibet. This development creates tensions behind the façade of unity of purpose that the government in exile tries to maintain. This official revisionism has affected the account of the Panchen Lama, too. To the exiles the Panchen Lama had become a blurred figure, whose special powers had faded in memory and whose followers had come to acknowledge the unchallenged supremacy of the Dalai Lama. In old Tibet, this was an altogether more qualified relationship.

The seventeenth century was a time of enormous change in Central Asia. As it opened, the fractured remnants of the Mongol empire still raged across the steppes, sometimes engaging in internecine warfare, sometimes directing their energies against their neighbours or the fortified frontiers of Ming China. By the time the century closed, the new power of the Manchu had conquered China and most of the Mongol tribes. Other powers, too, were beginning to make themselves felt in the region: Russia had begun her great expansion eastwards, and the scene was being set for the Great Game, that long-drawn-out battle for influence between the British and the Russian empires in Central Asia. It was a contest that was to provoke a response from the Qing emperors, nervous of movement on the periphery of their empire and aware, as all Chinese imperial power must be, that danger comes from that periphery. It was a lesson the Manchu, who had once themselves been that savage danger at the gates of China, had never forgotten.

Tibet had survived the upheavals of the century, and the Gelugpa had ended it immeasurably stronger than they began. They owed much of that strength to Lobsang Choekyi, whose life had spanned so much of that critical century. But a hundred years later the escalating competition for influence in Central Asia was to have dramatic consequences for Tibet – and for the relationship between the panchen and the dalai lamas.

It was during my second visit to India, in the autumn of 1994, that I set out to find the Panchen Lama's followers. I knew that they would have a direct interest in the search for his reincarnation, and I hoped to learn something of the character of the late Panchen Lama from people who had known him directly. The Dalai Lama himself, of course, had known him, but there was also, I learned, an exile version of the Panchen Lama's monastery of Tashilhunpo, near Bylakuppe, in the far south of India.

The Tibetan community in India was hugely scattered. Dharamsala was its administrative heart, but there were Tibetans living in many other cities, including Delhi. And though the Dalai Lama himself lived in the north, the great monasteries of Drepung, Ganden and Sera had been re-created more than a thousand miles away. This was an inconvenient arrangement, but one that had grown up by necessity.

When the number of Tibetans who fled Tibet after the failure of the uprising in 1959 reached the order of 30,000[6] the prime minister of India, Nehru, had asked several Indian states to donate land on which the refugees might be settled. Among the first to respond were the underpopulated states of the far south, and eventually settlements were built at Mundgod and Bylakuppe, Hunsur and Kollegaley. Several thousand people now lived in the south and the largest religious communities grew up there.

There are Tibetans who see design in the extreme inconvenience of their arrangements in India. When the Dalai Lama first came to India, he was lodged in the hill station of Mussourie. Mussourie was not exactly central, but it was only a few hours distant from Delhi. When the Dalai Lama first heard that Pandit Nehru planned to move the growing refugee colony to Dharamsala, a full day's travelling time from the capital, he wondered if the intention was to park the Tibetans in a place so inaccessible that the world would soon forget them.

In fact, he sent a senior figure to inspect two places where His Holiness and the by then several thousand refugees who had fled the Chinese occupation might make a home. His emissary returned with a glowing report on Dharamsala and the quality of the water in Himachal Pradesh. Dharamsala was approved, sight unseen, by the Dalai Lama. From that moment generations of Tibetans, not to mention Western pilgrims, Dharma-bums, journalists and Hollywood stars were condemned to deal with the challenge of getting there.

If communications between Dharamsala and Delhi are difficult, between Dharamsala and Bylakuppe they are next to impossible. There were, I was told, several obstacles in the way of a visit to Tashilhunpo. The monastery was remote, and it was not possible to stay there without permission from the security police. A request for such permission could take months to process and there was no guarantee of success.

From Dharamsala I made several attempts to telephone the settlement in Bylakuppe to inform them that I wanted to visit. I stood for what seemed like hours, listening to the whistles and thumps, the remote snatches of conversation, the whines and clicks of the Indian telephone system. But I never managed to get through to Bylakuppe, and the proprietor of the telephone did not trouble to hide his amusement that anyone should think it possible.

Letters, I was told, were unlikely to arrive, unless carried personally. An express telegram, perhaps, might get there, but it would take two weeks. Bylakuppe began to seem a place so distant and difficult of access I began to doubt its very existence. I gave up trying to communicate. Instead, I obtained a letter of introduction to the abbot of Tashilhunpo from the Dalai Lama's private office and set off to deliver it in person.

The journey took the best part of three days. It involved the bone-rattling taxi ride down to the railhead at Pathankot, an overnight train to Delhi, a flight the following day to Bangalore and a second perilous taxi ride.

This was a different India, lush and green, its roads slow with buffalo carts, an India of tropical gardens and warm, velvety nights, of thin, dark-skinned men selling fresh oranges and green coconuts by the roadside. When the Tibetans first came here, in the early sixties, they died wholesale from malaria and other sicknesses of the heat. Now there were new generations of Tibetans who had grown up in the tropics, more than a thousand miles from Tibet.

From Bangalore I had been driven for ten hours in an uncompanionable silence: the taxi was an Ambassador, India's universal home-produced motor, modelled on a British Austin of the 1950s, with high, rolling suspension and back-breakingly uncomfortable seats. I was told these cars were rugged, but I doubted it. I suspected it was what people found to say of a car that had few other redeeming qualities.

I was hot, sticky and ill-tempered by the time we pulled into a dirty and undistinguished village. It was Karanassie, the nearest Indian village to the Tibetan settlement. There was one flyblown hotel with collapsing plumbing and lighting so dim I sometimes thought I was imagining rather than seeing what was before me. The hotel did not serve dinner: for that, there was a restaurant, a cavernous and gloomy barn of a place at the other end of the long main street. I ate, then walked back along the rutted and barely lit street, my passage marked by silent stares from the knots of young men grouped around the intermittent pools of light. A sudden blast of damp air on my neck made me jump, and I turned, ready to let fly. The calf was as startled as I was and backed off to a safe distance, its head lowered, snorting wetly into the dust.

The next day I hired a motorbike rickshaw and asked to be taken to Tashilhunpo.

'Monastery! Monastery!' the driver yelled, nodding enthusiastically.

'*Tashilhunpo* monastery,' I said, firmly, knowing in my heart that defeat on the first attempt was all but inevitable.

'Monastery, monastery . . .' The nods were now emphatic, the motor roared into life, and the rickshaw began to vibrate with such force that had any mudguards or lights still been attached, they would surely have rattled off on the spot. We roared out of Karanassie, laying down a thick black vapour-trail that would not have shamed a jumbo jet, and thrummed our way steadily along a deserted tree-lined road.

After a few miles the driver suddenly plunged up a side-road. He screamed something over his shoulder. It was scarcely audible above the engine, but I knew, from the light in his eyes, he was saying, 'Monastery! Monastery!'

'*Tashilhunpo* monastery!' I insisted feebly. A short time later we pulled up at the gates of a monastery. It was Sera.

'Monastery! Monastery,' the driver grinned. 'Tibet,' he added, conclusively.

I shook my head. 'Wrong monastery,' I said.

We found it at the second attempt, guided by a young monk who had business near Tashilhunpo and was happy to take a lift. I found myself travelling along a narrow, dusty road between fields of maize in a landscape of gently undulating green hills. A glint of gold in the distance resolved itself into a roof, and we swerved around a corner to come to a triumphant halt before two large incense burners from which lazy threads of juniper-scented smoke were spreading their perfume on the air. A low murmur of male voices mingled with the high-pitched shouts of children playing.

'Monastery,' said the driver.

'Tashilhunpo,' I replied.

I climbed out of the trishaw just as another motorcycle roared around the corner and came to a halt in a cloud of red dust. A large, muscular, bare-armed Tibetan monk rode it in maroon robes and shades. He cut his engine, dismounted and grinned enquiringly. I started to be aware of the sensation that my arrival had generated. Monks were beginning to appear from the buildings. A head popped out of a doorway and disappeared, to be replaced immediately by two. A group of four or five monks had begun some urgent consultation, and eventually a young monk who looked about nineteen years old was pushed forward.

'Hello,' he said, frowning with the effort of concentration. 'I speak a little English.'

I began to explain – my letter of introduction, my curiosity about the Panchen Lama. The monk led me up a steep wooden staircase to an open first-floor balcony and into a large room that was almost entirely filled by a long table. One by one the monks began to crowd in – old men with gaunt cheeks and rheumy eyes, young men in maroon vests, their faces alive with friendly curiosity. They packed into the chairs around the long table and sat chattering like birds on a wire. I produced my letter and presented it, solemnly, to the monk I judged the most senior. It was examined carefully, then read out, line by line. A murmur of response and repetition, a flurry of nodding and a hurried consultation followed.

'Our abbot is away,' said the young monk, 'but you can stay here until he returns. We have a guest room.'

He led me along the balcony to a corner room. It was furnished with two beds, each covered with a Tibetan carpet. It was clean and light and I nearly danced for joy.

The monk sat down and struggled to frame his English sentences. 'This monastery,' he said, 'was founded in 1972 with eighteen monks. Now there are one hundred and twenty.'

'Did any of them know the late Panchen Lama?' I asked, abandoning subtlety.

'I did,' he replied. I looked at him in surprise and certainly with a renewed concentration.

'I was . . .' he groped for the words, paused, frowned and gave up. He succeeded on the second attempt.

'I was with him in prison,' he said. 'I told them to beat me.'

He stopped again.

'What happened then?' I asked.

'I died,' he replied.

'I see,' I said, my mind reeling slightly with the new narrative complications which had just been laid bare. 'Do you remember that?'

He grinned. 'No. It was in 1962. Maybe 1963. That was in my previous incarnation. Have you heard of Tina Turner?'

In the courtyard below the young monks were squabbling and teasing each other like puppies. One of them suddenly picked up a stone and threw it, hard, at a retreating tormentor. It caught him a glancing blow and he ran off, laughing.

My young companion had settled in. He was, he explained, the reincarnation of the late Panchen Lama's tutor, Ngulchu Lobsang Choephel. His father, it turned out, had been a monk in Tashilhunpo in Shigatse, but he had disrobed and taken a wife. The couple went to live in Ladakh where the disrobed monk was disturbed to find that his son, at the age of seven, himself showed signs of wanting to be a monk. His father had not escaped the monastic life to see his son enter it. He refused, but the child seemed constantly to dream of monasteries and monks. He even dreamed of the monastery of Tashilhunpo, and was beaten for his pains.

'When I was ten a monk came to Ladakh collecting donations

54

and I asked my father if I could be a monk. He said, Never. By the time I was twelve or thirteen I was drinking and smoking and I didn't want to be a monk any more. But then the abbot here discovered through a divination that I was the reincarnation: my father said he would believe it only if His Holiness confirmed it – which he did. So my father had no choice in the end.'

The story had taken some time and was full of twists and turns. Ngulchu sat on the bed, talking, asking questions. 'Do you have any music?' he asked. I had, but it was Mozart, and something of a disappointment. 'No Abba? George Michael? Michael Jackson?'

'Do you know,' he suddenly announced, 'that my mother married at twelve and had her first child at sixteen?' Then he got up and vanished through the curtained door.

Over the next few days he would appear, sometimes with his own tutor, a thin young man who had an altogether darker story to tell: he had left Tibet recently, the hard way, and was anxious to talk. Ngulchu seemed restless in this little community, buried in rural India. He talked of films he had seen before he became a monk and how, after his ordination, he would slyly sneak off to the cinema, excursions that earned him a beating from his tutor if they were discovered.

'Geerie,' he said one day, and waited for a response.

'Geerie?' I replied, bemused.

'Richard Geerie,' he explained. 'I saw him. In Dharamsala.'

Richard Gere, the actor, was one of the handful of celebrity Buddhists who attended the Dalai Lama's teachings in Dharamsala.

'I saw one of his films,' said Ngulchu.

'Which one?' I asked.

'*Pretty Woman*,' he said.

I laughed. 'That's not much of a film for a monk.'

Ngulchu showed me around. Tashilhunpo in exile is a relatively new and small monastery – a large courtyard of single-storey living quarters with a three-storey temple occupying one end. It quickly became clear that it was struggling to survive. There were four reincarnates, I was told, but few teachers, and it was difficult to attract monks. It also became clear that the great hope for the future of the monastery was that the Panchen Lama would be found and somehow brought here. The monastery had formed a search committee.

I asked how they were searching. Ngulchu shrugged. 'It is up to His Holiness the Dalai Lama,' he said.

But they were making one huge effort: outside the gate a large site had been cleared and slowly a new building was being erected. This, Ngulchu explained, was to be the Panchen Lama's palace.

From the roof of the main temple other monasteries could be seen, in particular the golden roofs of Sera monastery, large and prosperous in the middle distance. Sera, the monks explained, had many foreign sponsors. Sera was rich. If the Panchen Lama came here, they explained, Tashilhunpo, too, would prosper.

Ngulchu appeared one night after supper, keen to talk about movies.

'*Last Action Hero*,' he said. 'That was a good movie. Arnold Schwarzenegger ... very good muscles. Have you seen *Terminator?*'

I shook my head.

'I don't like lady movies,' he smiled. 'I like fighting movies. The abbot is coming back tomorrow,' he said, in one of those abrupt changes of subject that marked his conversation.

I met the abbot the following day, a sharp-eyed Ladakhi with a Roman nose. With the abbot's return a meeting was convened at which the monastery was to present its history and that of the panchen lamas. At the appointed hour we gathered around the long table in the upstairs room. It was a sultry evening; the monsoon season had begun. There was the boom of distant thunder in the heavy air.

The abbot began to speak. 'I will talk about the Panchen Lama, and about Tashilhunpo in Tibet. But first,' he said firmly, 'I want to talk about this monastery. Tashilhunpo was established late – in 1972. When we first came to India from Tibet the Tashilhunpo monks had no monastery, so they scattered. It has taken a great deal of hard work to set up this monastery – and the blessing of His Holiness – but it has no sponsors so we have not made much progress.'

There had been just eighteen of them to begin with, the abbot explained. He ran through an insistent list of the problems. 'On the advice of the Dalai Lama and the Panchen Lama this monastery will keep cultivating the tantric practices, but because of our financial strictures we are having great difficulty keeping the tradition alive.' There was the expense of the palace to meet and the problem of recruiting monks caused by the poor facilities. There was no dispensary and only two rooms for a school. Sometimes, he said, it was even difficult to feed the monks. He fixed me with his watchful eyes. 'We must ask our supporters to donate.

'Sera and Drepung and the others all have *foreign* support,' he stressed, in case I had missed the point. 'In Tibet, Drepung, Sera and Tashilhunpo were all on the same level. There were 5,000 monks in Tashilhunpo in Tibet, but here we are only a few. All the senior monks are over eighty and the next generation is very young. It is hard for them to study because they don't get enough to eat.'

The abbot's fund-raising speech was getting long. My eyes began to drift around the room. There was a line of framed photographs along the end wall which seemed to sum up the slightly eclectic spiritual and political concerns of the monastery, icons of authorities to be respected or appeased. The Gandhis were, of course, heavily represented: Nehru, Mrs Gandhi and Rajiv all looked down on our gathering. Then there was the obligatory photograph of the late Panchen Lama and the commemorative photograph of George Bush with the Dalai Lama, a souvenir of the first time the Dalai Lama had been officially received at the White House. Later a pious Tibetan was to describe to me how he had seen a vision of the White House in the holy lake of Lhamo Latso, a sign that even prophetic religious dreams can adapt to the demands of diplomacy.

As the abbot continued his financial report, the elderly monks began to doze and Ngulchu lounged across the table, chewing gum. Finally the bid for funds came to an end. The abbot paused, then began the speech I had been waiting for – the official history of Tashilhunpo and the panchen lamas.

Chapter Five

✺

'The first Panchen Lama,' the abbot said, 'was Kedrup Geleg Pelzang, the principal student of Tsongkhapa. He wrote many prayer books and established a new monastery in Gyantse.' He moved on through the list: Sonam Choglang, the second Panchen Lama, Lobsang Dondrup, the third. Until the third Panchen Lama, he explained, they were abbots of another monastery, but after the fourth, Lobsang Choekyi Gyaltsen – in fact, after the moment that the title was created – they had all lived in Tashilhunpo.

The names rolled on: 'The fifth was Lobsang Yeshe, and the sixth Palden Yeshe, who expired in China . . .'

In his recitation of names, the abbot was skipping rapidly through more than five hundred years of Tibetan history. His footnotes to the names were stories of acts of piety and miracles, the history of the panchens as he saw it. But there was another history which, if he knew it, he did not seem anxious to tell.

He skipped, for instance, over the figure of Lobsang Palden Yeshe, the sixth Panchen Lama, with scarcely a comment, though he had been one of the great figures of late-eighteenth-century Tibet. It had fallen to him to try to keep a balance between the competing foreign powers that were, by then, trying to consolidate an interest in Tibet.

By the time the sixth Panchen Lama was in his middle years, the British were established in India, and the first British Governor-General of India, Warren Hastings, was turning his mind to the challenge of trade beyond the Himalayas. The British knew little about Tibet; it had previously been visited by a trickle of enterprising foreigners, most of them missionaries, but memories of these visits were fragmentary and records sparse. The only maps that existed had been compiled by lamas trained by the Jesuit mission in Beijing and sent to Tibet on the orders of the Kang Xi emperor. The British had begun to remedy this lack of geographical data by sending in Indian pundits disguised as pilgrims, their surveying instruments concealed in their staffs. They surveyed the terrain by counting the miles on rosaries which had been specially re-strung to give an exact tally.

In 1774 Warren Hastings decided to send an envoy to the Panchen Lama with a mission 'to open a mutual and equal communication of trade between the inhabitants of Bhutan and Bengal'.[1] The chosen envoy, a young Scot named George Bogle, duly met the Panchen Lama in November of the same year in a small monastery to which the lama had retreated three years before to escape an epidemic of smallpox.

The man Bogle described had nothing of the hermit and little of the ascetic about him. He was, Bogle wrote:

... about forty years of age, of low stature and though not corpulent, inclining to be fat ... his hair, which is jet black, is cut very short; his beard and whiskers never above a month long; his eyes are small and black ... His disposition is open, candid and generous. He is extremely merry and entertaining in conversation and tells a pleasant story with a great deal of humour and action. Not a man could find it in his heart to speak ill of him.[2]

Bogle found the Panchen Lama full of curiosity and intelligence, and the two men became friends in the four months that Bogle stayed in Shigatse. The Panchen undertook to plead the East India Company's case in Lhasa.

Lhasa's view, however, was less friendly. The seventh Dalai Lama had died when the Panchen Lama was about twenty, and the eighth Dalai Lama was still in his minority. The government in Lhasa was in the hands of the regent, Demo Thupten Jigme, who was not disposed to admit the troublesome British. He was well aware that to do so would annoy the emperor of China.

In any event, this promising relationship between the British and the sixth Panchen Lama was cut short by the unfortunate fate that was to befall the Panchen Lama. In 1777 he was invited to Lhasa to administer the eighth Dalai Lama's final vows and spend the year in the Potala teaching him scriptures.[3] The following year, on the occasion of the Qing emperor's seventieth birthday, the Panchen Lama received an invitation to visit Beijing.

He accepted. It would be an elaborate journey of three years' duration, and he was to be accompanied by nearly two thousand people. His route took him north through Nagchu, then across the Tangla mountains to the great monastery of Kumbum in Qinghai, where he spent the five winter months. In the spring he continued through Ningxia, Gansu and Inner Mongolia until he arrived at the imperial summer resort of Chengde, where a palace had been built to receive him.[4]

It was a measure of the respect in which the Emperor held him that when the Panchen finally arrived at the summer residence, the Emperor was waiting at the gate to greet him. In contrast to the reception afforded the upstart representatives of the distant British crown, the Panchen Lama was not asked to kowtow.

The next stage of the visit was less auspicious. Shortly after arriving in Beijing, where he took up residence in the Yellow temple, which had been built for the visit of the Great Fifth Dalai Lama, at the age of only forty-two, the sixth Panchen contracted smallpox and died.

The body was embalmed and housed in a solid-gold stupa donated by the emperor, and the following year it began its arduous and doleful procession back to Tibet. In memory of the Panchen Lama, the Emperor built a second Yellow temple in Beijing, which still stands. A year after the death of the Panchen Lama, in April 1781, the enterprising George Bogle died in Calcutta.

There were two sequels to the death of the sixth Panchen Lama. Both were to echo across the years and influence the events of the 1990s. The first was a dispute that arose over the disposition of the treasures that the Qing emperor had given to the Panchen Lama. The Panchen's brother, Chumba, refused to share them with his other, surviving brother, a Kagyupa lama called Shamar. Enraged, Shamar fled to Nepal, where he incited the Gurkhas to invade Tibet.[5]

The Qing emperor sent reinforcements, ostensibly to help Tibet fight the Gurkhas, but meanwhile struck a secret deal in which the Chinese government promised that the Tibetans would pay the Gurkhas an annual tribute. When the Tibetans failed to pay, the Gurkhas invaded Tibet again. This time, they were categorically defeated.

Once order had been restored, the Emperor ordained that Shamar Rinpoche, who had fomented the invasion, should have his property confiscated, and that the monks of his monasteries should convert to the Yellow sect. As a final blow, Shamar's lineage was to be terminated. His subsequent reincarnations were not to be recognized – a severe punishment indeed for a living Buddha.

The prohibition was observed for over a century, but eventually Shamar did return. Many wish he had not, for he has proved to be as troublesome in the twentieth century as he was in the eighteenth. The present Shamar Rinpoche is the dissident regent in the current dispute over the Karmapa succession, the man who refused to accept the child agreed by his fellow regents and the Dalai Lama and who is now promoting a rival candidate.

The second enduring legacy of the sixth Panchen Lama's death was that, as a result of the quarrel between the Panchen Lama's brothers, the emperor began to doubt the authenticity of the Tibetan procedures for identifying senior religious figures. The fact that the fifth Panchen Lama, Shamar Rinpoche and Mongolia's Chumba Hutuktu had all been discovered in the same family – an aristocratic family from the province of Tsang – led the Celestial Emperor to wonder if the oracle who had been consulted in the choice had been entirely straight. Was it possible, he mused, that his trance had been tainted by bribes?

In order to prevent any fixing of a contest in future, the Emperor ordered the production of two Golden Urns, one for Mongolia and one for Tibet. It was agreed that, in the event of dispute over the recognition of the Dalai Lama or the Panchen Lama in Tibet, or the senior Hutuktus of Mongolia, the names of the candidates should be inscribed on tallies and drawn from the Golden Urn. The gift was accepted in Tibet with the idea that the Golden Urn lottery join the other forms of divination that could be used to reach such decisions. When circumstances demanded, lots would be drawn before the statue of Sowo, the historical Buddha, Sakyamuni, in the Jokhang temple in Lhasa.

The Tibetans attached no great significance to the gift, however, and the Urn was not always used. But as time went by, the government in Beijing began to insist that the Golden Urn lottery was an indispensable part of the process. In 1995, two centuries after the arrival of the Golden Urn in Tibet, the bitter dispute between the Dalai Lama and the government in Beijing was to turn on the significance of the lottery of the Golden Urn.

*

For nearly one hundred years, Tibet suffered from weak leadership as a string of dalai lamas died prematurely. It was not until the arrival of the thirteenth Dalai Lama on the throne, in 1877, that this curse seemed to end. He nearly came to an untimely end, too, but he managed to survive an assassination attempt organized by his outgoing regent and lived to steer Tibet through some of the most troubled times in her history.

As I listened to the abbot reciting names in that little room, outside in the gathering gloom of the southern Indian twilight, a torrential rainstorm had broken out. Water thrummed on the roof of the meeting room and splashed through the wire mesh of the open windows. From the courtyard below came the sounds of running feet and the slam of windows hastily being closed.

'The seventh was Palden Tenpai Nyima,' the abbot continued doggedly, 'who was ruler of Tibet for eight months. The eighth was Tenpai Wangchuk, and the ninth, Panchen Choekyi Nyima, who was born in 1883 in the province of Tsang. He was recognized as the Panchen Lama at the age of three. There was a sign in the lake and the boy left two footprints in stone. He entered Tashilhunpo monastery at the age of eight.'

At this point the abbot paused, and a monk was despatched to another room. He returned bearing a large photograph in a gilt frame.

'This is the ninth Panchen Lama,' said the abbot. 'This photograph commemorates the visit of the Panchen Lama to Delhi in 1906. He was twenty-four years old. The British,' he added, by way of explanation, 'were then in India.' A young man in robes stared stiffly at the camera. Behind him, standing in formal pose, was a British officer. I waited with interest to hear how the abbot would explain what had happened to the Panchen Lama following this visit.

'In 1914,' he continued, 'at the age of thirty-two, he made a nine-storey statue of Chamba Maitreya Buddha. It took four years to construct. This demonstrates that he was a very good man whose main concern was the Buddha. He carried out many good works.' (A prodigious list of good works followed.)

'In 1923, at the age of forty-one, he went to China. He celebrated the Kalachakra ceremony ten times in China. Abbot Bering went with him. Lobsang Gyaltsen was his servant, and Namgyal Sherab and Phurbu Tsering also went with him.'

'Why did he go to China?' I enquired.

The abbot plunged on. 'The Panchen Lama was not proud,' he said. 'He spoke very frankly and was very peaceful. He loved Tibet very much. That's why he made the great statue – for the peaceful settlement of all Tibetans in Tibet.'

'How long did he stay in China?' I asked.

'His eyes were slightly irregular,' the abbot went on, ignoring my question. 'But there was no defect in them. It was just that one was slightly higher than the other. You can see, in the photograph. He was five foot two, he was quite fat and his moustache was too long. The day before he died he bathed in spring water. There were designs on his hand of the chakra. He died in Kandze Dzong at the age of fifty-five in 1937 on the twenty-eighth day of the tenth Tibetan month.'

The abbot glared at me, daring me to insist on the question he was determined not to answer. The fourteen years that he had just tried to gloss over represented one of the most difficult and tragic episodes in recent Tibetan history: the epic quarrel that broke out between the ninth Panchen Lama and the thirteenth Dalai Lama. It was a quarrel that was to have enormous repercussions for Tibet, and I had hoped that the Panchen Lama's side of it would be part of the monastery's collective memory. If it was, then it had been deeply buried.

The immediate cause of the dispute was taxation, but the background lay in the escalating confrontation between the Chinese and the British over influence in Tibet. The run of premature deaths among the dalai lamas had afforded the Qing emperors the opportunity to establish a firm presence in Tibet. They had stationed two imperial representatives, or *ambans*, in Lhasa, who had found asserting the emperor's authority over the regents a relatively easy task, despite the fact that the empire itself was being weakened by both internal rebellion and foreign incursions.

The panchen lamas during this period emerged as champions of Tibetan independence against the Chinese. They used their relative independence from Lhasa, coupled with their longevity and prestige, to pursue their own diplomacy, including, when necessary, with the British. In doing so, however, Shigatse established a measure of autonomy from Lhasa that many in Lhasa resented.

That began to change when the thirteenth Dalai Lama survived his minority and assumed real power.

The ninth Panchen Lama was six years younger than the Dalai Lama and was described by the British envoy Charles Bell, who visited him in Tashilhunpo in 1906 as 'a sweet and modest man by nature'.[6] The thirteenth Dalai Lama, for all his qualities of leadership, was not a man whom anyone would describe in those terms. He was astute and intelligent. Contemporary photographs reveal him as a man whose mournful appearance was accentuated by his elaborate waxed moustache and large, pointed ears. Because he was the first strong dalai lama for more than a century he found his power compromised by a Chinese policy, developed during his predecessors' ineffectual reigns, of cultivating the panchen lamas as a counterweight to Lhasa. This meant that the panchen lamas and their courts had been able to increase their power virtually without challenge from Lhasa, and that, by the time the thirteenth Dalai Lama reached his majority, Tibet had two clear, and separate, centres of power.

The ninth Panchen Lama and the thirteenth Dalai Lama met only rarely, and as Tibet found itself increasingly threatened by outside interests, this lack of harmony between the two men (or at least between their respective courts) was to have a disastrous effect.

The international situation was, if anything, more menacing than before. The British were pressing on Tibet's southern frontier and the Russian expansion into Asia brought them into competition with the British. The Qing empire was suffering the encroachment of Western powers in the east and was anxious to keep both Russia and Britain at bay in Central Asia at least.

The thirteenth Dalai Lama took much of his advice on international diplomacy from a remarkable Buriat monk named Agvan Dorzhiev, who had known the Dalai Lama since he was thirteen years old and who was to be the Dalai Lama's inseparable attendant and close political adviser until 1913.[7] It was Dorzhiev who first explained to the Dalai Lama the differences between the various foreigners who had designs on Tibet. The British, he pointed out, having conquered India, were steadily swallowing the small states of the Himalayas. The Qing dynasty was too weak to play its traditional role of patron and protector. Only the Russians, Dorzhiev argued, could help Tibet beat off the British encroachment.

Other groups in Lhasa gave different advice. Some argued that Tibet should continue to rely on Peking, others that security lay in establishing good relations with the government of India. But for the first part of the Dalai Lama's career, at least, it was Dorzhiev who had the Dalai Lama's ear.

Dorzhiev had good contacts with the Russian Imperial court and, since the Russian emperors were believed by the pious Buddhists of Tibet and Mongolia to be the incarnation of the goddess White Tara, Dorzhiev's political arguments also had spiritual weight. The Dalai Lama began a friendly correspondence with St Petersburg with a view to developing a more solid relationship.

British policy was confused. The British of the Raj wanted to thwart what they saw as Russia's eventual purpose: to establish a presence in Tibet from which they could threaten Britain's greatest prize, India. For them, Agvan Dorzhiev's presence at the Dalai Lama's court was incontrovertible evidence of the Tsar's intentions. However, in London, the Foreign Office saw a wider picture of relations to be maintained both with China and Imperial Russia and never gave Tibet the importance the India Office did.

In any event, the Tibetans continued to refuse to respond to British overtures on trade. After Lord Curzon became Viceroy of India he wrote to the Dalai Lama, but his letters were returned unopened. Frustrated by the lack of progress, Curzon was persuaded in 1903 that sterner measures were required. He gave his approval to an expedition led by Francis Younghusband, the purpose of which was to force the Tibetan government to negotiate.

Younghusband crossed the Tibetan border from Sikkim in July 1903. He camped at Khamba Dzong, below the hill fort near Gyantse, and attempted to open negotiations with the Dalai Lama's representatives. It was a frustrating business: the Tibetans refused to talk until the British withdrew to Sikkim, and nothing Younghusband could say persuaded them otherwise.

More than a month later a delegation from Tashilhunpo monastery arrived and Younghusband's expectations rose, but the delegation repeated the government's insistence that the British must withdraw. Younghusband sat it out in Khamba Dzong for three months, then returned to India for consultations with Curzon.

London had given reluctant permission for a limited military expedition into Tibet, and in December Younghusband returned at the head of it and crossed the Tangla to set up camp near a small settlement called Tuna. The Tibetan forces, comprising a group of warrior monks from the three great monasteries of Ganden, Drepung and Sera, a local militia and horsemen and soldiers from eastern Tibet, dug in on the plain below Guru. They were pathetically ill-armed and were to face a military force equipped with weapons of which they knew nothing.

By March Younghusband's forces had been ordered to advance. The two sides met at a place called Chumi Shengo. The precise sequence of events that triggered what was to be a massacre of the Tibetan forces is still a matter of dispute, but there is no doubt about the slaughter of the Tibetans, penned up in a hollow under the British Maxim guns. It was all over in a few minutes. The British suffered six wounded; the Tibetans 628 dead and 222 injured.

The Tibetans mustered what further resistance they could, but the British marched on to Lhasa. When they arrived, in August 1904, they found that the Dalai Lama, accompanied by Agvan Dorzhiev and against the advice of the Chinese *ambans*, had fled.

In the Dalai Lama's absence the Tibetan government signed an agreement with the British under which Tibet recognized British overlordship of Sikkim and agreed trade terms with India through the trade marts that were to be set up in the Tibetan towns of Gyantse and Gartok. The Lhasa Convention, as it is called, was potentially an important foothold for the British in Tibet, but the gains were to be thrown away in a rerun of the vacillating British policy that had stifled Warren Hastings' initiative a century before.

Younghusband returned to India to find that the British government had repudiated his military expedition and that his career was effectively over. His great supporter, Lord Curzon, was hanging on by the skin of his teeth, trying to salvage a policy towards Tibet that was by now in tatters. The British government, instead of building on the Lhasa Convention, was anxious to mend fences with China. The Chinese, on the other hand, were so alarmed by the Younghusband expedition that they were anxious to establish direct control in Tibet, for fear that it would go the same way as Sikkim and become a British protectorate.

The Dalai Lama had gone north, ignoring the letters that pursued him from Francis Younghusband urging him to return. He spent two years in Mongolia, from where Dorzhiev was despatched to seek the assistance of the Russian Tsar. But the Russians had just lost the Russo-Japanese war and, troubled by internal unrest, were reluctant to offer more than sympathy and the promise of a gradual enlargement of support. Worse, the Qing government took advantage of the Dalai Lama's flight to announce that he had been deposed and stripped of his secular powers. 'The rank of the Dalai Lama is temporarily confiscated,' the proclamation said, 'and in his place is appointed the Panchen Lama.'

While the Dalai Lama was suffering the humiliation of exile and dethronement, the Panchen Lama was pursuing a line of diplomacy of his own. In 1903 he had sent an official to meet Younghusband at Khamba Dzong, and Tashilhunpo had been spared the hostility of the British forces that had marched on to Lhasa. In the autumn of 1904 the British renewed the contact with Tashilhunpo that had been interrupted for nearly a hundred years: the trade agent in Gyantse, Captain Frederick O'Connor, was sent to Shigatse to pay his respects to the Panchen Lama.

From the evidence of the diplomatic correspondence on the subject, it seems clear that, at this moment at least, the British were in no hurry to see the Dalai Lama return from his Mongolian exile; they had, after all, found him uncooperative and hostile. The problem that his absence created, though, was that it left a political vacuum in Lhasa that someone was bound to fill: if it was not to be the British, then it would be the Russians or the Chinese. The British needed some effective counter to that threat.

Captain O'Connor found the Panchen Lama receptive to the British approach, though how explicit the British intention was is not clear. Certainly it was in Captain O'Connor's mind – and in this he was supported by Curzon – that it served British interests to build up the Panchen Lama and help him towards his ambition of maintaining the autonomy of Shigatse as a counterweight to Lhasa.

Captain O'Connor wanted to open a trade mart in Shigatse and to make it clear that any consolidation of Chinese power in Lhasa would be matched by an expansion of British influence in Tsang. To reinforce this approach, he pressed on the Panchen Lama an invitation to India the following year: the Prince of Wales was coming, and it was to be a grand affair.

The Panchen Lama went into a characteristic dither. He wanted to go to India, to firm up British support. On the other hand, such a trip would certainly offend both the exiled Dalai Lama and the Chinese. He was eventually persuaded to accept the invitation, which, as he had rightly predicted, offended both parties deeply, on the promise that the British would protect him against the consequences. With that assurance under his belt, the timid Panchen Lama set out for India. No wonder he looked so apprehensive in the photograph the abbot had just showed me.

His apprehension was, indeed, fully justified. By the time the Panchen's visit to India took place, Lord Curzon had been replaced by Lord Minto, and Lord Morley was in charge of the Foreign Office. Lord Morley repudiated everything that Curzon had done, including any promises made to the Panchen Lama. Thus, under the urging of the British and bolstered by worthless reassurances, the poor Panchen had made powerful enemies, only to find that the promise of protection had evaporated. When Charles Bell visited Tashilhunpo in 1906 the Panchen Lama was still terrified of the consequences of what he had done. Retribution, he was sure, would follow.

For the time being, however, the thirteenth Dalai Lama was still suffering his lonely and difficult exile. He stayed for nearly two years in Mongolia, where the eighth Jetsun Damba Hutuktu was the spiritual leader. Unfortunately the Hutuktu, like his immediate predecessor, was not the most inspiring exemplar of religious virtue. He was fond of both alcohol and tobacco and, if that were not bad enough, notorious for both homosexual and heterosexual licence. Relations between the two prelates were not warm, and the Dalai Lama left Mongolia in 1906 to take up residence in Kumbum monastery in Qinghai. While he was there, his hopes of Russian support were finally dashed when the Russian–British convention of 1907 was signed. By this convention both parties agreed to respect the territorial integrity of Tibet, to respect Chinese suzerainty and to deal with Tibetans only through Chinese mediation, except where Britain enjoyed special rights under the Lhasa Convention. By the same agreement Russia agreed not to try to station representatives in Lhasa.

With no prospect, now, of help from the Russians, the Dalai Lama had no choice but to try to mend relations with the Chinese.

He eventually negotiated a visit to Beijing in 1908. He arrived by train and was ceremonially borne through the city to the Yellow temple[8] in a yellow state palanquin with sixteen bearers, escorted by a throng of Buddhist monks, soldiers and musicians. But despite the pomp the visit was a profound humiliation. Some of the titles that had been removed were restored to him, but he was treated with a studied lack of respect that emphasized the Qing government's desire to treat him not as a venerable religious superior but as a political vassal.

When the Dalai Lama tried to make his own diplomatic contacts in Beijing, the Chinese insisted that a Chinese official be present at the meetings. The contrast with the reception afforded the fifth Dalai Lama at the beginning of the Qing empire could not have been more poignant. The US ambassador to Peking, William Rockhill, concluded that he was witnessing the end of the temporal power of the leader of the Yellow sect. His observation was prophetic, if premature. The thirteenth Dalai Lama left Peking with a profound dislike of the Chinese and a conviction that he must look elsewhere for assistance. His only option now was the British.

In the Dalai Lama's absence the Chinese had been changing things in Tibet. They had occupied the eastern province of Kham, as they were to do again nearly fifty years later. Kham was attractive to China because it was contiguous with several Chinese provinces and its status was ambiguous: the Dalai Lama's temporal authority had never been established there, though the area was ethnically and culturally Tibetan.

Peking had proclaimed its own political authority over Kham and announced that the Khampa were now Chinese subjects and must pay taxes to Peking. The move provoked a rebellion in Kham, which became the pretext for a Chinese occupation. The Chinese also planned to try to secularize the government in Lhasa. British fears that the space vacated by the Dalai Lama would be filled by the Chinese appeared to be coming true.

The Dalai Lama returned to Lhasa on 25 December 1909, only to discover that a Chinese armed force was advancing towards the capital. He fled again. This time he went to India where he was courteously received and housed in Darjeeling at the Indian government's expense. He asked the Panchen Lama to join him in this second exile, reasoning that the exile of both the leading incarnates of the Gelugpa would serve to draw attention to Chinese action.

The Panchen Lama, however, refused and compounded what the Dalai Lama saw as this discourtesy by accepting an invitation from the Chinese *amban* to go to Lhasa. There, to make matters even worse, he was accommodated in the Dalai Lama's quarters. It was the most explicit attempt to date by the Chinese to replace the Dalai Lama with the Panchen Lama, and the popular view in Lhasa was certainly that the Panchen Lama had taken a step too far towards the temporarily vacant throne.

The emperor had once again stripped the Dalai Lama of his titles and, this time, in terms that were even more insulting than on the first occasion. The Dalai Lama, they said, had not only been deprived of his temporal power but he had, in the emperor's view, forfeited his right to be regarded as a high reincarnate. As the imperial decree put it:

He has been guilty of treachery and has placed himself beyond the pale of our Imperial favour. He is not fit to be a Reincarnation of the Buddha. Let him, therefore be deprived of his titles and his position of Dalai Lama as punishment. Henceforth, no matter where he may go, no matter where he may reside, whether in Tibet or elsewhere, let him be treated as an ordinary individual.

The emperor even abrogated to himself the right to find a new Dalai Lama, using, of course, the Golden Urn. His decree continued:

Let the Imperial Amban at once cause a search to be made for male children bearing miraculous signs and let him inscribe their names on tablets and place them in the Golden Urn so that one may be drawn out as the true reincarnation of previous dalai lamas.[9]

The Dalai Lama had been received attentively in India, but he failed to secure the military backing he hoped for. Nor did he receive any promise of help from the Russian Tsar, to whom he had again appealed in 1910. He did, however, make one friendship that was to prove enduring and have a profound influence on his thinking about the future of Tibet: he met Charles Bell, the government of India's political officer in Sikkim. Bell was to spend much of the rest of his career making tireless though not always fruitful efforts to persuade the British to support Tibet and to keep Tibet well disposed towards Britain.

By 1910 the Chinese had apparently abandoned their attempt to replace the thirteenth Dalai Lama with the Panchen Lama and invited the Dalai Lama to return to Tibet, where they offered him the opportunity to resume his spiritual, but not his temporal position. The Dalai Lama refused to discuss it. The Chinese, he now believed, could not be trusted. In future, he said, he would negotiate with the Chinese only through the good offices of the British. It was the last correspondence between the Dalai Lama and the Qing empire. In October 1911 revolution broke out in China and early the following year the last emperor of the Qing, the child Pu Yi, abdicated the Dragon Throne. China became a republic.

When the soldiers of the Qing in Lhasa heard the news they mutinied, and the Tibetans – or most of them – took advantage of the disorder to expel them. There were exceptions to this patriotic rule, however, whom the Dalai Lama was not to forget on his return. One monastery fought openly on the Chinese side and the Panchen Lama's seat of Tashilhunpo was reluctant to fight at all. Nevertheless, within a few weeks the entire Chinese garrison had surrendered and the soldiers were allowed to leave Tibet.

In 1913 the Dalai Lama finally returned home after nearly nine years of almost continuous exile. As Charles Bell wrote: 'Soon after their departure, daybreak broke and we could behold a gorgeous procession of men, joyful and determined, returning to govern their very own land, very different from the forlorn arrival of tired men on tired ponies that was witnessed two years before.'[10] Three weeks later the Dalai Lama issued a historic statement in which he proclaimed the political independence of Tibet and announced his firm intention to rule.

The shaky Chinese Republic that had been born from the ruins of the imperial system was headed by the unattractive figure of Yuan Shikai. He later tried, unsuccessfully, to restore the empire with himself cast in the role of emperor. Neither he nor the government he headed was in a position to do anything about Tibet's proclamation of independence. Mongolia was to make a similar declaration and, with Soviet support, succeed in maintaining independence, from China, at least.

But if Yuan Shikai was powerless, it did not mean that he or the governments that followed his short-lived reign had renounced the ambition to control Tibet conceived by the collapsed Manchu empire. It was an ambition that was to be handed on from the last emperor to the first president, through the Nationalist Guomindang (KMT) to the Communist government of Mao Zedong. Those various regimes may have disagreed over many things, but about Tibet they were strikingly unanimous in their ambition to establish Chinese rule. It was not until 1949, however, that there was to be a government in China that had both the strength of purpose and the ability to achieve this.

In 1913 the British tried to resolve the dispute that had arisen with the Dalai Lama's declaration of independence. They proposed a tripartite negotiation between China, Tibet and Britain in Simla. The convention that resulted divided Tibet into Inner and Outer Tibet: Inner Tibet – the provinces of Kham and Amdo – was to enjoy religious autonomy; Outer Tibet was to be under the political rule of the Dalai Lama. The convention was agreed by the Chinese representatives in Simla but repudiated by the government in Beijing. The British, whose motives were rarely altruistic, negotiated a separate agreement with Tibet which moved the north-east frontier between Tibet and India to a new line, known as the McMahon Line, adding to India the province that became known as Arunachal Pradesh.

The Dalai Lama had regained his throne but was faced with the urgent need to defend its independence. For that he needed a more effective army than Tibet had had for the best part of six hundred years. He listened with a favourable ear to proposals put to him to that effect by various British officials with modernizing ideas. But the burden of expanding and modernizing the army was crippling for a country with such a primitive tax structure. There was no manufacturing to speak of, and the British refused to allow the government to raise any import duties, pleading that it contravened a trade agreement arrived at in 1914.

The most obvious repository of wealth was in land, much of which was held by the great monasteries, and of these, the Panchen Lama's seat of Tashilhunpo was the richest. It seemed natural enough to Lhasa, therefore, that the Panchen Lama should be asked to make a significant contribution to the costs of bringing the army up to standard.

But many of the monasteries felt intimated by the direction in which the Dalai Lama was steering Tibet. For them an expanded army promoted by modernizing lay officials represented a threat not only to their finances but also to the dominance of the religious segment in the politics of Tibet, and they saw it as a direct challenge. All the great monasteries shared this sentiment. There was even a full-scale revolt by several monasteries against the policy of modernization. It was put down, but it made it inescapably clear how strongly sentiment was running in some quarters against the Dalai Lama's reforms.

In Tashilhunpo the resentment was felt more personally. Added to the general question of religious power was the long historic rivalry between the province of Tsang and Lhasa. On top of that, the thirteenth Dalai Lama's court was already suspicious of the Panchen Lama's autonomy, a suspicion that had deepened during the Dalai Lama's periods of exile.

Tibetans have blamed this dispute less on the two incarnates themselves than on their respective retinues. On the Dalai Lama's side, a senior official in the Lhasa court named Lungshar is blamed for nursing an old personal grudge against Tashilhunpo. On the Panchen Lama's side, the senior officials of his court are portrayed as small-minded and jealous of their authority: their respective spiritual leaders, the orthodox view has it, were above such considerations.

But though the two men maintained cordial personal relations, the Dalai Lama never lost the suspicion that the Panchen Lama's court regarded China as the best hope of preserving its own power against Lhasa.[11] When Lhasa levied its tax demand Tashilhunpo saw it as the retribution they had feared ever since 1906. The British had refused to supply the arms the Panchen Lama had requested 'for the defence of Shigatse'. As the quarrel between the two courts deepened the Panchen Lama was eventually to turn to China.

In 1922 the Panchen Lama appealed through the Gyantse trade agent, David Macdonald, to the British to mediate between himself and the Dalai Lama in the matter of the tax demand. The Panchen Lama, Macdonald reported, was being asked to contribute a quarter of the cost of the upkeep of the new Tibetan army. Some Tashilhunpo officials, he claimed, were already in prison for the monastery's failure to pay.[12] The British declined to mediate.

The Dalai Lama was persuaded that Tashilhunpo's reluctance to pay was not because the monastery lacked funds but because it rejected Lhasa's authority. The dispute became increasingly acrimonious until, in November 1923, some senior officials of Tashilhunpo were summoned to Lhasa for discussions of the Panchen Lama's tax bill. On their arrival, they were arrested and imprisoned.

When the news reached Shigatse, the Panchen Lama took it as the final signal that his own arrest was imminent. On the night of 15 November 1923 he fled, under cover of darkness, accompanied by only fifteen senior monks. The party rode furiously south, across the Tsangchen River to the grasslands, a journey that normally takes a month. Fifteen days later another group, consisting of the Panchen Lama's most senior officials with more than a hundred men and mules, slipped out of Tashilhunpo. They travelled at double time for five days and nights to rendezvous with the Panchen Lama.

At the news of the Panchen Lama's flight Lhasa had despatched a thousand armed men in pursuit, under the command of the implacably hostile Lungshar, but the Panchen Lama had turned north across the hideously inhospitable Changtang. The pursuers lost them, and defeated by the blizzards that now raged, turned back.

The Panchen's party, too, was ill equipped for a winter journey across the northern wastes of the Changtang. They were saved by a chance encounter with a caravan headed by two senior officials of the Jetsun Damba Hutuktu of Mongolia, who were heading back to Outer Mongolia from Lhasa. The Mongolians gave them food and shelter and accompanied the Panchen Lama as far as Gansu province, where delighted Chinese officials received him. A year after his departure from Shigatse, he reached Xi'an, in north-west China.

The Panchen Lama found himself in a country that was collapsing into civil war. The north-west had fallen prey to a succession of warlords. Outer Mongolia had fallen into the arms of the Soviet Union and would be devastated by Stalin. When Stalin's terror finished there would scarcely be a monk, let alone a monastery, left standing. In southern China the shaky government of the Guomindang would shortly be established in Nanjing and struggle, but fail, to establish its dominion over the whole country. The so-called northern government, based in Beijing, ruled northern China.

The timorous Panchen Lama, who demonstrated more than anything a desire for peace and a terror of danger, was now adrift in a landscape of violence, war and uncertainty. He had departed precipitately, leaving behind a reproachful letter to the Dalai Lama and condemning 'those officials' who had created his troubles. His absence, he said, would last only until someone could be found to mediate.

The Dalai Lama's reply was cold:

You seem to have forgotten the sacred history of your predecessors and wandered away to a desert ... like a moth that is attracted by the lamplight... (you) have run away with sinful companions who resembled mad elephants and followed the wrong path. It is difficult to believe that a person who thinks of himself only and who is not freed from the three sins should be regarded as a lama of Buddha.[13]

For the next fourteen years, the mild, courteous and pious Panchen Lama was to be buffeted by fortune, the instrument of the designs of others on his country. He never returned.

Chapter Six

✫

The rain had stopped, and a ceiling fan slowly revolved above the table in the upstairs room. A small tinsel decoration dangling from it twirled gently in the breeze. I looked around at the assembled monks, whose faces were now illuminated, unflatteringly, by the harsh central light that hung over the table.

As the abbot had explained, there was a wide age-gap in the company. There were the elderly monks, who included the abbot and an ancient lama with dramatically long fingernails and a wispy white beard. The single light cast deep shadows beneath his sharp cheek-bones so that he looked like a caricature of a venerable Chinese mandarin. These were the men who had known the original monastery of Tashilhunpo as young monks in Tibet and had left after the uprising of 1959. Their departures had not been dramatic, I discovered. Most of them were from Ladakh, a region with a long association with Tashilhunpo monastery and the source of many of the monastery's recruits in the old days. When the Chinese came, the Ladakhis simply left – quietly and legally. The other faces around the table were those of young monks. They were sitting quietly now, but usually they fidgeted with restless energy and curiosity. Many of them had been born in exile, but there were one or two native Tibetans who had made that perilous journey across the high Himalayan passes to India.

I had tried to prod the abbot into an explanation of the ninth Panchen's fourteen-year exile from Tibet, but all he was prepared to say was that 'Panchen Rinpoche gave the Kalachakra initiation many times and preached Buddhism in China.'

The Kalachakra teachings, the Wheel of Time, are considered the apogee of tantric teachings: they are believed to have been given by the Buddha and describe the destruction and renewal of the dharma (the doctrinal tradition of Buddhism). The Panchen did give the Kalachakra teachings several times in China, but the most important result of his exile was not to take Buddhism to

China but eventually to bring the Chinese, in force, into Tibet.

The ninth Panchen Lama was not to live to see that day, but his wanderings in Mongolia offered a foretaste of the fate that awaited his own land. In Mongolia, the Panchen became the focus of a bizarre myth of salvation that was to prove as ineffectual as magic potions were to prove against the might of the Chinese in Tibet.

The myth had its roots in the Buddhist dream of Shambhala, the pure land, the place where the blissful state of Buddhism will eventually be realized. It is both a mythological place and, for believers, a real land located somewhere in Central Asia, visible to those who are spiritually developed enough to see it. It was in Shambhala, Buddhist legend has it, that the Buddha's Kalachakra teachings were preserved for a thousand years until Indian tantric masters came to recover them and take them to Tibet.

The land of Shambhala is shaped like a lotus and surrounded by mountains. In its centre, within an inner circle of sharp-pointed mountains, sits the jewelled city of Kalapa, and to the south there is a three-dimensional mandala of the Kalachakra. From the city of Kalapa, the story goes, King Rudrachakrin will one day ride out on his stone horse to do battle with the forces of evil in the West, and an age of nirvana will dawn.[1]

The idea of Shambhala had been closely associated with the panchen lamas. The sixth Panchen Lama, Lobsang Palden Yeshe, even wrote a guidebook to it. Equally importantly, the realization of the Buddhist realm of Shambhala became an ambition of Agvan Dorzhiev's, the Buriat monk and friend of the thirteenth Dalai Lama whom the British suspected of acting as an agent of the Russian crown. Just after the turn of the century a pamphlet circulated in Lhasa that was attributed to Dorzhiev. It argued that Shambhala was located in Russia and that the emperor of Russia, as the reincarnation of Tsongkhapa, would eventually 'subdue the whole world and found a gigantic Buddhist empire'.[2]

Dorzhiev pursued this vision of a great Central Asian Buddhist empire under the protection of the Tsar through decades of tireless diplomacy conducted at either end of his long and dangerous journeys between St Petersburg and Lhasa. That this could ever have been more than a metaphorical reinterpretation of an old myth now seems fanciful, but in the early years of the twentieth century the slow collapse of the Manchu empire created a political vacuum in Central Asia in which many different dreams were to flower.

For a Buriat monk and a Tibetan dalai lama, it was not such an outlandish dream. In a region with fluid borders and a strong tradition of theocracy, a multinational Buddhist confederation backed by a sympathetic but happily distant Tsar might have seemed the perfect outcome of the competition of interests that was underway in the region.

If further evidence were needed for the faithful that Shambhala was imminent, it came in Mongolia a couple of decades later. By 1921 Outer Mongolia had become a Soviet-backed Communist state, and the slaughter of the Buddhists began. The Communists correctly identified Buddhism as the greatest threat to their ideological and political supremacy. The monasteries represented the most cohesive sector of Mongolian society and the only one that could pose both an organizational and an ideological challenge to the Party.

The catastrophic struggle between the Buddhist church and the Communist party in Mongolia seemed to many the Armageddon that was to precede the defeat of the forces of evil and the coming of the age of purity. Neither King Rudrachakrin nor his stone horse appeared, but as the believers waited for him, another highly significant figure was already in the region – the ninth Panchen Lama, teacher of the Kalachakra and the reincarnation of Lobsang Palden Yeshe, the author of the guide to Shambhala.

Throughout the 1920s and 1930s the figure of the Panchen Lama became the symbol of resistance in Mongolia. As the battle between the church and the Party intensified, rumours abounded that the Panchen Lama would ride in and save the situation. He would come, it was said, at the head of a Japanese army and drive the Soviet troops out of Mongolia to inaugurate a new age of Buddhism. He was rumoured, in the mean time, to be sheltering the infant ninth Hutuktu (whose identification the Communist party had refused to permit) in exile, as he prepared the invasion.

The myth of the Panchen Lama's invasion force had consequences for some that were all too real. It was decreed a matter of treason in Mongolia to insist on the recognition of the Hutuktu, and in the thirties a large number of lamas and members of the nobility were sentenced to death on charges of collaborating with the Japanese and the Panchen Lama to try to find the child.[3]

The Panchen Lama's status in Mongolia as a mythological hero of the religious resistance owed nothing to any real contribution he made to the fight. The ninth Panchen Lama was unlikely to ride to anybody's aid at the head of anyone's army: even had such a force been at his disposal, he was no martial hero. But there are traces of his involvement in battles that were real enough. He did, for instance, support the religiously based rebellion that broke out in Mongolia in 1929. The rebels hoped that China would intervene to expel the Russians and reintegrate Mongolia with China, and they asked the Panchen Lama for troops to secure the northern frontier against the return of the Russians.[4]

There is evidence, too, that the Panchen Lama corresponded with some of the leaders of the revolts against Communist rule that broke out in Mongolia after 1930 and that he encouraged the nobility and a group of monks to rebel in 1932, after the Party officials had committed a series of particularly gross acts of desecration in the Bandid Gegeen monastery. The rebellion grew into a full-scale civil war that eventually required the might of the Soviet army to suppress it, but neither the Panchen Lama nor his phantom forces came to join the fight. Shambhala was not to be.

These were dangerous times and hazardous places for a man of the ninth Panchen Lama's disposition and he must have longed for the peace of Tashilhunpo in his long years of exile. The British continued to work for his return in the hope of bringing the quarrel between Tibet's two high lamas to an end, and the Panchen Lama repeatedly asked the British for weapons, arguing that he needed a small armed force to guarantee his safe return to Tibet. The uncharitable view – and one that the actions of the Chinese did much to encourage – was that such a force would spearhead an invasion of Tibet with the express purpose of 'reuniting' Tibet with the Chinese 'motherland'.

The Chinese, who regarded the British actions with profound mistrust, became more fixed in their own determination to use the Panchen Lama's return to secure a firm foothold in Tibet. In 1929 the Panchen Lama's followers asked the British for a 'reasonable quantity of arms, ammunition and supplies' to enable him to raise a force on the Sino-Tibetan frontier. In November of the same year the authorities in Gansu offered to put 10,000 soldiers at his disposal, and in the opening months of 1932 it was again rumoured that he would return to Tibet with the help of a Chinese force. It was said in Lhasa that the Dalai Lama would immediately have him arrested if he tried.

Then, in December 1933, the thirteenth Dalai Lama succumbed to a sudden illness and died. He was only fifty-eight, but had long looked much older. He left behind a testament that was to prove eerily accurate in its predictions of the disaster that was to overtake Tibet. In it, he repeated his insistence that Tibet must develop an efficient and well-trained army – a plan that had occasioned so much conflict in Tibet and sparked the final phase of the quarrel with the Panchen Lama. He pointed to the unhappy example of Mongolia, where the establishment of a Communist system had meant that 'monastic properties and endowments were confiscated, the lamas and monks were forced into the army; the Buddhist religion destroyed, leaving no trace of identity.' A similar fate would befall Tibet if she could not defend herself:

In the future, this system will certainly be forced either from within or without on this land that cherishes the joint spiritual and temporal system. If in such an event we fail to defend our land, the holy lamas, including their triumphant father and son (the Dalai and the Panchen Lama), will be eliminated without a trace of their names remaining; the properties of the incarnate lamas and of the monasteries along with the endowments for religious services will all be seized. Moreover, our political system, originated by the three ancient kings, will be reduced to an empty name; my officials, deprived of their patrimony and property, will be subjugated like slaves by the enemy; and my people, subjected to fear and misery, will be unable to endure day or night.[5]

After the Dalai Lama's death, the Guomindang despatched a delegation to Lhasa, ostensibly to observe the mourning rites, but in fact to open negotiations on the status of Tibet with the regency. The question of the Panchen Lama was high on the list for both sides. With the Dalai Lama dead, the Tibetan government was anxious to have him return but still not willing to allow a Chinese military force across the border with him.

The Chinese still believed that the British aimed to control Tibet, and in China the option was discussed of converting Tibet into a

Chinese province or, alternatively, of splitting it into three administrative regions centred on Batang, Lhasa and Shigatse. Neither of
these options found much favour in Tibet itself.

The British continued to try to mediate. The Panchen Lama's
absence, they could see, added an unwelcome instability to Tibetan
politics at a time when the regency was unlikely to be capable
of maintaining Tibet's independence from China. Negotiations
between the spiritual leaders had always foundered on the mutual
suspicion between the Dalai Lama's court in Lhasa and the Panchen
Lama's officials in China. By the time of the Dalai Lama's death,
the Panchen Lama had spent so long under the protection of the
Chinese that he had lent himself to their demand that he return
only at the head of a substantial military force to 'guarantee' his
safety.

The Panchen Lama moved to Jyekundo on the Sino-Tibetan
border in anticipation of a successful conclusion to the negotiations
for his return. He even sent some advanced luggage on to Nagchuka,
but when it was opened it was found to contain weapons and
grenades. It seemed to confirm Lhasa's worst suspicions and the
Panchen Lama's onward journey was again delayed.

He was still in Jyekundo when a party of senior monks in search
of the Dalai Lama's reincarnation passed through in December
1936. They consulted him as to the child's likely whereabouts. The
Panchen Lama gave them three possible names and told them,
accurately, where the child might be found. It was an intervention
for which the present Dalai Lama remains grateful to the Panchen.

In July 1937 external events dealt another blow to the Panchen's
hopes of return: Japan invaded China, and total war was imminent.
Chiang Kai-shek's government had other matters to attend to and,
dependent on British and American help to fight the Japanese, was
forced to lower the pressure on the Panchen Lama issue.

The Panchen Lama dropped his insistence on a swift return at
the head of a Chinese force and forlornly settled in Qinghai to wait
the war out. He was not to see the end of it. In a magnificent if
remote monastery in Jyekundo, Qinghai at 2.25 on the bitterly
cold morning of 1 December 1937, the ninth Panchen Lama died.
In the days that followed, hundreds of devotees waited in the
freezing winds of the Qinghai winter to pay their last respects and
present one final *khata* to their beloved Panchen. Prayers began

immediately for his swift rebirth. His dying wish, after fourteen years of exile, was hope that the rights enjoyed by successive panchen lamas in Tibet would be restored one day.[6]

'He was always loyal to His Holiness the Dalai Lama,' the abbot insisted. The evidence was against him, but there seemed little point in debating it.

A small party of boy monks erupted into the room bearing tea kettles. Hot sweet tea was handed around and drunk, in silence, as the company reflected on the loyalty of the Panchen Lama.

Then one of the monks from Tibet began to talk. 'I was told the story of what happened then,' he began, earnestly. 'Panchen Rinpoche died on the border between Tibet and China and his body should have been brought back to Tashilhunpo, but the Chinese wouldn't let him go. They wanted the Panchen's treasure. The military commander said that they could take the body, but not the treasure. So two monks from Tashilhunpo made a statue of the body, a copy, and they left it there. They brought the real one back to Shigatse.'

Old heads were nodding in agreement as though distant memories were stirring. The young monk's eyes were bright as he warmed to his story. 'There was fighting between two parties. The people from Tashilhunpo had to fight the Chinese, but they licked the salt off the Panchen's body and it made them safe from the Chinese bullets. The Chinese shot at them, but the bullets just fell harmlessly to the ground.'

I glanced at the abbot, then at the faces of the other old men, looking for some hint that they recognized the story as myth. They were leaning forward, nodding, captivated by the wonder of it. There was no hint of scepticism. They were simply enchanted.

One of the old men took up the story. 'I was in Tashilhunpo at that time. The body arrived before the stupa was built. They kept the body in Tashilhunpo for two to three years while the stupa was completed. I remember there were many ceremonies. At the time we were all young and we all went to pay our respects to the body before it was interred in the stupa.'

The abbot was anxious to bring the story up to date. 'The monks of Tashilhunpo were looking for the Panchen Rinpoche's reincarnation for a long time,' he said briskly, 'but only the Dalai Lama could settle it. The Panchen Rinpoche was born in 1938 in the tenth month. He was fifteen when he was enthroned. When the search party first found him they could see he was the exact reincarnation of the Panchen Rinpoche. His Holiness,' he added firmly, 'has also written that.'

Perhaps, but even the abbot could not disguise the fact that the age of fifteen was late for the enthronement of a Panchen Lama. The fifteen years that passed between the tenth Panchen Lama's death and his enthronement concealed another story that the abbot did not want to tell: that when the tenth Panchen Lama finally arrived in Tibet, he was accompanied by the Chinese armed force that the Tibetans had resisted throughout the ninth Panchen's exile.

But in that dim upper room in the far south of India, history had been cast aside. The abbot was elaborating on the authenticity of the tenth Panchen Lama. 'The search parties went to look in the lake,' he said. 'And they saw a pastureland with one small hill and a white stupa. In the centre there was a tiger, asleep, and on each of four sides a rabbit. The tiger meant that the Panchen would be born in the year of the tiger.' He pressed the point, anxious that I understand its significance.

'There is a palace in Tibet that the Panchen Rinpoche used. The ninth Panchen Rinpoche had a special painting made on the wall, of a sedan chair with nobody inside, just a tiger. That meant he would be reborn in the year of the tiger.'

Another old monk chimed in. 'The ninth Panchen Rinpoche died in the Ox Year. The tenth Panchen Rinpoche was born in the Tiger Year. In fact, there was only three months,' he explained triumphantly, 'between the death of the ninth Panchen Rinpoche and the birth of the tenth.'

I looked at him in surprise. This did not seem like a strong argument in his favour.

'This means,' the old monk continued, patiently, 'that there were also strong candidates from the Rabbit Year.' He nodded at the attentive table and several monks nodded back. He sank back in his chair, his case complete.

The abbot took up the argument again. 'These highly realized beings can come and go at any time,' he explained. 'The Gautama Buddha stayed for six years in his mother's womb. One man,' he added, triumphantly, 'was sixty years in his mother's womb. He was born with grey hair.' He, too, looked around the table for confirmation. The old monks buzzed with melodious excitement at this revelation, nodding rapidly.

'At the age of thirteen' – the young monk from Tibet had picked up the thread – 'the Panchen Lama was recognized by the Dalai Lama and brought to Tashilhunpo. He was enthroned at the age of fifteen, in 1952, in the fifth month.

'It was very windy in Shigatse at that time,' he said, 'and there was a sandstorm the night before his arrival. But then it rained and everything was clean when he got there. There were many signs when the Panchen Rinpoche was born: a flower grew in his room – and when he was four, he recognized the previous Panchen Lama's servant and remembered that he had beaten his dog. Then, at the age of eight, while he was getting dressed, he made a four-sentence prophecy.'

'Fetch the prophecy,' said the abbot, and a monk raced out of the room. He returned a few minutes later with a loose-leafed book. It was handed to the elderly monk with the white beard and the mandarin face. With immensely long fingers he untied the book and began to search slowly through the pages, turning each over and laying it neatly on the pile. He began to read, then stopped. 'No, that's not it,' he said.

The abbot grew impatient and took the book. 'Here it is,' he said and began to read. The administrator struggled to translate. 'Gautama Buddha is equal to everyone. Buddha feels merciful towards the poor, and few people have problems because of previous karma. And rulers feel they are proud, but they still have problems and Buddha feels mercy for them, too. Whether he is rich or poor, he has problems. And Buddha is the only one who sees rich and poor as the same. He makes no difference between all sentient beings. He gives thanks for that.' He stopped. 'It's something like that,' he said, apologetically.

The pages were reverently placed back in order and the book tied up again with its yellow silk strings. The account of the miraculous signs continued. 'It is written in the prayer books that in the year 1985 the Panchen Lama went to Kathmandu and visited Buddha's birthplace. There is a stone statue there of Buddha's mother, and during the Panchen Lama's visit a kind of liquid from heaven came . . . heavenly water.'

The young monk from Tibet had more. 'He showed magic many

times during his stay in prison,' he said. 'In 1966 he was brought to Lhasa and paraded in public with his hands behind his back. [The Chinese] pointed guns at people and told them to beat him, and he was beaten very badly at that time. Then he was taken to China and put in prison. At that time his body was tied up with electric wire, but he blew on it and it fell away. That's what he told his servant.

'There was a place in prison with lots of mosquitoes. He was sent there with no clothes. There were two Chinese with protective clothing, but the Panchen Lama said some prayers and the mosquitoes couldn't come within a foot of him.

'The Chinese tried to shoot him, but the bullets didn't hit him. One time he disappeared from the prison for a few days and they hunted high and low for him; then they found him in the meditation posture in the middle of a lake.'

From the darkness outside rose the melodious chanting of the boy monks at their evening prayers. It was getting late, but the young monk still held the company entranced. 'In the 1970s the Chinese held a pistol to the Panchen Lama's head and told him to curse the name of the Dalai Lama. He said he wouldn't curse His Holiness's name. He said he would write it on his hat and take it around the universe. He also said that he brought his old patched prison clothes to show them in the temple in Lhasa. It was known to everybody that, when he was in prison, the Chinese once said he was lost. They hid him and were planning to kill him, but when they went to kill him he had disappeared. He came back the next day. He did that four times.'

As his stories went on, the mythological powers of the Panchen Lama and the old dream of Shambhala began to take on flesh before my eyes. To these men, the fabulous was part of daily life: if the Panchen Lama was the real incarnation, then no miracle was beyond him. For them there seemed to be no doubt. It was not for me to quarrel with their faith, but I was still trying to marry the abbot's version of history with political realities. I made one last attempt.

'People say,' I ventured cautiously, 'that there was a quarrel between the ninth Panchen Rinpoche and the thirteenth Dalai Lama.'

He glared at me. 'There was no quarrel,' he said. 'The ninth

Panchen Rinpoche was a great spiritual master. He built the three-storey Maitreya Buddha. This proves that he wanted the happiness of the Tibetan people.'

Chapter Seven

✳

When the travellers and writers Peter Fleming and Ella Maillart passed through the city of Xining in north-west China in 1935, at the start of their epic trek across Xinjiang to northern India, it was still a remote and fabulous walled city, the gateway to the Silk Road, the great trade route of Central Asia. Approaching from the east, they sighted the walls at three o'clock in the afternoon at the far end of a long, open valley. They reached them, finally, at dusk and entered the gates, where sentries armed with automatic rifles looked down on them from above. They passed, as Peter Fleming wrote, 'like dusty ghosts through streets where rich food smells hung on the frosty air and paper lanterns were golden in the darkness'.[1]

Within the walls, the streets of the city thronged with camels and heavy carts loaded high with bales of wool; the people were no less exotic – Mongols from the Tsaidam, the huge salt marshes to the west, and Tibetans, hung about with amulets and daggers. The city then was the domain of Ma Bufang, the young military governor of Qinghai. Ma Bufang was a Tungan, of Mongol descent. He was a Muslim and a warlord whose powerful family had grown rich on the caravan traffic and who was to extract his own heavy tax from the Tibetan religious search parties that found their way twice to Qinghai in the thirties, looking for their most revered reincarnates.

My own arrival in Xining was more prosaic: by air from Beijing one dank autumn morning in 1995. The passengers on the little plane reflected the mosaic of peoples that still make up the population of Qinghai: there were Tibetan women in *chubas*, with hair in waist-length plaits and silver amulets around their necks; there were dark, Mongolian-looking people and flat-featured men with Muslim skull-caps, and Chinese in black leather jackets carrying small attaché cases, the new breed of travelling businessmen.

I caught a bus towards the town. I had come from a smog-filled capital that had lost itself in a frenzy of rebuilding. The road I was now on in this remote north-west corner of China seemed like a sleepier, more familiar country: the traffic consisted of tiny chugging 'walking tractors', the curious but sturdy little three-wheeled machines that had been the rural workhorses of Mao's China. They were pulling small carts with peasants crammed into them, muffled against the cold. The bullock carts, each with a driver dozing on top of a toppling load of straw, were another sight from an earlier age. The road from the airport wound along a river valley that cut deep in into the sandy soil. Eroded sand cliffs dropped abruptly to the stony riverbed and such land as was not eroded had been meticulously cultivated by the peasant women in coloured headscarves who were bent over their small crops under the leaden sky. It was bitterly cold.

When we arrived in the town proper, I saw that the Xining of Peter Fleming's visit had vanished. Gone were the great city walls and the alleys thronged with camels. Instead I found dreary rain-swept streets choked with a deafening mixture of buses and lorries that belched black smoke into the damp air. Xining sprawled along the river valley, a jumble of tawdry new buildings interspersed with old, ramshackle courtyard houses. Gimcrack modern office blocks marched side by side along the main thoroughfare and, no doubt the pride of the municipal authorities of Xining, a vast concrete pedestrian bridge arched across the central junction in front of a grim, oversized post office.

The signs of the modernization fever that was sweeping the more metropolitan parts of China were sporadic. The post office was undergoing a refurbishment of which the main result was a deafening hammering that made long-distance and international phone calls even more hit and miss than usual. The city was spotted with high-rise construction sites, and one gleaming building, the Qinghai Bank of Commerce, had opened earlier that year, according to the plaque fixed to one of its walls. Mysteriously flanking the door of this glistening glass tower were two unmistakably British bronze lions. I could only wonder how they had come to be there.

From the grimy windows of my hotel room I looked across the city, struggling to imagine the pad of camel hooves through narrow alley-ways and between the high walls that once secured this frontier town against barbarian marauders. The most prominent feature of the view from my window was a large square department store topped with a green dome. I was told that it had once been the warlord Ma Bufang's headquarters, though it did not seem likely. Smaller buildings, most of them square, concrete blocks, formed up in a regimented line that headed towards the hills. On one of the summits sat a forlorn pagoda, a memory of a more graceful past, now dwarfed by pylons. A cacophony of motor horns and engine noise rose from the street below.

Xining is the capital of Qinghai, the vast, mountainous north-west province, the borderlands and, for centuries, the badlands of the Chinese empire, where troublesome tribes would rise to harry the settled civilization to the east. It is a place of spectacular and pitiless geography: to the west of Xining lies the vast salt lake of Kokonor and, far beyond, at 10,000 feet above sea level, the immense Tsaidam plateau, the place to which, for centuries, Tibetans had come to dig for salt. Beyond that is the merciless Taklamakan desert, the graveyard of countless camel trains.

Qinghai is still a patchwork of nationalities – in spite of strenuous Chinese settlement, more than half the population are of other ethnic origins – Tibetan, Muslim, Tangut and Mongol. Under the Communists, Qinghai acquired another, more sinister claim to fame: it became the Chinese gulag, the place of *laogai*, reform through labour. In the camps that are scattered across the bleak province an untold number of people – thousands of them Tibetan monks – have died of cold, hunger and exhaustion.

Qinghai is known to the Tibetans as 'Amdo', and for them, too, it was a borderland. It was part of what became known as Inner Tibet – 'Inner' because it was close to China and a place where the Dalai Lama commanded spiritual allegiance but did not hold temporal power. It was not governed from Lhasa, but it was a place of strong Tibetan traditions. A few miles from Xining is the great monastery of Kumbum, built on the birthplace of the great reformer and founder of the Yellow Hat sect, Tsongkhapa. The ninth Panchen Lama spent many years there, waiting for his chance to return to Tibet.

When Peter Fleming visited Kumbum, in 1935, the camels and yaks were being assembled for the great caravan that the Panchen planned would take him home. He was still hoping to return to his native land when he died in Jyekundo, a hundred miles to the south.

And in this same province, to the south of Xining, the most recent reincarnations of each of Tibet's two most important lamas were born – the fourteenth Dalai Lama and the tenth Panchen Lama, whose passing in 1989 precipitated the current crisis. On the Panchen Lama's death, both the Communist state and adherents of the Buddhist faith hailed him as a hero and claimed him as a loyal servant of their opposing causes. I had come to Qinghai to try to find the truth.

There was little encouragement in Xining to explore the legacy of either of the province's two illustrious incarnates. There was a glancing reference in an official guidebook to the fact that both were born in Qinghai, but the details of the location were fuzzy and it was clear that going there was not officially encouraged.

The cold that came with nightfall brought lethargy and there was little in my grim hotel to rouse me from it. I huddled down in my coat in the dim light cast by the one weak and crookedly shaded bulb that hung from the centre of the ceiling. In the bathroom, a steady stream of cold water from the back of the lavatory had flooded the floor. From below came a monotonous rumbling sound that I later tracked down to a cavernous and ill-lit roller-skating rink on the first floor. I fell asleep to the twin lullaby of the leaking lavatory and the roller-skaters, telling myself things would look better in the morning.

It was still grey the next day, but at least I now had company. A telephone call had resulted in a visit from Dhondup, a tall, good-looking Tibetan man, a minor official and a friend of a friend. If he was surprised by my call, he was too polite to show it, though we both knew that contact with foreigners is never without risk for citizens of the People's Republic of China, especially if they are Tibetan.

Dhondup cast a glance around my room. It was clear from his expression that even by local standards, the hotel was dismal. He looked at me quizzically. 'There's not much to see in Xining,' he said. I could hardly contradict him.

'I want to visit the birthplace of the tenth Panchen Lama,' I said. 'And perhaps meet people who knew him.'

Dhondup looked puzzled, then alarmed. 'It's a long way to the birthplace,' he said. 'I don't think people go there.'

I opened my government-issue guidebook and pointed to a page. 'The former residence of the tenth Master Panchen,' it read, 'is situated in Xunhua county. It is splendid, dignified, solemn and elegant. In front of the residence lies a thousand-year-old tree.' This brief paragraph was my talisman against any official disapproval that I might encounter. If challenged, I would produce it as evidence that the Panchen Lama's birthplace was on the list of Qinghai's official sites. Dhondup shrugged. It was clear I was going to have to go it alone.

In the thirties Xunhua county was both impoverished and remote. Its largely Tibetan population seemed to have been forgotten even by Tibet itself and the region's only claim to fame was as the birthplace of a celebrated religious scholar, Geshe Sherab Gyatso, who once described his homeland as 'undeservedly obscure'.

But on the night of 19 February 1938, as the villagers of Wendu were celebrating the beginning of the year of the tiger, there occurred an event that was to earn Xunhua county a permanent place in the official canon of blessed earthly spots: the village headman's wife, Sonam Dolma, gave birth to a son.

The term 'headman' was, by then, something of an anachronism. It indicated only that the family had once been important in a system of local government that had fallen into disuse. They had once been wealthier, too, but now, though not at the bottom of the social heap, they were a modest, hard-working family who managed to sustain a reasonable standard of living. The headman himself was something of a local character. He kept a concubine called Trik-trik, no doubt to the irritation of Sonam Dolma, his industrious and long-suffering wife, and though he is remembered as an entertaining companion, he also had a reputation for irascibility.

The birth was not thought particularly remarkable at the time, though the arrival of a son is always a mark of good fortune. Later there were to be claims that it had been accompanied by miraculous signs: a rainbow had appeared in winter, the villagers said, recalling the observations of one villager who had been widely mocked for drunkenness at the time. Nobody else in the village had noticed – or been expecting – anything unusual. They were not aware that the forlorn figure of the exiled ninth Panchen Lama had died near by two and a half months previously, let alone that the search for his reincarnation would soon begin.

Even had they been aware of this momentous search, the villagers of Wendu might not immediately have thought their headman's baby a likely candidate. Reincarnation, they could have pointed out, takes at least as long as gestation, and the two and a half months that elapsed between the death of the ninth incarnation and the birth of the headman's son might not have been judged adequate.

That was a conundrum that the high clerics and religious authorities involved in the process would wrestle with later. For now, though, they were preoccupied with a more pressing political problem. The dispute that remained unresolved at the death of the ninth Panchen was continued by his exiled retinue. Some of the deceased's followers returned to Tibet with his body, but a large contingent – the 'Field Headquarters' – remained in Qinghai, living on a somewhat reduced allowance from the Chinese government and worrying about how their situation was to be resolved. Since they were still reluctant to risk going home to Tibet and facing the anger of the Lhasa government, their options were limited. As the Panchen Lama's closest followers, they had both a religious responsibility and a keen political interest in finding and attaching themselves to his reincarnation. But given that they could not go home, they would have to find the reincarnation in one of the Tibetan communities of Qinghai.

They were not the only group anxious to find the next Panchen Lama. The Panchen's home monastery of Tashilhunpo in Shigatse, as well as the government in Lhasa, at the time a regency that ruled Tibet on behalf of the boy who was the fourteenth Dalai Lama, took a keen interest. And for reasons that had little to do with religious faith, the Guomindang government of China was determined to keep a close eye on developments. The two men whose quarrel had caused so much heartache in Tibet, the ninth Panchen Lama and the thirteenth Dalai Lama, were both dead, but the consequences of their quarrel were to be felt by their respective reincarnations and by all the interested parties.

In the search for the reincarnation, each of these interested parties was moved by political as well as religious considerations. The ninth Panchen Lama's Field Headquarters was the most explicitly pro-Chinese faction among the late Panchen's followers: it represented the group that had always been suspicious of Lhasa's authority and anxious to preserve the autonomy of the Panchen Lama's court in Shigatse. When the quarrel between the ninth Panchen Lama and the thirteenth Dalai Lama began, it had only confirmed what they had long suspected – that Lhasa and the government of the Dalai Lama were trying to assert an improper degree of control and that the best hope of protection against the threat to their local hegemony lay with China.

Since the dramatic moment of the ninth Panchen's flight from Shigatse in 1923, these men and their families had lived in exile on the charity of the Chinese government. Not only were they deeply indebted to the Chinese, but they saw in the power of the Chinese government their only hope of a safe return to their lost positions of privilege and authority in Shigatse. The key to occupying those positions was the next incarnation of the Panchen Lama. They needed no further incentive to begin the search for the child and had every reason to keep closely in touch with the Chinese government.

Back in Shigatse, more than a thousand miles away, the *labrang* of Tashilhunpo monastery – effectively the regency of the monastery – was also, as tradition demanded, planning the search for the Panchen Lama. And because of the singular importance of the Panchen Lama and the spiritual ties that had traditionally existed between the dalai and panchen lamas, the Lhasa government expected to be kept informed by Tashilhunpo. The Dalai Lama himself would expect to be the final arbiter and give the chosen candidate the seal of approval.

In the summer of 1938 the Tashilhunpo search began one of its most important phases, the examination of the sacred lake of Lhamo Latso. The task was given to Bilung Rinpoche, a senior monk from Tashilhunpo and himself a reincarnate lama. He was assisted by a *geshe* scholar (a holder of the highest degree in Buddhist studies, equivalent to a doctorate). Although there were rival interests at play, each group acknowledged that the consultation of the lake should be done only once.

The two men took an oath before the Buddha that they would carry out their task with honesty and devotion. After three days of prayer and offerings at the lakeside, they gazed into the waters. It was a bright day and the pure colours of the lake were dazzling. After two hours of silent contemplation the two monks prayed, prostrated and withdrew to their tent where, in silence, each man wrote and sketched what he had seen.[2]

Neither man knew what visions had appeared to the other, but the images that each man recorded were to be decisive nearly five years later. On that clear, sunny day in 1938, the two documents were sealed on the lakeside and sent to Tibet where the leadership of Tashilhunpo monastery and eventually, the Dalai Lama himself, would be expected to read them.

The lake consultation over, the monastery prepared to send out search teams – monks were to travel throughout the country to identify exceptional male children with roughly the right birthdate. Tradition dictated that they disguise their purpose to minimize the risk of fraud and deception.

If any clue had been left by the deceased incarnation as to his preferred place of return, the search would have begun there. But the ninth Panchen Lama left no such hints behind, and the monks of Tashilhunpo had to make their own decision about where to begin. The Nechung oracle had predicted that the ninth Panchen Lama would return in the east. From Tashilhunpo monastery, this indicated they should search in Qinghai, where, conveniently, the Panchen's Field Headquarters, now settled in Kumbum monastery near Xining, could be asked to help.

In 1941 the two search groups, that of the exiles, led by Lobsang Gyaltsen, and the Tashilhunpo team, headed by Ngulchu Rinpoche, joined forces in Qinghai. It was Ngulchu Rinpoche's movie-loving reincarnation whom I had met in south India and who had told me, with justification, that Ngulchu Rinpoche had been close to the tenth Panchen Lama. From the beginning of the search to his tragic death in a Chinese prison, this learned monk had been an influential figure for the boy who would be recognized as the tenth Panchen.

Ngulchu Rinpoche had been the first to pick out Gonpo Tseten, the son of the headman of Wendu village, when he made a preliminary sweep through Hualung and Xunhua counties in 1941. In late 1944 and again the following year, the boy was among ten candidates who were taken to Kumbum monastery for observation and tests. Six of that group, including Gonpo Tseten, took the final test – identifying objects that had belonged to the previous incarnation. But though he correctly identified all of the late

Panchen's possessions, Gonpo Tseten was not the search party's final choice. He returned to Wendu village, where his father agreed to allow him to be educated at the local monastery, though he opposed the idea that his son should finally become a monk.

The search appeared to be over. An intelligent boy with strong religious connections had emerged from the tests as the clear leading candidate,[3] but then began an alarming series of misfortunes. The boy, who had impressed all who met him with his piety and intelligence, suddenly died.[4]

The search group hastily identified the next most likely candidate on their list. Their dismay when he died, too, can only be imagined. The third boy selected was the son of a village headman from Kham who had been brought in as a late contender. He lived no longer than the others. Even in a country with a high rate of child mortality, a less auspicious series of events is hard to imagine.

By now, no doubt, alarmed and embarrassed by this series of disasters, the search group returned to their depleted list. Gonpo Tseten had originally been at the bottom of the list, but as his case was re-examined the merits of it seemed to grow stronger. Not only had he scored well in the test of objects, but, as members of the late Panchen's retinue belatedly decided, the child had appeared to greet them as familiars. They turned to the evidence of the lake for confirmation of their growing certainty that Gonpo Tseten was the child they were looking for.

The lake evidence, too, was in his favour. Five years before, Bilung Rinpoche had seen an image of three rabbits chasing a tiger on the moving surface of Lhamo Latso. His companion had reported a vision of a lion asleep in the monastery followed by an image of a religious building shadowed by tall trees.[5] By the traditional Tibetan calendar Gonpo Tseten had been born in the year of the tiger and two of the dead boys had been born in the year of the rabbit. A similar building was discovered in Wendu monastery, and outside the gate of the Wendu headman's family compound grew two tall and ancient trees. Gonpo Tseten, the searchers in Qinghai concluded, was their candidate.

That was not the end of the matter, however. Back in Tibet, the government in Lhasa had also ordered a search and another group of eminent lamas had identified two further candidates.

One of them was a boy from Lithang, in Kham. He had the

virtue of strong family connections to the job: his father had been a servant of the previous incarnation and his mother was the niece of the highest lama of Lithang monastery.[6] The boy's great uncle was convinced that the child was the true reincarnation. As befits a strong candidate, miraculous signs began to be attributed to him, too. In Dharamsala an eminent Nyingmapa lama who had known the boy told me that for fifteen consecutive days during the third month of each year, one syllable of the Kalachakra mantra would appear on the child's forehead. He himself, he said, had seen it.

'It was quite clear,' he insisted. 'It was as though the veins of his forehead stood out to form the letter. And when he was asked where his monastery was, he would reply that it was Tashilhunpo and he would invite you to go there. I used to ask him if it was bigger than the one he was in and he would say, yes, it was much bigger and had golden roofs.'[7] The boy was taken to Tashilhunpo monastery to begin his religious studies, his case, like that of his rivals, still not settled.

The second candidate was an even stronger favourite of the Lhasa government. He was born in 1939, also in Kham. At the age of four he was identified as a reincarnate and sent initially to a Kagyupa and then to an important Gelugpa monastery. He spent four years there before he was picked out as a possible reincarnation of the Panchen Lama and sent to Lhasa, where he lived in Drepung monastery. There he was befriended by the fourteenth Dalai Lama's younger brother, Ngari Rinpoche.

Ngari Rinpoche, by his own account, spent much of his young monastic life playing practical jokes on his fellow monks, but recalls that the boy monk from Kham was a different and altogether more serious character. 'He was a very studious fellow,' he said. 'Very quiet and good-natured. I was very naughty and used to play a lot of tricks. I remember once in one of those long prayer sessions he was in front of me and I sewed his robes to the cushion. He never seemed to mind.'

All three candidates were destined to become monks but only one would be recognized as the Panchen Lama. A decision would have to be made, but who was to make it and how?

The Lhasa government had no doubt about how to proceed. In a statement issued on behalf of the Dalai Lama, the government ordered that the Qinghai candidate and the boy in Tashilhunpo be brought to Lhasa for a final round of tests and, if necessary, the final decision should be made by drawing lots from the Golden Urn.

When the Qianlong emperor sent the Golden Urn to Tibet in the late eighteenth century, he was making both a religious and a political gesture. In the nineteenth century, as the Qing dynasty sought to consolidate its rights over Tibet against the challenge from Russia and Britain, the use of the Golden Urn became an even more urgent symbol of Chinese sovereignty. The imperial representative in Lhasa tried to insist on the use of the urn as a demonstration of the emperor's symbolic right to nominate and legitimize Tibet's most important religious and political figures. The Tibetans resisted the idea of 'normalizing' the lottery of the urn but they did not reject it outright. Rather, they used it, among other methods of divination, when there was an argument to settle.

In 1995, in the search for the eleventh Panchen Lama, the Golden Urn lottery was once again to be invoked by the Chinese government as the key act of legitimation, an act that symbolized Chinese sovereignty over Tibetan spiritual practice. It was, the government argued, the indispensable final stage of the selection. By the same token, the use of the Urn was resisted by anyone who saw the Dalai Lama as the final authority in the process.

But in the search for the tenth Panchen Lama, these positions were reversed. The Dalai Lama's government, faced with conflicting claims, wanted to use the Golden Urn. But in this elastic dispute over symbols, it was the pro-Chinese faction in the Panchen Lama's entourage who most bitterly resisted it: they knew that if the Golden Urn was used, their candidate might not win, and without their candidate, they were nothing.

Even if their boy were to be selected, the exile Field Headquarters would be in a weak position. If Gonpo Tseten went to Lhasa and was successful in the lottery, there would be no reason for him to return to Qinghai: he would go directly to Tashilhunpo and be educated there until his majority. His retinue in Qinghai would have lost the opportunity they still hoped the process was going to offer them: to restore them to their former position and to establish the Panchen Lama's Tashilhunpo, with the support of the Chinese, as at least the equal of Lhasa and perhaps even the dominant power in Tibet. The Qinghai faction refused to send the boy to Lhasa.

They had no doubts, they said, that Gonpo Tseten was the tenth Panchen Lama and they intended to notify the Nationalist government of China in Nanjing to that effect.

But the KMT government had other things on its mind. The defeat of Japan by the allies had brought only a brief respite in its doomed struggle for survival. Months after the end of the war, the Nationalists were engaged in a full-scale civil war with Mao Zedong's Communist armies. Tibet was no longer a priority, and to intervene in a disputed recognition might seem provocative. For the time being, the Chinese government stayed its hand. The young Gonpo Tseten left Wendu village and his family home for the last time. He was never to live there again. With his parents, he moved to Kumbum monastery to await the settlement of his destiny.

In the normal course of events, the birthplace of a dalai or a panchen lama would have become a place of pilgrimage and veneration. The close family of such a high incarnate would immediately be elevated to a position of wealth and power and his native village would bask in reflected glory. But it was the fate of little Gonpo Tseten to be named as an incarnate at one of the most difficult moments in the history of his religion. Instead of passing his life as the unchallenged object of the devotion of his followers, he was to be caught up in the violent political struggles of his age, and the practices of his religion were to be all but stamped out by a government bitterly hostile to any set of beliefs that challenged its own.

By the time I visited Xining, the government had declared itself more tolerant on matters of faith and claimed that religious freedoms were now restored. But the fact that the tenth Panchen Lama's birthplace had joined the bird sanctuary of Lake Kokonor in the official guide to Qinghai's tourist attractions did not necessarily mean tourists were actually welcome.

The next day, I broached the subject of a trip to Xunhua with the taxi drivers outside my hotel. They seemed to spend most of their time, in this out-of-season season, trying to keep the ambient grime from settling on their cars. The first driver was frankly incredulous: it was as though I had proposed driving to Mars. Nevertheless, after a prolonged bout of bonnet-polishing, he proposed a price of 350 yuan – around £30.

I put on my anxious look.

'Well, how much would you pay?' he asked.

'Three hundred,' I replied. The sums of money were not large, given the distance, but I had discovered that, in what I had begun to think of as post-Communist China, if you wanted to be taken seriously, you had to demonstrate a lively interest in the price of everything.

He shook his head. A circle of onlookers had built up around us and a general discussion began about the proposed journey. Would the car make it? What was a fair price? Why did the foreigner want to go there? Where was it? Exactly how far away? The next taxi driver on the rank joined in. I offered him three hundred and he took it, with every appearance of satisfaction. I got into the back of his taxi and *both* drivers climbed cheerfully into the front. We set off.

No journey in this region is undertaken without some gesture of deference to the gods of hazardous travel. Our departure from Xining that morning was a protracted affair that carried faint overtones of the preparation of a camel train for the crossing of the Taklamakan desert. First there was a stop at the spares shop to pick up a fan belt. Then the petrol station, where I was relieved of 100 yuan for fuel. Then a stop at a food stall, and several stops to announce news of the journey to friends and acquaintances. Finally, we got on to the road for what both drivers had assured me was likely to be a five-hour journey.

As we headed south from Xining I realized that there was one ingredient of the journey to which I had failed to pay proper attention: the vehicle itself, a Toyota saloon, superficially in good order but already, with only five miles of our journey behind us, beginning to display alarming signs of eccentricity. It rattled and swayed on the uneven, metalled road and if we ventured above forty miles per hour, the unmistakable judder of poorly balanced wheels set in. The driver coped with this by severely limiting his speed. It was going to be a long day.

In the little town of Ping'an we negotiated a small traffic jam caused by a queue of walking tractors that were waiting to load stoves on to their small trailers. Qinghai was preparing for a winter which would turn out to be disastrous. Temperatures plunged to thirty degrees below zero and both people and livestock on the high grasslands died of cold. But for now, it was autumn and the trees that lined the little terraced fields in the valleys beyond Ping'an were ablaze with colour. We were now well into the countryside but following the river course and avoiding the high plateau: here it was still arable land and the peasants were ploughing their autumn fields with mules and oxen. Others had roped themselves into heavy wooden wheelbarrows loaded high with cabbages and were hauling them laboriously across muddy fields.

The road wound along the side of the valleys, hazardous for the unpredictability of the traffic: loose mules, walking tractors that pulled out without warning, trucks that blithely pursued their right to drive in the very middle of the road, mule carts loaded with winter fodder. My two drivers plied me with questions. How old was I? How old were my children? What did my husband do? Was I interested in Buddhism? Did my 'work unit' pay for the trip? How much had I spent? Neither of them was Tibetan, though one of them was married, he said, to a Tibetan.

The first breakdown came a few miles beyond Ping'an. 'Just a little defect,' said the driver cheerfully, as he emerged from an inspection of the engine. 'It won't take a minute.'

The car jerked violently, then began to move forward along a road that led uncompromisingly upwards in the direction of a towering set of snow-covered peaks. As we followed it, the Toyota began to protest. We inched our way up above the snow line and passed the great jagged bulk of Qingsha mountain, its summit lost in thick cloud. Our Toyota was now being nursed along at ten miles an hour, and even the crowded public minibus had overtaken us. The two drivers seemed confident: 'It's just had a service,' they said. Moments later, we came to a halt. Clouds of steam were pouring from beneath the bonnet.

Miraculously we managed to get going again and crawled to the summit, marked in the Tibetan style by a pile of stones topped by prayer flags. As we breasted the peak I found myself looking across the next valley to a range of spectacularly grim mountains that fell away into the distance. The car ran gratefully down the winding road.

At the next village, we were flagged down by a knot of men in uniform: the People's Armed Police. The driver got out and words were exchanged. My drivers looked embarrassed and, without further explanation, two of the men squeezed into the back seat beside me. Men in uniform in the People's Republic of China are not usually to be argued with, but our suffering Toyota was in no state to accommodate two uninvited passengers.

'This isn't a bus,' I protested to the man who had crammed himself in next to me, a thin-faced figure whose eyes were hidden behind the mirror shades beloved of security services everywhere.

'It is now,' he replied.

'This car's no good,' I insisted. 'It won't take the hills with five.'

'Yes it will,' he said flatly, smiling with the satisfaction of a man who wears a uniform in a police state.

We drove off, barely scraping into second gear. We stopped at a bridge to add water to the boiling radiator and a basinful was thrown over the engine for good measure. After another four hundred metres of steep ascent we ground to a halt.

The overloaded car was clearly not going to make it. Equally clearly the police would find it impossible to get out without losing face. The two drivers exchanged glances and one of them got out, leaving an opportunity for the junior policeman to do the same. We made another, unsuccessful stab at the hill. We were down to a hard-core stand-off. Of the three of us left in the car, only the driver was clearly necessary. The policeman and I were now locked in a contest of face. He stared mulishly in front as the driver tried to coax the car into motion. Clouds of steam were beginning to escape again from under the bonnet. The driver struggled for five minutes, then turned and shot a desperate glance at us.

'Shall we?' I said to the policeman.

Wordlessly, he opened the door and got out of the car. We walked up the hill behind the taxi, which, relieved of its burden, had found the strength to continue. At the summit of a spectacular pass, we remounted and rolled down the further slope. The sensation of speed was almost intoxicating. The little taxi had recovered its spirits and we limped on to the next town, Hualong. The policemen got out and silently went on their way.

Now we were following a rough single-track road through a much starker, narrower valley, alongside a stream that had cut a deep channel through the mountains. Great weathered sandstone pillars towered over us like ancient fortresses guarding the passes. We emerged into a beautiful valley bounded by sandstone crags and lush with glorious bright autumn trees. Sheep and goats browsed on the sparse dry grass and groups of men with scant beards and white skullcaps stared at us curiously. Weathered conical sandstone peaks rose sheer from the valley floor and the turned earth and the walls that bordered the fields were a deep vibrant pink. Muslim women in black headscarves and the occasional Tibetan in a *chuba* bent over the fields.

By four in the afternoon we had crossed the Yellow river, which, even in these upper reaches, was already wide and powerful as it set off on its epic journey to the sea. An hour later, we were in Xunhua. A group of men looked up from the sheep they were butchering as we sped through the little square past high courtyard walls with richly decorated carved gateways. We climbed out of the town along a deeply tree-shaded road, weaving through small flocks of chickens and goats that seemed to view the highway as their own. We asked our way and were directed to a mud-walled compound.

Two monks in maroon robes were playing billiards on a table set up beside the road. Behind them, at the gate of the compound, stood two tall trees – the trees that Bilung Rinpoche's companion had seen in his vision at Lhamo Latso lake that far-away summer of 1938.

'Is this the birthplace of the tenth Panchen Lama?' I asked one of the monks.

He stared sullenly and silently at the ground. His companion was gazing at our little group as though we had descended from a distant planet. The thrill of the chase had emboldened my drivers to forget their apprehension. One of them forged his way down the alley and made enquiries of one of the growing crowd of the curious who had appeared, out of nowhere, to wonder at our arrival. He came back, triumphant. 'Yes,' he shouted, 'this is it. They've gone for the key.'

The caretaker appeared, bearing a large key-ring. He looked at us suspiciously but consented to undo a large padlock that secured the main gate to the compound. We entered, past a small fleet of parked Land Cruisers into an inner paved courtyard that lay in the centre of a low rectangular building. We were steered up a steep wooden ladder to a flat roof terrace off which opened a series of rooms that had been given over to the memory of the Panchen. In the first a large photograph of him sat by a Buddhist altar, flanked by glass-fronted bookcases. The monk stayed behind the threshold. I asked if I could go in. He nodded, coldly. Neither that room nor the next contained much of interest: a few photographs of the young Panchen with his parents, a formal portrait of one of his teachers.

I asked the monk if he had ever met him.

'Once,' he said, 'when I was fourteen. Now I'm twenty-three,' he volunteered. What did he remember? He shrugged.

'Panchen Rinpoche came here four or five times,' he said, by way of reply.

The final rooms were locked and there was no move to open them. Peering through the dusty window, I made out a little bedroom and sitting room furnished with heavy armchairs. The bed was hung with embroidery, but it seemed implausibly small for the Panchen Lama, a man who grew to such a bulk that a friend of his in Beijing once showed me the sofa that he had been fond of sitting on. Years after the Panchen's death, the sofa still sagged drastically in the middle.

'That's all there is,' said the monk, in a manner that firmly discouraged further questions. I hung about, stubbornly. Was this all I was to get for my ten-hour round trip? As I hesitated, reluctant to depart, a young girl appeared at the top of the ladder and smilingly offered tea.

I followed her back down the steep steps and she led me to an elderly man who was sitting on a wooden chair in a passage at the foot of another staircase, his chin resting on hands that grasped a walking stick. He looked up and I felt a flash of recognition as I saw his slightly drooping lower lip and prominent ears. 'Panchen Rinpoche's little brother,' said the girl.

The man gave me a long, slow look then smiled. He nodded, unformed sounds coming from his mouth. He pointed to his ears and gestured. This was Gonpo Kyab, the tenth Panchen Lama's only sibling, his deaf mute brother.

He reached out and took my notebook from my hand.

'Name?' he wrote. 'Work unit?'

I squatted down beside his chair and we began a conversation in my notebook, scribbling by turns in Chinese. The dialogue was friendly, if not profound. It was interrupted by a slightly formal session of photograph-taking, to which Gonpo Kyab supplied the caption: 'English–Chinese friendship.' He beamed at me. I was clearly the former. For the latter, he gestured to the drivers, then placed his hand on his own breast. He seemed to be trying hard to make the point that, if nothing else, the Panchen's family was politically reliable.

The photographs taken, he led us slowly into a side courtyard. He walked along the covered veranda, leaning on his stick, his legs stiff, and sat heavily in an armchair beneath an imposing clock that had stopped at 12.30. He gestured us to some stools beside him and pointed to a tray of bread and tea that had been placed on the table. Our written conversation continued.

He pointed to his ears again, made the sign for the number two and banged his head. 'Explosion,' he wrote.

'High blood pressure,' explained the girl who had come to sit at his feet, 'when he was two years old.'

'Is your prime minister a woman?' wrote Gonpo Kyab.

'Not any more,' I scribbled back. Was there nowhere in the world, I wondered, that I could forget Margaret Thatcher?

Gonpo Kyab was growing chatty. Before his death in 1989, he told me, he had seen his brother regularly. He himself was fifty-four and had two children. In a burst of inspiration, he wrote 'English–Chinese friendship' again on a clean page of my notebook, then scribbled, 'Write your name in Big Nose writing,' grinning at his own audacity. I reached for the pad, then I saw his face suddenly darken. I turned to follow his gaze and saw a man framed in the doorway. His face seemed to be made of stone. My drivers froze into the wooden blankness of men who smell trouble and are trying to render themselves invisible.

'*Ganbu*,' they muttered. 'Official.'

The *ganbu* walked round the veranda and came and stood behind Gonpo Kyab, looking hard at the remains of the bread and tea, as though inspecting it for signs of conspiracy.

I wrote my name, with the date and my thanks, tore the page out and handed it to Gonpo Kyab. The *ganbu* took my notebook and slowly flipped over the pages, scanning the record of our written conversation.

The drivers began to fidget with self-conscious *bonhomie* and to chatter about the immense distance of the return journey and the lateness of the hour. I said goodbye to the Panchen Lama's little brother and we left him in the gathering dusk, his minder still towering over him. A light rain was falling as we set off on the long journey back.

Gonpo Kyab had other, more painful memories that he had not shared: during the Cultural Revolution he had been present in one dreadful session of mass criticism of his elder brother at which the Panchen Lama faced the monstrous charge of raping his own sister-in-law. Those memories were publicly buried now, but Gonpo Kyab's private scars were another matter. What reverses of fortune might the next incarnation of the Panchen Lama have to endure?

'They haven't found the child,' my driver suddenly volunteered, cutting through the heavy silence that had fallen, as though he had read my thoughts.

'The child?' I said.

'The next incarnation,' he replied. 'The government . . . are very interested in finding him.'

I debated with myself whether to pursue this opening, but decided I was in enough trouble as it was. I had been discovered in the tenth Panchen Lama's childhood home, an unusual place for a foreigner to visit. If the taxi drivers were questioned, any untoward curiosity about the current search, a far more sensitive matter even than the controversial history of the tenth Panchen, would be reported.

'Really,' I replied, noncommittally.

The following day, my reservations were confirmed. After much persuasion, a former official of the tenth Panchen Lama's office agreed to meet me in a teahouse in Xining. He sat, uncomfortably, a faint, disengaged smile on his face, parrying my enquiries about the search. We talked about many other things, but he did not seem to hear my questions about the long process of discovering the eleventh Panchen Lama. Finally, he rose to go. As we left the teahouse, he shook my hand. 'Have you ever noticed,' he said, 'how long some people can spend on one page of a newspaper?' I glanced back into the dim interior of the teahouse and met the eyes of the man who had occupied the table next to us. He had been engrossed, apparently, in his reading, but now he was staring at us as we said goodbye. As I looked at him, he turned, unsmiling, back to his copy of the *People's Daily*.

Chapter Eight

*

A few days after my encounter with Gonpo Kyab, there was an unexpected message. If I wanted to see the late Panchen Lama's mother, it could be arranged. I met up with Dhondup: I needed his expertise to help me choose the appropriate *khata* for the visit – the long white silk scarf that Tibetans exchange on every occasion from a simple visit to a grand religious ceremony. *Khatas* come in many lengths and qualities, and it was important to find one that would express the proper degree of respect for the mother of the man who had been such an elevated figure in Tibet.

Dhondup studied a selection of *khatas* in a local shop, turning them over, examining the fringed ends. Finally, he chose two, then selected some tea and sweets for me to take. I paid for our purchases and he rolled the *khatas* carefully. One went into his pocket, the other joined the tea and sweets in my rucksack.

We made our way to a soulless compound of regulation low-rise apartment blocks and climbed the concrete steps to the second floor. Sonam Dolma was waiting for us in a drab but comfortably furnished room: a large television set sat in the corner; a telephone, two Thermos flasks, two armchairs and a sofa all but filled the remaining space. On a low metal and plastic table were dishes of raisins and fruit.

Sonam Dolma was, I had heard, respected by both the exiles and the Tibetans in Tibet. This is not an easy position to maintain in a culture riddled with quarrels – Amdo against Lhasa, exile against resident. Tibetan records are full of complaints about the exigencies and high-handed behaviour of close relatives of the dalai and panchen lamas. Their automatic elevation to the aristocracy made them rich, but not always popular. But in Dharamsala, those who had known Sonam Dolma had told me that she was revered as a devout and hard-working woman who had never succumbed to the temptations of arrogance and who had borne her husband's philandering with stoicism. They remembered her sufferings, too

– the dark years of the Cultural Revolution, when the entire family was reviled for its association with the then disgraced Panchen Lama.

Now both her son and her difficult husband were dead and Sonam Dolma had been restored to a position of official respect, entitled to the modest comforts allotted her by bureaucratic regulations. She sat in an armchair opposite me, a small woman, plainly dressed in a brown jacket and black trousers, her grey hair plaited in two long pigtails. She held a rosary in her hands, and slipped the beads through her fingers as we talked. A young man, an attendant, hovered, pouring tea. The conversation was polite but strained.

I asked her what she had felt when her son was recognized as the Panchen Lama. She replied with a lack of enthusiasm that I found disconcerting.

'I lived in the countryside and didn't pay much attention to things like that. My son went to the monastery in Wendu when he was three. He was recognized when he was seven. It was before liberation,' she went on.

'There were five boys who were brought up to Xining for a month and they were examined by Ma Bufang. Then they scattered again and later they went to Kumbum.'

Seven is late enough for the recognition of a high lama. But, in fact, Gonpo Tseten was not finally accepted as the tenth incarnation of the Panchen Lama until 1951, when he was nearly thirteen, and even then recognition was won only at the point of a gun. By the time he was seven, though, the ninth Panchen's Field Headquarters had settled on him as the most promising surviving candidate and he was taken to live in the great Kumbum monastery, outside Xining.

Ma Bufang, the Muslim warlord who controlled the region, would have had little to contribute to the spiritual recognition of the Buddhist reincarnate. But as he was well aware, high lamas were political figures and, as such, potentially both valuable and troublesome. Ma Bufang had succeeded in extracting a large ransom from the Tibetan delegation that had come to fetch the young fourteenth Dalai Lama to Lhasa. No doubt he hoped the search for the Panchen Lama would provide similar opportunities for extortion.

It was January, his mother recalled, when the party set off to Kumbum, and the weather was terrible. It took them two days on the road. When they finally reached Kumbum, the boy was given into the care of Gyagyab Rinpoche, a Kumbum monk of Mongolian origin who had looked after him when he had visited the monastery for the initial tests. An aged monk who had been tutor to the ninth Panchen Lama, Lakhog Rinpoche, was named the child's tutor, and he asked Gyagyab to assist him in the task of instilling in the child the knowledge of scripture he would require to fulfil his elevated religious role.

The monastery arranged a grand ceremony for the child, and asked for the approval of the Chinese government for his formal enthronement. According to the official notice sent from the Field Headquarters in Kumbum to the chairman of the Commission of Mongolian and Tibetan Affairs of Chiang Kai-shek's government:

At eleven in the morning (on the fifteenth of the first month by the lunar calendar) the reborn person, Gonpo Tseten, accompanied by monks holding religious articles and playing religious musical instruments, was brought in to worship the Buddha before he was confirmed as the new Panchen. The ceremony was attended by more than 100,000 people, including representatives of the government of Qinghai province, Living Buddhas, Mongolian and Tibetan princes . . . It is our duty to report the ceremony to you and ask you for approval.[1]

For the monks of Kumbum and the ninth Panchen's retinue the boy's status as Panchen Lama was now beyond question. With the Tibetan government, though, the stalemate persisted and the KMT was curiously reluctant to give an immediate endorsement. For them the young Panchen candidate was a card to be played when necessary, but they were engaged in negotiations with Lhasa over the question of Tibetan independence. They were aware that the Tibetan government had its own Panchen candidates and, for the time being, did not want to antagonize the Tibetans by taking a unilateral position.

The head of the Panchen's office in the KMT capital Nanjing, Chen Jigme, one of the most pro-Chinese of all the Panchen's court, tried his best to persuade the KMT government to endorse the boy who was the Qinghai group's only asset. He made repeated visits to senior officials in the Nationalist government, sweetening his argument with substantial presents of gold and Tibetan medicines. Finally, in the very last months of the Nationalist government, after Chiang Kai-shek had stepped down from the presidency in favour of Li Zongren and on the brink of defeat in the civil war, the KMT formally recognized the boy. Chen Jigme had his endorsement, but it was not the simple victory he had hoped for. As Chen Jigme was soon to discover, the KMT's real intentions towards the child were not straightforward.

It was not until 3 June 1949 that the government of the acting president Li Zongren issued a mandate exempting Gonpo Tseten from the Golden Urn ceremony and recognizing his claim. The chairman of the Commission for Mongolian and Tibetan Affairs, Guan Jiyu, was sent to Qinghai for the tonsuring ceremony, which duly took place on 10 August. The Nationalist government had scarcely a month of mainland life left. Chiang Kai-shek and as many of his supporters as could escape were preparing to flee offshore, to the island of Taiwan. They took with them as many cultural treasures as they could carry and the pretension that they were still the legitimate government of China. They had also hoped, according to the Tibetan scholar Jampal Gyatso, to take the young Panchen Lama.[2]

Jampal Gyatso has argued that the Nationalists were running a two-pronged policy: on the one hand they wanted to enlist Lhasa's support against the Communists, perhaps even to use Lhasa as the final Nationalist stronghold. In order to avoid offending Lhasa, they had withheld recognition from Gonpo Tseten. But by the summer of 1949 it was clear that there would be no last stand anywhere on the mainland. The final retreat was to be to Taiwan, there, perhaps to regroup and fight on, and, if not, at least to survive. A young Panchen Lama had potential as a political asset and both Ma Bufang, who was on the Nationalist side, and the KMT planned to add him to the luggage.

As the Nationalists prepared for their own flight, they applied steady pressure on the ninth Panchen's former entourage to come along and to bring the young Gonpo Tseten with them. Ma Bufang had led the military resistance to the Communist advance with troops largely made up of his own Muslim cavalry, allied with local Tibetan and Mongol fighters. But now he, too, was planning his own departure and offered to fly the boy from Xining to Chongqing and from there to Taiwan.

It was a difficult choice for the Panchen's circle. They had had no contact with the Chinese Communists and were uncertain what to expect from them. The Nationalist government had supported them for nearly twenty years but now it was facing defeat and an uncertain future in exile. A life in Taiwan as a pawn in the hands of a defeated and exiled government was not a particularly attractive prospect for a group of Tibetans whose one wish was to secure Chinese backing for their return to Tibet. The entourage could not reach a decision and Chen Jigme was summoned to Qinghai from Chongqing for a summit.

He left a colleague, Enge Palden, in the Chongqing office with instructions to determine what the Communist party's attitude towards religion would be. The KMT, meanwhile, tried to lure Enge Palden to Taiwan by promising him the chairmanship of the Commission for Mongolian and Tibetan Affairs and of the Tibetan Affairs Bureau if he did so. In the end, for whatever reason, Enge Palden decided that the young Panchen should throw in his lot with the Communist party.[3]

Had he turned his eyes to Mongolia and contemplated the fate of the Mongolian religious establishment under their own Russian-dominated Communist party, Enge Palden might have hesitated before recommending this course of action to Chen Jigme. But the habit of trusting the Chinese was now ingrained in the Panchen Lama's entourage and now they decided to throw in their lot with Mao Zedong. No doubt in the short term it seemed like a sound decision: it was, in all likelihood, their best chance of a ticket home.

But in the end most of the men who made the decision and who had nurtured a pro-China policy through the long years of exile were to die at the hands of their new allies. Some perished in labour camps, others in prisons, some died of torture, some of hunger, and others still committed suicide, their spirits broken by the ruin of a world which they had, unwittingly, helped to destroy.

Once the decision was taken, there was nothing for it but to wait. It was not to be long. In September 1949 Ma Bufang made good his escape, with his wives and treasure, on two DC10s, and the PLA occupied Xining. The loyal Chen Jigme was sent to Xining to make the first contact.

On 1 October 1949 Chen Jigme sent what was to become a notorious telegram to Mao Zedong in the name of his eleven-year-old master. In it, he congratulated Mao on the founding of the People's Republic of China and reminded him of two key points: the Panchen Lama was eager to return to Tibet; and he was counting on Mao's assistance to do so. In return for this favour, Chen Jigme offered a Faustian pact – the Panchen's unqualified support for the Chinese cause in Tibet. As he wrote:

For more than twenty years . . . I have been campaigning for the integrity of Tibetan sovereignty without a moment of negligence . . . Though I am staying in Qinghai, I am waiting to return to Tibet at your command . . . From now on, the peace and happiness of the people can be anticipated, the restoration of our country is hopeful and liberation of Tibet is expected.[4]

There was neither peace nor happiness in Lhasa, nor had there been for some time. The regency of a Dalai Lama was often a period riddled with conspiracy and instability, and that of the minority of the fourteenth Dalai Lama had been no exception. Things had become so chaotic and corrupt that there had even been a brief civil war in 1947. While the government mismanaged, the Guomindang (Kuomintang, or KMT), who had an ever larger representative office in Lhasa, had been quietly peddling influence in the capital.

In 1949 the Lhasa government hurriedly expelled the Chinese as the realization came, belatedly, that there was about to arrive in power in China something which had not been seen since the nineteenth century: a force that had both the capacity and the will to invade Tibet. Worse still, there was no sign of a counterbalancing foreign power: the British had left India, and Russia was also a Communist country – unlikely therefore to thwart Chinese Communist designs. The Tibetans were to make belated efforts to gain international support for independence, but in the post-war world, nobody was interested. After the British departure, Britain's international treaty obligations – and to some extent her strategic interests – had been inherited by India. But India was nervous of provoking China and unlikely to offer any robust support.

In Lhasa the young Dalai Lama knew little about Communism, except, characteristically, that he was acutely aware of the devastation it had wrought on the religious institutions of Mongolia. Of the Chinese Communist Party, there was apprehension, but little knowledge.

Even if there had been greater understanding, it would have given the Tibetans small comfort. Despite their formal ideological differences and their sworn enmity, the Communist party had inherited the Nationalist party's ambition, derived in turn from the Qing dynasty, to consolidate Chinese power in Tibet. When the Qing collapsed in 1912, the republic that was founded declared its ambition to convert the lands of the Mongols and the Tibetans into Chinese provinces, as they had with Xinjiang after the defeat of Yakub Beg's principality.[5]

This was, in part, an evolution of the Manchu relationship to Tibet. But now, devoid of the religious connection which had underwritten the Manchu emperors' dealings with the dalai lamas, the argument for Chinese control of Tibet drew on an older process: the steady assertion of predominance of the Han Chinese over their smaller and weaker neighbouring peoples. The boundaries now claimed by the Communist government were much wider than those controlled by pre-Qing Chinese dynasties. The justification for them was expressed in terms of nationalism and Han cultural superiority over the barbarian peoples of the fringe.

Sun Yatsen, revered by both sides in the Chinese civil war as the father of the Chinese revolution, believed that China was essentially one nation, that the state and the nation were synonymous, and that the cultural differences – which he acknowledged – would disappear. Mao Zedong's vision had some of the same elements, fortified by his utopian conviction that Communism would prevail over ethnic and cultural divisions to create national harmony in the socialist ideal and, eventually, the common consciousness of international proletarianism.

Mao's attitudes to what were to come to be defined as 'China's minority nationalities' had evolved partly from traditional Han chauvinism and partly from his reading of the Communist canon. Marx, of course, believed that nationalism was a transitory phase, progressive in its moment but fated to be superseded with the end of capitalism. Lenin wrestled with the problem of Communism in his own pre-capitalist society and the role of the minorities in the revolution. His solution to the theoretical conundrum was that the Communist party should act on behalf of the non-existent minority proletariat. He believed that all minority nationalities would choose to identify with the advance guard of the revolutionary activists because that was where their true interests lay. They should, theoretically, have freedom of choice. But since the revolutionary activists were deemed to be the agents of their revolution, the choice was made for them in their 'best' interests.

Mao combined the worst of traditional Chinese superiority and revolutionary dogmatism. In the early stages of the revolution he, too, upheld the idea of self-determination. But by the time the People's Republic of China was founded Mao was impatient to get on with the business of transforming mankind. Since national identities were fated to surrender to international proletarian consciousness and minority peoples were bound to recognize where their true class interests lay, he reasoned that all nationalist consciousness was really a question of class.

Nationalism, he thought, would have no base once class was eliminated. The problem of the minorities, therefore, was essentially the same problem of class as existed in the rest of China, only in a slightly more acute and more exotic form. The solution – class struggle – would settle all these issues.

The first step towards this transformation was to gain control of all the so-called minority areas. On New Year's Day 1950 Radio Beijing announced that 'the tasks for the People's Liberation Army for 1950 are to liberate Taiwan, Hainan and Tibet'. On 16 April Lin Biao attacked Hainan island in the Gulf of Tongking and defeated its Nationalist defenders within days.

The Tibet on which Mao Zedong now set his sights was not a nation in the modern sense. Its vast territory was sparsely populated by a people who spoke a multitude of related but often mutually incomprehensible dialects, intelligible through a universal written language. Their sense of national identity corresponded neither to Marxist theory nor to the realities of a modern nation state.

Tibetans identified strongly with their native region, be it Kham, Amdo or central Tibet, a region further divided into the sub-regions of Ü, Tsang and Do-pa. Their religious affiliation gave them a common allegiance to the culture of Buddhism but not necessarily a strong loyalty to the person of the Dalai Lama. Stronger were the more immediate ties to a particular teacher or a local religious figure.

Across this cultural continuum ran political divisions. Eastern Tibet, the land of the Khampas, was politically semi-detached from the Lhasa theocracy and offered the Chinese a foothold for their ambitions. The ground, indeed, had been prepared by history.

After Francis Younghusband's military adventure into Tibet in 1904 an alarmed Qing dynasty sent an imperial official to Batang in eastern Tibet to begin the process of reasserting Qing control. When the local population rose in revolt and killed him, Beijing sent a punitive expedition led by General Zhao Erfang. Zhao became frontier high commissioner and was ordered to proceed with the sinification of the area around Batang. He abolished the powers of the Tibetan local leaders and appointed Chinese magistrates in their places. He introduced new laws that limited the number of lamas and deprived monasteries of their temporal power and inaugurated schemes for having the land cultivated by Chinese immigrants.

Zhao's methods in eastern Tibet uncannily prefigured the Communist policies nearly half a century later. They were aimed at the extermination of the Tibetan clergy, the assimilation of territory and repopulation of Tibetan plateaus with poor peasants from Sichuan. Like the later Chinese conquerors, Zhao's men looted and destroyed Tibetan monasteries, melted down religious images and tore up sacred texts to use to line the soles of their boots and, as the Communists were also to do later, Zhao Erfang worked out a comprehensive scheme for the development of Tibet that covered military training, reclamation work, secular education, trade and administration.

In February 1910 Zhao Erfang invaded Lhasa, prompting the thirteenth Dalai Lama's flight to India. Zhao Erfang's brief was to institute reforms in Tibet with the express purpose of breaking the grip of the ruling religious élite, but the collapse of the Qing dynasty cut his project short. His soldiers mutinied and he himself was beheaded. The longer-lasting consequence, however, was that eastern Tibet had been radicalized by the experience of Zhao's reforms.

Although his reforms were resisted by the religious establishment and were, in many ways, offensive to Tibetans, they had two important effects: they introduced a concept of reform that was to challenge the conservative Lhasa theocracy at the same time as they awakened a Tibetan nationalism in eastern Tibet. This led to several political initiatives from the region in the next two decades, aimed at persuading Lhasa to modernize the political and social regime. The fact that they were systematically rebuffed led, in turn, to the growth of radical political ideas in eastern Tibet and some sentiment in favour of an independent, or at least autonomous, Khampa state.

The religious establishment was at its strongest in central Tibet, but on the fringes of the Tibetan polity other political ideas had begun to take hold among progressive Tibetans frustrated by the rigidity and conservatism of the religious élite. In the thirties a Khampa from Kandze called Sangye Yeshe founded the first Tibetan Communist area in Kham and later marched to Yan'an to join Mao Zedong, inspired perhaps by the fact that the 1931 constitution of the Chinese Soviet still promised full rights of secession, self-government and self-determination for each ethnic group or nationality.

A year later the Khampas asked for a separate state, and in 1939 the eastern portion of Kham was appended to China by the K M T government as the short-lived Chinese province of Sikang.[6] It was on the ground that had been fertilized by this history that the Chinese Communist Party was to sow the seed of its conquest of Tibet.

By the early spring of 1950 advance PLA units had driven out the remnant K M T forces in eastern Kham. By May the first probing attack was launched across the Yangtze river to the town of Dengkok. Two weeks later it was recaptured by the Tibetans, a victory which boosted morale but which, as a portent of what was to come, was to prove illusory.

An important obstacle to the immediate invasion of Tibet was the reluctance of the war-weary Chinese armies to take on the task. Mao Zedong first asked Peng Dehuai to form a plan for the invasion. Peng Dehuai was in Moscow with Stalin and he took a month to respond to his leader's message. When he did, he was discouraging. A military conquest of Tibet, he said, would take five years.

Mao was less than pleased with the reply and sent a telegram to Chengdu, where Liu Bocheng was commander and Deng Xiaoping political commissar. Liu Bocheng asked each of the seven armies in the area, but each of them refused. The men were weary, said their commanders, and they had been promised a rest and some civilian life. Eventually, the 18th army was persuaded, but on hearing the news, 30 per cent of its troops deserted.

Despite these difficulties, on 7 October 1950, 40,000 soldiers of the 18th Route Army, led by Zhang Guohua, rowed across the Drichu river east of Chambo and attacked. When Peng Dehuai heard that the 18th army had agreed to undertake the invasion, he hastily despatched a small unit to join the fight, a move that failed to improve his position with Mao Zedong but laid the ground for an enduring rivalry between competing PLA units in Tibet.

The Tibetan standing army totalled only 8,500 men. The Tibetan forces in Chamdo, commanded by a handsome young aristocrat called Ngabo Ngawang Jigme, were outmanœuvred and defeated in days. A telegram Ngabo had sent to the Tibetan government, informing them of his desperate situation and asking for instructions, had gone unanswered for days because Lhasa's senior officials were away from their posts, attending their traditional three-day picnic. As the Chinese advanced, Ngabo asked for permission to surrender, then fled. Eleven days after it had begun, the battle was over. In Lhasa, the terrified government heard the Chinese radio announcement that the 'peaceful liberation' of Tibet had begun.

Belatedly, Tibet sought international support. The Indian government, backed by the British, protested, and on 7 November the Tibetan cabinet, the Kashag, appealed, fruitlessly, to the United Nations. The West was prepared to fight for Korea, but the invasion of Tibet took place with hardly a squeak of protest.

Lhasa was thrown into panic and the regency rapidly collapsed. When the state oracle was consulted about this new danger facing Tibet, he gave a decisive answer: the Dalai Lama must assume power. On 17 November the Dalai Lama was invested with full political powers. He was fifteen years old.

The Dalai Lama and his advisers waited nervously for news, still uncertain as to the intentions of the Chinese invaders. Such news as did come through was ominous. At the beginning of November the Dalai Lama had received a visit from one of his two elder brothers, a figure whom, because of their respective monastic upbringings, he hardly knew. Thupten Jigme Norbu had been recognized in infancy as the reincarnation of the Takste Lama and had left home as a boy to begin his religious life. In 1949 he was abbot of Kumbum monastery in Qinghai, the brothers' native province. The Dalai Lama had scarcely met him, but now his elder brother had made the long journey to Lhasa to deliver a message. It was not a reassuring one.

He was, the Dalai Lama recalls, in a terrible state – tense and full of fears that were explained when he told his story.

Qinghai had been conquered by the PLA in 1949, and Thupten Jigme had more than a year's experience of the intentions of the Chinese Communist Party towards the religious establishment. As he told his younger brother, he had been a virtual prisoner in a monastery from which many monks had already been driven out. His new Chinese masters had subjected him to intense political indoctrination and had released him only to make this journey to Lhasa. Its purpose, he explained, was to persuade the Dalai Lama to accept Chinese rule without further resistance. If he did not agree, Thupten Jigme Norbu went on, his instructions were to kill him.

There was no doubt, Thupten Jigme Norbu said, that the Chinese would do the same in Tibet as they had begun to do in Qinghai. The only course open to the Dalai Lama was to flee abroad and to try to rouse international support for Tibet. He himself had resolved to renounce his religious vows and to go to Washington to seek help from the United States.

The Dalai Lama did not hold out much hope of international help, but he left Lhasa for Yadong, two hundred miles away on the Sikkim border. There he received a message from his defeated commander, Ngabo Ngawang Jigme, informing him that Chamdo was now in Chinese hands, and if no settlement were reached the Chinese force would march on Lhasa.

In April 1951 a Tibetan delegation, led by Ngabo, arrived in Peking. It had no cards left to play. Its role was now to negotiate a treaty that would legitimize the Chinese takeover of Tibet.

The Panchen question figured largely in those negotiations. To the surprise of the Tibetan delegation, young Gonpo Tseten and forty of his entourage had been summoned to Beijing to attend the conference.

On the way to Beijing, the boy had made his first acquaintance with a high-ranking Communist party official, in Xi'an. By all accounts, the meeting had gone well. The thirteen-year-old Gonpo Tseten had been well schooled in the language that Communist party officials like to hear and pledged his support for the liberation of Tibet and the 'unity' of all Tibetan peoples.

On 27 April, when Gonpo Tseten arrived in Beijing, the surprised Tibetan delegation was informed that they were expected to greet him at the railway station. It presented them with a diplomatic problem: the boy hadn't been recognized by Lhasa and they could not, therefore, offer him the respect appropriate to the rank he claimed. They resolved the dilemma by sending their most junior official in layman's dress, with strict instructions not to perform the acts of reverence due to a Panchen Lama.

The delegation was painfully aware that recognition of this candidate was one of the Chinese side's most pressing demands. It had been raised on the second day of the negotiations and every day thereafter. As the Tibetans continued to insist that they had no authority to recognize the boy, the Chinese gave an ultimatum: the boy, they said, had accepted Mao Zedong as the new leader of China and Mao Zedong had accepted him as the true incarnation of the Panchen Lama. It was now a question of face.

A telegram was sent to the Dalai Lama, still in Yadong with his retinue. There, they were debating whether to continue towards India and exile or to return to Lhasa. The telegram from Ngabo in Beijing informed them that the Chinese were refusing to continue the negotiations until the Qinghai candidate was accepted. Only the Dalai Lama could make the final choice, and he favoured the candidate in Drepung monastery. The decision that had been postponed for years was now inescapable. The Dalai Lama performed a divination. It confirmed the Qinghai candidate. Under these inauspicious circumstances, Gonpo Tseten was finally accepted as the tenth incarnation of the Panchen Lama. The news was telegraphed to Beijing. The next day, Ngabo Ngawang Jigme went to pay his full respects to the boy.

With the Panchen issue out of the way, the negotiations began in earnest. In truth, there was little to gain on the Tibetan side and little to give on the Chinese, beyond a list of promises that were soon broken. The Seventeen-Point Agreement on Measures for the Peaceful Liberation of Tibet, to give it its full title, was signed on

23 May 1951. The news surprised the Dalai Lama, not least because Ngabo had only been given authority to negotiate – not to sign – an agreement. It was an agreement with many of the characteristics of an international treaty, despite the Chinese claim that Tibet had been an integral part of China since the Yuan dynasty.

Under the Seventeen-Point Agreement, central Tibet survived as an entity that was later to become the Tibet Autonomous Region, but the Tibetan provinces of Amdo and Kham – half of traditional Tibet – were to vanish, eaten up by the Chinese provinces of Qinghai, Gansu, Yunnan and the short-lived province of Sikang. The Tibetans who lived in these parts were to come under direct rule from Beijing, as any other citizen of the People's Republic of China. The Chinese justified this dismemberment of Tibet as a reflection of demographic reality. Only in the TAR, they argued, was the Tibetan population 'unmixed'. In the other provinces, they pointed out, Tibetans were one minority among a mosaic of different nationalities. Where they were numerous, they would be allowed local autonomy in so-called autonomous districts.

It was a fallacious but self-fulfilling argument. The old boundaries of Tibet, including Kham and Amdo, encircled a homogenous Tibetan population. But if the political boundaries were redrawn, as they now were, to include the many minority nationalities of the contiguous Chinese provinces as well as the Chinese themselves, the Tibetans were transformed into a minority within the newly defined provincial borders.

With the signing of the Seventeen-Point Agreement, the struggle to maintain the independence that the thirteenth Dalai Lama had proclaimed on the collapse of the Qing empire was finally ended. The Tibetans conceded sovereignty to the Chinese, and their country was to be pillaged for its territory and its resources. In return, the Chinese guaranteed a system very similar to the one they were to offer to Hong Kong more than forty years later – known in the case of Hong Kong as 'one country, two systems'.

The Dalai Lama was guaranteed the continuance of his position and functions in the Tibet Autonomous Region. The Panchen Lama saw the end of a period of exile that had begun for his previous incarnation two decades earlier. Point five of the agreement provided that 'the established status, functions and powers of the Panchen Erdeni shall be maintained', and point six that 'by the established status, functions and powers of the Dalai Lama and of the Panchen are meant the status, functions and powers of the thirteenth Dalai Lama and of the ninth Panchen Erdeni when they were in friendly and amicable relations with each other.'

The Dalai Lama's decision in favour of the Chinese candidate ended, of course, the expectations of the rival candidates – the boy in Drepung monastery and the child in Tashilhunpo. Of the two, the boy in Drepung had most to complain about. He had been the clear favourite of the Dalai Lama and he had been, to take an uncharitable view of the process, unceremoniously dropped for political reasons.

He did not complain, though. He pursued his religious studies and won respect as another manifestation of the Panchen Lama, being accorded the title Panchen Outrul Rinpoche. 'It is,' one eminent lama told me, 'as though he is the reflection of the moon in the water, rather than the moon itself.' He fled Tibet in 1959 and now runs a small religious centre in Ireland. He is a retiring, scholarly man who gives the impression that he is, if anything, relieved that the name that came out of the lottery in 1951 was not his.

The third boy, the Lithang candidate in Tashilhunpo, had a sadder fate. He was caught trying to escape from Tibet in 1959 and was never heard of again.

At the banquet that was held on 24 May 1951 to celebrate the signing of the agreement, Mao Zedong made a speech praising the newly established unity between the dalai and the panchen lamas and the Tibetan and Chinese peoples. 'The unity,' he said, 'is a brotherly unity, not a result of one side pressing the other, but rather of efforts contributed from all sides. Starting from now, on the basis of this unity, we shall, among all races, develop and progress in politics, economics and culture and in all other aspects.'

Under the agreement, Tibet was to be allowed to run its own internal affairs, the so-called 'democratic reforms' were not yet to be implemented in what was to become the Tibet Autonomous Region, and the status and functions of Tibet's religious authorities were to remain. China guaranteed that the status quo in Tibet would continue.

The promises were broken within months.

*

As the formal celebrations of the agreement were held in Beijing, the Dalai Lama and his entourage were still undecided what to do: should they return to Lhasa or continue their flight into exile? Thupten Jigme Norbu, who had made plans to travel to the United States to make a personal appeal to President Truman, was pressing his brother, the Dalai Lama, to go to India. At this late stage, the United States began to suggest, over British objections, that if the Dalai Lama wanted to go into exile, and repudiate the Seventeen-Point Agreement, then help would be available.

An agreement was drawn up under which the United States promised financial and military assistance for a resistance movement to the Chinese, if the Dalai Lama would agree to the US demands. The Dalai Lama was to leave for India on 12 July. But the major monasteries were urging their leader to return to Lhasa, and a Chinese emissary, General Zhang Jingwu, was already on his way to Yadong, where he was to promise the Dalai Lama that life in Tibet would go on much as before, with Chinese help. Once the foreign imperialists had been driven out – there had been six foreigners who remotely answered to that description in Lhasa when the Chinese invaded, and all had now gone – religious freedom would be guaranteed and China would help Tibet to modernize.

The Dalai Lama cast a divination to determine whether he should return to Lhasa or leave his country, perhaps for ever. The answer was that he should return. On 21 July, a week after General Zhang's visit, he set off. On 24 October 1951 Lhasa formally accepted the Seventeen-Point Agreement and on 26 October, 3,000 PLA troops entered the city.

The Panchen Lama's entourage, meanwhile, was preparing for its own historic journey, accompanied by troops of Peng Dehuai's 1st Route Army which, from its base in Lanzhou, was conveniently placed to travel to Xining to form the Panchen Lama's escort. Direct contact between Tibet's two highest lamas had resumed on the signing of the Seventeen-Point Agreement, when the Panchen Lama had sent the Dalai Lama a telegram confirming his intention to return. In due course the Dalai Lama replied, asking for information as to the route that the Panchen Lama planned to take on his journey to Tashilhunpo. A large welcoming party made up of lay and clerical officials was sent to Qinghai that September and arrived in Kumbum monastery in December. There the preparations were already in train for his return.

On 19 December 1951, according to his official biography,[7] ten thousand people assembled in Xining to see the young Panchen Lama depart. It was a two-thousand-mile journey in the hardest months of the year and an impressive party had been assembled. The Panchen was accompanied by his council of abbots and their families, along with his own parents and attendants. Now that the Panchen Lama's position had been confirmed, his parents could look forward to a life of wealth and high status. They said goodbye to Qinghai and the party set off with 3,000 camels, 7,000 yaks, along with their food and fodder, 200 mules and some horses. It took three months to cross the Tangla mountains, and by the time they reached Nagchuka, in March 1952, 2,000 camels had died. The fate of the yaks is not recorded.

By the time the caravan finally arrived in Lhasa in April 1952 a further 20,000 PLA soldiers had reached Tibet. Within a few months the influx had doubled the population of Lhasa and the strain on Tibetan resources was beginning to tell. Food shortages and inflation, two afflictions hitherto virtually unknown in Tibet, had set in, and a resentful populace had started to compose and sing disrespectful songs about their new masters and the PLA commander, Zhang Jingwu.

Despite the strained conditions of the capital, a grand reception was prepared to welcome the Panchen Lama. Tents had been set up in the eastern suburbs of the city and the entire government, as well, of course, as the PLA commanders, turned out for the ceremonies. That afternoon, the fourteenth Dalai Lama and the tenth Panchen Lama, three years his junior, met for the first time. It went better than might have been expected, despite the unwelcome intrusion of a Chinese security man. The two lamas sat in the Sunlight palace in the Potala and talked. He was, the Dalai Lama recalled, 'very sincere. We spent a few days together. He was very nice, very open, very genuine.' He thought him, he said, an honest and faithful young man who had an innocent air.

It was the first direct contact between Tibet's most venerated spiritual leaders in nearly three decades and there was still much unfinished business to settle. The month that the Panchen Lama stayed in Lhasa was filled with negotiations as the officials of the two great reincarnates tried to agree the details of the restoration of the Panchen Lama's status and powers according to the provisions of the Seventeen-Point Agreement. For this, they had to fix the date at which the two previous incarnations were deemed to have enjoyed friendly relations. They settled on 1897, a year when Qing imperial power was at its height in Tibet and the previous incarnations of the Dalai Lama and the Panchen Lama had been respectively twenty-one and fourteen years old.

It was agreed that the Dalai Lama's officials would be withdrawn from Tashilhunpo. In an echo of the old quarrel, they disagreed about how much tax Tashilhunpo should pay for the upkeep of the army. History was on the point of repeating itself as farce when Zhang Jingwu pointed out that Tibet's defence was now in the hands of the PLA.

Then, on 6 June, the Panchen Lama and his retinue set out for Shigatse, and on 23 June they finally arrived home. An exiled monk remembers that day. For him it was another miracle. 'It snowed,' he said. 'It was summer and it snowed.' The 1st army accompanied the Panchen Lama to Shigatse and made its headquarters there. The 18th stayed in Lhasa. As things had turned out, at the moment when the Chinese had succeeded in imposing a solution to the long quarrel between the Dalai Lama and the Panchen Lama, the Tibetan rivals had acquired Chinese military patrons who were themselves developing what was to be a prolonged and bitter rivalry.

From the outset, the rival PLA armies each promoted their respective Tibetan prelates: the 18th army, in Lhasa, argued to Beijing that the Dalai Lama was the key to controlling Tibet and must be supported. The 1st army, in Shigatse, maintained that the Panchen Lama, by virtue of his court's long-term loyalty to China, was the only reliable ally. At the moment when the Tibetans might have been ready to bury the past, the Chinese had invented a fresh quarrel.

Chapter Nine

✡

The Panchen Lama's mother chatted, distantly, searching the past for memories that were suitable to share with a foreigner. Many were not. The family household was big, she recalled, but they never had any problem with food when they lived in Qinghai.

'Later?' she murmured. 'Ah, later. Later there were difficulties.'

Later there was the 70,000-character petition that the Panchen Lama wrote to the Chinese leadership, a document that was to bring about his disgrace. Had she known about it?

She knew he was writing something, she said. But she herself could not read, so she never really knew what it said. She tacked back to her earlier life, to the peace and relative prosperity of the village. There was a school there, she said. And later, in the eighties, the Panchen Lama himself had established a Tibetan school.

'There had been the time of leftist errors,' she said. The words sounded out of place; this was the Party euphemism for the Cultural Revolution. 'We lived apart then,' she said, 'for seven years.'

In Dharamsala the Dalai Lama's sister had told me how the Panchen Lama's mother had wept as she described those years for her. For seven years she had not known whether her son was dead or alive. But now, those emotions were shut away.

'We didn't suffer personally at that time,' she said to me.

The atmosphere grew slightly heavy. Her attendants began to check their watches. 'She is an old lady,' they said. I took the hint and began to thank her for the visit. She rose and went to the next room, reappearing with a *khata*, which she placed around my neck. We left, down the dark staircase and out into the grey afternoon light, feeling suddenly conspicuous in that official compound with its unseen, watching eyes.

I walked back to my hotel, through the dirty streets of Xining, reflecting on all the unspoken suffering that lay between Sonam Dolma's happy memories of that long-vanished life in Xunhua and the watchful, guarded present.

Her time as the honoured mother of the new Panchen Lama, living in comfort in Shigatse, had been desperately brief. The Panchen Lama enjoyed a short honeymoon in his relationship with the Chinese Communist Party. He was given political status and recruited to act as figurehead for the Party's policies. But the Party's internal ideological disputes and power struggles were soon to bring tragedy to Tibet, as they did to the rest of China, and the Panchen Lama was to join the ever-lengthening list of its victims.

The Communist party that had invaded and now ruled Tibet had been forged over nearly thirty years of armed struggle. Its military adventures were to continue with occasional external engagements – the Korean war, already begun as the Tibetan invasion took place, a brief border conflict with India in 1962, and in the seventies, the tortuously named 'self-defensive counter-attack' against Vietnam. But, after 1949, most of the Party's destructive energy was turned in on itself.

The internal Party struggles revolved around the personality and ideas of Mao Zedong. Once the People's Republic was established, in 1949, Mao set about transforming China into the model Communist society of his dreams. By the time he died the pursuit of that dream was to have cost the lives of more than thirty million of his fellow countrymen. In Tibet, Mao's 'vision' was to bring starvation, rebellion, mass imprisonment and the virtual destruction of the Buddhist church.

Like Stalin, Mao believed in the forced collectivization of agriculture, which would, he thought, enable China to skip the capitalist phase of development and move straight to Communism.

The shorthand for Mao's disastrous theories was the innocent-sounding word *reform*. The question of when, where and how to implement reforms in Tibet was to be the crux of the argument between Lhasa and Beijing from the moment the Seventeen-Point Agreement was signed. Within the Tibetan élite, there was already an appreciation of the need for reforms in Tibetan society. The impulse to enact major changes to Tibet's political and social system had first been stirred by the thirteenth Dalai Lama. After the shock of first the British then the Chinese occupations of Tibet, he had been persuaded by the British diplomat Charles Bell that a degree of modernization was necessary to equip Tibet for survival in an increasingly dangerous world. As has already been discussed, the thirteenth Dalai Lama's desire to finance an army was one of the main causes of the quarrel with the ninth Panchen Lama. He also tried to introduce secular education but was finally defeated by the uncompromising hostility of the conservative monks, who saw in such a move a threat not only to their institutional monopoly of education, but to Buddhism itself.

The stifling intransigence of much of the religious élite had had two effects: Tibet had drifted on, isolated, internally divided and unmodernized, until the Chinese invasion in 1950 revealed its true helplessness. And many progressive Tibetans who had failed to have their ideas accepted in Lhasa turned towards China as the hope for the future. Some had become Communists; others, though not Party members, were nevertheless disposed to see the Chinese as a modernizing force.

But to the Chinese Communist Party, reform was not a matter of rejuvenating Tibet's traditional society but of destroying it. This was the first step, in their eyes, towards the creation of a Communist society. It began with land reform, which forced landless peasants to confront and, in many cases, eliminate their landlords, creating, the theory went, allegiance to the Communist party by rewarding the peasants with land and tools. That stage completed, the peasants were to be encouraged to form co-operatives and, finally, they were to be collectivized.

In this last stage, agricultural communes would achieve modernization and efficiencies of large-scale production. Surplus labour would be released for collective undertakings such as terracing, dam-building and irrigation. It was a process that foresaw both an economic and a political revolution, transforming both the landscape and the people in it. It would turn superstitious – or religious – peasants into fully-fledged members of the new society. Mao Zedong was impatient to get on with it.

Mao began in China proper, with results that anyone familiar with the history of the Soviet Union could have predicted. By the end of the fifties Chinese agriculture was wrecked, hunger was well established and China's prison camps were full to bursting.

On paper, Tibet should have escaped the worst effects of the disastrous reforms of the fifties. Under the Seventeen-Point Agreement, central Tibet, which was to become the Tibet Autonomous

Region, was not to be subject to reform. A long shadow was cast, nevertheless, as the Tibetan government was drawn inexorably into the events that were taking place in China.

The agreement promised Tibet autonomy in all areas except defence and foreign policy. Initially China adopted a 'United Front' policy, under which the Tibetan ruling élite was to be induced by the offer of good jobs and large salaries to co-operate with the Chinese. Some, particularly the small urban élite and the aristocracy, who were rewarded with official posts, were inclined to co-operate anyway, seeing in the Chinese a force that could bring about a modernization which Tibetan society could not achieve for itself.

But the fifties saw a steady tightening of the Chinese noose around the Tibetan administration. In March 1952, in Lhasa, a 'People's Congress' was set up to protest against the food shortages and inflation caused by the presence of the PLA. It petitioned Zhang Jingwu, demanding that the army units withdraw and requesting that only the representatives of the central government remain, as had been the practice in the early Qing dynasty.

Mao appeared to draw back. His reply is contained in the 'Directives on the Guideline for Tibetan Work' prepared for the Central Committee on 6 April 1952. Tibet, he said, lacked the material base for a full implementation of the agreement and forcing it would do 'more harm than good'. Mao gave instructions that the Party should confine itself to solving the material problems and developing trade. They should be prepared to compromise, he said, and wait until 'the time is ripe for a future attack'.

In spite of Mao's apparent concessions, the People's Congress petition nonetheless led to the dismissal of the Dalai Lama's two most senior officials and the restructuring of the Tibetan government to allow a more direct grip. In 1953 Mao decided to invite the Dalai Lama to Beijing in order to inform him that he had decided to rule Tibet directly from China. The occasion was the first National People's Congress in Beijing the following year. Both the Panchen and the Dalai Lamas were to attend and Tibet's two great incarnations were once again to become the key symbols in the political struggles of Tibet.

The young Panchen Lama had settled into Tashilhunpo, and under the care of his tutors, had embarked on the long process of mastering the Buddhist texts when, in 1954, he and the Dalai Lama were 'elected' as delegates to the first National People's Congress in Beijing.

In July 1954 the Dalai Lama set out, under the gaze of the population of Lhasa, who had gathered, anxious and suspicious of the reasons for the journey, to see him off. Five hundred of his chief dignitaries accompanied him on his journey eastward to Chamdo, where he was greeted by a PLA guard of honour. From there he continued to Chengdu where, for the first time in his life, he boarded a plane and flew to Xi'an.

In Xi'an his party met up with that of the Panchen Lama, who had taken a different route, and the two continued their journey to Beijing by train. Relations between the two incarnations had cooled since their first meeting. Shigatse was not inclined to bow the knee to Lhasa, and Lhasa was nervous about the reality of Chinese intentions. There seemed to be every reason to suppose, at the dawn of the fifties, that the historic quarrel between the thirteenth Dalai Lama and the ninth Panchen Lama would be renewed, in all its vigour, by their respective reincarnations.

For if there had been suspicion between Lhasa and Shigatse in the twenties and thirties, how much more reason was there for mistrust now: the Dalai Lama headed the government that had just lost the struggle for Tibetan independence. The Panchen Lama had arrived at the head of the conquering army. It was not likely to be an easy relationship. As the political conditions imposed by the Chinese began to take shape, the old tensions returned. On that trip, the Dalai Lama recalls, things had begun to turn a little sour between them.

'He was a little bit, shall we say, spoilt,' he recalled. 'He had developed a sense of competition with the Dalai Lama. He had been influenced by his officials and when we went to China there were some silly incidents. The Panchen Lama himself was OK, but some of this entourage – some of them were quite silly.'

Both the panchen and the dalai lamas had been assigned the roles of exotic *apparatchiks* in the Chinese machine. In a contemporary revisiting of the Qing dynasty practice of distributing titles – now overlaid with a false veneer of democratic rhetoric – the two young men were nominated to a series of empty positions in bodies that carried grand names but held little power. The Dalai Lama emerged as Vice-Chairman of the Standing Committee of the first National People's Congress and the Panchen Lama a standing committee member. The Panchen was then named Vice-Chairman of the Chinese People's Political Consultative Congress and the Dalai Lama a standing committee member. Honour was satisfied on both sides.

But the power structure had changed for good. During that long visit to Beijing the state council set up the machinery that would eventually usher in the new government of the Tibet Autonomous Region. Under the Chinese administration, political power would no longer be vested in the Dalai Lama's government but in the preparatory committee for the TAR, which would ready Tibet for assimilation into the political structure of the People's Republic. Mao sent no less a figure than the vice-premier, Marshal Chen Yi, to Tibet to supervise the work of the committee, with instructions to proceed slowly and to endeavour to win over the Dalai Lama and the Kashag in order to avoid provoking any resistance.[1]

The preparatory committee was made up of four groups: the Panchen Lama's representation, the Chamdo party, the Dalai Lama and his Lhasa government and the Chinese authorities. The Dalai Lama was nominally the chairman but could control only one quarter of the committee. The Panchen Lama was vice-chairman, but the real power lay with the second vice-chairman, the Commander-in-Chief of the Tibetan Military Area Command, Zhang Guohua. Ngabo Ngawang Jigme, the young governor of Chamdo who had surrendered to the Chinese at and subsequently led the negotiating team in Beijing, was secretary-general. The arrangement effectively partitioned the Tibetan government and removed control from the Dalai Lama.

Still, the Chinese had promised not to institute 'democratic reforms' in the TAR and their strategy at this stage remained to form alliances within the traditional ruling class. The Tibetan areas that lay outside the TAR – Kham, which included Chamdo, and Amdo, which included parts of Qinghai, were not so lucky. Democratic reform was to be implemented there at the same time as in the rest of China.

As the process got underway in these areas it became clear that, as in Mongolia under Stalin's influence, the Buddhist church was a prime target. There should have been no surprise in this: the

Communist party could not, finally, tolerate any ideological rivals. But it came as a rude shock to the religious establishment, which had hoped to avoid persecution.

Although in the TAR reforms were meant to be delayed at least for the duration of the second five-year plan, the Panchen Lama's group and the Chamdo party's Chen Jigme also 'demanded' reforms. The Panchen Lama offered Shigatse up as an 'experimental zone'. The Dalai Lama and the Kashag were, of course, opposed.

By the time Chen Yi and his delegation of more than five hundred people arrived in Lhasa in 1956 to supervise the workings of the committee, the first Tibetan rebellion had already broken out, in Kham, the present-day Kanze Tibetan Autonomous Prefecture in Sichuan.[2]

The rebellion had been provoked by the first stage of reform that had begun in Sichuan, Yunnan, Gansu and Qinghai in the winter of 1955. Even before then, regional leaders had begun to rebel and the Chinese had responded with force against them. Village heads, tribal leaders and prominent religious figures had been arrested as the PLA attempted to disarm the local population.[3]

In these areas the religious establishment had begun to feel the effects of Chinese rule. Monasteries had been disbanded, the monks and nuns forced to live a secular life, and religious treasures stripped out and stolen. As the Chinese cracked down, the population resisted. Soon, the Chinese were facing a full-scale revolt, which had begun in Kham and was to cover almost a million square miles.

The rebellion attracted the sympathy and support of both the KMT and the US government, who began to supply material assistance. This had little effect on the military balance, but it allowed the central authorities to define the rebellions as a 'counter-revolutionary armed rebellion supported by reactionary factions of the US and Chiang Kai-shek'. As the fighting spread, refugees began to flood into Central Tibet. From 1956 to 1958 up to sixty thousand people fled from Kham into Tibet. Some of them were local leaders, but the vast majority were ordinary lay and religious people. The Dalai Lama, who was struggling to maintain a balance between his Buddhist devotees and the occupying Chinese, found himself in an increasingly untenable position.

It was against this background that, in 1956, the Panchen Lama and the Dalai Lama were invited to visit India to celebrate the

2,500th anniversary of the Buddha's birth. By then, revolt against the Chinese in Kham and Amdo was well established, and the trip presented the Dalai Lama with an opportunity again to appeal for outside support. At the first opportunity, he broached the possibility of seeking asylum in India with Prime Minister Nehru. Nehru was unenthusiastic, but he did agree to make an appeal on behalf of the Dalai Lama to the senior Chinese leader Zhou Enlai, who was due to visit India.

When Zhou Enlai arrived, the Dalai Lama laid out his complaint about the reforms in progress in eastern Tibet. He received a pledge from Zhou Enlai that any abuses that existed would be corrected. The Panchen Lama, on the other hand, took advantage of the occasion to assure Zhou of his support for Chinese policy. A few weeks later Zhou returned to Delhi to urge the Dalai Lama to return to Tibet and to make it clear to him that China was ready to use force to put down the rebellion.[4] In February 1957, while the Dalai Lama was still undecided about whether to return, Mao Zedong made a speech in Beijing in which he declared that Tibet was not ready for reforms and that they would not be implemented for at least six years. Reassured, the Dalai Lama decided to return to Tibet.

Back in Tibet, the tensions between the two prelates continued. When the Dalai Lama visited Shigatse, Tashilhunpo expressed its coolness by failing to send its monks out to line the streets in greeting as protocol demanded. The Dalai Lama, in turn, had expressed his disapproval of the monastery's slight by staying not in Tashilhunpo but in the *dzong*, the ancient fort opposite the monastery, the site of what had been the stronghold of Tsangba Khan. It was a decision resonant with history and its significance escaped nobody. The stately quarrel became public knowledge, and the populace, always ready to comment on the conduct of their leaders, expressed their disapproval of the Panchen Lama by withholding gestures of respect.

But if there were personal tensions, they were to pale before the catastrophe that was overtaking the People's Republic of China and in which Tibet was to become inexorably entangled. Even the Panchen Lama, accustomed by now to view Lhasa's opinions unsympathetically, was soon to be confronted with the warning signs. They were to come from his own province of Amdo, now the Chinese province of Qinghai. There the reforms had begun, as they had in the rest of China, in the fifties. By the end of the decade, the catastrophe was well advanced.

In 1958 Mao launched the Great Leap Forward, a crash programme of communization and forced industrialization that was to wreck Chinese agriculture and lead directly to the death by starvation of more than thirty million people between 1959 and 1961.

There was opposition to Mao in the higher reaches of the Party, but it was not strong enough to stand against the tide of 'revolutionary optimism' that Mao had engendered. Among his opponents was the defence minister Peng Dehuai, the son of peasants, who knew the signs of famine from his own experience of it in his youth. In the autumn of 1958 Peng Dehuai toured the country and discovered the dismal truth. He challenged Mao the following year, at the six-week Lushan summit, where he presented a 10,000-word report on the catastrophe that had engulfed the country. Peng was backed by a small number of other Party luminaries, but Mao still refused to acknowledge that anything was seriously wrong.

The two men clashed again at a Politburo meeting in July. Peng accused Mao of acting like a despot and Mao, perhaps still nursing his grudge against Peng for his reluctance to liberate Tibet, called Peng a rightist and accused him of trying to sabotage the dictatorship of the proletariat. Few people present spoke up for Peng Dehuai and the meeting ended in a victory for Mao. The policies of the Great Leap Forward were reaffirmed and Peng Dehuai was condemned as an 'anti-Party element' and a 'rightist opportunist'. He fell into disgrace and was imprisoned, and later tortured and killed, in Mao's next great upheaval, the Cultural Revolution.

By this time, the revolt in Kham had begun to affect Lhasa and matters were to come to a head at the New Year celebrations in 1959. Over the previous two years, some sixty thousand people from Kham and Amdo had fled to Tibet, and six thousand armed Khampa rebels were in Lhasa itself. The population was further swelled by the thirty to forty thousand monks from the major monasteries who traditionally came to Lhasa for the Monlam prayer festival immediately after New Year. The arrival of so many monks in Lhasa for Monlam always generated tension, as they were by tradition an unruly and unpredictable throng. Wealthy Lhasa citizens often took the precaution of hiding their valuables before the New Year in case the monks caused trouble. But this year, the trouble was to be of a different order.

What followed is well known: at the New Year festival of 1959, the Chinese military commander invited the Dalai Lama to attend a drama performance at the army base. When news of the invitation reached the streets of Lhasa, crowded with pilgrims and monks, rumours began to fly that the Chinese planned to kidnap the Dalai Lama. The rumours were given added weight by the impassioned street-corner testimony of the Khampa pilgrims who had come to Lhasa to ask for the Dalai Lama's support in their armed resistance to the Chinese.

As the rumour of the Chinese plan to kidnap the Dalai Lama spread, the Khampas harangued the Lhasa crowds with dreadful stories of Chinese atrocities and warnings that, on other occasions, such an invitation had served as cover for an arrest. Now thoroughly alarmed, crowds began to surround the Dalai Lama's summer palace, the Norbulingka, to try to prevent either the Dalai Lama visiting the Chinese camp or the Chinese coming to get him. A monk official, a member of the TAR preparatory committee, who appeared at the gate of the Norbulingka in plain clothes and was discovered to be carrying a pistol, was taken for a Chinese spy and stoned to death. In the fevered atmosphere Lhasa was rising in revolt.

The Dalai Lama, anxious not to inflame the situation further, sent a delegation to the military commander to beg to be excused from attending the performance. The commander, Tan Guansan, reluctantly permitted the Dalai Lama to postpone his visit, in a letter delivered by Ngabo to the Dalai Lama on 11 March. He also instructed the Kashag to find and punish the instigators of the revolt.[5]

The Dalai Lama appears to have tried to mediate between a genuine popular uprising which he had not encouraged and the Chinese military on the ground. From Beijing, though, the revolt had a different aspect: it presented an opportunity to show who was boss and to deal with the recalcitrant Tibetan 'reactionaries'.

Perhaps there were echoes, for Beijing, of the Hungarian uprisings in 1956. As Khrushchev hesitated then, over whether or not to send the tanks into Hungary, Deng Xiaoping, in Moscow for a meeting with the Russians, had argued that the Hungarian uprising was not Nationalist but anti-Communist in character and that it had to be crushed. Now, from Beijing, Mao ordered Tan Guansan to crush the Tibetan revolt. As he put in his telegram to the military area command in Lhasa, 'Judging from the developing situation, the Tibetan problems are very likely to be resolved by force. (This kind of force is good.)' The Chinese, said Mao, should abandon the alliance with the upper class and look for allies below. If the conspirators tried to flee, he added, they should be allowed to do so.[6]

By this time the revolt was in full swing. A 'Tibetan People's Congress' had been declared and the Seventeen-Point Agreement rejected. The Dalai Lama still tried to keep his balance as the ground beneath his feet began to give way. On 12 March he wrote to Tan Guansan condemning the 'unlawful behaviour of the reactionary faction' and informing him that he had ordered the illegal congress dismissed. Mao instructed that the Dalai Lama should be warned that if he did not co-operate in putting down the revolt he would be 'jettisoned by his own people'.[7]

These thoughts were passed on, along with the accusation that the Dalai Lama's government had been faking its compliance with Chinese instructions and had in fact encouraged the revolt. If it did not stop soon, Tan Guansan warned, 'the centre' would have no choice but to act. He offered the Dalai Lama the protection of the military compound. Ngabo had included a note of his own in which he warned that Chinese were preparing to shell the Norbulingka. He begged the Dalai Lama to indicate where in the compound he would be, so that the artillery could be directed away from his hiding place.

The Dalai Lama wrote back, promising to come, in secret, when he could. Instead he turned to his traditional source of advice and consulted the Nechung oracle. When the Dalai Lama asked the oracle what action he should now take, the reply from the medium was unequivocal.

'Go!' he screamed. 'Go tonight!' Still in his trance, the medium hastily wrote down the route the Dalai Lama should take, then collapsed.[8]

Almost as the medium spoke, the first Chinese shells exploded in the grounds of the Norbulingka. That afternoon the Dalai Lama performed another divination that confirmed the oracle's instructions. Shortly afterwards, his tutors and four members of the Kashag made their escape from the palace hidden in the back of a lorry. After dark, his mother and younger brother left in disguise. The Dalai Lama made one last farewell before the statue of the Protector. Then, disguised in trousers and a long coat and shouldering a rifle, he joined a small group of soldiers who announced to the surrounding crowds that they were going on patrol.

They made their way through the crowds and slipped, unnoticed, out of Lhasa. Once across the river, the Dalai Lama was reunited with his family and the party rode hard towards the Indian border. They reached it five days later. They were, it seems, allowed to leave. In a telegram to Tan Guansan, Mao had instructed: 'We should split up the upper echelon and educate those below; if they are fleeing, our armies must not categorically block them, whether they are going to Lhokha or India, let them go.'[9]

Thousands of Tibetans fled in the months after the suppression of the rebellion. Many died on the high Himalayan passes. Many more died in India, victims of grief, shock, unfamiliar climate and disease, and the rigours of the road gangs which were the mainstay of their existence in the first traumatic years of exile. The Chinese attack had begun on the morning of 20 March 1959. Forty-eight hours later, the monks who had been holding out in the Jokhang, Tibet's holiest cathedral, surrendered. The uprising was over and the last vestiges of Tibetan autonomy were shattered.

When the 18th army first discovered the Dalai Lama's absence, they were mystified. Supporters of the Dalai Lama, they concluded he had been kidnapped by 'reactionary elements'. Their confusion was understandable. In the course of an exchange of correspondence with Tan Guansan during the uprising in Lhasa, the Dalai Lama had repeatedly written of his fear for his life and the concern he felt for the activities of 'reactionary elements'.

In his last note, written on the afternoon of 16 March, he had said, 'I am trying to use some tactful methods to divide internally the line between the progressive and anti-reformers among the government officials. After a few days, once I have a certain number of reliable forces, I will go to the military base by secret means. By then I would write to you first. I hope you would adopt some dependable measures. Please inform me often with your views.'[10]

It was only after the Dalai Lama made it clear at his first press conference in exile that he had not been kidnapped but had chosen to flee that the Chinese were forced to find another explanation. Thus was born one of the abiding hate figures of Chinese propaganda – the reactionary Dalai Lama and his anti-China clique, the 'traitor' who sought to 'split the motherland' with the help of international imperialism.

Thus Tibet's supreme spiritual leader had become a pariah to the Chinese. But there was still the Panchen Lama. With the Dalai Lama gone, the Chinese hoped that the compliant Panchen Lama, client both of the Communist party and of the 1st army, would be a willing substitute. He was swiftly promoted to acting chairman of the TAR preparatory committee, and the way seemed clear for Beijing to create a puppet theocrat whose spiritual influence would bring the rebellious Tibetans to an acceptance of Chinese rule.

From Beijing's vantage point, it must have seemed likely that the proposition would succeed. The ground had been long prepared, beginning with the exile of the ninth Panchen Lama in China. This time, it seemed, the Chinese had a more likely candidate even than the mild and retiring ninth incarnation. The tenth was a young man on whom Chinese influence had been strong from early childhood. And there was no more pro-Chinese Tibetan than his trusted administrator, Chen Jigme. The Panchen Lama owed the Chinese his return to Tibet and it was Chinese support that had elevated the Panchen Lama's political position even as it had undermined that of the Dalai Lama.

How much the Panchen Lama supported the Chinese Communist Party remains a matter of dispute. But it seems clear that at this stage in his life at least, he believed he shared a vision of a modernized, progressive Tibet with his new masters. It was to be a Tibet free of the abuses of the past, free of serfdom and cruel punishments, a country in which the overblown religious sector would be pared down to those monks who had a genuine vocation, and the peaceful practice of religion would be encouraged. It would be a Tibet in which the rule of law would replace arbitrary personal power.

He was to express this vision later, in the long petition to the leadership that was to prove his downfall, and it is clear from his command of the Party's language that he saw no contradiction between the ideals the Communist party proclaimed and his own religious and nationalist convictions.[11]

He supported land reform and praised the Party for building modern schools, hospitals and roads. He supported the vision of a socialist society in which Tibetan traditions and culture would be respected. However rudely he was to be disenchanted later, in the fifties he still seems to have believed that this was what the Chinese Communist Party would bring to Tibet. He had the makings of an ideal puppet.

The Dalai Lama today takes a different view of the Panchen's position. The two had their differences, he says, but by 1959, he was convinced that the Panchen Lama had doubts, at least, about the effects of the Chinese occupation. One incident, in particular, stuck in his mind.

'In 1958 I was preparing to take my final examinations and I received a letter from the Panchen Lama,' he told me. 'The examinations were due to be held in the Monlam prayer festival of March 1959 and a delegation arrived from Tashilhunpo. It was brought by a special old monk official who was well known as unbiased, not pro-Chinese,' the Dalai Lama recalled. 'He brought a handwritten letter from the Panchen Lama and a verbal message which was very encouraging. It said that he had realized how very bad the Chinese had been in his area, in the Amdo area, and that he had understood how important it was that there should be unity amongst the Tibetans.

'This monk official told me that the Panchen Lama was much changed, that he had become more mature and thoughtful and that he was beginning to think that any differences between lamas were insignificant: it was all between officials. He went to the extent of telling me about plans to resist and saying that he supported them. That was in 1959. That was almost the last communication between us.'

Many exiles believe that the Panchen Lama both supported and prepared for an armed resistance to the Chinese in the fifties. That seems unlikely, but there is certainly evidence that he had formed his own small army under the aegis of the school that he set up in 1956. The school taught Hindi, Tibetan and Chinese to some three hundred young men. They also learned cavalry skills, driving, photography and shooting.

A light-engineering factory belonging to the monastery, as the monks of the exiled Tashilhunpo had told me, was making machine-guns. In 1958, another story goes, the Panchen Lama had given instruction for the secret purchase of large numbers of fast horses and, after the Dalai Lama's escape, 96 horses were purchased, bringing the total in his stables to 150.[12] And, finally, there is the evidence of Jigme Kongga.

Jigme Kongga is an exiled Tibetan who, after many years as the Dalai Lama's driver, now runs a small shop in McLeod Ganj. He is a native of Amdo and his father and the Panchen Lama's father were sworn friends. As a child, Jigme Kongga had played with the young Gonpo Tseten and shared his enthusiasm for riding, fencing and target practice. When Jigme Kongga's own father died, the Panchen Lama's family took an interest in the boy and, in 1956, after they had moved to Shigatse, Jigme Kongga went to live with them.

'The Panchen Lama's father was very short tempered, but very devout,' he said, 'and very anti-Chinese. He hated it that the family was seen as pro-Chinese but he couldn't do anything about it.

'After the Tibetan guerrillas started to fight the Chinese I wanted to go and join them. People from different parts of Tibet formed an armed movement called the Voluntary Army of Buddhism with the headquarters in the Lhokha district. But the Panchen's father told me to wait. They had established this special school and their aim was to build up an armed force. They didn't welcome visitors because they were worried about their secrets being known. I saw students riding horses, being trained to swing swords from horseback at dawn every morning. They were being trained as cavalry. I also saw students being trained to shoot. I'm sure of it. They were planning their own armed rebellion, he said, and he wanted me to join them.'

It is unlikely that the Panchen Lama seriously planned an armed rebellion, but perhaps he saw his own small force as some guarantee of his own security. When the confrontation came, though, it caught him by surprise.

'When the Lhasa uprising happened,' Jigme Kongga explained, 'I think they couldn't get away. The Panchen's father came and told me that I had better go quickly and join the guerrillas or I would be in danger. I left and never saw them again.'

After the Dalai Lama's escape the Panchen Lama was visited by a group of Chinese officials who formally informed him of the uprising in Lhasa, by then almost over, and of the 'kidnapping' of the Dalai Lama. If he had harboured a desire to join the rebellion, it was already too late. There was still heavy fighting in Lhasa but, in Shigatse, the Panchen Lama promised his visitors that he would do his best to maintain calm and to keep the situation under control.

His own five hundred troops were disarmed, along with the local Tibetan garrison in Shigatse, and the local civil and religious administrations were dismantled (a precaution, the Chinese explained, in case they threw in their lot with the rebels). The Panchen Lama gave a response that more than pleased the Chinese visitors.

'This confrontation was unavoidable,' he said. 'It was only a matter of time. A running sore has to be cut open. Once it is open, Tibet work will instead be easier and democratic reforms can also be implemented earlier.'[13]

The Panchen Lama was meant to hold his new position as acting chairman of the TAR preparatory committee for as long as the Dalai Lama remained 'under duress'. He spent a week in Lhasa, then left for Beijing for the Second National People's Congress and several urgent meetings with China's leaders.

The Chinese leadership had, by then, designated the rebellion the work of a 'handful of reactionaries' acting in concert with foreign imperialists. They declared the Seventeen-Point Agreement in abeyance and removed all restraints on the implementation of reform in Tibet. As Zhou Enlai said to the Panchen Lama at a banquet in Beijing, the rebellion had 'created extremely favourable conditions for the democratization of Tibet'. The Panchen Lama agreed. The work was to begin at once. The Third Plenary Meeting of the Preparatory Committee, with the Panchen Lama as its acting chairman, passed the first resolutions on land reform in September.

Reform in Tibet was to include the religious sector. The Party laid down that the number of lamas would be reduced, and those willing to resume a secular life would have to work. But under the Party's principle of freedom of religious belief, 'patriotic and law-abiding religious disciples' would be permitted to remain in the temples to continue religious activities.

The Party promised that only the most reactionary minority would suffer from the consequences of the rebellion. All others would be protected, as long as they approved of and supported democratic reform. The Tibetan delegation, perhaps not sorry that the defeated remnants of their old enemies in Lhasa were now finally to be removed, were enthusiastic in their support. They returned to Tibet, eager to begin their historic mission.

For the Panchen's veteran servant, Chen Jigme, it must have seemed the fulfilment of all his ambitions. More than thirty years after the thirteenth Dalai Lama had fled to India, leaving the ninth Panchen Lama behind to be wooed by Chinese officials, history seemed to be repeating itself. Now that the Dalai Lama was out of the way, what could prevent the tenth Panchen Lama from taking that final step towards the throne? The long quarrel between Ü and Tsang, between Lhasa and Shigatse, would be settled firmly in Shigatse's favour and the reactionary Lhasa élite could no longer obstruct the modernization of Tibet. As one of the architects of this triumph, Chen Jigme could look forward to a period of security and prosperity under Chinese patronage.

It was a tempting vision but, within four years, it was in ruins. All those who had facilitated the Chinese occupation and considered themselves progressive and pro-Chinese were to receive a rude awakening. Few of them – with the notable exception of Ngabo Ngawang Jigme – were to be spared.

Many more monks were to die, in the labour camps and prisons of Tibet and Qinghai. Before long, the Panchen Lama himself was to endure the process of violent struggle that the Chinese Communist Party habitually released against its enemies. By the time his own position began to slip, he had become painfully aware that Chinese rule in Tibet was not producing the benefit he had anticipated: the world in which he had been brought up, the world of religion, of learning and spiritual contemplation, had been shattered beyond repair.

Chapter Ten

✻

The morning was dank and grey as I left my hotel in Xining to walk to the bus station. I was on my way to visit Kumbum, once one of the greatest monasteries of them all. It was built around the birthplace of the great reformer and founder of the Gelugpa sect, Tsongkhapa, and had been the refuge of the ninth Panchen Lama's entourage as well as the tenth Panchen Lama's point of departure for that great trek to Tibet. Now, according to the guidebook, it had become one of Qinghai's major tourist attractions.

At the bus station a small fleet of 'luxury' minibuses lay in wait for the thin tourist traffic. Behind, a more dilapidated version was already filling up with Tibetan travellers. Most of the seats were already occupied, and I squeezed in beside a large Tibetan man. He was wearing a brown *chuba* and held an assortment of cloth-wrapped bundles on his lap. The passengers kept piling in, folding down the jump-seats. Finally, when the minibus would take no more, a Chinese conductor appeared at the door and began to harangue the passengers.

'Get up!' he shouted. 'Move! Can't you see I can't get in.'

The man to whom this request was addressed was a small Tibetan with a nut-brown face which had assumed an expression of rigid blankness. He stared ahead as though deep in meditation and deaf to the increasing volume of abuse that now rained down on him. Finally the conductor lost all restraint, seized the passenger by the coat and bundled him off the bus.

'Why is it always Tibetans who have to get up?' a woman behind me muttered. An old man in rags who had been watching the scene from outside thrust a filthy hand through the window. 'I'm hungry,' he intoned. 'I'm hungry.' The bus jerked forwards, forcing his arm out again. The bus conductor occupied the seat he had claimed and gave vent to a long, loud stream of invective.

Nearly two hours later we came to an abrupt halt and the bus rapidly emptied. I got out and looked around at the dismal town.

I assumed it was Huangzhong, my destination, but there was little beyond the sudden disappearance of my fellow passengers to tell me so. Four roads opened off a straggly square. 'Kumbum?' I enquired of a woman who was selling dusty dried fruit from a small stall. She pointed to a steep hill that many of my fellow passengers had already begun to climb.

I followed them up a street lined on both sides with open stalls selling tourist knick-knacks – butter lamps, fur-lined *chubas*, striped Tibetan aprons, rugs, *khatas*, amber and turquoise beads and silver amulets. The stall-holders called out their wares as I passed. Further up the street a craftsman was beating out huge golden ornaments for a temple roof. At the top of the hill, a ticket kiosk and a line of eight white *chortens*[1] told me I had arrived.

The monastery was laid out on a hillside, across which a freezing wind was blowing. The tops of the hills were lightly dusted with snow and, further down, a steady sleet had turned the ground to slimy red mud. A steady trickle of Chinese tourists trudged around in the cold. Between them darted bands of pilgrims, hurrying from shrine to shrine.

There were whole families of Mongolians, small, round-faced, dark-skinned, the women's long plaits encased in embroidery and silver covers. Their heavily embroidered fur-lined robes, tightly sashed with orange, swayed as they passed, the silver ornaments that hung from their waists bouncing gently. A flock of tiny children scuttled behind the adults as they made their rounds, touching their foreheads to the Buddhas, their movements urgent, hurried. The Chinese tourists watched them, amused, then posed for each others' cameras, their hands resting on the temple's huge prayer wheels.

I tramped around, following the Mongolians, in and out of the dark temples, past a vast scene sculpted in butter of the sixth Panchen Lama's visit to Beijing. Butter sculpture is one of the emphemeral arts practised in the winter months by Tibetan monks. The sour smell of the butter filled the chilly room. Thirty monks, the notice said, worked on it for four months. I looked at the little world they had created – the joyous scenes of the Panchen's triumphal procession through the capital of the Chinese empire. It was huge, a riot of gilded and coloured ornament, but it omitted, of course, any reference to the trip's final chapter: the Panchen's death from smallpox.

Much of the monastery was under scaffolding and on top, in the Panchen's palace, vivid new colours were being painted on the sandalwood pillars and roof beams. The official explanation for the damage the monastery had suffered in the past was that it had occurred in the Cultural Revolution. But when I asked a monk with whom I had fallen into conversation about this, he shrugged. 'The monastery was virtually empty by then,' he said. 'It wasn't the Cultural Revolution, it all happened much earlier. This monastery was destroyed in the Great Leap Forward.' He looked at the ground and began to speak rapidly, in a low voice. 'It's happening again, now,' he almost whispered. 'It's like the anti-rightist movement all over again. Anyone who raises his head is driven out.'

The immediate cause of the new wave of ideological terror was the conflict over the search for the reincarnation of the tenth Panchen Lama. But that conflict was part of a pattern that had begun when Chinese troops first occupied Tibet and Beijing realized that the strength of the Buddhist religious establishment and the faith of the Tibetan people were the main obstacles to the new order. The Cultural Revolution was only one of the confrontations between Beijing's ideology and Tibet's religious faith. The Cultural Revolution is now officially described as 'ten years of disorder' – a terrible mistake. But though the crimes of that period, when Deng Xiaoping was in political disgrace, are acknowledged, the story of the devastation of the late fifties and the mass starvation of the early sixties, a time when Deng played a full political role, is still mired in Party obfuscation. It was this period that was to bring the downfall of the tenth Panchen Lama.

In May 1959 Mao Zedong and Zhou Enlai had promised the Panchen Lama that the Tibetans' religious freedoms would be protected and that those monasteries that had not taken part in the March rebellion had nothing to fear. There would be reform of the religious sector, they said, only in order to eliminate those elements of exploitation that had crept in. The number of monks would be reduced, but traditional practices, they promised, would continue.

The Panchen Lama was a supporter of reform in the monasteries as in the rest of Tibetan society. He, too, believed there were too many lamas and that those who had been coerced into monasteries by their families, or driven into them by poverty, should be encouraged to return to secular life. Those who had a genuine vocation and who would devote themselves to the rigorous spiritual traditions of Tibetan Buddhism, he believed, should be supported by the government.

Any change in the religious sector was sensitive in Tibet, not only because of the conservatism of the monks but because the monasteries held such a central place in the system of belief to which most of the Tibetan population adhered. Any reform, the Panchen Lama told the Chinese leadership, should, therefore, be carried out cautiously and with sympathy for that religious faith.

He wanted to see democracy in the monasteries. 'Capable individuals from all fields should be put forward as candidates,' he wrote, 'and the monks and masses should, under the leadership of the Party, elect a chairman, vice-chairman and members of a democratic management committee. Under the policies of democracy and leadership, this democratic management committee should act in accordance with the actual conditions.' At the same time, those temples in Tibet that had historical significance, as well as Buddhist images, sutras and *chortens* should be protected.

When the reforms began in Shigatse, Chen Jigme, who had been in the forefront of those Tibetans who had pressed for them, promised full co-operation. A Party work team was sent into Tashilhunpo monastery. The Panchen Lama's closest entourage was now to experience the misery of the reality behind the fine-sounding words.

The impact of the work team on Tashilhunpo monastery was devastating. Respected lamas and reincarnates were attacked as reactionaries. A song and dance troupe made up of young men and women was installed in the monastery as part of the propaganda effort, and their constant noise and unsuitable behaviour infuriated the monks. When the monks protested, their complaints were taken as signs of resistance and those who had spoken out were subjected to humiliating 'struggle sessions' – mass criticism at the hands of a Party-led mob. Several committed suicide.

When the head of the religious affairs committee in Shigatse attempted to negotiate a truce, he, too, was attacked. He went on hunger strike in protest and, when the work team ordered him to be force-fed, cut his own throat. He survived this suicide attempt but never spoke again. His throat wound did not spare him from the further humiliation of having the charges against him repeated in another denunciation. In despair, he wrote to the Panchen Lama:

Abiding by your order, I joined the revolutionary work after the liberation. In the past seven years, I followed the Communist party's instructions and worked for the Communist party. I have supported and been actively involved in the democratic reforms since they started. I would never foresee that mere suggestion would bring upon me such persecution that makes neither living nor dying easy.[2]

It was October 1959, only seven months after the Lhasa rebellion had been crushed. The Panchen Lama was absent, in Beijing celebrating the tenth anniversary of the founding of the People's Republic of China. He returned to Tibet to find that even his own parents had been under attack. Their property had been confiscated and they had been the victims of a 'struggle session'. Even Ngabo's family was not entirely unscathed: his wife had been put to repairing roads.

As the effects of Chinese rule began to come home to the Panchen Lama and to his court, he began slowly but inexorably to move towards a devastating confrontation with the leaders he had once so admired. His own monks were beginning to suffer. All over Tibet, in the aftermath of the rebellion, the process of neutralizing suspected rebels and implementing land reform began. The Party had promised that slavery and *corvée* (obligatory unpaid labour) would be abolished, rents reduced and land distribution set in train. The monasteries were to be judged by whether they had joined the rebellion and whether they were large – and therefore exploitative – institutions.

But the people who were to implement this policy, the Panchen Lama soon realized, were not seasoned political activists, and as they wielded their new power, justice was not their first consideration. They had grasped certain elements of the message: that the rebels and the well-to-do were fair game. Officially, the policy was to forgive those rebels who repented or who had been misled, and only to punish the so-called ringleaders. But as the Panchen Lama was later to complain, many of those who surrendered suffered violent struggle sessions, arrests and imprisonment. Some cadres fabricated crimes, he discovered, and the people accused of those crimes were added to the ever-lengthening list of criminals, rebel elements and counter-revolutionaries. Even the Panchen Lama himself was not immune.

Arbitrary arrest, confiscation and false accusations became commonplace and the battle soon began to affect Tibet's delicate economy. In the pastoral areas the cadres pursued violent 'struggles' against herd owners and in the ensuing chaos herds were neglected and livestock numbers dropped rapidly. The fate of any individual depended on whether he was classified as a 'feudal lord' or a serf, but while some serfs benefited, others found themselves classified as exploiters and attacked along with their masters. The political education that was meant to accompany this process was a failure, partly because of the ignorance of the activists themselves, but also because the necessary texts were not translated into Tibetan, a language that the Chinese regarded as backward and inadequate for the new Tibet. Mass meetings were convened at which the apprehensive Tibetans listened to reports and speeches in Chinese without understanding the meaning of such elementary terms as 'reform' and 'mobilization'.[3]

The cadres, the Panchen Lama complained later, were 'impatient and lazy in helping the masses to gain understanding. [They] behave grudgingly and use coercive methods . . . The cadres believe that as long as they carry out the campaigns of reform and mobilization quickly, vigorously and with intense struggle sessions, then they have completed their task.'[4]

Had they heeded the Panchen Lama's warnings, the Party leadership might have understood that the reforms in Tibet, far from winning over the people to the Chinese side, had created deep resentments that would return to haunt them. But the message that the Party leadership received from their newly appointed cadres was different. The Panchen Lama became convinced that the leadership was being given a false picture of the results of the campaign.

As he was to report to them:

If one goes to an area and asks the masses how the campaign is going the cadres will say it is going well, the main reasons being the large numbers of activists as a percentage of the general population and the liveliness of the movement. But what about the masses' knowledge of the democratic reform movement? The distinction between their enemy and ourselves? Revolution and class-consciousness? What about the sincerity of the activists in the campaign? How much love is there of the Party and the people? Is the work fair or not? Has trouble been caused?[5]

The results of the first moves towards collectivization were no better. Instead of encouraging voluntary participation, the cadres applied the same coercion that had been practised in land reform. Some who wanted to join mutual aid teams were not permitted to do so. Those who joined found themselves forced to contribute heavily to the state accumulation funds and were put to work by the activists on the large-scale projects that Mao believed were the key to raising production.

As the local Party leaders reported ever increasing production figures, which resulted in ever heavier demands for grain for the state, the reality, as elsewhere in the People's Republic, was an exhausted peasantry and declining yields, which led, in turn, to shortages of animal fodder and seed.

As grain became scarce, for the first time in living memory, people in Tibet began to go hungry. The Panchen Lama was deeply shocked and complained to the Chinese:

Although Tibet was in the past a society under the barbarous rule of feudalism, grain was never this scarce. This was especially due to the wide influence of Buddhism, which ensured that everyone, no matter if they were noble or humble, had the good custom of aiding the poor. People could live by begging for food, and it wasn't possible for someone to starve to death. We have never heard of such an occurrence.[6]

The hunger, the Panchen Lama knew, was man-made – a direct result of Chinese policy. Herdsmen and farmers had traditionally exchanged products – the herdsmen supplying the farmers with butter and meat in return for *tsampa*, the roasted barley meal that is Tibet's staple grain. But in 1959 they were forbidden to trade and many herdsmen resorted to slaughtering and eating their livestock. The prohibition on trade led to shortages and panic-buying in the towns. Families who were found to have concealed a little grain or *tsampa* were punished.

It was hardly surprising, then, that within two years of the implementation of reform, discontent was widespread and the number of 'underground reactionaries' had grown. The Panchen Lama wanted the Party to stop and listen, to examine its own contribution to the disaffection of the Tibetans and, belatedly perhaps, to take account of the realities of the nation they now ruled. But the Party was not in the mood to listen. From Mao Zedong to the lowest ranking cadre, criticism of the Party was judged, at best, a symptom of low political consciousness, and, at worst, a sign of reactionary thinking.

The Panchen Lama tried to use his nominally high position as acting chairman of the preparatory committee of the TAR to influence the cadres below him. But he soon discovered that he held no real power. The Party bureaucrats ignored the committee, he complained, or presented false reports. He was aware, though, that the brutality of the methods they had employed had already produced an unprecedentedly large number of detainees in prisons and labour camps. Many of them, he protested, were guilty of nothing. In prison, they lived in appalling conditions, prey to cold and hunger and the regular beatings administered by their jailers.

If things were bad in Tibet, in Qinghai, the Panchen Lama's native province, where the dismal process of forced collectivization was more advanced, they were even worse. Qinghai had been occupied by PLA troops in 1949 and the occupation had been troublesome from the beginning. It is a sparsely populated province, its high grasslands inhabited by unbiddable nomads, its valleys and river bottoms intensively cultivated. The mountainous terrain makes for poor communications and strong traditions of local independence among the various nationalities, of which Tibetans and Muslims form the largest groups. None of this fitted well with the newly arrived People's Liberation Army's mission to enforce uniform enthusiasm for the revolution.

There was local resistance to the PLA from the start, and it was to escalate rapidly once the Chinese began their reform programme. It was this situation that had been described so graphically to the Dalai Lama by his brother, Thupten Jigme Norbu (Takste Rinpoche), the abbot of Kumbum monastery.

Many of his monks had fled Kumbum at the outset. Takste Rinpoche himself had gone into exile in the United States after delivering his warning to the Dalai Lama. Those monks who stayed behind had suffered successive waves of 'reform' that reached a climax in the anti-rightist movement in 1958.

The first major incident occurred in the Panchen Lama's home county of Xunhua in the spring of that year. The Qinghai authorities sent a work team to Xunhua county to impose socialist reforms. In April 1958 the team invited the local community leaders, including the deputy county magistrate and a leading Buddhist scholar, Jamphel Rinpoche, who was a former teacher of the young Panchen Lama, to a 'study session'. Once there, these local dignitaries found they were not allowed to leave.

The detentions provoked an uprising in the town of Wendu and 200 armed men, accompanied by the monks of Wendu monastery, laid siege to the village government and demanded Jamphel's release. When this was refused, more than 4,000 people attacked the neighbouring town of Xunhua. In the PLA counter-attack the next day, 500 people were shot dead. In the days that followed, more than 2,500 people were arrested out of a total Tibetan population in the county of only 11,000. Jampal, meanwhile, committed suicide.[7]

Far from being alarmed at this revolt, Mao Zedong was delighted that his theory – that class was the main contradiction in minority disputes – had been, as he saw it, confirmed. In June 1958 he wrote to the provincial Party committee:

It is wonderful that the Qinghai reactionaries are revolting, for the time of the liberation of the working people is approaching. The policy of the Qinghai provincial committee is absolutely correct. Tibet should prepare for an overall uprising there. The greater the disturbance they create the better.[8]

In September 1958 co-operatives were set up throughout Xunhua county and in the aftermath of the uprising the Party itself was purged. The monasteries were the next target, and middle- and high-ranking lamas were brought to Xining for study sessions. In all, seventy-four mosques and twenty-six Buddhist temples were closed, and religious practice among the people was banned.

Wendu was subject to severe reprisals: there were mass arrests of men of fighting age and much of the rest of the population was forcibly transferred. The people of more than thirty villages were relocated to communes elsewhere, and 5,000 young people were brought in from Hunan to help farm the land and to form the basis of a Han militia. Unfortunately, these young people fared no better than the local population when the famine hit Qinghai. More than half of them died of starvation. A few years later the survivors were allowed to return home.[9]

The experience of Wendu was to prove a template for what was to happen throughout Qinghai. Tamdin Tsering is the ex-Party secretary of Tzekhog county in Qinghai. His birthplace is two hours on horseback from where the Panchen Lama was born. He was ten years old in May 1959 and clearly remembers the day when he saw his first Chinese.

'Some of my neighbours and I had taken the animals up to the high pastures. In the evening, one of the elders came and told us to come home. "The Chinese war has come to the village," he said. When I got back to the village I saw two Chinese soldiers guarding the gate to our house. Inside there were about fifty soldiers and they had machine-guns. There were Chinese soldiers stationed in all the vantage points in the mountains: they had occupied all the roofs and hilltops. I wasn't scared, just curious.'[10]

The Chinese collected all the guns the 900 villagers possessed. Then they called the people together and read out a list of sixty-seven names. Those on the list were loaded on to a truck and driven off. It was later discovered they had been taken to one of the string of labour and prison camps that were established in Qinghai in the fifties.

'One man who tried to resist was shot in front of everybody,' said Tamdin Tsering. 'Four years later twenty-three people came back. The rest had all died in prison.' Within a month a rebellion had begun.

Following the 1959 uprising in Lhasa, the PLA set about mopping up any pockets of resistance in Qinghai, Gansu and Sichuan from their base in Lanzhou, in Qinghai. More than 80,000 people were killed or arrested.[11] Officially, they were all classified as counter-revolutionaries but, in fact, the Chinese campaigns were directed at anyone who resisted the imposition of communal canteens, backyard steel furnaces and the enforced construction of the largely useless irrigation works that were imposed in the Great Leap Forward.

The Panchen Lama was now the most senior religious and political figure left in Tibet from the old regime. Pro-Chinese though he was, he could hardly ignore the growing numbers of desperate pilgrims who came to tell him of the disaster that had struck his home province. After the Xunhua incident, he began to formulate his own plan.

In 1960 he set out on a tour of Qinghai and was devastated by what he found. Everywhere he went he found that the population was dropping because of hunger and poverty. In September 1960 the Panchen Lama went to Beijing to attend the celebration of the eleventh anniversary of the founding of the People's Republic of China in October. In public, he told the National People's Congress, 'a wonderful situation prevails in Tibet today. Prosperous scenes of labour and production are found in every corner of the vast countryside and the towns.' But the reality, as he knew, was very different.

By 1960 the disruption caused by Mao's Great Leap Forward was so severe that even the Party leadership could no longer ignore the fact that China was in the grip of a terrible man-made famine. Mao's influence began to decline as the Party attempted to restore some normality to the country and regenerate China's food production. The backyard steel furnaces were abandoned and the peasants were allowed to return to their fields. Chairman Mao, however, was not a man to give up without a fight. In the political battle that ensued, the Panchen Lama was, finally, to become a victim of the man whom he had been taught to admire from his earliest youth.

In October 1960 the Panchen Lama was sent on an extensive tour of southern China, accompanied by Li Weihan and Wang Feng, who was First Secretary of the Gansu Provincial Commission and Deputy Head of the United Front Work Department. On the journey the three men talked at length about the situation in Tibet and the Panchen Lama laid out for his Chinese travelling companions evidence of the Party's 'mistakes'. Li Weihan kept extensive notes and later drew up a report to the central government on what the Panchen Lama had said.

While the Panchen Lama was away, the abuses in Tibet had continued. Chinese troops had even surrounded his own monastery of Tashilhunpo and arrested nearly 4,000 monks. Several were executed and others sent to labour camps. But initially the Panchen Lama's representations seemed to have had some effect. In January 1961 Deng Xiaoping ordered that 'Tibet must now prevent leftism . . . and maintain stability . . . co-operatives should not be established for five years.' Later that month, when the Panchen Lama returned from his tour, Mao, Zhou Enlai and other leaders agreed with him that the moment had not yet come for Tibet to be collectivized.

Instead, the peasants would be organized into so-called 'mutual aid teams' and the Party would continue its policy of co-operation with the upper classes. Reform, in so far as it was to be initiated, would be a relatively gentle affair in which the property of the landed gentry would be purchased by the state, not confiscated, and the aristocracy would not be subjected to intensive propaganda.

Mao also accepted the Panchen Lama's suggestion that some of the out-of-work monks should be given work training Buddhist scholars, and he even agreed that the Communist cadres should acquire some knowledge of Buddhism. Mao admitted that the confiscation of the Panchen's parents' property and that of Chen Jigme had been a mistake and promised to hold elections for the TAR government.

Although the Panchen Lama felt that he had made some headway with the Chinese leadership, he had not understood that when the leadership acknowledged 'leftist errors' they meant the excessive speed of the reforms. They did not query the fundamental wisdom of the policy. The Party leaders had almost no direct experience of Tibet and, given Mao's conviction that the Tibetan resistance was primarily a manifestation of class struggle, it was not long before he began to view the Panchen Lama's protest as a sign that he was defending the interests of Tibet's upper classes.

In 1961 and 1962 the Panchen continued his inspection tours and his dismay only deepened. There was destitution everywhere. In Kanze, in Sichuan, where the PLA had been trying to suppress a rebellion for nearly six years, there was now a generalized revolt. As he struggled to reconcile the reassurances that Mao and Zhou Enlai had given him with the dismal reality that he found in the villages and towns he visited, the Panchen Lama became increasingly convinced that the problem lay in the mediocrity and indifference of the officials on the ground. If only the leadership could be made aware of the true situation, he concluded, then they would put things right. At the end of 1961 the Panchen Lama retreated to his Beijing residence and began to write his own fateful report.

At the beginning of 1962 there seemed to be grounds for hope that a frank report to the leadership might have the effect he hoped for. Mao's opponents in the Party had gained ground, and a cautious liberalization was underway. In Tibet, there were even the beginnings of a religious recovery. That New Year, for the first time in several years, the old rituals were observed.

The liberal atmosphere continued through the spring: in April, Li Weihan called a major meeting on the so-called 'nationalities question' at which he encouraged delegates openly to voice their criticisms. The result was a torrent of complaint – of indiscriminate arrests, of damage to temples and cultural relics, of the violation of religious beliefs, including Muslims being forced to rear pigs, the sacking of monasteries and the secularization of lamas.

Among the boldest of the critics was Geshe Sherab Gyatso, the widely respected Buddhist scholar who was deputy governor of Qinghai. As he rose to speak, he was aware that, in the past, invitations to criticism had been followed by retribution, but this time, he had resolved to be bold. The Party's policies, he said, were worse than those pursued by Chiang Kai-shek and the warlord Ma Bufang.

Some applauded his speech. Others trembled at what they saw was a foolhardy act. But Li Weihan was fulsome in his assurance that the meeting was not a plot to entice the opposition into the open in order to suppress it. He promised there would be no retribution.

For a time, Li Weihan's promise held true. For the best part of a year there were no reprisals, but nor was there much improvement. The Panchen Lama continued to work on his report, more convinced that he had to persuade the Party's leadership that things were going badly wrong. As the only person who both knew the problems and had the necessary high-level access, he was convinced that if he could describe the effects of the Party's policies in his native Amdo and in Kham, the abuses would be stopped.

His entourage, however, far from sharing his faith in the goodwill of the Party leadership, were deeply worried by the Panchen's determination to set down his thoughts. Both Chen Jigme, by now the vice-chairman of the TAR preparatory committee, and Ngulchu Rinpoche, the Panchen's elderly tutor, attempted, vainly, to dissuade him.

When he had completed the first draft, the Panchen Lama showed his report to Ngabo Ngawang Jigme, the man who had negotiated the Seventeen-Point Agreement and was now a key figure in the Chinese governing apparatus, and to Geshe Sherab Gyatso. Ngabo, who saw only too clearly what the likely result of the Panchen's report would be, suggested he confine himself to verbal criticisms. Sherab Gyatso merely complained that both the Panchen Lama's writing and his use of language were a disgrace. Stung by the criticism, the Panchen's tutor, Ngulchu, set about polishing the manuscript. Even as he did so, his own apprehension grew.

In the early spring of 1962 the faithful Ngulchu made one last attempt to dissuade his illustrious pupil from the course he had chosen. He lit the butter lamps in the temple at the Panchen's residence and kowtowed to the Panchen Lama – an unusual procedure for a tutor. The formalities complete, Ngulchu laid out his argument.

There had, he pointed out, been numerous investigations on the ground and the government was perfectly clear about the situation. Had they wished to correct it, they would already have done so. To put the case in writing, Ngulchu said, would only bring disaster. Besides, he argued, he had consulted the oracle several times and the omens were not good. However cordial relations might be now, the Chinese leadership was subject to frequent changes of mood and there was no guarantee that this benign atmosphere would last. Ngulchu argued for hours, but at the end of it the Panchen Lama had not changed his mind.[12] The most he was prepared to do was to excise some particularly virulent sections and to add, at Ngabo's suggestion, a preamble in praise of the Party and all its works.

When the report was complete, the Panchen ordered its translation into Chinese, then had it retranslated, so that errors could be checked. By early May 1962 the laborious checking and rechecking was complete. The Panchen Lama entitled it 'A report on the sufferings of the masses in Tibet and other Tibetan regions and suggestions for future work to the Central Committee through the respected Premier Zhou'. It ran to 70,000 Chinese characters.

He was ready to present it to Zhou Enlai and, through him, to Mao and the Politburo. Zhou Enlai was due to go on a trip to north-east China, so a meeting of senior military and Party officials was hastily arranged at which the Panchen Lama would make an oral presentation of his report. On 18 May the Panchen Lama duly summarized the contents of his report in an atmosphere which grew steadily colder as he spoke. He was, after all, directly criticizing many of those present. Even Zhou Enlai, a man whom the Panchen Lama had always respected for what he saw as his kindness and his wisdom, was less enthusiastic than the Panchen Lama had hoped.

Zhou promised a full response when he returned from his trip. Despite the cool reception he had received, the Panchen Lama ordered the report to be printed in both Tibetan and Chinese. In mid June 1962 he formally submitted it.

The text that the Panchen Lama produced removes any possibility that the Communist party leadership was unaware of the consequences of their policies for the Tibetan people. The cumulative effect of the Panchen Lama's detailed reporting and fluent writing was devastating. Like a slowly gathering storm, the report details the situation in the Tibet Autonomous Region, which the Panchen Lama describes as problematic, but improving. Then he moves on to the sufferings of the Tibetans in the four Chinese provinces of Qinghai, Sichuan, Gansu and Yunnan. There, the picture he paints adds up to the most detailed and informed attack on China's policies in Tibet that would ever be written.

He had merely, as he saw it, written down what he had witnessed in the hope that once Mao and Zhou understood the reality that he described policies would be changed and the dream that he still believed in – the peaceful modernization of Tibet under Chinese leadership – would, at last, be realized.

As he wrote in his concluding paragraphs:

Now, forsaking all idea of personal gain, I courageously submit this report in order to benefit the Party and the people. This is a matter of great significance in my life. I have already pledged to do good works for the benefit of the Party and the people in the future and do not wish to be remembered as having brought any trace of dishonour to the reputation of the industrious and courageous Tibetan nationality . . . I would ask that you exercise magnanimity and generosity of spirit when examining the above.[13]

He was to receive neither. His petition, as his tutor had predicted, brought disaster. The text itself was suppressed, as far as the Party was concerned, for ever. More than three decades later, as I began to research the Panchen Lama's story, I had, of course, made many enquiries in China and in Tibet about the Panchen Lama's petition. The answer was always the same: it had disappeared. I spoke to people who had seen it, years before, even to one man who had contributed to the translation, but the petition itself was still regarded as too explosive to be revealed.

Then, one day in the summer of 1996, a package was delivered to my home in London. It had been hand-carried out of China. I opened it, and realized I was holding a copy of the Chinese translation of the Panchen Lama's petition. I still do not know the details of how or where the copy was made, but after more than thirty years of suppression, the Panchen Lama's petition – the document that Mao Zedong had described as a 'poisoned arrow' aimed at the heart of the Party – finally saw the light of day.

Chapter Eleven

✲

When the Panchen Lama wrote his plea for justice for his people, he must still have had some faith in the wisdom and good intentions of the Chinese leadership, the men in whom he had placed his trust since childhood. He continued to believe that if only Mao Zedong and Zhou Enlai could be made to understand the mistakes of the lower-level bureaucrats, those unworthy instruments of policy whose actions had caused such suffering to Tibetans, they would act to put the Tibetan revolution back on course. The Promised Land was still attainable.

At first the reaction appeared to confirm his faith in Mao and Zhou. Meetings were called and reports were written in response to his criticisms. At the beginning of August 1962 he returned to Lhasa, where on instructions from Beijing, even General Tan Guansan seemed to have been galvanized into a response. The Panchen Lama felt vindicated. Things were going to happen.

He would not have been so confident had he been aware of the ominous developments that were taking place within the Communist party. The failure of the Great Leap Forward, far from sobering Mao's vision, had merely convinced him that his fundamental analysis was correct: class struggle was the dominant problem. Conflicts over national or ethnic identity and religious faith were all, he believed, manifestations of reactionary class-consciousness.

Mao had retreated from the claim that Communism could be achieved in fifteen years, but he had substituted for it an assertion that the phase of socialist transition would be long and arduous. His position in the Party was severely weakened, but he had begun his fight back. As Mao started to identify his enemies and plot his revenge, the shadow of his displeasure crept inexorably towards the Panchen Lama. The Panchen Lama thought he had made a reasoned contribution to the Party's understanding of Tibet. Mao Zedong came to believe that the Panchen Lama had exposed himself as a true reactionary.

That summer the Central Committee held its annual meeting in the seaside resort of Beidahe. In some fringe meetings Mao criticized Li Weihan and the United Front Work Department for failing to 'grasp class struggle' and giving in to 'capitulationism'. High on Li Weihan's list of errors was his overfondness for the Panchen Lama who had, said Mao, become too proud.

Li Weihan was a veteran of the Chinese revolution. He had been both a schoolmate and a comrade of Mao's in the early revolutionary struggle. He had fought in the revolutionary war and was a veteran of the Long March. Since 1947 his job had been to secure the co-operation of ethnic minority leaders, including, of course, the Tibetans.

But despite his long revolutionary record, by October 1962 Li Weihan was in disgrace. He was accused of revisionism, a charge made more serious by Mao's now open quarrel with the new Soviet leader, Nikita Khrushchev. Mao regarded Khrushchev's denunciation of Stalin as a betrayal of the revolution, and as relations between the two former allies slid to the brink of armed hostilities, anyone accused of revisionism was, in Mao's new orthodoxy, a deadly enemy.

In a progression that was already familiar to students of Stalinism, the charges widened. Not only was Li Weihan headed for trouble, but everyone who had been associated with him was now in danger. Li Weihan could no longer protect himself, let alone those, like the Panchen Lama, whom he had encouraged to speak out.

In October 1962 the Panchen Lama was accused of 'reactionary arrogance' and ordered to make a self-criticism by the head of the Tibet Work Committee. It was time for the revenge of all those cadres whom the Panchen Lama had criticized in his 70,000-character petition. The Panchen Lama, still unfamiliar with the relentless process of Party purges and bewildered by the change of policy, refused.

He was still the acting chairman of the TAR preparatory committee, but as soon as Li Weihan began his vertiginous descent, the Panchen's titles became meaningless. Mao had now launched the Socialist Education Movement, a mass campaign designed to enforce revolutionary orthodoxy and rid the Party of his enemies. The Panchen Lama was to become the movement's principal target in Tibet.

Many years later the Panchen Lama was to describe what happened to his supporters and family as he began his slide into disgrace. 'In the beginning,' he said, 'we were told great things about peaceful reform and policies of fraternal relations. However, when the reforms were undertaken, people belonging to our establishments were subjected to untold suffering. This filled people with disgust and disbelief . . . all my family members were subjected to *thamzing* (public struggle sessions).'[1]

The Panchen Lama went on to relate the excitement of a group of interrogators who overheard the wife of a member of his staff complaining, 'This man called Panchen has caused me so much suffering that I will die of depression.'

Her interrogators were eager to collect denunciations of the lama, now targeted for criticism, but the woman continued, 'If he had led us in rebellion against the Chinese our condition today would be better than this . . . But this man told us to be progressive and patriotic. And this is what we get for following his advice. Now it is not possible to flee to India. Our people, both men and women, are being persecuted here. We are experiencing hell on earth.'

The Panchen Lama responded badly to his impending disgrace. The Chinese Communist Party insists that a transgressor must not only be punished, but that he must also confess and acknowledge that the Party is correct in the punishment it orders for him. But the Panchen Lama, trained as he was in the rigorous intellectual methods of his religious order, could not abandon his conviction that what he had done was both just and correct.

Throughout 1963 he was confined, isolated and ordered to admit his mistakes. He read the works of Mao and reread his own petition. But the more he tried, the less he could understand what his crime was. Cut off from contact with Zhou Enlai and Mao, he fell back on his own spiritual training to try to make sense of his situation: he used divination and examined his own dreams for clues as to how events had taken this terrible turn. He made a record of his dreams and wrote his own long commentaries on them. He did not, however, write a self-criticism.

At the beginning of 1964 the Panchen Lama was offered what might have been a chance to rehabilitate himself, at least partially. At the Monlam Chenmo, the Great Prayer festival in Lhasa, he was brought before a rally of some 10,000 people and ordered to denounce the Dalai Lama as a reactionary and a tool of foreign powers. The Panchen Lama began to read his prepared statement before the expectant officials and his huge audience. But instead of delivering the expected message, he paused. When he resumed, he said, 'Today, while we are gathered here, I must pronounce my firm belief that His Holiness the Dalai Lama will return to the Golden Throne. Long live His Holiness.' To the dismayed Party officials, the Panchen Lama seemed bent on his own ruin.

In 1964 the Four Clean-Ups campaign began. At first its aims were prosaic, focused on minor administrative improvements. But soon the Four Clean-Ups came to stand for the key ingredients of a full-scale purge in politics, the economy, ideology and Party organization.

From 18 September to 4 November Zhang Guohua chaired a conference, the Seventh Enlarged Meeting of the Preparatory Committee for the Tibet Autonomous Region. The main point of the meeting was to criticize the Panchen Lama, whom Zhang Guohua described as the most 'dangerous enemy' of socialism. The once-revered religious leader was now reviled and humiliated before an audience which had been brought from all over Tibet to witness the process. The Panchen still refused to acknowledge his 'mistakes' and argued that the conference contradicted the thoughts of Chairman Mao. The attack steadily widened from the Panchen Lama himself to include those around him. By November he was accused of heading a 'treasonous clique' that was charged with betraying the country and working for Tibetan independence.

The prominent members of Tashilhunpo's management council, including the architect of the Panchen's pro-China policy, Chen Jigme, the Panchen's elderly tutor Ngulchu, and Enge Palden, the former head of his Beijing office, were all labelled as members of the clique. A huge exhibition was mounted in Lhasa and 'emancipated serfs' were bussed in to Lhasa to criticize the Panchen. His property was confiscated and when his writings on dreams were discovered, they were used as further evidence of his crimes.

The horses he had kept were cited as evidence of cavalry training, his dogs were described as 'counter-revolutionary' and the technical school he had set up in Shigatse was evidence of secret militia training. A jeep that he had had fitted with extra water tanks was produced as proof of his intention to escape to India. In the Party's eyes, the Panchen was now the main 'enemy' of the Tibetan 'people'. In the Party meetings the audience was encouraged to spit on him and curse him, and some were prepared to attack him physically. At the end of this 'trial' the Panchen was labelled anti-Party, anti-People and anti-socialist. He was only twenty-four years old.

In December 1964 Zhou Enlai announced that the Panchen Lama had been dismissed from all his posts. He gave instructions that the Panchen be brought to Beijing, where he was lodged, at first, in the house of a former official. Once in the Chinese capital the Panchen Lama continued to try to make his case to the supreme leaders whom he had once so admired, but the door was now firmly shut to his entreaties.

Speaking of his time in later years he said, 'In 1964, when I was called to Beijing, some leaders told me, "You are turning against the Motherland. Are you trying to start a splittist rebellion? Even if the whole of the Tibetan population were armed, it would only be just over three million people. We are not scared." On hearing this, I felt very sad and realized this is how it is to be without freedom.'

The Panchen Lama was not yet in prison, but he was shunned. No religious pilgrims were allowed to visit him, and his staff was reduced to a handful of attendants. In Tibet the struggle against him, now defined as a struggle against counter-revolution, continued.

Then, in 1966, the power struggle within the Communist party took its most violent turns as the Cultural Revolution began. One evening in August that year a group of Red Guards broke into the Panchen Lama's residence and seized him. Once again he was to be subjected to the humiliation of mass criticism, this time in a meeting hall at the Central Institute of Nationalities. His tormentors 'interrogated' him, tying his arms tightly behind his back with a nylon cord that cut deep into his ample flesh. They spat on him and abused him, then paraded him through the streets as they denounced him through loudspeakers as the 'biggest reactionary serf owner' and the 'biggest parasite and bloodsucker in Tibet'.

The Panchen Lama's story might have ended there. But, on the orders of Zhou Enlai, he was rescued and transferred to the custody of the PLA, despite the protests of his student persecutors. After prolonged negotiations it was agreed that he would undergo one more such session of 'criticism', and then he would be kept in PLA detention. The criticism session was duly held in a Beijing sports stadium, and when it was over the Panchen Lama was taken to an army artillery camp in the eastern suburbs of Beijing. A few months later he was allowed to return home and lived under house arrest for another year.

In the summer of 1968, as all the heads of the Party, the government and the military from Tibet met in Beijing to plan the setting-up of a revolutionary committee that would form the new government of the TAR, the Panchen Lama was again incarcerated, this time in solitary confinement. He did not know that he was sharing his prison in the College of Politics and Law with many other veterans of the revolution, including Peng Dehuai, who was to die there, still refusing to acknowledge his own 'errors'.

For years there was no news of the Panchen and most people assumed he was dead. He remained cut off from the world: his prison guards fed but never spoke to him; his own family had no idea of his fate. In those long years of imprisonment the Panchen studied the reading material he was permitted – the thoughts of Mao, Marx and Lenin, and the Party's theoretical magazine, *Red Flag*. He learned Chinese and emerged well versed, if nothing else, in the Marxist canon. The irony was that by the time he was released these sacred texts of the revolution were themselves on the way out.

In 1974 Zhou Enlai tried to have him freed, but himself came under attack that year from the Gang of Four. It was not until Zhou Enlai and Mao Zedong were both dead and the Gang of Four had fallen that the Panchen Lama was finally released – on 10 October 1977. It took another eleven years for his designation as an 'anti-Party element' to be revoked.

What were the crimes for which the Panchen Lama endured those long years of imprisonment? He had, no doubt naïvely, maintained his faith in the goodwill of Mao Zedong and the Chinese Communist Party towards Tibet. So strong had his conviction been that he could trust Mao and Zhou that he had been deaf to the reasoning of those closest to him. Now, those who had tried to dissuade him from writing his petition were dead.

The Panchen Lama had not been the only Tibetan to cling to his faith in the Communist party, despite the suffering and the persecution. Many, like Chen Jigme, had died lonely deaths in prison, unable to accuse their tormentors. Others had fled and become bitter critics of the regime in exile. A few had been imprisoned, but like the Panchen Lama himself, had survived long enough to benefit from a partial rehabilitation.

What had the Panchen Lama thought during those years in prison about his misguided faith in Chairman Mao and his millenarian dream of the perfectibility of human society? He was no longer there to ask, but one man who, like the Panchen Lama, had been frustrated by Tibet's conservatism and thrown his energies into the Chinese revolution, had survived the long years in prison and was living still. One cold November afternoon in Beijing I went to find him.

The apartment I was looking for was one of hundreds in a huge, ugly block with several numbered entrances. A high wall protected it from casual passers-by. Outside the gate the traffic from the main road roared past. I took the lift and found the right door. It was opened quickly by a tall, handsome man, whose large frame still seemed scarcely big enough to contain a superabundance of restless energy.

Baba Phuntsog Wangyal was a Khampa and had been one of those young idealists who had joined the Communist party in the thirties. He had helped the Chinese to plan the 'liberation' of his own country, only to fall in 1957, in one of the first purges, for having tried to persuade the leadership of the wisdom of a less confrontational approach to his native Kham.

His apartment was spacious and well furnished. The shelves were crammed with books and photographs and mementoes marking the passage of a life spent first in the service of the Party, then in its prisons. I admired a photograph of him in the uniform of a Guomindang cadet.

'That was Nanjing,' he said, proudly, 'in 1940. We were the first Tibetan group.' Another framed photograph showed him as a young man, sitting with Ngabo and Mao at the banquet to celebrate the Seventeen-Point Agreement. Beside it, photographs of Zhou Enlai and Chen Yi, all of them reminders of days of solidarity and shared hopes.

Phuntsog Wangyal had been educated at a Christian Mission school in Batang, in Kham, and was one of the first and most committed Tibetan Communists. After the Chinese occupation he had tried to mediate between the Chinese and the Tibetans and had earned the continuing respect of the Dalai Lama.

When the Dalai Lama and Phuntsog Wangyal met in Beijing in 1954, the two men had talked and argued about Buddhism and about the future of Tibet. Phuntsog Wangyal had idolized Chairman Mao, the Dalai Lama recalled, but wrote of Phuntsog Wangyal, 'In the final analysis, we were both Tibetans thinking of the future of our country.' The Dalai Lama requested that Phuntsog Wangyal be posted to Tibet as Party secretary, the only Tibetan who was equipped to occupy such a post.

Then it all came to an abrupt and cruel end. Late in 1957 a Chinese official told the Dalai Lama that Phuntsog Wangyal would no longer be coming to Tibet. He was, the official said, a dangerous man. In 1958 Phuntsog Wangyal was sent to Beijing for thought reform. In 1960 he was jailed.

Phuntsog Wangyal spent eighteen years in prison, most of them in solitary confinement. Now rehabilitated, he was a member of the National People's Congress. His prestigious apartment block was, he told me, a colony of battered survivors: Wang Guangmei, the widow of the disgraced party leader Liu Shaoqi, who herself had undergone unspeakable torments in the Cultural Revolution, was a neighbour. Her husband had died a miserable death in prison, the victim of a deliberately untreated illness.

'Lots of people in these flats have been in jail,' said Phuntsog Wangyal, beaming widely. 'Some of them are quite mad.'

'But you want to talk about the Panchen Lama?'

His face instantly lit up with remembered affection. 'He was a wonderful man.'

By 1980 both men had been released from prison, but both still had their 'hats'. The hat was the label of their crime: in the Cultural Revolution, victims were often made to wear a dunce's cap on which the charges against them were written in large characters for all to see. Even after a sentence had been served the labels remained. A man could carry the stigma of being a 'rightist' or a 'capitalist roader' for years, vulnerable to any renewed upsurge of persecution.

'[Panchen Rinpoche] came to see me one day,' said Phuntsog Wangyal, 'at my home. When he first came he talked about the years in prison. But he was so full of plans. He said he still had his strength and there was so much he wanted to do. I said, "So have I! I can help you."'

'Then we had nearly ten years of close friendship. He telephoned me every single day. He called me his *jiu-rou* friend, his wine and meat friend. He used to come and sit on that sofa where you're sitting. Stand up. I want to show you something.'

I stood up. He pointed to the legs of the sofa.

'See that? Specially strengthened. I had to have that done because it was collapsing under him, he sat on it so much and he was so fat!'

He roared with laughter, delighted, it seemed, by the memory of his friend's enormous bulk. 'One day he called me. He was down below and the lift was broken. He said, "How am I going to get up to the twelfth floor?" We all had to go downstairs and help him up!

'What did he really think about it all? I'll tell you. I knew his political philosophy. He loved four things: his country, the Communist party, the people – and religion.'

My doubts must have showed in my face. Phuntsog Wangyal became insistent. 'He always talked about those *four* things. But people don't want to believe it. Some people are willing to believe that he loved the first two. Others think he only cared about the last two. But I'm telling you he loved all four. He didn't separate them and you can't understand him if *you* do.'

Which country did he mean, I wondered – the 'Great Motherland' of the People's Republic or Tibet? For Phuntsog Wangyal it was clearly the Motherland.

'How,' I asked, 'could he love the Communist party *and* his religion, given what happened?'

'The Communist party policy isn't to ban religion,' Phuntsog Wangyal replied. 'They don't believe in it themselves, but they don't stop others.'

I looked at him, sceptical. He continued, unabashed.

'He was never a Party member, of course. But he always said that they were the country's leadership. So you had to love them.' He grinned and continued with his exposition of the Panchen's beliefs. 'For Tibet, he wanted three things: self-government, to heal the wounds and friendship – friendship with China. He wanted

real self-government and to heal the wounds of the reform period
– and he wanted development.'

I was beginning to think that this was going to turn into a Party speech. But then Phuntsog Wangyal paused.

'There are seven thousand monasteries that are not there any more,' he suddenly said. 'How many wounds are there? How many mistakes?'

And as though to banish an unworthy train of thought, he added, 'The Panchen Lama didn't agree with independence, but he did not want real autonomy. Under today's conditions you can't get independence, but it is very important to get your own language, your own politics and economics. Language was particularly important: it's a matter of the cultural transmission.'

On the wall, facing where I sat, there was a picture of a prisoner coming home to a joyous welcome from his family. Beside it hung a painting of a prisoner about to be shot. Phuntsog Wangyal followed my gaze. 'It's by a Russian artist,' he said.

'I was in a cell seven foot by nine foot for eighteen years.' Again that infectious smile. The horror of what he had just said left me groping for a response.

'What did you think about?' I asked.

He laughed. 'I read books! That's to say, after the first two years, I read. No books for the first two years, and no literature ever. That wasn't allowed. But I read everything else – economics, logic, natural sciences.' He talked with enthusiasm, as though describing a memorable evening at the theatre. 'I wrote a book, too,' he added.

Outside, the light slowly faded as he talked on about his life, trying to explain to me how it had all turned out badly. 'It was all fine in the beginning, back in 1939. I met Ye Jianying in Chongqing. We went to Yenan and to Moscow. But after 1956 things went wrong. In the autonomous districts it was all terribly wrong. The Panchen complained but a lot of people didn't agree with him. He told them they were shooting too many people.' Phuntsog Wangyal shook his head. 'Peng Dehuai and the Panchen Lama were the only people who talked about it,' he said.

'Then came the Great Leap Forward and from 1960 to 1965 it was worse and worse. In 1965 the whole country went mad. The *ganbu* thought they didn't need to speak Tibetan. They felt like big men because they spoke Chinese. They are all still there, from top to bottom. They still don't want to listen to any criticism.'

He leaned forward. 'There's a saying – perhaps you know it,' he said. ' "You can bend the willow." But those people, they didn't bend it. They just broke it.'

I asked Phuntsog Wangyal why the Panchen Lama had married after his release. He shrugged. 'His parents opposed the marriage,' he said. 'They said a Panchen Lama shouldn't marry. So relations weren't good. But look at his life: he was a leader, he was admired. Then he was criticized. He was put in jail. Finally, he just felt like an ordinary person. I can understand it. You lose your bearings. For nine years nobody spoke to me. Then, when somebody did, I was so shocked, I cried. I had forgotten my own name. It was the same for him.'

So, I asked, did he regret helping the Chinese all those years ago?

Phuntsog Wangyal shrugged. 'They had already decided to go into Tibet. Nothing could change that. I just thought I could help to make it peaceful.' He lapsed for a moment into reflection, then shook it off. 'Mostly I just write these days, I don't talk politics.'

Then suddenly his enthusiasm returned. 'Let me show you something.' He reached up to the bookshelf and took down a book. 'It's the book I wrote in prison.'

I stared at the unfamiliar characters of the title, trying to make it out. Phuntsog Wangyal was alight with his eagerness to explain. 'It's a book of natural sciences . . . I explain a lot of Hegel . . . many things . . . look at this diagram.' He talked on, much of it over my head as I tried to follow his scientific Chinese. Then he paused and looked at me.

'You know my dearest wish? This is the product of my eighteen years in prison. My dearest hope is that it will be published abroad. Here –' he gestured to the window and the muffled roar of the traffic far below '– people are only interested in money. I think in England there would be real interest in the ideas. I would so much like to go and discuss it with people in England.'

It was a touching view of England. He brushed my scepticism away. He inscribed the book to me and we said goodbye. He had told me that he longed to live in Tibet, but the government refused to permit it. I realized that all further questions about the present – and about the search for the Panchen Lama's reincarnation, had been skilfully side-stepped.

'Next time you come,' he said, 'perhaps we can talk again. This is a difficult time for conversation.'

Under the dim lights of my hotel room, I pored over that precious book, that monument to eighteen years' endurance. It was a thesis on the existence of water on the moon. Two years later, in an announcement that caused a stir in the scientific world, NASA announced that they had, indeed, discovered the existence of water on the moon.

There was no such tangible monument to the Panchen Lama's prison years, occupied as he was with studying the thoughts of his tormentor, Chairman Mao. He had taught himself Chinese with the aid of a little, battered dictionary. He had had more than enough time to reflect on the meaning of the words of poor Ngulchu Rinpoche. The leadership knew what was happening, the wise monk had said. If they had wanted to change things, they would have done so.

But the Panchen Lama never appeared to regret the petition that had brought his downfall: it did little to alleviate the sufferings of the people of Qinghai or Tibet, but written as it was by a young man still in the grip of devotion to the Party, it stands as a unique account of the disaster that Chinese rule inflicted on a society that had lived in relative peace and prosperity for nearly three centuries. It is the only such account, for the truth about that period was never officially told.

In 1997 China, for the first time, acknowledged that the poverty in Qinghai was still so severe that Western agencies were to be invited to help to alleviate it. It was the enduring legacy of the Great Leap Forward. Even after the deaths of Mao and Zhou, when Deng Xiaoping had begun his own transformation of China into a proto-capitalist society and Mao was subject to the judgement of his heirs, the injustices of the anti-rightist movement, of the democratic reforms in Tibet and the Great Leap Forward were suppressed. The famine that took the lives of thirty million people is still described as the result of three years of natural disaster. The devastation of the monasteries is blamed on the Cultural Revolution.

Chapter Twelve

✻

The monk was waiting on a bench just by the gate of Beihai, the beautiful park on the north side of the Forbidden City that Jiang Qing, Mao's last wife, had ordered closed for her private pleasure in the Cultural Revolution years. Now it was open again, and on this warm, bright day, it was thronged with families, sightseers and lovers seeking a measure of respite from the city's polluted air. The monk sat in that style that develops over years of cross-legged prayer and meditation, squared on his haunches, his maroon robe hitched up slightly to let the sun warm his muscular calves.

He was a large, solidly built man with a heavy head flanked by two impressively prominent ears. We had met and talked several times before, and I knew that despite this forbidding exterior he was devout, wise and often witty. I had learned to appreciate the rare smiles that would transform his broad face. But today that face was closed and serious. I sat beside him, briefly, on the bench. After a few moments, he glanced quickly round at the busy park entrance, then rose and set off in the opposite direction. A small gesture of his head told me I should follow.

We walked for less than ten minutes. 'Wait here,' the monk said, then crossed the empty street and rang the bell of a tall iron gate that was set into a high brick wall. After a few minutes' conversation at the gate, he disappeared inside, then reappeared and beckoned me to join him. I slipped through the door and the attendant shut it firmly behind me.

Inside, a courtyard led on to a large, Tibetan-style house which nestled against the moat of the Forbidden City. We climbed the steps to the main door and entered a spacious hall. Three women in Tibetan dress appeared, their slippered feet silent on the highly polished floor. They showed me into a waiting room decorated with Buddhist scrolls. 'Wait here, please.' We sat down, and after a few moments the monk began to speak.

'Li Jie is much misunderstood,' he said. 'It was a happy marriage

and she was a great help to the Master. She's a devout Buddhist –
her family was Buddhist for many years. But there is trouble
between her and the Qinghai people. They say bad things about
her.'

'But why did the Panchen marry?' I asked.

He shrugged. 'You can't imagine what it was like when he came
out of prison. There was nothing left in Tibet. There was no
religion left anywhere. He'd been in solitary confinement for ten
years; he'd been beaten, spat on, humiliated. I think he just wanted
to feel he was alive. He was a good husband. He cared for her.

'Besides,' he continued, 'after the Cultural Revolution it was
much easier for him to work if he was married, if he conformed. He
remained the Panchen. He wasn't allowed to live in the monastery
anyway, so why not? A lot of people didn't like it. They said he
should have married a Tibetan. After he died, they turned against
her.' He paused, and fixed me with a warning look. 'Be respectful,'
he said. 'She has had a lot of disrespect. And no difficult questions.'

A few moments later, the woman whose very existence had
caused outrage among pious Tibetans appeared in the doorway.
She looked about forty and was heavily made up. She wore a bright
green Tibetan dress and high-heeled shoes that made her walk with
exaggerated care. The woman had materialized with an air of drama
that entirely fitted the occasion. She was Li Jie, granddaughter of
a Guomindang general, former PLA doctor, widow of the tenth
Panchen Lama.

It is no small matter when one of Tibet's highest lamas disrobes
and breaks his vows of celibacy. Even the sixth Dalai Lama, a
celebrated womanizer, drinker and poet, had not gone that far; he
had simply refused to take his final vows. But the tenth Panchen
Lama had done what was once unthinkable: he had abandoned
his vows to marry a Chinese woman and father a child. Mao
Zedong had not lived to see it, but still it seemed as though, even
from beyond the grave, the Chairman had scored another triumph
over Tibet.

Many Tibetans believed the Chinese had forced the marriage
on the Panchen Lama, and for those who saw it that way she
became a final symbol of the humiliations they had suffered at the
hands of her fellow countrymen. Some whispered scurrilous stories
about her sexual behaviour. Others murmured about her arrogance

and claimed the Party had put her in the Panchen Lama's bed to spy on him. Since his death, Li Jie was rarely seen in public. She lived on as an embarrassing reminder of bad times, in this vast mansion, with her daughter, who was, by then, twelve years old.

Smiling graciously, the Panchen's widow led us into the reception room, and directed us to the heavy armchairs that were arranged in a dull square, in the formal style of Chinese official meeting-rooms. Outside, the sun lit up the walls of the Forbidden City, and the reflections from the water of the moat played back across the high ceiling. The room was quiet, the clamour of the overcrowded city streets reduced to a distant murmur.

The conversation began stiffly. She told me that her father now spent his time in the Beijing public library, engrossed in genealogical records. He had discovered a family connection to Princess Wen-Ch'eng, the T'ang dynasty Chinese bride of the great Tibetan king Srongtsen Gampo, whom the Chinese credit with converting the king to Buddhism.

She told me of her first meeting with the Panchen Lama, at Beijing railway station, and the difficulties they had had to overcome to marry. Many Tibetans objected, of course, but some Chinese, who thought it would reduce the Panchen's authority and therefore his value to the Communist party, also opposed it. Now, she told me, she spent her time in religious practice. Life, she hinted with heavy sighs, was difficult, and she had many enemies.

The thought of them made her suddenly indignant and her mouth set hard. 'There are people who say that I married him for his money and his position.' She flushed, her face twisted in theatrical disdain. 'When I met the Panchen, he had nothing. Nothing! He had a miserable state salary that would hardly buy him a bowl of noodles. When he walked along the street people who had once been friends would hide in doorways so they wouldn't be seen greeting him.'

Now she was leaning sideways in her chair, her words suddenly tumbling out, loud and insistent. 'Do you know what he had suffered? What had been done to him in that prison? I'll show you what the Panchen had when I met him.'

She called a servant and gave some rapid instructions. He disappeared and reappeared a few moments later bearing a large bundle wrapped in saffron silk, which he placed on the armchair next to her. Tenderly, she untied the bundle and folded back its bright wrapping to reveal a carefully folded pile of shabby clothes.

'This!' she gestured dramatically. 'This is what he had. You see?'

She held up a threadbare grey cotton jacket, laid it on the neighbouring chair and reached for a worn pair of shoes. 'Look! He mended them himself. Ten years he wore these clothes!'

There was a sudden, choking cry as the monk fell on his knees and, tears streaming down his face, touched his forehead repeatedly to the clothes. 'Master,' he sobbed. 'Master!'

Li Jie was still producing garments – a pair of patched trousers and finally a pair of enormous grey underpants. She held them up. 'That's what the Panchen had. Nothing.'

The monk continued to prostrate himself before the relics.

Li Jie had fallen back into her chair, as though exhausted by the weight of her memories, when a tall, good-looking young man appeared tentatively in the doorway. Li Jie introduced him as the Panchen's nephew. Moments later her daughter – taller than her mother, shy and sweet-natured – came home from school. We posed for photographs in a spacious shrine room dedicated to the Panchen, that huge man who had once dominated this house. Now, his wife and daughter, Li Jie had told us, were under pressure to leave. She walked us to the gate to say goodbye, her make-up pink in the bright afternoon sunshine. 'Come and see me again,' she said, 'the next time you are in Beijing.'

The Panchen Lama was only thirty-nine years old when he was released from his prison on 10 October 1977. Zhou Enlai, whom the Panchen had seen as his protector, was dead. Mao Zedong lay, waxen yellow and inexpertly embalmed, in his hastily constructed mausoleum in Tiananmen Square. Things were undoubtedly changing.

Deng Xiaoping was in power, and his grey, exhausted country was on the edge of another revolution – this one aimed at reversing the damage done by Mao Zedong's. The theory of 'class struggle' was not yet entirely dead, but it was on its way out as the dominant political discourse. In another twenty years it would be history.

But these changes had come too late for the world of the Panchen Lama's childhood and youth. Though the Panchen's prison days were over, he was now a lonely relic of a civilization that had all but been destroyed. All of the hundreds of the monasteries in which he had been venerated as a living Buddha were closed, and most had been demolished, stone by stone. In Lhasa, the Jokhang temple, the holiest of all Tibet's holy places, had been sacked and its precious scriptures scattered to the four winds. In Tashilhunpo, his monastery, a third of the buildings had been destroyed. The tombs that had held the bones of his five predecessors had been smashed open and their contents scattered. The Potala, once home to the Dalai Lama, was empty and barricaded, floating above a city from which all traces of colour and joy had been drained.

The Panchen's monks, his servants, his council of abbots were mostly dead. Like the courageous Geshe Sherab Gyatso, most had been victims of the chain of labour camps that still thrived in his native Qinghai. The Panchen Lama was out of prison, but what did life have to offer him? The answer given by the Chinese government was membership of the Chinese People's Political Consultative Conference Standing Committee. He was not even allowed to live in Tibet.

While the Panchen Lama had been in prison things had gone from bad to worse in Tibet. He had seen the beginning of the famine that reached central Tibet in 1963, three years after the rest of the People's Republic, but by the time the Cultural Revolution razed so many of Tibet's religious buildings to the ground, he was already in jail. In the Cultural Revolution Tibetans had been pushed, finally, into communes. Some had risen in revolt in 1969, others had simply gone hungry as they struggled to meet the unrealistic production quotas. The Cultural Revolution completed the destruction of the religious order, though it also gave young Tibetans an excuse for rebellion against the authority of the Chinese cadres. In the name of Chairman Mao they attacked the Chinese Party apparatus in Tibet, and various rogue groups still existed at the time of the Panchen's release.

Before his fall, the Panchen Lama had been worshipped by his fellow countrymen as an incarnation of the Buddha. Now, he was adrift in Beijing, a freak survivor. Still, it was a dawn, of sorts. The reformers who surrounded Deng Xiaoping set about reviving the idea of the United Front – tentatively seeking the co-operation of what was left of Tibet's old order. For the first time in nearly two decades, there was direct contact between Beijing and the exiled Dalai Lama. The go-between was Gyalo Thondup, one of the Dalai Lama's elder brothers. Of all the Dalai Lama's large family, Gyalo Thondup was the most 'sinified'. He had been educated in China, spoke the language fluently and had married a Chinese wife. By the end of the seventies, it seemed that both Beijing and Dharamsala were ready for a new phase of relations.

In 1978 Beijing suggested, through Gyalo Thondup, that exiled Tibetans be permitted to return to visit their relatives and see for themselves what conditions were like in Tibet. In October 1978, as the first step in response to that initiative, a group of fifteen Tibetan exiles applied for visas at the Chinese embassy in Delhi. But things turned sour when, shortly before their visit was due to begin, the Chinese insisted that the exiles be described in their visas as 'overseas Chinese'. The Tibetans found this unacceptable. The Chinese did, however, allow Tsultrim Tersey – a Tibetan resident in Switzerland – to visit his homeland, the first exile legally permitted to do so.

In spite of the setbacks and mutual suspicions, the diplomatic mood continued to be encouraging. The Dalai Lama received an invitation from Deng Xiaoping to return to Tibet. He replied that he would first like to send four fact-finding delegations to Tibet. The Party leaders in Tibet assured Beijing that Tibet was prosperous and settled, that Tibetans no longer had any interest in the Dalai Lama and that there was nothing to fear from a visit by his representatives.

It came as a terrible shock, then, to the Beijing leadership, when the first delegation from the Dalai Lama to visit Tibet, in August 1979, was greeted with scenes of extraordinary mass emotion. When the second delegation visited in June 1980, general public joy at this oblique contact with the Dalai Lama gave way to shouts for independence among the crowd in Lhasa. The visit was cut short and the delegation was asked to leave, six days early. The third delegation, led by Jetsun Pema, the Dalai Lama's sister, was already in the country and had completed its mission, but the planned fourth delegation was postponed and only finally allowed to visit in 1984, and then only the Tibetan areas of Qinghai and Gansu.

Nonetheless, sporadic contacts continued, and it even seemed possible that the Dalai Lama might, indeed, return. The Chinese even issued their conditions, which included a prohibition on his living in Lhasa. But, perhaps because he saw that accepting such conditions would mean that he would be reduced to a kind of functionary for the Chinese government, the Dalai Lama issued a statement in December 1983, saying that he would not be visiting Tibet, as had been rumoured, in 1985.

The public displays of emotion that the Dalai Lama's delegations had provoked brought home to the Chinese government how far adrift from reality the reports they had been receiving from Tibet had been. The Party secretary, Ren Rong, was sacked, and in 1980 two senior members of the government, Hu Yaobang and Wan Li, made a personal visit to Tibet. Hu Yaobang was surprised and shocked by what he found. Instead of the prosperity and content-ment that had been reported to Beijing, there was penury. The reports had spoken of the improvements that the Chinese had brought. Hu Yaobang discovered that the local economy had been ruined by collectivization and the Chinese cadres were utterly dependent on supplies from the mainland. The Tibetans themselves could not have been more miserable and demoralized.

As a result of this visit, Hu dictated a new policy for Tibet: the autonomous government should exercise its autonomy; Tibetan farmers should be exempt from quotas and taxes; increased sub-sidies and flexible economic policy would be introduced; Tibetan culture would be allowed to revive; and the numbers of Chinese officials in the TAR government reduced.

Hu's measures made an immediate difference. The land was decollectivized, and the surplus permitted by the tax holiday began to be spent, with great enthusiasm, on rebuilding the temples that the Chinese occupation had destroyed. Once again, Tibetans were allowed to cultivate their lands and rear their flocks in the ways they knew best and Tibetan *chubas* began to replace the Chinese Mao suit. Young women could, once again, wear their hair long and, gradually, the ornaments and jewellery beloved of the nomads began to reappear.

The Panchen Lama, though not formally rehabilitated, was allowed a limited participation in the new reformist mood. His wealth and his status were partly restored and for the next ten years he was to use his position and his influence to save what he could of Tibetan culture, language and religious practice.

1. The Dalai Lama with the author

2. Dharamsala street

3. The ninth Panchen Lama, 1905

4. The Dalai Lama and the Panchen Lama, Beijing, 1954

5. Mao Zedong, Beijing, 1954

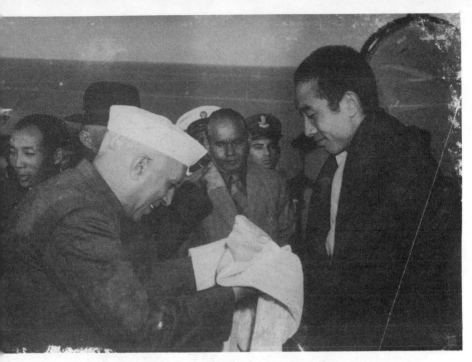

6. Nehru and the tenth Panchen Lama, India, 1956

7. The tenth Panchen Lama and
the fourteenth Dalai Lama, 1956

8. The fourteenth Dalai Lama with his
brother, Ngari Rinpoche (Tenzin Choegyal),
leaving Tibet, 1959

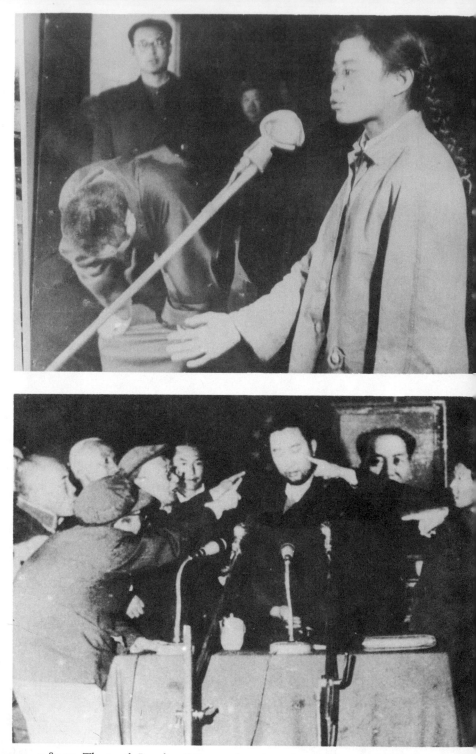

9 & 10. The tenth Panchen Lama undergoing a 'struggle session', Lhasa, 1964

11. The Potala Palace

12. Ruins of Drepung monastery, near Lhasa, destroyed in the Cultural Revolution.
Taken by the Dalai Lama's first delegation, 1979

13. The tenth Panchen Lama receiving members of the Dalai Lama's first delegation. Ngabo Ngawang Jigme and Baba Phuntsog Wangyal are directly to the Panchen Lama's left.

15. The tenth Panchen Lama in his office, Beijing, c. 1987

14. The tenth Panchen Lama with his wife and daughter, Beijing, c. 1984

16. The author with the tenth Panchen Lama's widow and daughter, Beijing, 1995

17. Chadrel Rinpoche, leader of the search for the eleventh Panchen Lama

18. Lhamo Latso oracle lake

19. People's Armed Police entering Tashilhunpo monastery, Shigatse, 12 July 1995, to crush the monks' protest

20. Chinese security personnel sightseeing in Kumbum monastery, 1995

21. The symbolic enthronement of the eleventh Panchen Lama, Tashilhunpo monastery, southern India, 1996

Life had improved materially and, perhaps, emotionally since the day in 1978 when he had first set eyes on Li Jie at Beijing's main railway station. 'They lived well,' recalled a young Tibetan who had grown up in that privileged Beijing-based élite. He remembered watching the couple arrive at a special film show that had been laid on for important cadres – the Panchen Lama, a huge man, dressed in a Mao suit, his wife wearing a leather overcoat, high heels and an elaborate hair-do. 'Everyone called her Princess Wen-Ch'eng,' he said. 'It was like royalty arriving.'

The couple enjoyed all the trappings of Beijing high society: a large house with servants, a villa in the western hills where the Panchen could indulge his love of horses and dogs during country weekends. In the summer they stayed in a villa near the beach at the resort of Beidahe, near to that of the great survivor, Ngapo, and his family. Wherever they went Li Jie was careful to respect Tibetan habits. She would take dried yak meat when they went to the seaside at Beidahe and serve *tsampa* and butter tea – Tibetan peasant food that most Han Chinese would consider repellent.

The Panchen Lama took up his political duties as a member of the National People's Congress, despite his lack of formal rehabilitation. Pilgrims began to appear in Beijing, tentatively at first, then in greater numbers, to assure themselves that he was, indeed, alive and to prostrate themselves before him. In 1980, when the Dalai Lama's sister, Jetsun Pema, met the Panchen Lama in Beijing, she found him living in some splendour with his parents and his younger brother. In deference, perhaps, to the sensibilities of the Tibetan visitors, Li Jie was not presented to her.

Jetsun Pema's visit was another sign of official relaxation. All the same, the Panchen Lama himself had still not been permitted to visit Tibet, and he plied the visitors with questions about the state of his homeland.

'He seemed very sad when I told him what we had seen,' Jetsun Pema told me. 'We travelled over 13,000 miles in Tibet, visiting schools and meeting people. We ourselves had been in tears every day because people were so dreadfully poor and the conditions were so hard. The stories people told us were heartbreaking. But Panchen Rinpoche seemed sure that things would improve. He asked me to give a message to the Dalai Lama, that things were going to get better.'

In 1980 the Panchen, too, formally applied for permission to visit his own country. It took two years for it to be granted. In June 1982, for the first time since he was shipped out as a prisoner in 1964, the Panchen was on his way back home.

However, while ordinary devotees might long for his return, the fact was that the political and religious world in which the Panchen Lama was to work in his remaining years had changed. The visit was heavily resisted by those who had benefited from his disgrace and his absence. The local administration contained hard-line Tibetans who hated Deng's reforms as much as their Chinese colleagues. The religious establishment, too, was riddled with figures who, because of the sides they had chosen in the struggle, had no reason to welcome the return of the Panchen Lama.

Eighty-four members of the Panchen's immediate entourage had been sent to prison, but others had avoided that fate by taking the side of his persecutors. His former secretary, I had been told in Lhasa, had betrayed him and held a senior post for a while before succumbing to a fondness for alcohol. Another of his persecutors was to rise in the nineties to the position of vice-chairman of the religious affairs office. Two senior religious figures – Sengchen Rinpoche and Phagpa-lha – had earned popular opprobrium by their willingness to join the physical assault on the Panchen in the prolonged struggle session of 1964. Both were to continue to play damaging roles in the drama of the tenth Panchen's life and, later still, in the search for his reincarnation.

Sengchen had come from a small monastery on the outskirts of Gyantse, which was under the jurisdiction of Tashilhunpo. In 1959 he moved to Tashilhunpo monastery, where he was an ordinary lama until he won the favour of the authorities with his willingness to raise his fist to the Panchen Lama. Like many religious figures in the Cultural Revolution, Sengchen had abandoned his vows and married, so that by the time of the Panchen Lama's visit to Tibet in 1982, he no longer lived in Tashilhunpo monastery. But by virtue of his status as a reincarnate lama and his position as a trusty of the regime, he retained an important position in the religious bureaucratic hierarchy and in the monastery's affairs. When the news reached Tibet that the Panchen Lama was to visit his homeland, Sengchen and Phagpa-lha drafted letters in opposition, arguing that his presence would generate instability. Several members of the local bureau of religious affairs and local Party officials supported them, arguing that the visit would lead to a revival of 'superstition'.

'When the Panchen Lama arrived at Lhasa airport,' recalled one lama who witnessed the visit, 'he was well aware of these letters. The bureau of religious affairs was responsible for his visit to Tibet, and once they had lost the battle to prevent him coming at all, they fell back on the argument that he should be given a very low-key reception. The Panchen Lama was to demonstrate that the determination that had got him into trouble nearly two decades earlier had been undiminished by his years of incarceration. He came off the plane furious. "What are you going tō do?" he shouted at the officials who reluctantly came to greet him. "Here I am and you're not treating me properly."'

There was a stand-off at the airport. 'The Panchen Lama was in a terrible temper, banging his fist on the table, shouting at them, sulking,' the lama recalled. 'He refused to leave the airport until it was sorted out. It took all day. He talked about the Cultural Revolution and how negative it all was. He complained about Tibetans who had been carried away and didn't think for themselves, who had got involved in struggles that were nothing to do with them. He called a meeting at the airport and spoke from the platform. He said that even among the people up there on the platform with him – there were people who caused a lot of trouble and did a lot of harm. The meeting started at three in the afternoon and he made it drag on until eight at night. He told them that they were going to get hungry and so was he. People had no choice but to stay.'

When the visit was finally allowed to proceed there were scenes of mass rejoicing and emotion similar to those that had greeted the Dalai Lama's first delegation. After two decades of sustained Communist party assault on religion in all its manifestations, the people of Tibet seemed to desire it now more than ever. But the Panchen Lama also saw for himself the devastation that had been wrought on his religious world. It only confirmed him in his decision to devote the rest of his life to rebuilding what had been destroyed.

During that first visit a group of Buddhist devotees from Shigatse came to pay their respects to the Panchen Lama and handed over to him some fragments of bone they had rescued, at great personal risk, from the desecration of the tombs of the panchen lamas in Tashilhunpo monastery. The Panchen resolved to rebuild the stupa and re-inter the bones.

This material damage could be repaired, but as the Panchen Lama was to realize the human devastation was harder to remedy. The majority of the most learned teachers had died in labour camps or fled abroad, and centuries of unbroken transmission of learning from teacher to pupil had been severed. The recognition and education of reincarnate lamas, who had once been the spiritual and financial mainstay of their monasteries, had also been interrupted. The level of their education had been in decline since 1958, but in the Cultural Revolution the recognition of incarnate lamas was labelled feudal superstition and banned outright. Though some devotees continued to seek them out in secret and covertly offered devotion, these *trulkus* now received no religious education at all. As a result, some were scarcely worthy of respect, let alone the veneration they were given.

The tax holiday granted as the result of Hu Yaobang's visit and the easing of state controls over agriculture alleviated the worst of the poverty in Tibet relatively quickly. As soon as a surplus was in sight people began to rebuild the temples and the monasteries. But the scale of the task was huge. The great monasteries of Ganden and Sera were in ruins and abandoned. Tashilhunpo had lost about a third of its buildings, and there were only nine monks left out of the tens of thousands who had thronged its steep, narrow passageways when the Panchen Lama first arrived there in triumph.

As he toured the wreckage, the Panchen Lama formed a plan. To finance the rebuilding of the monasteries, he decided to take another step away from his traditional religious role and set up a business corporation, based in Tashilhunpo monastery. The profits, he reasoned, would benefit the monastery directly, but the business would also be an example of economic development for the benefit of Tibetans, rather than Han Chinese.

Future funds could be used to advance other causes dear to his heart – such as the use of the Tibetan language in education, the rescue of Tibetan culture and the religious upbringing of *trulkus*. He decided to set up series of *trulku* schools of which the most important would be in the old Lama temple in Beijing, the temple that had been built by the Qing emperors in honour of the visit of the fifth Dalai Lama to Beijing. The Buddhist Association approved the plan for the *trulku* schools in 1983, but it took another three years to find the premises in Beijing's Lama temple and recruit the staff. Work finally began on the school in March 1987.

It began with a staff of eighteen, seven of them teachers and the rest set to building and repairs. Li Jie took an active part in the management, and within six months the repairs were finished and teaching began. Almost all of the scattered communities of Tibetans were represented in the first group of students – they came from Qinghai, Gansu, Yunnan, Tibet, Sichuan, Mongolia, Xinjiang and Wu Taishan. But whereas in the past a *trulku*'s religious education would begin in childhood in the monastery, these were already young men with no experience of the rigours of monastic life. Some were barely literate.

Despite the Panchen Lama's return to favour, the authorities continued to impose restrictions on his activities. The school was limited in numbers and not allowed to recruit new students until the first batch had graduated. In addition to religious subjects, of course, they were also obliged to teach politics. In spite of the difficulties, the Panchen, according to those who worked with him in the eighties, was a whirlwind of impatient, autocratic energy. 'If he was angry,' said one former teacher at the *trulku* school, 'he would say so straight away. He was very frank and liked people to be frank with him.'

In the evenings, he recalled, the Panchen and his staff would gather to talk and eat together. 'We'd all sit on the floor and eat, including the cook. The Panchen loved mutton and he could eat a kilo of it a day. He would take a whole leg of lamb and eat it. He was very lively and he liked tall, strong people. He liked dancing and when the monks were dancing he would often join in. Later, he got too fat to dance properly.'

The Panchen's business ventures had mixed success. He hoped that, by employing and training Tibetans in business, he could encourage his fellow countrymen to win their place in an economy that was increasingly dominated by Chinese.

His enterprises traded under the umbrella of the Gyang-gyen corporation, founded in September 1985 and based in Tashilhunpo monastery. That year, the government returned part of the Tashilhunpo property that had been confiscated during the Cultural

Revolution, including land and buildings in some of Lhasa's central sites.

A company that exported wool, mostly to Nepal, was profitable, and a carpet factory, established near the monastery under the supervision of a Tibetan from Nepal, Lobsang Gelek, was a modest success. But other ventures fared less well. Several projects foundered because of incompetence and petty rivalries. A planned school, for instance, that the Save the Children Fund had offered to guarantee, was never opened because the Gyang-gyen corporation's building division never managed to build it. And though the shops that the corporation owned in Lhasa made a profit, the Panchen's reputation in the capital was badly damaged when the corporation evicted several small shopkeepers without compensation. In Tibet, the Panchen acquired the pejorative nickname, 'the fat businessman'.

Throughout the eighties, and despite his detractors, the Panchen's status in Tibet continued to grow. He was still obliged to live in Beijing and forced to run his many projects from afar. His visits to Tibet required the permission of the authorities in Beijing and Lhasa. The latter, especially, remained nervous about his residual popularity, especially as in the second half of the eighties there was an explosion of political unrest in Tibet.

The immediate cause was a five-point peace plan unveiled by the Dalai Lama in a speech to the US Congress in September 1987. When news of the plan reached Tibet, there was an instant response. On 27 September twenty-one monks from Drepung monastery led a demonstration in Lhasa. They marched through the streets of the capital calling for Tibetan independence and displaying the Tibetan flag.[1] The authorities' response was unequivocal. The monks and some lay people were arrested and the crowd that they had attracted dispersed, but the damage had been done. The example of their courage had lit a fire that was to continue to burn, despite the repression it provoked.

There was a second demonstration the following month, this time led by twenty-three monks from Sera monastery, eight from the Jokhang temple and three from Nechung monastery. This time the demonstration was violently broken up and the monks and some thirty other demonstrators arrested. They were taken to a police station in central Lhasa. A crowd of two to three thousand now attacked the police station and set fire to it, and a confrontation began that was to last for much of the rest of the day. By the end of it the police station had been looted and burned, and at least eight Tibetans shot dead.[2] In the days that followed, soldiers armed with automatic weapons patrolled the streets of Lhasa. Despite this, the monks from Drepung monastery staged a third demonstration five days later.

The demonstrations and their subsequent brutal repression created an atmosphere of simmering discontent that was soon to boil up again. On 5 March 1988, the last day of the Monlam Chenmo prayer festival, monks from Ganden monastery surrounded a group of government officials in Lhasa and demanded the release of Yulu Dawa Tsering, a prominent scholar and member of the Chinese People's Political Consultative Conference (CPPCC), who had been arrested in December 1987 for talking about Tibetan independence with a foreigner.

A unit of the People's Armed Police entered the Jokhang temple and attacked the monks who had retreated there for sanctuary. Several monks were killed and many more were arrested. Another major demonstration followed in which one Chinese and at least eight Tibetans were killed and hundreds were arrested. The demonstration erupted into a riot, which in turn led to large-scale arrests, imprisonment and torture.

On 15 June that year the Dalai Lama made a speech to the European Parliament in Strasbourg in which, for the first time, he publicly abandoned his claim for Tibetan independence. He proposed instead that Tibet should enjoy genuine autonomy within the Chinese state, a proposal not far off the original terms of the Seventeen-Point Agreement.

The plan met with some criticism in the Tibetan exile community, but it roused considerable interest inside Tibet and, initially, met with a favourable response from the Beijing regime. They offered to negotiate with the Dalai Lama in any place he chose. But when Dharamsala tried to follow up on this offer, the Chinese interest had cooled. Once again Tibet was to fall victim to a power struggle in Beijing.

Hu Yaobang, who had been the most senior government figure to visit Tibet, and who had personally insisted on the liberalization of Beijing's Tibet policy, had now fallen into disgrace, and his appointee as Party secretary in the Tibet Autonomous Region, Wu Jinghua, was replaced in December 1988 by the hard-line Hu Jintao.

The Panchen had never publicly encouraged the protests that had broken out in Tibet. On the contrary, in public he condemned disorder and often made speeches in support of the Chinese occupation. For some, this was confirmation of his quisling status. For others, such remarks were the price of his freedom of manœuvre. But what is indisputable is that he blamed the Party cadres for exacerbating the situation and worked behind the scenes for the release of many of the demonstrators arrested in the disorder of the late eighties. While he never supported rebellion, he was not afraid to criticize Chinese rule.

In March 1987, for instance, the Panchen made a lengthy speech to a closed meeting of the TAR Standing Committee of the National People's Congress in Beijing, in which, unrepentant, he repeated many of the charges he had levelled against the Chinese in his 70,000-character petition of 1962. He also added a few new points for good measure. Chinese policies in the last twenty years, he said, 'have been very detrimental. The effects of these policies are being felt even today. Good as the present policy of liberalization is, the Tibetans are apprehensive that it might not last long.'

In this speech, he attacked the Chinese policy of keeping large numbers of Chinese bureaucrats in Tibet and encouraging Chinese migration. It cost four times as much, he complained, to keep a Chinese in Tibet as it did to sustain a Tibetan. He could see no reason why Tibetans should pay this heavy price.

Although China had officially made large investments in Tibet, the money, he continued, had been embezzled by corrupt officials. He criticized every aspect of Chinese policy in Tibet, from the appalling state of education to the neglect of the Tibetan language. He censured the lavishly funded Institute of Tibetology in Beijing, and its head, Dorje Tseten, by name.

'How can people not well versed in the Tibetan language and culture,' he asked, 'do research on Tibetan studies?' In the unlikely event of a war with India, the Tibetans were so disaffected that they could no longer be counted on to support the Chinese side. And despite the relative liberalism of recent years, the Panchen Lama complained that strong 'leftist' influences persisted in Tibet. 'Those with leftist ideology are suppressing everything. When comrade Hu Yaobang was disgraced recently, the leftist officials exploded firecrackers and drank in celebration. They said that this stalwart supporter of the Tibetan people had been defeated. They also said that Wu Jinghua, Panchen and Ngabo would not be able to return to Tibet. Why can't we return to our homeland?'

It was an extraordinarily bold and direct speech, and one that afforded a glimpse of the Panchen's true beliefs. As his friend and adviser, the exile Tsultrim Tersey told me, 'The Panchen Lama's speeches grew stronger as time went on. He would say Tibet is part of China, because that's what he had to say. Then he would say that Tibetans should stand up and help themselves. Those who criticize him don't understand. The Panchen told me not to talk about independence. He said, "We have to divide our duties. The biggest mountains in the world lie between the Dalai Lama and me. There are so many things that I can do that the Dalai Lama can't do and so many things that he can do that I can't."

'He explained to me that he saw Tibet like a naked child. Clothes can be sent from outside, but we have to feed the child and make him strong. To do that, we had to keep quiet about politics. He was a very strong-minded nationalist. Whatever he did he thought about carefully and discussed with his closest friends. When he had made a decision, he didn't change his mind.'

Despite the warning signs that the liberalization of the eighties was coming to an end, the Panchen had won some important battles, and his steadfast defence of Tibetan rights had earned him a reputation in Tibet as a leader who would risk much to defend their interests. One of the Panchen's most significant victories was to win government support for his plan to rebuild and re-consecrate the tombs of his predecessors. From 1980, he had kept the bones of past panchens in a strongbox in his Beijing home and set about raising the money and winning the permission to fulfil his spiritual obligation to his predecessors. By the end of 1988 his task was complete. The inauguration was set for the beginning of 1989, when the Panchen Lama planned to visit Tibet for the New Year celebrations.

Tsultrim Tersey remembers the planning of the trip and also, in retrospect, his own feeling that perhaps this would be a trip from which the Panchen Lama would not return. 'In November or December 1988 His Holiness invited the Swiss ambassador to lunch,' he told me. 'When the ambassador invited him in turn, at first he didn't reply. Then he repeated that he was going to Tibet. He had no expectation of returning.'

In January the Panchen Lama set out from Beijing for a visit that was full of symbolic value: he was to restore the relics of the past panchens to their rightful resting place in the monastery. A historic wrong would be put right. It was a visit from which, indeed, he was never to return.

Chapter Thirteen

✧

It takes the best part of a day to drive from Lhasa to Shigatse, along a winding mountain road. If you were to continue for another two days, along the road the Chinese built and called the Friendship Highway, you would reach the border with Nepal. Shigatse sits in a wide, fertile valley at around 14,000 feet. It is now a nondescript town, its ancient fortress – the stronghold of the king of Tsang – reduced to rubble in the Cultural Revolution and the harmony of its architecture destroyed by the sprawl of gimcrack development – Chinese hotels, a Friendship Store, an army camp.

But on the hill opposite the ruins of the fortress the damaged but defiant Tashilhunpo monastery still stands. It remains a place of haunting beauty. Behind the heavy main gate a complex of whitewashed buildings climbs up above the town. Beyond these, steep steps and narrow paths lead to ochre buildings, topped with resplendent golden roofs. A little further still lies the palace of the panchen lamas. In 1960 it was designated a site of historic importance by the Chinese government. Six years later it was devastated by Red Guards.

In old Tibet Tashilhunpo monastery had had an ambivalent standing. It had been relatively late in joining the first rank of the great monasteries, and though its status as the seat of the panchen lamas had given it great wealth and power, the quarrel between the thirteenth Dalai Lama and the ninth Panchen Lama had brought the monastery under suspicion of political unreliability.

After the Chinese invasion the fate of the monastery had continued to depend on the favour enjoyed by the Panchen Lama. While he had prospered, so had Tashilhunpo. When he fell, the monastery, too, was targeted for destruction; when he returned, Tashilhunpo emerged from its time of nightmares and began to enjoy again the privileges of being associated with the Panchen Lama.

Circumscribed though his powers were, the Panchen Lama

nevertheless disposed of far greater influence and wealth after 1959 than any other religious figure in Tibet. As long as the Panchen Lama remained in favour, then the monastery, too, could be seen as reliable. As Tibet began to open up to foreign tourism the authorities needed monasteries – and monks – who would give the impression to outsiders that religious life was once again thriving under a benign government. Tashilhunpo fitted the description exactly.

By the mid eighties Tashilhunpo could boast several hundred monks and though the building that housed the tantric college was the only one of its teaching departments to have survived the Cultural Revolution, the functions of the other three colleges were revived.

But even this showpiece monastery was not permitted to run its own affairs as it had before the Communist party had imposed its will on Tibet. It was administered by a 'democratic management committee'. A reincarnate lama of a relatively minor lineage called Chadrel Rinpoche was elected head of the committee.

Chadrel had entered the religious life at the age of seven, and in 1954, when he was fifteen, he was sent to study at Tashilhunpo. In 1960, at the behest of the Panchen Lama, Chadrel left for Beijing to study at the China Buddhist Institute. He spent five years there, coincidentally escaping the worst consequences of the democratic reforms in Tibet. When the Cultural Revolution broke out the institute was disbanded and Chadrel returned to Tashilhunpo.

He discovered that few of his fellow monks still lived there. He and a handful of survivors remained in the monastery, but they were forced to dress as laymen and spent their days working the fields. In 1979, when China's Tibet policy relaxed, Chadrel was permitted to return to religious life and was appointed deputy head of what was left of the monastery.

Chadrel's religious studies had been curtailed by two decades of political upheaval, and he had no great reputation as a scholar. But he did have some rare management skills, and his monks respected his honesty and fair-mindedness. He was extremely strict on disciplinary matters and would readily expel any monk who had committed even minor breaches. Nor would he tolerate open political activity in the monastery: anyone discovered in possession of such subversive material as the speeches of the Dalai Lama could expect no support from Chadrel.

Chadrel had reason to be cautious. Like all the monasteries, Tashilhunpo had its share of police informers who watched and listened for signs of dissent. The monks knew who they were: they worked out of a small security office and were rumoured to carry guns, but their main function was to report on their fellow monks and the growing number of tourists who were, by the mid eighties, beginning to visit Tibet's few remaining monasteries. The monastery retained only some traces of its former magnificence – one third of its buildings had been destroyed in the Cultural Revolution and its treasures had been looted – but now the main religious disciplines began to revive. There were three main colleges, which specialized in, respectively, tantric practice, dialectics, and ritual, including dance.

The numbers of monks were restricted by the local authorities, and to join a monastery a boy had to be physically fit, to have the permission both of his parents and of his local Party officials, and to have a tutor in the monastery willing to take him on. The novice had to promise to observe the monastery's discipline, and his first task before ordination was to master the *Chajo Rabsel*, the 134-page prayer book. It could take a year or two to achieve this, and the initial vows were followed by a further year of study.

Those who were successful in the examinations at the end of that year joined the élite main college and continued their religious studies and spiritual training. The others became worker monks, responsible for agricultural tasks and maintaining the monastery, as well as performing the many rituals that marked the religious calendar. Both the college monks and the worker monks attended prayers twice a day on pain of punishment. Drinking, smoking, wearing layman's clothes and even riding bicycles were banned. Monks could earn money by performing prayer ceremonies for the monastery's patrons but otherwise lived on a modest cash allowance, from which they were expected to buy their own meat, soap and butter, and a basic ration of grain. They were also obliged to attend a political meeting once a week.

It was a rigorous life, but one that always had more young men anxious to take it up than the monastery could accommodate. If the monasteries no longer had a monopoly of education in Tibet, they were still almost the only places to study Tibetan tradition, language and culture in any depth.

By the late eighties the monastery was held to be a model of its kind. Tourists could safely be taken there and the management, under Chadrel Rinpoche, was held to be reliable. Chadrel was rewarded with an official post – he was appointed a member of the National Committee of the Chinese People's Political Consultative Conference – and his status brought him a large car and a high salary. He was also devoted to the Panchen Lama, and as he prepared for the ceremonies that would mark the Panchen's visit and the inauguration of the newly built tombs of the past panchens, Chadrel could reflect with satisfaction on the fact that the future of the monastery over which he presided seemed at last, after all its recent tragedy, secure.

27 January 1989 was a bitterly cold winter's day, but Tashilhunpo, nevertheless, wore the air of a grand festival. The Panchen Lama had been in Tibet for nearly three weeks, and his visit had reached its climax – the five days of ceremonies at Tashilhunpo to celebrate the completion of the project he had conceived some nine years previously.

It was a national celebration, and also a family affair. His wife and daughter had stayed in Beijing, as they usually did, but the Panchen Lama's parents had come to Shigatse and were staying with him in the Dekyi Podrang (the Palace of Happiness), the Panchen's residence just outside the gate of the monastery. The Panchen's personal retinue of monks from Beijing was also with him.

It was a trip, full, as the Panchen's visits to Tibet inevitably were, of ceremony and huge crowds. 'There were seventeen to eighteen in the party and another thirty would join us locally,' recalled one of his attendants. 'Even more at Tashilhunpo. There were twenty to thirty cars in the procession. His Holiness worked hard on that trip. He got up at 5 a.m. and went on till ten or eleven at night. More than a thousand people came to be blessed each day. It seemed as though he could do anything. He was never tired, and he would always see things through to the end. He did everything thoroughly. He seemed really happy on that trip.'

The inauguration of the stupa was to be a major propaganda

event for the government as well as the celebration of an important piece of religious restoration. The construction itself was imposing – the stupa, a dome-shaped memorial shrine, was nearly twelve metres high and housed within a hall nearly thirty-two metres high. Both the Panchen Lama and the Chinese government had invested large sums of money in a project that would certainly add to their prestige.

Official propaganda meticulously listed the government's gifts in materials: 109 kilos of gold, 1,000 kilos of silver, 665 kilos of mercury, 5,639 kilos of bronze, 1,100 cubic metres of timber, 116.8 tons of steel, 1,105 tons of cement and 71,782 pieces of stone. The monastery itself had supplied a further 669 kilos of silver, and the Panchen personally donated a large amount of precious stones and jade. It was the largest stupa to be built in a monastery for fifty years and the biggest state investment in religious building in Tibet to date.

The lavish expense of the construction was intended to symbolize the end of the blackest time Tibet had endured since the Chinese occupation. Perhaps, as the day approached, the Panchen Lama reflected not just on the desecration of the tomb but on his own humiliations and suffering, on the occasions when he had been paraded in bonds through the streets, his head forced downward, a placard around his neck, to be jeered and spat upon.

Perhaps he recalled those epic struggle sessions, when thousands of people had been brought in to denounce him, or the occasions on which two monks he knew well, Sengchen Rinpoche, from his own monastery at Tashilhunpo, and Phagpa-lha, still an important figure in religious circles in Tibet, had physically manhandled him in front of the crowd. He must have recalled when he had learned that Red Guards had stormed Tashilhunpo, and the tombs of the panchens – the richest parts of that fabulously wealthy monastery and once so splendid they were said to gleam like the sun and moon in the sky – had been broken open, and the bones scattered as if for the dogs.

That anything had survived that desecration was a tribute to the faith of the devout people of Shigatse, who had braved the wrath of the Chinese and retrieved what they could. Now, more than twenty-five years later, they were assembled to see the relics of the Panchen's lineage interred, once again, in splendour.

The inauguration ceremony on 22 January was blessed with official Chinese approval and attended by such figures as Hu Jintao, Tibet's Communist party chief and Mao Rubai, the vice-secretary of the TAR Communist party. It was a useful opportunity for the Chinese authorities to demonstrate their contention that, after the riots that had broken out in Lhasa for the two previous years, Tibet was once again a place of harmony and religious freedom.

On the day of the inauguration the Panchen Lama made a speech. 'I am elated,' the official version goes, 'at this historic moment . . . All the deceased panchen lamas [were] patriotic religious leaders who had made outstanding contributions to China's unification and national unity.'

'A festive atmosphere prevailed,' reported *Ta Kung Pao*, the pro-Beijing Hong Kong newspaper.

Other ceremonies were held in the days that followed. On 27 January there was another public audience and a reception for those who had saved the relics and the craftsmen who had been involved in the construction of the stupa. That evening, there was a reception with dancing and Tibetan and Chinese songs. The Panchen Lama grew tired and, telling the guests to enjoy themselves, he retired to his room in the palace at about 1 a.m.

The Panchen Lama planned to read for half an hour before he slept, and he asked his attendant, Lobsang Tsultrim, to bring him an extra blanket. Lobsang hurried to get it, but when he returned, he found an unusual number of Chinese security personnel had surrounded the Panchen's room. They refused to let him in. The blanket was snatched from him and he was told to leave. He noticed, to his alarm, that all the security personnel were new and that they seemed to be under the command of a senior security officer whom he had never seen before.

At about 4 a.m. on the morning of the 28th, according to the official account, the Panchen Lama felt a chest pain and called a doctor. He was given some medication, after which he slept again. He woke at around 8.00 that morning, the 28th, and his heart was checked by medical staff. He told them that he felt much better. Five minutes later, he collapsed and died.

'I think he was poisoned,' Tsultrim Tersey told me: 'He died between 8 and 8.30 a.m. and after that, they closed the door, and three to four Chinese doctors spent the whole day with the body. It wasn't necessary, if he was already dead. And if he wasn't, if they were trying to save him, why would they close the door?'

With that hindsight which faith translates into prediction, there were stories, of course, about the Panchen Lama's death. Some said that he had known, when he made that last visit, that something would happen. It is reported that he said goodbye to his wife in a more than usually final fashion. It was her custom to offer him a *khata* when he departed on journeys. This time, he paused at the door, returned to her and said, 'Now you must offer me one more.' Others said that he had commanded two craftsmen to make a clay image of himself for his burial stupa, and a rainbow was seen in the open sky the day before his death.[1]

His attendants recalled a moment during the inauguration of the tomb that, even at the time, had sent a *frisson* through those who had witnessed it. The remains of the panchens had been placed in five safe-deposit boxes for which the Panchen kept the keys. During the ceremony, the Panchen locked the boxes, then stamped and sealed them and placed them inside the tomb. When his attendants left the tomb, the Panchen Lama stayed inside. 'Close the door,' he had said to Lamdrak Rinpoche. 'Do I look good in here?' A joke, perhaps, since this was certain to be his final resting place. Nonetheless, his attendants had been alarmed and pressed him to come outside.

But all of these stories came later. What happened at the time was that the suspicion that the tenth Panchen Lama had not died a natural death spread like a blaze in a dry pine forest.

From the official accounts there seems to be little ground for questioning the circumstances of the Panchen's death. He was only fifty, but he was a huge man who gloried in his bulk. It was January and bitterly cold, and the ceremonies had been long. The main speech-making had taken place when the stupa was consecrated. On that day, according to the official reports, the Panchen made a speech of unusual sycophancy: 'The rebuilding of this magnificent complex,' *Ta Kung Pao* reported him as saying, 'shows the correctness of the Communist party's present policies on religion and nationality affairs, the unity between the Tibetan and Han peoples as well as the patriotism of religious people in Tibet.'[2] (A slightly different version was published later by the Chinese government in which some detected a coded message in support of the Dalai Lama.)

But the remarks that resonated and gave rise to the tenacious conviction that he was murdered were delivered at a high-level meeting between government and religious leaders on Monday 23 January 1989 in Shigatse, and give a clue as to his real feelings about the occupation of his country. He condemned the extremism that had destroyed the stupas during the Cultural Revolution 'and earlier' and said, 'Since liberation, there has certainly been development, but the price paid for this development has been greater than the gains.'

It was 'leftism', he said – the dogmatic attitudes that had ruled Tibet since the era of 'democratic reform' – that remained the biggest threat to Tibet. While most policy-makers had learned from the tragedy of the Cultural Revolution, some had already forgotten and were beginning to make the same mistakes all over again. As for 'rightism', which, in this language of references, meant the economic relaxation of the eighties, he hardly saw it as a threat at all. 'We must pay attention to it,' was all he said.[3] Unusually, his comments were reported on the front page of the *People's Daily* overseas edition and the *China Daily*. Was this, his followers speculated afterwards, the speech that precipitated his death?

When the news of the Panchen Lama's death was announced in the monastery, Lobsang Tsultrim was unable to contain himself. He shouted out that the Panchen Lama had been poisoned by the Chinese. A Chinese official snapped at him to shut up or face the consequences. He did shut up, but not for long. In April 1990, over a meal in a restaurant in Lhasa, he told his mother and sister of his conviction that the Panchen Lama had been murdered. Two days after returning from Lhasa to Shigatse he was woken at 2 a.m. by the Chinese police. They played him a recording of the conversation. The episode earned him three months in prison.

For Sonam Gyalpo, who is now in exile in India, the news was the beginning of the end of his life at Tashilhunpo. Tears filled his eyes as he described the shock of that day.

'It had been the best week of my life,' he said. 'The presence of the Panchen Lama, the restoration of the tomb, it all seemed so full of hope.' But as he waited with his fellow monks in the early afternoon of 28 January 1989 for the Panchen Lama to arrive to lead a lavish prayer ceremony, he heard that the Panchen had caught a cold. Shortly afterwards came the news of his death. 'People just couldn't believe it at first. The monks were beating their heads against the walls so hard that the walls were stained with blood. Some fainted and others felt sick. They were crying that there was no point in staying in the monastery any longer.[4]

'Then we heard that the Chinese wanted to take the body. We saw the Chinese helicopters arrive and rumours went round that they were planning to take the body away to China. So we all had a meeting and we gave them three demands – that they leave the body in the monastery, that a golden stupa be built to house it, and that the authorities acknowledge that only the Dalai Lama can recognize the reincarnation.'[5]

Arrangements for the official mourning ritual were set in train, but behind the solemn façade an unseemly tussle had been taking place. Among the many anxious faces who flew into Lhasa on the 28th was the Panchen Lama's widow, Li Jie, who swiftly presented herself at the palace and demanded a small brocade bag that the Panchen always had about him. It was handed over to her and she departed again for the airport. When she had left, the head of the monastery, Chadrel Rinpoche, discovered that the bag contained the keys to the many safe-deposit boxes in which the Panchen kept his valuables. He sent word to the airport that Li Jie was to be intercepted and the keys returned. It was the beginning of a row about the Panchen Lama's assets that was to continue for six years.

On 3 February, 800 Tashilhunpo monks paid their respects to the Panchen Lama, lining up outside his residence to view the body and present *khatas*. They noticed that his flesh had turned black, another sign, for those who were convinced of foul play, that the Panchen had not died a natural death. In an adjoining hall, tens of thousands of people paid homage to his photograph. In the first five days in February, 30,000 people paid their respects to the Panchen Lama in Shigatse. Butter lamps were lit in his memory, and as a Party newspaper commented, 'the free market was much slower than usual'.

On 3 February a memorial service was held in Lhasa, too, attended by the Panchen's parents and younger brother, along with the usual cast of officials of the Tibet Autonomous Region. The eulogy was delivered by Hu Jintao, the Party secretary. He quoted Deng Xiaoping, who had described the Panchen Lama as 'the most outstanding patriot of our country'.[6] By 'our country' Deng did not mean Tibet.

If the Panchen Lama had been a controversial figure in life, his status was no less complicated after his death. The Tibetans wanted to assert their claim on him as a high religious leader and follow the traditional rites of mourning and burial. But the state also wanted to claim him as a significant leader of a troublesome minority people who had maintained his 'patriotic loyalty' to the Beijing government. The National People's Congress had set up its own funeral committee with no fewer than seventy-one members, including China's president and Tibet's Communist party chief.[7] They were charged with upholding the official line that the late Panchen Lama had been 'a devoted friend of the Communist party of China'.[8]

But if they hoped to inter him according to the rituals of the Chinese Communist Party, they failed. On the same day that the civil authorities in Lhasa staged their mourning ritual, in Shigatse, Chadrel Rinpoche announced that the body would be preserved according to traditional Buddhist rites and that a mausoleum would eventually be built in the monastery to house it.[9]

And so the preparation of the body of the tenth Panchen Lama for its final interment began. This is an elaborate process. To draw the moisture out of the body, it was rubbed with saffron, sandal oil, spices and salt and wrapped tightly in silk. After five months of this treatment, the by now rather sunken body was gilded. One man who took part in this process described to me what was involved.

'When his body had been embalmed, my teacher and I coated it with gold. We did it at night, with the door closed. Nobody was permitted to enter. The face had shrunk a bit and the internal organs had been removed. When we gilded the body, we applied a paste of precious pills, then a layer of gold paint to the hands, over the face and down to the upper part of the chest. It took about two hours to apply two or three coats. We didn't do it every day, just when it needed it. It peels off a bit and we would have to repaint it. We carried on doing it until the body was entombed.'

Outside the secluded prayer chapel where the Panchen's mortal remains were being gilded, trouble was stirring once again in Tibet. A month after the Panchen's death came the most resonant month of the Tibetan year: March was a time the Chinese authorities had learned to fear. The Tibetan New Year, which falls in late February or early March, was traditionally followed by the greatest religious event of the year, the Monlam Prayer Festival – a week of teachings and prayer in Lhasa. Late winter is the pilgrimage season and the capital was always swollen with devotees. Added to their numbers were the monks who poured in from the surrounding monasteries for the festival. It was during this time that resistance to Chinese rule would swell to its highest level.

March of 1988 had been marked by protests and 1989, the year of the Panchen Lama's death, was the thirtieth anniversary of the uprising. It was important for their own propaganda that the Communist party put its stamp on the memory of the Panchen Lama. To do that, it was important to stage memorial meetings at which the official message could be reinforced – that the Panchen Lama had been a loyal servant and supporter of the Communist party.

But the month of March was the worst possible time to hold meetings in Tibet. To gather Tibetans together for any event was always a risky enterprise. A Tibetan crowd could never be trusted to behave like the contented citizens of the motherland that official propaganda described, and the Chinese generally judged it safer to avoid big public events entirely. As March 1989 approached, the authorities became nervous.

Extra units of the People's Armed Police were drafted into Lhasa. On 13 February 1989 there was a small street demonstration. It was to be the first of many. Posters went up, demanding that the Chinese authorities prove that they had not murdered the Panchen. On 16 February the authorities abruptly cancelled memorial cere-monies in Lhasa and Shigatse,[10] and on 17 February, in an unam-biguous show of force, 1,700 PAP troops paraded in Lhasa's largest open square, around the People's Cultural Palace Memorial.

It was only in the safety of distant Beijing, nearly two thousand miles away, that the Chinese state could guarantee that the Panchen Lama's solemn memorials would be celebrated without fear of displays of nationalist sentiment. On 15 February, in the Great Hall of the People, China's president, Yang Shangkun, the Communist party general secretary, Zhao Ziyang, who was shortly himself to fall victim to political turmoil, and the prime minister, Li Peng, led a ceremony that, bar the addition of some Tibetan *khatas*, was a traditional Chinese state occasion.

The assembled dignitaries stood in front of a huge portrait of the Panchen Lama, beneath which were arranged some young pine trees and a collection of wreaths that bore the names of the most powerful figures in the land – Deng Xiaoping, Chen Yun, Peng Zhen and Deng Yingchao, Zhou Enlai's widow. The numbers were made up with friends and family of the deceased and representatives from Tashilhunpo.[11] Even Li Jie, who later complained bitterly that the Chinese government had made her pretend to be the Panchen Lama's secretary during their life together, was allowed to attend, though she had had to fight for the right to be there. She told a Hong Kong magazine that it was because the Chinese government was afraid that the Tibetans would be offended. Indeed, when Li Jie argued her way in, the Panchen Lama's mother was reportedly furious.

According to official reports, the occasion was deeply satisfying to the Tibetans who were present. But if there was satisfaction in Beijing, in Lhasa things grew ever more heated. Scattered street demonstrations continued, despite the authorities' show of force, and on 5 March police opened fire on a demonstration, killing at least ten Tibetans.

This sparked off a full-scale riot, which was savagely suppressed. Two days later, for the first time in what Beijing considers its national territory, martial law was declared. Units of the People's Liberation Army took over the city. By this time, the death toll was in the hundreds, and the arrests ran into the thousands. Martial law was not to be lifted for two years.

The monks of Tashilhunpo did not take part in the Lhasa demonstrations, but their determination to retain control of the memory of the Panchen Lama was undiminished. When a year went by with no sign of the promised mausoleum they grew suspicious that the Chinese might renege on their agreement. But if the central authorities would not fund a stupa, the monks decided they would do so themselves.

They demanded that they be given passports to go abroad to solicit donations. Failing that, they demanded that the Chinese return the many treasures they had stolen from the monastery. If that was refused, said the monks, they would sell their own property to build it, and if *that* was denied them, they were prepared to die.[12] In September 1990 their pressure brought results. Chadrel Rinpoche convened a meeting to announce plans for the construction of the Panchen's mausoleum. Work on the mausoleum began at last, but there was another matter that was not to be so easily resolved.

The death of the Panchen Lama immediately raised the question that was to dominate the thoughts both of the supreme spiritual leader of Tibetan Buddhism, the Dalai Lama, and the highly secular government of Peking for nearly six years. Who was to be the Panchen's successor – or rather, in which child was the next incarnation of the Panchen Lama to be recognized? At stake was the future of Tibet and her unique religion.

When the Panchen Lama died, in January 1989, the Dalai Lama was fifty-four. He was in robust health, and in the religious view, would return in the next incarnation of the Dalai Lama. But even at the Dalai Lama's senior religious level, reincarnation – the voluntary return to the material world of a highly realized spiritual being – carries with it the disadvantages of human life. In human form, even the Dalai Lama is mortal. The time was in view when he would take temporary leave of the world and seek a fresh rebirth. At that point, the highest spiritual authority in Tibetan Buddhism would be the Panchen Lama. And just as it fell to the fourteenth Dalai Lama to find the eleventh Panchen Lama, it would naturally fall to the eleventh Panchen Lama to find the fifteenth Dalai Lama, if, indeed, there will be a fifteenth Dalai Lama.

The implications were clear. To a regime in Beijing which had spent decades seeking the key to the pacification of Tibet, the opportunities offered by this situation were boundless. If they could control the selection, then they were in sight of establishing a hold over the spiritual process of Tibet. The Dalai Lama, watching from his exile in northern India, was equally sensible that this was the most critical diplomatic and spiritual issue that he had faced since the catastrophe of 1959. Badly handled, it would leave him stranded on the sidelines. But if it went well, it could allow him to reaffirm his spiritual supremacy and mark out once again the limits of Chinese power. Within days of the death of the tenth Panchen

Lama, the players were staking out their positions in the search for the eleventh.

The demand that the monks of Tashilhunpo had put forward on the day of the Panchen's death – that the Chinese government bow to the spiritual authority of the Dalai Lama and acknowledge his right to choose the Panchen Lama's reincarnation – met with an implacable refusal from Beijing. A couple of days after the death of the Panchen Lama, the Xinhua news agency published an article on reincarnation. It was designed to demonstrate that the central choices of Tibetan Buddhism – the selection of the panchen and the dalai lamas – had always been the prerogative of the Chinese government. Under the Qing empire, it said, the task had fallen to the emperor. Now, the implication was, the last word lay with the emperor's successor, a self-proclaimed Marxist, materialist government that, since 1949, had campaigned actively against religion and had frequently condemned the whole idea of reincarnation as feudal superstition.

Despite the absurdity of Beijing's pretensions to control the spiritual practices of Tibet, in this stand-off for the hearts of the Tibetan nation, all the cards appeared to be in Chinese hands. The Chinese were in full occupation of Tibet. They controlled the monasteries: they determined how many monks were permitted to join, they insisted on political study, they regulated the activities of the monastery and the economic regime. When carrots failed, there were sticks: arrest, torture, beatings and dismissal from religious life.

Yet the Dalai Lama, too, held some cards. Most crucial were his unflagging prestige and the profound respect in which the Tibetan people, who had not seen him and had heard only intermittent news of him for thirty years, still held him. Whatever proclamations might emanate from the state council in Beijing, the faithful found it laughable that the Chinese, whom the Tibetans considered to know nothing of religion and to care less, could have any standing in a choice that went to the heart of their beliefs. Simply put, if the Dalai Lama did not choose the next Panchen Lama, nobody in Tibet would acknowledge the choice.

For Beijing, the dilemma was that a puppet with no popular legitimacy was not worth having. For the Dalai Lama, it was a matter of forcing the Chinese to acknowledge that, though they had deprived him of the secular side of his role as a god king, his spiritual authority was inalienable. What is more, his own religious beliefs aside, he also had a political position. As leader of the exile community, bound to him by ties of shared memory and diminishing hope as well as of religious faith, it was unthinkable that the Dalai Lama should not be the one to authenticate the next incarnation.

As soon as the news of the death reached Dharamsala, the Kashag, the cabinet of the government in exile, held an emergency session. Little emerged from it, beyond a request that the Dalai Lama pray. The Dalai Lama sent an immediate telegram of condolence to the Panchen's family and declared three days of official mourning. He also issued his own assessment of the Panchen Lama in which he both described him as a patriot – in this case to the cause of Tibet – and made it perfectly clear that his reincarnation was the Dalai Lama's business.

There were, then, two opposite poles to what was to become the dispute over the Panchen Lama's succession. But there was also a third important player in the game. In old Tibet, the task of searching for the reincarnation of a high lama falls first on the senior lamas of the late incarnation's monastery. Only in the later stages, or in the event of a dispute, need it involve such a senior figure as the Dalai Lama. In the case of the Panchen Lama and the Dalai Lama, there was an established custom of mutual recognition. But still, the search itself was conducted by other respected religious figures. The third player in this more complicated version of the rules was Tashilhunpo itself and its chief administrator, Chadrel Rinpoche, who, though he may not have known it, was about to embark on the most complicated and dangerous game of his life.

It was of prime importance to the monks of Tashilhunpo monastery that they assert their standing in the process. The monastery's privileges and status, its protection and such room for manœuvre as it had, depended entirely on its position as the home base of the Panchen Lama. It was imperative, if this status was to be maintained, that the new incarnation be found and installed again in Shigatse.

The position of the Tashilhunpo leadership was delicate. Their own monks had made it clear that they regarded the Dalai Lama as the final arbiter in the matter, but if the Chinese government demurred, the monastery could hardly stand against Beijing. Above all, the monastery's leaders knew that a Panchen Lama who was not recognized by the Dalai Lama was of doubtful religious value. Worse still, if no agreement could be reached between Beijing and the Dalai Lama, there might be two Panchen Lamas – one inside the People's Republic and one discovered in the community in exile. The monastery would be forced to accept the internal candidate but the exile candidate would carry the spiritual authority of the Dalai Lama's approval. However they examined the problem, the obstacles to a happy outcome were formidable. The first step, though, was to ensure that the search would take place and that they would have a firm hand in it.

On 25 August 1989 Chadrel Rinpoche announced from Tashil-hunpo monastery that on orders from the state council, Tashil-hunpo, and he himself as its leader, were to be responsible for searching for and recognizing the new Panchen Lama. The search, he explained, would be limited to 'within the country'. He cited in support of this condition both 'established historical practices' and the constitution of the People's Republic of China (PRC).

Quite which clause in the constitution of the PRC lays down that reincarnate lamas must be found within national boundaries Chadrel did not say. As for 'established historical practice', the case is open to challenge. Until the events of 1959 sent more than 100,000 Tibetans into exile there were no compelling reasons for looking outside Tibet's borders for reincarnate lamas, but there were important cases, notably among the early dalai lamas, of discoveries in Mongolia. If the argument was flawed, there was no mistaking the point. Tashilhunpo could have its Panchen Lama, but only if the game was played by Beijing's rules.

Chadrel Rinpoche did not carry this burden alone. He named a number of other high-ranking Tibetan lamas who would assist in the search, all of whom occupied senior positions in the official religious organization. Most were respected and trusted. But there were others whom the Tashilhunpo monks regarded as Chinese placemen, forced on to the committee to watch over Chadrel and ensure that the central government stayed informed and in control. Foremost among these were Phagpa-lha Gelek Namgyal, notorious for his willingness to support the official position, and Sengchen

Rinpoche, the man who had raised his fist to the Panchen Lama during the Cultural Revolution and who had been so roundly rebuked by the late Panchen for trying to prevent him visiting Tibet. He was also, as students of Tibet's complex religious politics remembered, the reincarnation of the Sengchen Lama who had, in the late nineteenth century, been so cruelly drowned on the thirteenth Dalai Lama's orders for offering hospitality to the Indian explorer, Chandra Das. How much this past history was to matter – or how much it was believed to have influenced the course of events – would only emerge much later.

Finally, there was another interested group, though at this stage in the proceedings their opportunity to influence events seemed marginal. The monks of Tashilhunpo in exile, that pale southern twin of Tashilhunpo monastery proper, had received the news of the Panchen's death with their own sadness and their own hope. Small and unconsidered, even among the reduced splendours of the exile monasteries, lost in the lush countryside of southern India, the little monastery struggled for everything – its dispensary, its sponsors, its teachers, its grocery bill and, finally, its monks.

The monastery's ageing abbot and its benefactors set about fulfilling the prayer rituals due to the departed soul and began making their own, forlorn preparations. Where the new incarnation would be discovered and where he would be brought up was a potent question for them. If he were to be discovered in exile – better still, if they were to be the agents of discovery and later have the care of him – the fortunes of Tashilhunpo monastery in India would be transformed overnight. They, not Sera, whose golden roofs they could see, tantalizingly large and prosperous, from their own more modest roof, would become the most prestigious Tibetan monastery in the whole of southern India. Benefactors, pilgrims and monks would flock there, the coffers would fill and they could become a centre of learning and of spiritual pilgrimage at last. With due ceremony and the blessing of the Dalai Lama, they, too, formed a search committee.

Chapter Fourteen

✻

The search for a panchen or dalai lama was always a matter of state, prone to intrigue and conducted in great secrecy. It began with the observation of any remarkable signs associated with the death or the corpse of the deceased lama. Natural phenomena such as a rainbow or a sudden growth of fungus might be read as clues, marks on the body itself might point a particular direction, and words uttered by the deceased, unheeded at the time, could, with hindsight, give an indication of his intentions. Unlike the Karmapa, neither the Panchen nor the Dalai Lama had the custom of leaving written instructions.

Dreams mattered, also, for they could contain codes, and the visions that appeared on the moving surface of the sacred lake of Lhamo Latso were judged the most telling of all. All these factors were to play a part in the search for the Panchen Lama. But now there was a new variable to take into account: this was the first time such a search had been undertaken under such close supervision by the Chinese government.

In July 1989, after a meeting of senior lamas and Party officials at the late Panchen Lama's residence in Shigatse, some ground rules were laid down for the search. It was to be carried out, the *People's Daily* reported, 'according to Buddhist tradition and Chinese law' and it was to be confined to what the newspaper called 'Chinese territory'.[1] The late Panchen Lama's aged teacher, Gaya Rinpoche, was to be in charge, and the search party was set up a month later. On 20 September 1990 Gaya Rinpoche, leaving Chadrel Rinpoche as the senior administrator of the monastery, and so in charge of the search.

Throughout Tibet thousands of monks in hundreds of monasteries prayed regularly for the Panchen Lama's early rebirth. But little information was available inside or outside Tibet about the progress of the search itself. Such matters were traditionally kept close, and given the delicacy of the political situation, secrecy was vital to all concerned.

In 1990 a group of senior lamas from Tashilhunpo, including Ngagchen Rinpoche, head of the tantric college, and Chadrel, made the arduous journeys to two sacred lakes – Yumboli lake in Rinbung county and Lhamo Latso – to watch for visions. They returned from Lhamo Latso convinced that they had seen important signs. The evidence was strong enough to start the preparations for the search parties that would begin to survey the likely children. Once that had been done, a shortlist of candidates would be tested to see if they recognized items that had belonged to the last incarnation.

As far as the test involving the identification by prospective candidates of the late incarnation's property was concerned, however, there was an unexpected complication – a problem for which tradition offered no solution. A dispute had arisen between the monastery and the Panchen Lama's widow, Li Jie, over ownership of the Panchen Lama's property.[2]

It is one of the deficiencies of the Chinese laws of inheritance that they take no account of reincarnation. As in other countries, widows and children have a strong claim on the property of the deceased. But in the religious view, a reincarnate lama is only considered dead in the rather narrow sense that his body has stopped functioning. His property is kept in trust until another body is inhabited.

In spite of her Buddhist faith, Li Jie was also, as she was to demonstrate, attached to a more secular view of her own property rights and those of her daughter. Bruised by her treatment at the hands of the Chinese authorities and sensitive to the embarrassment her existence caused the religious powers, she was the more determined to insist on a proper provision for herself and her child from the considerable wealth that her husband had enjoyed in the last years of his life. Tashilhunpo monastery, on the other hand, already depleted of many of its treasures by the Cultural Revolution and all that had gone before, was bent on preserving what remained of the Panchen Lama's wealth for the next incarnation.

Since the Panchen Lama's death, Li Jie's own position had become uncertain. Even the large and imposing house that she had shared with the Panchen in his final months did not, in the Tibetan view, belong to her. Widows simply did not figure in the arrangements of a religious order in which celibacy was a founding rule. The Panchen Lama's personal items – his rosary, for instance, which a regular widow might expect to keep for sentimental reasons – would be required in Tibet for the recognition tests, and the monastery repeatedly requested the return of the property. Li Jie repeatedly refused. The argument was to drag on for years, in tandem with the search itself.

After the visits to the lake, though, the search seemed to be marking time. There were periodic reports, but no real progress seemed to be made. Then, on 26 September 1992, Chadrel informed the Xinhua news agency that the first stage of the search for the reincarnation had been completed.[3]

The first stage, according to the report, included the reading of the sutras, praying, consulting senior religious figures and visiting the lakes. Chadrel said that there had been three visits to the prophecy lakes in the three years since the death of the Panchen and vital clues as to his identity – the animal representing the boy's birth year and the direction of his home – had been confirmed. It was believed that the boy was born in the Year of the Horse – an appropriate choice for the Panchen Lama who had, in his previous incarnation, been a great lover of horses. The Year of the Horse had begun in 1989. If the clue was accurate, the child, wherever he might now be, was three years old. But Chadrel gave no prediction in his report as to how long it would take to find him. Searches, he observed, vary in length, and some can take many years.

Chadrel may have been biding his time. There seemed to be little hurry, on his part at least, to reach a conclusion while the question of who should have the final say in the child's recognition was still in dispute. The Tashilhunpo monks had made it clear to the government that, for them, the involvement of the Dalai Lama was essential. But since the Panchen Lama's death, according to Sonam Gyalpo, the government position had hardened.

'At some point towards the end of 1991 or the beginning of 1992,' he recalled, 'the Chinese authorities held a secret meeting to discuss the search. Our own committee had done a great deal of work, also in secret, prior to this meeting. At the meeting, the Chinese authorities emphasized that they would not allow the reincarnation of the Panchen Rinpoche to be recognized by Gyalwa

Rinpoche [the Dalai Lama]. They said he had to be recognized by them. The Chinese began to pressurize the committee and they even bribed some rinpoches from Amdo to declare that they would not accept Gyalwa Rinpoche's recognition of the Panchen Rinpoche. Then Chadrel Rinpoche told the meeting that if the reincarnation wasn't going to be recognized by Gyalwa Rinpoche, then his committee would resign and leave the Chinese to do the job, as they couldn't do it without Gyalwa Rinpoche's recognition.'

Chadrel's gesture of resistance earned him the vocal support of some of Tibet's most eminent and respected lamas, including Gungthang Rinpoche, the most senior lama in Amdo. This was not something, he stressed, that was a matter of personal choice: it was part of Tibet's tradition and the committee was powerless to change it, even had its members been inclined to do so. Faced with the possibility of a revolt of Buddhism's most elevated hierarchs, the Chinese authorities did not press the point. Nor, however, did they give express permission for the search committee to contact the Dalai Lama.

On his return to the monastery Chadrel called a meeting of his monks and told them that he had committed his life to the search for the candidate that the Dalai Lama would recognize as the true reincarnation and to the completion of a reliquary stupa worthy of the late Panchen Lama. If he were to accomplish these two tasks, he told them, he would die happy.

It was not only the Tashilhunpo monks who felt strongly about the right of the Dalai Lama to have the final say. In July 1990 posters had appeared on the walls of Drepung monastery in Lhasa, challenging Chinese authority over the search for the Panchen Lama: 'The reincarnation of the late Panchen Lama would be acceptable to us Tibetans only if it has been approved by our leader, His Holiness the Dalai Lama. In no way can we accept a nominee of the Red Chinese.'[4]

The Chinese showed no sign of backing down. They repeatedly used the argument that was to be the crux of Beijing's claim to a 'historic right' to choose the 'local' Tibetan leaders: that Chinese sovereignty over Tibet had been demonstrated by the imperial gift of the 'Golden Urn', the vessel from which the names of Tibet's highest lamas had sometimes been drawn in the past.

The case was a weak one. The Qianlong emperor, whose gift it was, had been both a Buddhist and a Manchu. His offering, therefore, had both a religious and a geo-strategic meaning. His relationship to the dalai lamas of Tibet was that of a patron to a religious superior. The gift of a vessel for a religious ceremony did not carry command, nor was it received by the Tibetans as such.

The Tibetans had accepted the urn, but used it only rarely: they preferred to avoid the kind of deadlock that might have been resolved by the urn. When they did use it, they did not see it as handing over the choice to the emperor but as another element in a religious process which they conducted: it was on a par with other methods of divination – the use of carefully weighed balls made of *tsampa* dough, the observation of a candle flame, or even the use of dice. All of these were, to a secular eye, the operations of chance. But in a religious ritual they were interpreted as manifestations of the will of a higher power.

Finally, as history could demonstrate, more dalai and panchen lamas had been identified *without* the use of the Golden Urn than had been selected with it. The Chinese acknowledged this, but as the Xinhua agency argued in 1990:

Some 'soul boys' did not have to be chosen through 'drawing lots from a gold urn', but their names always had to be submitted to the central government for ratification before they could assume their positions. During the last century or more, this has become usual practice. This demonstrates that China's central authority had exercised the power over ratifying the 'soul boys' of the Dalai Lama and Panchen Erdeni and conferring their title . . . The central government also had the right to abolish the titles. So, the ratification and conferment procedures were an important exercise of the administrative authority of China's central government over Tibet.

The debate about the use of the Golden Urn continued throughout 1993. At a meeting that year in Beijing, Chinese officials proposed that the Golden Urn be used as the final stage of the search. Chadrel argued fiercely against it. The Golden Urn had only been used to identify a Panchen Lama, he said, when there had been no Dalai Lama to settle the matter. Any departure from the tradition that the two most senior figures have a mutual obligation to recognize the other's incarnation would, Chadrel argued, discredit the choice. In this most critical of searches it was obvious that, if the Golden Urn was to be avoided, a candidate must be found who was beyond challenge. But that, in turn, came back to the question of who had the authority to recognize such a child.

Had relations between the exile leadership and Beijing continued along the track on which they seemed to be set in the late eighties, the search for the reincarnation of the Panchen Lama might have afforded an opportunity for co-operation and reconciliation. But the riots in Lhasa in early 1989 and the tragedy of Tiananmen Square later that year had rattled the Chinese leadership. When the PLA was sent in to clear the demonstrators in Tiananmen Square, the carnage that resulted fatally undermined the government's claim to moral authority both inside China and abroad. Ideologically weak and morally on the defensive, Beijing retreated into authoritarianism. The liberal voices in the Party were disgraced, and the government turned to a combination of political repression and rapid economic development to maintain its rule. Any chance of a *rapprochement* with the Dalai Lama was destroyed.

Dharamsala continued all the same with its efforts to establish a dialogue, struggling to maintain a thread of contact both with the Beijing leadership and with the monastery in Shigatse. Communication, though, was sparse. The Dalai Lama's immediate response to the death of the Panchen Lama had been to ask for permission to send a religious delegation to observe the funerary rituals. The request was refused. In March 1991 the Dalai Lama sent a further message through the Chinese embassy in Delhi, this time to the effect that he wished to assist in the search for the reincarnation by sending a religious delegation to observe the visions in Lhamo Latso. Three months later a message came back. There was no need, said Beijing, for 'outside interference'.

There was no further communication for two years. Then, in July of 1993, as a result, apparently, of a brief thaw in Beijing's hostility, the only direct meeting between Chadrel and the Dalai Lama's representatives took place. That month, Gyalo Thondup, the Dalai Lama's elder brother and, at the time, the minister of security in Dharamsala, travelled to Beijing. He was accompanied by a man who has held a number of senior posts in the exile government, and was then the secretary of political affairs, Sonam Topgyal.

Gyalo Thondup had brought a message from his younger brother to the Chinese authorities, repeating his request that the Dalai Lama be allowed to send a delegation to the lake. According to Sonam Topgyal, the official response was that the matter was in the hands of the Tashilhunpo search committee and the request must be addressed to them. The Chinese were at pains to maintain the fiction that the search committee was operating without government interference and strictly on religious principles.

The two men requested a meeting with Chadrel Rinpoche but were despatched, instead, to Beidahe to meet Ngabo Ngawang Jigme, an excursion that consumed four days of their visit. On their return to Beijing they were told that Chadrel Rinpoche had asked to meet them: they discovered later that Chadrel Rinpoche had, in fact, been waiting to see them for eight days.

Finally, on 17 July 1993, in a hotel in Beijing, they came face to face with Chadrel and his private secretary, a monk called Champa Chung-la. The meeting was held under the watchful eye of a Chinese figure in the United Front, the arm of the Party charged with controlling non-Party groupings, including Tibetan leaders, who spoke good Tibetan. It was a nervous encounter, but still a breakthrough: the official mourning period for the Panchen Lama had just ended, and Chadrel told the two visitors that he, too, wanted contact. He had brought a request for the Dalai Lama's prayers and assistance in the search. He gave them a letter and offerings to take to Dharamsala. Sonam Topgyal and Gyalo Thondup told Chadrel that they had asked the Chinese to permit communication between Tashilhunpo and Dharamsala.

Chadrel, in turn, stressed his concern that the reincarnation be authentic and said that he wanted to discuss the matter with the Dalai Lama in person. Sonam Topgyal told him that he should not be nervous, it was a question of religious freedom, and that Chadrel should not be afraid to speak in front of the Chinese official. Chadrel replied that, religious freedom or not, the monks had to do what the central government wanted. To the delegation's request that the Dalai Lama be allowed access to the lake, Chadrel did not respond.

The meeting concluded with Gyalo Thondup pressing his point again to the Chinese present. The Dalai Lama's role was central, he stressed, and it was vital that the Tashilhunpo search committee be allowed to contact him. Gyalo Thondup promised to talk to higher authorities and did so, later in the visit, when he met Hu Jintao, the former TAR party secretary and later a Politburo member.

The delegation returned to Dharamsala tolerably encouraged by their visit. Gyalo Thondup told the exile parliament that there had been a change in the Chinese attitude, though not all the members of the Kashag were convinced. The Dalai Lama, too, took Chadrel's letter as a hopeful signal. After all, if the Chinese had vetted its contents, which of course they had, it was tantamount to an official invitation to the Dalai Lama to assist in the search. The Dalai Lama hastily issued an invitation to Chadrel Rinpoche to visit him in Dharamsala. The letter was handed in to the Chinese embassy in New Delhi to be forwarded to the United Front. In Dharamsala, they awaited the reply.

They waited, hopefully, for two months. But in September the Chinese ambassador in Delhi made a belligerent public statement on Tibet, and the Dalai Lama concluded that his optimism had been misplaced: the Chinese attitude had not changed.

Back in Tibet, Chadrel was at the mercy of these events. After the meeting in Beijing, he continued to steer a narrow course between the Chinese-imposed bureaucracy and his spiritual duty to the Dalai Lama. From 20–23 July 1993 he presided over the second meeting of the search group and reported to it on the progress made in the four years since the Panchen Lama's death.

It consisted of little more than a repetition of the religious formalities that he had followed, though he did take the opportunity to scotch a rumour that had begun to circulate that a boy had already been found and taken to the monastery. The search was continuing, Chadrel said, in accordance with procedures established since the time of the fourth Panchen and the fifth Dalai Lama – an era, of course, that preceded the founding of the Qing empire and the existence of the Golden Urn.

Apart from the search for the eleventh incarnation, Chadrel's main preoccupation was with the construction of the memorial stupa to the tenth Panchen Lama at Tashilhunpo. It was almost complete. Beijing had allocated 11 million yuan (US$1 million), 614 kg (1,353 lbs) of gold and 275 kg (606 lbs) of silver to the project. It was spectacularly ornate, inlaid with precious stones, jade, amber and coral.

On 30 August the mummified body that had been sitting in state in the monastery for four years and had shrunk, noticeably, in the process, was taken, wrapped in yellow silk, to the newly completed structure and enshrined. A more elaborate ceremony was planned for the following month to mark the formal inauguration of the tomb.

Beijing was not going to miss the opportunity of publicizing its generosity. A foreign film unit – an obscure Japanese company – had even been given permission to film the ceremony. CCTV was also in attendance as the senior Party leaders gathered for the celebrations at Tashilhunpo. The Party leaders and officials who flew in from Beijing were welcomed in Shigatse with socialist slogans of a kind by then long out of fashion elsewhere in Beijing's empire. Lhasa's streets were hung with banners hailing 'the unity of all Chinese nationalities' and expressing 'the thanks of the Tibetan people for the cordial attention of the Chinese Communist Party Central Committee and the State Council'.

Senior Chinese officials, visiting Shigatse for the ceremony, tried to present the event as an example of China's religious freedoms and of the central government's financial generosity towards Tibet. The Panchen Lama was lionized in appropriate terms: 'The Panchen Lama . . . is remembered as a celebrated leader of Tibetan Buddhism, a sincere friend of the Communist party, an outstanding activist in state affairs and a great patriot,' the official Xinhua news agency said.

The late Panchen's father had died, but his mother and his younger brother were in attendance. More than 2,000 Buddhist lamas and laymen assembled for the inauguration ceremony on 4 September 1993. It was a gathering of all of Tibet's senior religious figures, a group historically divided by regional and personal feuds and now further compromised by their role as functionaries of the Chinese state. Many of these men remained on an honourable path. But just as every monastery maintained its quota of spies and police informers among the monks, so the leadership of the religious community, too, was infested with Chinese placemen.

Chadrel Rinpoche presided over the ceremonies as Luo Gan, the secretary general of the state council, made a speech on behalf of the National People's Congress, the Chinese People's Political Consultative Conference and the state council. The government, he told the assembled monks, had chosen to honour the Panchen Lama because of the contribution that all the panchen lamas had made to 'safeguarding the unity of the motherland'. The stupa, he said, would be placed where pilgrims could honour the tenth Panchen Lama's soul and remember his patriotism.

But despite the lavish ceremonial, the occasion served to remind the Panchen Lama's watching followers how much had changed since his death four years earlier. Traditionally, the monastery had been at the heart of their rituals and belief. When major ceremonies took place, people would travel large distances to attend, and there would be days of feasting, picnics and dancing in the monastery. But this ceremony had been co-opted by the government and the invitation list was under the control of the TAR. The public was not invited.

Only important cadres and officials were allowed inside, most of whom, as the local people well knew, did not believe in Buddhism. The monastery was full of plainclothes and uniformed security personnel and when the local people came to take part in the ceremony with their picnic baskets, as they had in the past, they were turned away. In a final humiliation for the Tibetans who watched their ceremony on television, the inaugural ribbon was cut, not by the monastery's religious leader, but by a government cadre.

'When we looked at him,' one Shigatse resident said later, 'we felt humiliating pain. We couldn't hold back the feeling that the abbots of Tashilhunpo and the monks there had been humiliated and shamed. But if we said so openly it would be against their law and we would be condemned as criminals.'

The day after the ceremony, Chadrel again turned his attention to the search. It was, he said, progressing smoothly, but it probably would be 'two or three years' before the boy was located. The traditional rites at the two sacred lakes had already 'pointed the direction'.

'We are currently making preparations for the search, which is set to begin officially in 1994,' Chadrel said of the latest of a series of postponements. 'It is the common wish of all monks in our lamasery, as well as all Buddhists, to search for and choose the reincarnated child as soon as possible.' He might have added that it was also their common wish that the Dalai Lama perform the final recognition. Several months had passed since he had sent his letter to Dharamsala, but the Dalai Lama's eager reply had never been passed on to him.

From the little that Chadrel and his search committee had given away, 1994 was to be the year in which the search was to end. The Chinese were growing impatient for a conclusion, and once the final interment of the tenth Panchen was over, they saw no further reason to hold back. Chadrel himself had been proceeding cautiously, delaying as long as he could in the hope that relations between China and Dharamsala would improve. But the following year there was to be a major shift in Chinese policy, which was to render his task infinitely more difficult.

In July 1994 the Beijing authorities held a top-level meeting on Tibet. Called the Third Forum, its importance may be judged by the fact that Jiang Zemin himself, already being groomed as the heir to the power of the failing patriarch Deng Xiaoping, addressed it. The conclusions of the meeting were not released at the time, but as they leaked out in various policy documents, it became clear that there had been an important hardening of the Chinese position *vis-à-vis* the troublesome religious sector. In particular, there had been a change in the view of the role and standing of the Dalai Lama in the loyalties of Tibet's religious community. The Chinese had toyed with the idea of *rapprochement*, but now appear to have concluded that extermination of the Dalai Lama's influence was the better option.

This was a policy to be pursued on several fronts: the religious sector would be tolerated only within strict limits of numbers and under firm ideological control. As far as the general population was concerned, the encouragement of Chinese migration into Tibet was to be stepped up and the secularization of Tibetan society through rapid economic development pursued with renewed vigour.

Chinese hostility to Buddhism was not new. But after the Third Forum even the limited tolerance that had been won in the eighties was eroded. By November the directives of the Third Forum were being circulated in Tibet itself. On the 25th of that month the *Tibet Daily* published an article based on the Third Forum documents, which carried the general title of a 'Golden Bridge to Reach a New Era'. The article, issued by the Propaganda Department of the TAR Communist party, was entitled 'Never Let Religion Spread Unchecked'.[5]

There was, the article explained, too much religious activity. Monasteries had been opened without permission, 'wasting' manpower, materials and money. Even Party members were 'quite enthusiastic about participating in religious activities', and religion, it appeared, was 'interfering in administration, law, education, marriages, and family planning'. More directly threatening was the assertion that 'a number of religious institutions have been used by a few counter-revolutionaries to plot against us and have become counter-revolutionary bases.'

This official complaint adds up to an admission that, in the contest for the hearts and minds of Tibet, Communist doctrine was running Buddhism a poor second. Despite decades of absence and virulent propaganda against him, 'the influence of the enemy outside, especially the Dalai clique, has been slipping into the monasteries of our region more than ever.'

The tactics proposed to try to turn the tide in Beijing's favour had a familiar ring:

We must pay attention to the Dalai clique's [strategy of] making use of religion for the cause of separatism. We must expose the way the Dalai is using religion as a pretext for his political purpose. The Party members, government personnel, monks and nuns in the monasteries must all make a clear political distinction concerning the Dalai clique. Those few separatists who are making use of religion for their own political purposes must be exposed and punished according to the law.[6]

The number of monks and nuns was to be reduced and the management of the monasteries brought under strict government control:

We must teach Tibetan Buddhism about self-reform, and teach them to adapt themselves to the socialist system. They must adapt themselves to the developments of Tibet and to the necessity of stability. They must learn to reform all tenets and practices of religion which do not comply with the socialist society and develop religion according to this way.[7]

A year had elapsed between Chadrel's brief meeting in Beijing in 1993 with Gyalo Thondup and Sonam Topgyal and the Third Forum. It was a year in which, in Tashilhunpo, Chadrel had waited in vain for the reply to his letter to the Dalai Lama. The Dalai Lama's invitation to Chadrel to visit him in India had borne no fruit either. As the two men waited, the political background to their tenuous communication had grown several degrees colder. The brief promise of co-operation, held out at that meeting in July 1993, shrivelled in the chill and died.

By August 1994 Tashilhunpo monastery was coming under increasing pressure to bring the search to a conclusion. When this news reached Dharamsala the Dalai Lama issued a sharp statement to the effect that the search for the Panchen Lama was a spiritual matter. Another round of recrimination had begun. From this point on the search for the Panchen Lama would take a more dangerous tack.

Chapter Fifteen

✳

October 1994: Dharamsala was bathed in a golden, autumnal light. During the day, a warm sun lit up the peaks of the Himalayas high above. At night, the chill hidden in the deep daytime shadows thickened and penetrated every corner. On the terrace of Kashmir Cottage, where the Dalai Lama's mother had lived out her exile years, the arch of oleanders was crimson and gold. Kashmir Cottage was now a guest-house run by the youngest of the Dalai Lama's siblings, Ngari Rinpoche, more familiarly known as Tenzin Choegyal or TC.

The elderly staff, family retainers of many years' standing, served morning porridge and tea and evening vegetarian meals to the few guests. From the terrace the valley spread out below, its detail melting into a blue haze from which the muffled sounds of the Indian bazaar drifted up. At night, explosions of firecrackers and the faint smell of gunpowder announced the celebration of the Hindu festival of Diwali.

In Dharamsala, as in Tibet, people went about their daily business, oblivious to the drama that was unfolding in the search for the Panchen Lama. The details were as closely guarded in the Dalai Lama's entourage as they were behind the high crimson walls of Tashilhunpo, hundreds of miles to the north, and most of the Dalai Lama's followers were content to trust the matter to their supreme spiritual leader. But high up on the steep hill, in the compound that housed the Dalai Lama himself, there was a growing anxiety about the long official silence from beyond the mountains.

The Dalai Lama still held weekly public audiences, in which long lines of pilgrims, dressed in their best clothes and clutching *khatas*, would wait in line for a brief blessing. It was easy to spot those who had made the journey from Tibet: their faces were deeply tanned, their clothes rougher, their emotions more visible as they came into the Presence.

There were private audiences, too: overseas visitors, many of them active in the network of support groups, delegations from Korea and Japan, Americans with show-business connections, officials from the Indian government or the armed forces who must be treated with respect – a kaleidoscope of visitors for whom the Dalai Lama, in his many roles – international media star, religious icon, political leader – was a point of pilgrimage.

The waiting room of the Dalai Lama's reception hall is festooned with the souvenirs of his long journey from boy-king of Tibet to international icon: presentation medals from European civic groups, certificates of freedom of cities, awards of this and that from peace movements. His greatest civic accolade, the Nobel Prize for Peace, awarded in 1987, is not on view. Nor are the symbols of a more subtle and complicated role displayed – that of spiritual and political leader of an exile community that carries in its memory a country that no longer exists and maintains as its unifying principle the dream of return.

As the leader of this community the Dalai Lama must preserve that dream. But it is no longer a simple dream of restoration of a lost theocratic state – a state that threw away its slim chance to defend itself when it turned its back on that brief encounter with the modern world in the 1920s. The old Tibet has been savagely dismantled, most of its ruling class killed or forced to flee. In exile, the fragments of its old society have been forced to adopt the image of the politically modernized state they had rejected fifty years before.

The government in exile is a template, set up at the request of the Dalai Lama, who continues to suggest to his reluctant people that they must eventually choose a leader other than himself and, perhaps, not his successor either. But though the democratic structures are there, it is no secret that the unity of the Tibetans in exile, and their continuing sense of identity as Tibetans, owes most to their loyalty to the Dalai Lama.

Even in old Tibet that was not always the case. Tibet was a cultural entity that was embraced by the Tibetan people. Most held Buddhism in common and defined themselves as 'insiders' – believers in Buddhism – as against the outsiders, the non-believers. But politically, the government of the Dalai Lama neither held a monopoly of power nor commanded the allegiance of all the Tibetan people. In the east, for instance, many local Khampa leaders felt as close to the influence of China as to that of Lhasa.

Nor was the Dalai Lama acknowledged as the leader of all the sects of Buddhism. The Gelugpa was the dominant sect, but other Buddhist sects had their own high lamas, as had the practitioners of Bon. It was in exile that the Dalai Lama came into his role as protector of all the Buddhist sects, a role that calls for a constant balancing between the demands of the more sectarian of the Gelugpa conservatives and the interests of unity among the traditionally competing sects. The politics of that struggle are complex, obscure and, sometimes, violent.

In the exile community's religious politics the search for the Panchen Lama, too, had an important symbolic role. For the religious exiles, lay and monk, it was an unchallengeable article of faith that the Dalai Lama must be the one who recognized the new Panchen Lama. Anything else would be spiritually invalid. It would also be an uncomfortable failure of his religious and moral authority and one that could erode what was an already difficult proposition that eventually the Dalai Lama's spiritual authority would triumph over the political might of Beijing. Beijing possessed the temporal power, but the magic and mystery rested entirely with the Dalai Lama. In the dream of return, for a small powerless community, magic and mystery are potent components.

In late October 1994 I climbed the steep steps towards the audience hall in the Dalai Lama's compound in the hope that I would be able to uncover the process so far. I wanted to ask him how he planned to ensure that the search did not escape from his authority. Below and behind me, I could hear the deep bass notes of the long trumpets being sounded by monks of the Namgyal monastery. Bright geraniums bloomed in the clay pots that were carefully arranged beside the path. Inside, it was spacious and quiet, a large room hung with Buddhist *thangkas* (religious paintings) and furnished with deep armchairs. The Dalai Lama appeared, moving quickly, direct and energetic, filling the large room with his presence.

He had agreed to be frank. I had agreed to be discreet, until such time as the process reached its conclusion. I wanted to know what was in his mind: whether he had any hope of intervening directly in the process from which he had, politically at least, been excluded. I wanted to know, though I doubted whether he would tell me, whether he was planning some *coup de théâtre* along the lines of the smuggling out of Tibet of the Nechung Rinpoche, the operation executed so successfully by the monk Dorje seven years before.

The Dalai Lama settled in the armchair opposite and his face assumed that air of expectancy – just short of impatience – which signals that a moment of high seriousness has arrived. From the moment he first heard of the Panchen Lama's death, he told me, his fear had been that the Chinese would politicize the process.

'This,' he said, leaning forward to emphasize his words, 'is a spiritual matter.' It was clear to him now, five years later, that the end-game was in sight, though precisely what the conclusion would be was still not clear. He did not even know, he told me, whether the child would be found inside Tibet or in exile. 'To me there's no difference,' he said, 'whether he appears inside or outside Tibet. The point is he should be genuine.'

Was it not possible, as the medium of the state oracle had suggested, that the Panchen Lama himself might elect for a life in Dharamsala, given what he had endured in China in his previous incarnation?

'Yes,' the Dalai Lama replied. 'But there is another interesting point, which we take very seriously. One opinion is that the Panchen Lama's reincarnation should be close to Tibetans but should not be in Chinese hands. According to this point of view, even if the reincarnation is found in Tibet, he should be brought outside. But there is another point of view, which says that if the Panchen Lama's reincarnation is found outside Tibet, then China, naturally, will not recognize him. So they will be compelled to find another child whom they would install in Tashilhunpo monastery. That means two reincarnations, which eventually might create complications.'

They were complications that he had hoped to avoid with the recognition of the Karmapa. The Chinese government had recognized the same boy as the Dalai Lama, but the Chinese had permitted the rival candidate to leave Tibet for India, where he had become the focus of that violent and continuing dispute. A similar outcome in the case of the Panchen Lama could cause a disastrous split in the ranks of the Dalai Lama's own sect. Even if the Gelugpa in exile remained loyal to the Dalai Lama's choice, an equally undesirable division of loyalties between Buddhists inside Tibet and those in exile was easy to foresee.

Given the risks, the Dalai Lama explained, even if the reincarnation were to be found in exile, there was a case for sending him to Tibet where he could be formally recognized.

'This is the very point I want to discuss with the concerned lamas of Tashilhunpo monastery,' he said. 'If they really want the Panchen Lama in their monastery, that is the end of it. So I want to discuss what they feel so I can act accordingly.'

He himself had initiated his own investigations, a mixture of the religious and the mundane. He had, he said, consulted the Tsangba oracle, an oracle which had, in the past, had a particularly close relationship with the panchen lamas. And from all over the Tibetan world had come names.

'So far, I have received a list of names – one in Ladakh, four to five in Tibet. Who it is going to be is not yet finalized.'

What was it, I asked, that qualified these boys to be considered as candidates?

The Dalai Lama smiled and began to enumerate the signs. 'There is a boy from Gyaltang,' he said. 'I have some information about him because he has a distant relative here in India. There does seem to be something remarkable there. I don't know whether it is true or not, though I don't think those parents would be lying to me.'

He warmed to the theme. 'While this child was still in the mother's womb,' he said, 'he recited a mantra. The mother heard it. Then the day the child was going to be born, he spoke from inside the womb, and said, "I am going to be born today" – exactly as it happened.' He laughed. 'Talking before birth – and immediately afterwards.' He shook his head. 'Curious,' he said.

I felt the ground give way as the foundations of the conversation shifted. Moments before we had been analysing a grim political game. Now we were discussing a talking foetus. My eyes were fixed on the Dalai Lama's face. I was hoping to be thrown a rope – some clue as to how literally I was meant to take this, but the exposition continued, unchecked by my surprise.

'There were some other indications . . . a certain light, things like that. Then there is a child in Amdo, who also seems to be very bright. In both cases the previous Panchen Lama had a special connection with the families. That also is generally taken,' he explained, 'as a clear indication. Then there is another one in Lhasa. Then there is another in the Amdo area. On that one I haven't received any definite information. I have just heard about him through third persons. Then one in western Tibet. This is five. One in Ladakh – that's six. There's one that local ladies say had declared himself to be the Panchen Lama's reincarnation. You see, there is competition,' he laughed again, 'particularly among the local ladies.

'Then there is another one in Dharamsala. The father is a lama inside Tibet, who had some close connection with the Panchen Lama. This mother, when she was there, inside Tibet, received some special kindness from the Panchen Lama's wife. She escaped while she was pregnant. Then, a few months later, there were some strange dreams. I think, in the dream, the Panchen Lama comes and asks for certain things. So that young mother wanted to see me before birth, but somehow I could not manage it. Then after one or two months I saw her with that baby. That baby was very small but he looked at me and smiled –' The Dalai Lama beamed at the memory – 'very beautifully.'

The list complete, we were back in the realm of the secular. The official channels of communication between Beijing and Dharamsala had dried up, but it was now clear that the Himalayas were porous. Messages came and went. Secrets were exchanged, covert arrangements were attempted. In Dharamsala, the Dalai Lama was trying to penetrate the mystery of the list of names, searching his own responses for clues as to which child might be the real incarnation.

'Frankly speaking,' he said, 'at the moment, my mind is in a state of confusion and indecision.' Again that laugh. When the Dalai Lama found himself in such a state of indecision, he turned to religious tradition for inspiration. If the other clues were obscure, he thought, perhaps the lake would offer further guidance.

'My plan now is a further check in the lake of Lhamo Latso. You see, in my case,' he explained, 'that lake gave a clear indication – it showed the place where I was born.' The lake had been consulted already, as I knew, and there had been several visions, among them a house, the Dalai Lama said, with a guard who looked like a Sikh policeman. It had been taken as an indication that the child had been born in India, but since then the claims of the boys from Tibet had been put forward and the evidence in their favour also seemed strong.

'So in order to share some of my burden with more people,' he said, 'I want to meet some of the concerned monks from Tashilhunpo, inside Tibet. I don't want to create discomfort in their minds. I want to listen to their views. They trust me one hundred per cent, but meantime they have their own suggestions and views.'

He leaned forward. 'Recently I sent a message to these concerned people, in Tashilhunpo, in the monastery, that they should go to the lake. I haven't received any report since, so now, most probably, I am going to the Kalachakra initiation. I received a report that one of the high lamas is trying to get permission from the Chinese discreetly, to come to India, without any mention of the Panchen Lama. His main concern is to discuss the matter with me. He would attend the Kalachakra, so if he comes there, to south India, I shall discuss all their information and my information. And if possible, I want to have one test, a search party, as happened in my case, to carry some articles that belonged to the previous Panchen Lama, to check each candidate. Then, finally, I don't know, whether in Lhasa, or Dharamsala, there would be some spiritual investigation.'

Had he any indication, I asked, from the Chinese government, as to how they envisage his role?

'The lamas,' he replied, 'regard me as the only one who can decide, but what if the Chinese government put pressure on them? So far the monks in Tashilhunpo have been very resistant to the Chinese and said that unless the Dalai Lama approves, they won't accept it. They have been quite stubborn. But what if the Chinese government puts real pressure on them? The Chinese government can have some of these people dismissed and other people appointed. The Chinese government could produce someone more compliant. Recently this very person applied for permission to come to India, but the Chinese government refused. This name is confidential, but this name is Chadrel Rinpoche. Unless things really become clear,' he said, 'you must not mention this name.'

The Dalai Lama was trying to judge the relative weight of the contestants in what had become an increasingly tense process in Tibet. At the beginning, he explained, the government had decreed that the Panchen Lama's reincarnation must be found within the People's Republic of China and had issued periodic instructions that the Dalai Lama must not be involved. But as time went by the Chinese government had appeared to make concessions, partly under pressure from senior religious figures. One of the most respected religious figures in Amdo, Gungthang Rinpoche, had been asked to become involved in the search, but he declined. The Panchen Lama is the second most important lama in all Tibet, he said. How can I select him? If I do, the Tibetan people won't accept him. Only the Dalai Lama has the authority. Tashilhunpo had given the same message.

But there had also been, the Dalai Lama told me, a recent message from Beijing. 'According to that message, the Chinese government will announced the new Panchen Lama very soon. They were enquiring as to my response. This is a little illogical, a little delicate. My main concern is that the Panchen Lama's reincarnation should be the genuine one. And all the tests should be carried out, all these should be conducted according purely to the traditional spiritual way without any political interference or political reason.

'So the Chinese government is trying to find some way to deliver,' said the Dalai Lama. 'Recently they sent an official message saying they are going to select a reincarnation and asking what the Dalai Lama's response would be. They want me to say yes.' He chuckled. 'I don't think I will say yes. What do you think? Yes or no? I think no, don't you?' His voice trailed off into a gale of laughter.

I left, the sound of the Dalai Lama's merriment still in my ears. But despite the mirth, it was clear that the process had reached a critical stage. The Chinese were pressing to complete the selection, but the Dalai Lama was hoping it would be delayed until he could talk directly to Chadrel Rinpoche himself. The Kalachakra initiation – one of the most important teachings in Buddhism – would take place in Mundgod, southern India in January 1995, and the Dalai Lama hoped that Chadrel Rinpoche would be able to attend. At the very least, the Kalachakra was to be the moment when a message would arrive which would offer the Dalai Lama the further information he needed to make his next decision. Then, he hoped, his choice would be confirmed by the search parties whom he hoped to send out in April or May of 1995. If there was co-operation with the Chinese authorities, the search parties could proceed openly. If not, then they would travel clandestinely. That, as he observed mildly, would be much more complicated. If Tashilhunpo told him that they were content that the child be brought up in India, then, he had explained, the child would be brought to India. 'It would take two or three months,' he said, 'and then we would make the announcement. No problem.'

As I descended the steps of the compound, I tried to digest what I had been told, to gauge the relative strengths of the complicated loyalties that were in play. Did the fact that the Chinese had sent a further message mean that, even now, despite the hostility at a public, official level, they were trying to retrieve the situation, to ensure that the next Panchen Lama was acceptable to all the Dalai Lama's devotees in Tibet? And how, given the high level of official hostility that was now being demonstrated in China's propaganda, had the message been sent? Some time later, I discovered the answer, to the second question, at least.

In 1988 the Chinese government had chosen two unlikely candidates, both Hong Kong residents, to act as messengers between Beijing and the Dalai Lama. Nancy Nash is a veteran campaigner for many causes, from the conservation of the panda to the preservation of Tibet. She is an outspoken American woman who is no fan of Chinese policy in Tibet. (A visit to Tibet financed by the Chinese government to convince her that Chinese policy was on the right lines had backfired completely: 'I saw the bloody robes of the monks who had been shot in the Jokhang,' she said, 'and I knew that everything was not OK. Not OK at all.')

The second messenger, T C Wu, is a Hong Kong newspaper proprietor who was an anti-colonialist under the British and who was imprisoned for three years by the Hong Kong government during the Cultural Revolution. While T C Wu was imprisoned in Hong Kong, the Reuters correspondent in Beijing, Anthony Gray, was being held in the Chinese capital by Red Guards. When both men were released, Nancy Nash, in a characteristically imaginative gesture, arranged for them to have lunch together. Despite their ideological differences, they became friends.

In March 1988 Nancy Nash accompanied T C Wu to Dharamsala for an audience with the Dalai Lama, in the hope of opening a dialogue with Beijing. The Dalai Lama discussed where and when such a dialogue might take place and gave them documents and letters for transmission to Beijing, but a year later, in 1989, Deng Xiaoping froze the process.

Then, in October 1994, TC Wu telephoned Nancy Nash to tell her that he had received a request from 'his government' to go to Dharamsala, and to take Nancy with him. She replied, with less than revolutionary zeal, that she would only undertake what was an uncomfortable journey if she could fly business class. Wu assured her that he had been given money by Beijing and that he was on a specific mission entrusted to him by a member of the state council.

TC Wu remains a supporter of the Beijing government, but he has no illusions about the dirty nature of politics. On the flight to India he told Nancy that he could, of course, have paid for the trip himself but he had insisted that Beijing pay in order that he might have an official record of the trip. 'After all,' he said, 'what would happen to me if the Chinese government decided to deny that this was official business?'

On 17 October they contacted the minister of information of the exile government, Tempa Tsering, who put them in touch with the Dalai Lama's private secretary, Tenzin Geyche. He told them to come immediately to the palace, where they met the Dalai Lama for an hour and gave him the letter they had brought. Wu took notes throughout the meeting and agreed to take a letter in reply.

Wu and Nash left immediately for Pathankot railway station and reached Delhi again on 19 October. The next day they returned to Hong Kong and, two days after that, TC Wu set off to Beijing to deliver the Dalai Lama's letter. He was later told that the Dalai Lama's reply was under consideration.

In his letter, the Dalai Lama said that he was looking for a peaceful way forward, and that the true candidate would emerge soon. He also issued an invitation to the Chinese to discuss the matter with him directly and repeated his request that the leaders of the search process in Tashilhunpo be allowed to come and talk to him.

The letter was delivered, but there was to be no reply. The reason, Wu explained to me, lay in political rivalries in Beijing. The United Front have poor relations with the People's Liberation Army, who in turn despise the government of the TAR. Each pursues its own policy.

From this exchange of correspondence delivered by TC Wu, the pressures that Tashilhunpo was under were clear. It was also clear that some elements in the Beijing leadership were still looking for an accommodation with the Dalai Lama, albeit one that would give him little influence over the process. The Dalai Lama, in turn, was pursuing a double track. He continued to make his demands to Beijing that there be direct contacts with Tashilhunpo, but at the same time he was in fact in unofficial communication with Chadrel Rinpoche. Chadrel, in turn, had understood by now that it was unlikely that Beijing would permit the Dalai Lama to have the final say in the choice.

Chadrel had reached a crossroads in his life. If he went along with Beijing's demands and pursued the search to its conclusion, his career would continue on the upward path that it had followed since the early eighties. He would earn Beijing's approval and would bask in the prestige that the new Panchen Lama brought to him and to his monastery. There was only one disadvantage to such a course: he would earn the contempt of at least some of his fellow countrymen and many of his own monks. The difficult path he had walked – of keeping outright rebellion in check inside Tashilhunpo while allowing the monks to maintain their essential loyalty to the Dalai Lama – would become impossible. There would be some rebellion at least, and he would be forced to side with Beijing to put it down. There was also, of course, his private, religious conscience. He had maintained his faith through the hardest times. Now he was faced with the prospect of betraying it, or risking everything to keep true to it. He chose the route of faith.

In entering into a clandestine correspondence with the Dalai Lama, Chadrel embarked upon a course that Beijing would regard as treasonable. Beijing's definition of the act, of course, depends on the acceptance of two propositions: the Dalai Lama is primarily a political, not a religious, figure; and his political objective is to 'split the motherland' by working for the independence of Tibet. It seemed to make little difference to Beijing's argument that the Dalai Lama had abandoned his demand for Tibetan independence in favour of a plan that would have returned Tibet to the conditions laid out in the Seventeen-Point Agreement. And though it can hardly be denied that the Dalai Lama is a political figure, he is also, for any Gelugpa monk, the most important and venerable religious leader. For Chadrel, obedience to the Dalai Lama was a fundamental matter of conscience. His room for manœuvre, already much reduced, was shrinking daily. Perhaps he himself did not realize how small it had become when he embarked on the last, great gamble that was to bring the long-drawn-out process to a conclusion.

It was bitterly cold on the afternoon of 17 October 1994 as Chadrel Rinpoche arrived at Dakpo Shatruling, a large and ancient monastery in the county town of Gyatsa, on the banks of the Tsangpo river in central Tibet. Dakpo was once a Sharmapa monastery and was one of the few that survived the Cultural Revolution intact. Chadrel was accompanied by his secretary Chung-la and the head of the tantric college of Tashilhunpo, the highly respected monk and incarnate lama Ngagchen Rinpoche, along with some twenty Tashilhunpo monks. It had been a long drive and they were tired. They checked into the hotel near the monastery and slept.

The next morning the weather was no better as they faced another laborious day's travel. They were a large party and travelled in several Land Cruisers, with a truck to carry the luggage. Ahead of them, in that bitter weather, was another three days' journey before they reached their destination, Lhamo Latso lake.

It was not, of course, their first visit. Four years earlier, both Chadrel and Ngagchen had consulted the lake at the beginning of this most difficult search. They had stayed nearly two weeks and had been rewarded with what Ngagchen, a venerable seventy-year-old and one of the most senior tantric practitioners alive in Tibet, regarded as clear and unambiguous visions: in the moving and changing waters of the lake, he had seen a small child with a birthmark in the shape of a number two on his body. He had also had a clear vision of two Tibetan letters – Dra and Ra. For Ngagchen Rinpoche, it was then only a matter of finding the child who corresponded to these visions.

Later, Ngagchen was a member of one of three search parties whom Chadrel had entrusted with the task of visiting some of the children from the list of twenty-eight compiled from numerous reports which had reached him from all over the country. It fell to Ngagchen to visit two boys in Nagchu, in central Tibet. One of them had made a deep impression upon him, and he was never to lose the conviction that this was the child for whom they had been searching. The vision in the lake seemed to be confirmed by unusual weather as they approached the child's home, and the boy had been warm and friendly to the strange monk. He had even tried to accompany him when he left, a sign frequently reported in accounts of such searches and understood to be a manifestation of the will of the reincarnate to resume his religious life.

But despite this powerful evidence, Chadrel had insisted that a further search of the water of Lhamo Latso lake be made. It was already late in the season, and Chadrel was anxious to go quickly. Time – and the Chinese government – were pressing. The Chinese wanted an announcement by March. Soon the winter weather would make any visit to the lake impossible.

The next day the party were up before dawn and continued towards the monastery of Choekhorgyal. From Choekhorgyal, a valley opens to the north-east, leading to the lake. The weather was more than cold. A bitter wind had sprung up, so severe that when they stopped for the night it was too stormy for them to pitch the tent they had brought. There is little accommodation in these inhospitable parts, but there was a small hotel. It had no electricity but the alternative was the outdoors, and no doubt the Tashilhunpo party was grateful for it.

At around five in the afternoon the next day, the convoy reached Choekhorgyal, which was once a monastery as big as Ganden and was the lodging place of the dalai lamas when they made their obligatory pilgrimage to the lake (a pilgrimage which several dalai lamas did not survive). Now it is largely ruined, though a small section has been rebuilt and houses some dozen novices and three or four elderly monks. There, the party from Tashilhunpo was housed in the administrative offices. In Gyatsa county, though, another group of pilgrims who had reached the same spot had picked up an unwelcome addition to their group – two public security bureau officers, who now proposed that they accompany them to the lake.

The Tashilhunpo party, too, had come under observation two days earlier, as they had approached the town of Tsethang, 93 kilometres to the south-east of the lake. They had been overtaken by a vehicle they recognized as belonging to the Chinese security forces. Chadrel's secretary Chung-la was immediately nervous, in spite of Chadrel's reassurances. From Tsethang, the security services alerted their colleagues in Gyatsa county, where Lhamo Latso lies, to instruct them to keep the Tashilhunpo convoy under surveillance.

After a day's rest, on 19 October the Tashilhunpo party set out for the lake. They had hired some twenty yaks to carry their luggage, cooking things, firewood and religious instruments and anticipated a two-day trek around the mountain to Lhamo Latso. Chadrel was, he knew, taking a risk. He had already satisfied the bureaucratic requirements for the search by visiting the lake some four years previously, but now he was prepared, if necessary, to spend a further week at the lake, to find the answer he was looking for.

The Tashilhunpo party spent three days watching for visions from the high ridge known as the throne, about a kilometre above the lake itself. Chadrel, Ngagchen and two assistants sat in a row on the throne, wearing ceremonial cloaks and hats, facing the lake and reciting mantras. They held the bells and *dorjes*[1] of tantric ritual, and from time to time picked up a pair of binoculars to scan the surface. Behind them, three serving monks made tea and prepared food, while a third filmed the ceremony on a video camera.

Frustratingly, the visit proved inconclusive from a religious point of view. The monks saw visions of Tashilhunpo monastery and of monks in procession – impressive enough, but not a conclusive guide to the identity of the child they were looking for. But if the religious results were marginal, the political effects of the visit were not. When they returned to Choekhorgyal, where their vehicles had been left, the Tashilhunpo party found two security men waiting for them. They were followed back to Gyatsa, where they were stopped and questioned. Who were they, the security forces wanted to know, and what were they doing there? Their documents were closely examined, and then the officers left, only to return at eleven o'clock and again at one.

On the third visit Chadrel Rinpoche protested. He was, he told them, a man with a certain status bestowed on him by the government. The monks were conducting a religious ritual and, if the police were not satisfied, he invited them to contact the main security office in Lhasa.

The police became less threatening and it seemed that the incident was closed. But when the party returned to Tashilhunpo, it was clear that the episode had aroused serious suspicions. Chadrel was summoned to Lhasa to give an account of himself to the Lhasa security bureau. From their interrogation it was clear that they suspected Chadrel of making an assignation with the foreign party, led by a monk from Dharamsala, Tashi Palden, who happened to be making a pilgrimage to the lake at the same time and with whom Chadrel's party had, indeed, mixed.

Chadrel was now under close surveillance, and in the security bureau he heard the unwelcome news that the security forces now believed he was in contact with the Dalai Lama. Their evidence of this was the chance encounter with Tashi Palden and his group.

Chadrel tried to bluff it out. Many people from all over the world visited Lhamo Latso, he said. He had seen the monk, and also some foreigners, but he had not stayed in the same place and had not talked to them. Let them prove it, he said. Chadrel was not detained, but the suspicions of the authorities had been aroused. From then on, his every move was watched.

The incident had consequences for two foreigners, too. On 1 November a pair of Australian tourists who had encountered both Buddhist groups during their own visit to the lake, were called upon by the police in Lhasa, who asked them for a list of all the places they had been during their stay in Tibet. The next morning they set off for Nepal but were taken into detention in Shigatse police station and questioned, separately, for two days. Their belongings were subject to a search that left little doubt of the seriousness of the police suspicions. All the seams of their clothes were checked and tubes of insect repellent squeezed out. The two were body-searched and their personal papers minutely scrutinized. Had they, the police wanted to known, given or received anything from the Tashilhunpo party? At the end of the third day they were allowed to go, after paying a 500 yuan fine for visiting the lake without a special permit. The police confiscated their letters, film and maps.[2]

Chadrel had obeyed the Dalai Lama's instructions to search the lake for further clues, but the visions had not advanced his understanding. All that remained for him to do was try, somehow, to communicate the results of the visit to the lake to the Dalai Lama, together with all the other information on the candidates that the monastery had collected. But it was clear now that the Chinese government was both overtly hostile to communication with Dharamsala and impatient for the process to be finalized. Getting a message out had never seemed more urgent. The time had come for the choice to be made.

Chapter Sixteen

✻

In mid January 1995 the telephone rang at my home. It was two o'clock in the morning. Down a terrible line I made out the familiar voice of Tsering Tashi, from the Dalai Lama's private office in Dharamsala. Such calls were rare, and he sounded excited. Could I come to India immediately, he said. His Holiness wanted a meeting. I asked him why, but that was all he knew. The Dalai Lama was in southern India, giving a Kalachakra teaching, and had sent a message to Dharamsala asking them to set it up. It was not Tashi's place to ask why, and even had he known, he might have hesitated to explain on the telephone. We both knew that, whatever the exact reason, it was connected to the search for the Panchen Lama. The urgency in Tashi's voice suggested something critical had happened.

I went back to bed, but not to sleep. There was no doubt in my mind that I would go. Four days later my week's appointments had been cancelled and with visa and tickets speedily arranged, I boarded a plane to Delhi, the beginning of the long, slow journey to Dharamsala. I still had no idea why.

I had by now tried several routes to Dharamsala. On this occasion, I flew to Jammu in Kashmir and drove. That day, as we crossed Kashmir, heading for Himachal Pradesh, there was the usual parade on the road: slow-moving water buffalo, gaunt cattle, an occasional moth-eaten camel, a troupe of monkeys. People huddled by open fires, muffled by large shawls against the morning chill. Once in a while a bare foot would be held over the flames, apparently without ill effects. Flocks of neat schoolchildren in bright uniforms straggled along the margins, the boys with white topknots, the girls in uniform saris or neat box-pleated gymslips. At mysterious checkpoints papers were perused and stamped as policemen and soldiers lolled in glass booths beneath signs which tried to keep drivers alive by exhortation: *Stay awake, stay alive! Better late than never! Use horn!*

As we crawled up the final ascent to McLeod Ganj the car finally broke down. The vehicle clung to the road on a vertiginous bend; stones were hastily stuffed under the wheels. I got out and stretched. The late-afternoon sun was painting the valley a mellow gold. The familiar sound of voices and snatches of music floated up from the bazaar a couple of miles below and nearer at hand children played, birds sang, dogs barked. There didn't seem to be any hurry to cover the last two hundred yards.

I picked up a bag and strolled along the path to where Kashmir Cottage lay deep in woodland shadows. From the bushes came the familiar, though unexplained rustling of small creatures. The dogs broke into a deafening fusillade as I approached, and the cook and housekeeper came out to greet me. I settled in to await developments.

Tashi arrived before long. He knew no more than he had told me on the telephone but informed me that I was expected the next day for an audience. The following morning I walked up the steep hill towards the palace. It was brilliantly sunny and cold, and the sound of my own laboured breathing blended with the dry thud of my steps on the path. Groups of old ladies greeted me as they circumambulated, prayer wheels turning, counting off their rosaries. I made my way up to the top path and then walked along the perimeter of the Dalai Lama's compound to the crossroads by the dialectical college.

It was a busy crossroads in Dharamsala terms, marked by a large rubbish bin in one corner into which sacred cows like to climb and then stand, devouring the contents. One road dropped precipitously, a single van wide, down to the library and the government buildings. Another road climbed the hill equally sharply but was impassable to car traffic. Two others made more reasonable demands, one running along the side of the hill to McLeod and the second winding gently up to the temple and the palace beyond.

I walked up the steps through the Dalai Lama's personal monastery and across the courtyard in front of the temple to the gate of the palace compound. Inside, I was searched by the Indian security guards and led on up the steep steps to the audience room. There was a pile of camera boxes in the corner, and shortly a two-man team appeared from inside the audience chamber and began to pack their gear away. It was my turn.

After the briefest of greetings the Dalai Lama came directly to the point.

'You see, the last time we met,' he began, 'I said that I was waiting, to see if this concerned monk could come to India. Maybe news in January . . .'

I remembered that conversation and the Dalai Lama's hopes that Chadrel Rinpoche would somehow manage to attend the Kalachakra initiation in Mundgod, far away in the south of India. Chadrel, the Dalai Lama now explained, had not obtained permission. But he had succeeded in conveying a message. It had come through a monk who had managed to communicate to Tenzin Geyche, the Dalai Lama's principal private secretary, that he wanted an audience.

'Actually, we told him to go away and stop making a nuisance of himself,' said Tenzin Geyche, later. 'I told him there were thousands of people who wanted to see His Holiness. I told him to wait or at least to tell me what it was he wanted to see His Holiness about. But he wouldn't. He insisted that he could only tell His Holiness. The fellow wouldn't go away. He made a real nuisance of himself. Eventually somebody said that his brother had been an important rinpoche and he was a *geshe*, so in the end, I arranged an audience.'

The monk had an extraordinary story to tell. He had just returned, he said, from a visit to Tibet, in the course of which he had made a pilgrimage to Tashilhunpo monastery. There, some monks had expressed a wish to send the Dalai Lama a present. He had agreed to bring a set of scriptures back to India to present to the Dalai Lama.

The *geshe* had planned to return to India for the Tibetan New Year, in March. In early January, however, he was summoned to Tashilhunpo and told that it was imperative that he return to India at once. That was not all. He had to travel through Nepal, where he would be given a message that should be taken at once to the Dalai Lama.

In a state of some agitation the monk prepared to leave, taking the southern route through Shigatse and Dram to the border crossing with Nepal. At the border he was joined by a travelling companion who went with him as far as Delhi, then handed over a package that he had taken to Mundgod. The package the *geshe* had brought threw the whole process of the search for the Panchen Lama into high gear. When the Dalai Lama opened it, he discovered that it contained a complete list of the boys whom the Tibetan search committee had under consideration. There were also more than twenty photographs and a long letter from Chadrel explaining the evidence in each case. It also contained a proposal as to how matters should proceed.

There was already, as the Dalai Lama was to find, a candidate whom the team in Tibet favoured. But the final choice would be his. What was to happen after he made that choice was the subject of Chadrel's proposition.

Chadrel had maintained two clear objectives throughout: firstly, that it should be the Dalai Lama who made the final selection; and, secondly, that the new Panchen Lama should take up his historic residence in Tashilhunpo in Tibet. Though conditions in Tibet were difficult, they were, Chadrel felt, not impossible. There was a precedent in the young Karmapa, who, though occasionally produced for state occasions in Beijing, when he was required to remember his Marxist catechism, was, in between such trips, left in the relative peace of his remote and beautiful monastery of Tsurphu in central Tibet. His presence there brought hundreds of pilgrims to the monastery each day to receive his blessing, and the huge financial resources of the Karmapa operations world-wide came within reach of the monastery. As long as he was there, the monastery would thrive. And so, reasoned the monks, would the young Karmapa, shielded from the corrupting influences to which rinpoches brought up in the West are exposed and given the benefit of a traditional spiritual education.

Perhaps Chadrel envisaged the young Panchen enjoying similar privileges, and Tashilhunpo monastery entering a new Golden Age. For the monastery, the advantages of having the Panchen Lama were obvious: not only would they, too, attract a huge following of devotees, but they would also be given the opportunity to bring up a child who, it seemed certain, would play a critical role in the future of Tibet. As the Dalai Lama grew older and a generation grew up in Tibet which had no memory of the old society, the new Panchen represented the generation that would take the question of Tibetan identity and culture forward, if it was not to perish entirely.

The Dalai Lama was willing to grant this request. While the tenth Panchen Lama had been alive, despite the vicissitudes of his life, he had been able to perform an important pastoral and political role. The Dalai Lama, himself all but powerless to affect conditions inside Tibet, considered it reasonable that the second in rank in the hierarchy should be within reach of his followers in the country. Chadrel's careful planning had reached its most delicate moment, and the success of his plan to bring the young Panchen Lama home in triumph hinged on the proposition that he now laid out in his letter to the Dalai Lama.

The main obstacle to Chadrel's plan remained the conflict between what Beijing insisted was his political and patriotic duty to the Chinese government to conduct the search according to the rules they had laid down and the demands of Chadrel's spiritual conscience that the child chosen be the authentic reincarnation as selected by the Dalai Lama. It was pointless, he knew, to go along with the Chinese, since the spiritual value of any candidate they proposed would not survive the critical scrutiny of the Tashilhunpo monks or the wider Buddhist public in Tibet. It would be a victory for the Chinese, but a hollow one, and a total loss for Chadrel. Somehow he had to satisfy both demands. He had tried for six years to do so through the correct channels, but now the Chinese had closed that door and were pressing for an end to the delays. He thus proposed an innocent subterfuge: the Dalai Lama would identify the child and convey the result to Chadrel, but his choice, and the fact that he had made a choice, would remain a closely guarded secret.

Once Chadrel had the name of the boy he would take the Chinese search through its closing stages, ensuring that the Dalai Lama's candidate emerged as the choice of the Tashilhunpo search committee. The child would be presented to the Chinese, approved, proclaimed and installed in his monastery, all without a sign of life from Dharamsala. Only then, when all the formalities were complete and Chinese approval irrevocably given, would the Dalai Lama make it public that the boy was his choice. If it worked, Chadrel argued, they would have pulled off the impossible: the right choice of reincarnation would be accepted by the Chinese, and he would, by virtue of the Dalai Lama's endorsement, also enjoy the allegiance of the exile community. However angry the Chinese might be at the deception, it would be too late for them to renege on their recognition of the child. But if any hint of it were to leak out in advance, they were sure to reject the Dalai Lama's choice and impose their own candidate. The resulting confusion might take a generation to sort out and, in the meantime, do untold damage to the people's faith.

As the Dalai Lama read Chadrel's letter he reflected on this extraordinary proposal. Not without reservations, he told me, he had agreed to it. He took the view that Chadrel was in the best position to understand how to play the Chinese game and that he, the Dalai Lama, had little choice but to try to make it work.

There was, however, enough of the politician in the Dalai Lama for a doubt to have surfaced about one aspect of Chadrel's plan. For nearly four decades the Dalai Lama had run what might be termed a highly successful public relations operation: it had several components, the prime one of which, for the wider world, was his unquestioned moral authority. For his community, however, there was another important element: he was the guiding light of their faith. In such an important spiritual matter, there could be no suspicion that the Dalai Lama had merely followed the Chinese lead. Although under Chadrel's plan he would have the satisfaction of seeing his own candidate accepted by the Chinese, he was now concerned that if he was merely seen to recognize the candidate the Chinese government acknowledged, his own sceptical and anti-Chinese following might entertain doubts that the boy was the true incarnation.

There was no particularly easy answer, and I was beginning to understand why my telephone had rung in the middle of the night. The Dalai Lama needed to be able to demonstrate at some point in the near future that he had, indeed, made the choice before the Chinese government acknowledged the child. The solution he had hit on was to invite a Western journalist who had already declared an interest in the process to witness the fact. Better still, he said, to film it. He paused in his explanation.

'Then, later,' he said, smiling widely, 'there will be no argument.'

I listened, astonished by the speed of events and the proposition that was unfolding. The Dalai Lama had, he said, conducted a divination while he was still in the south of India to establish whether the moment had come to make the choice. The answer was positive. In two days' time the monk-messenger would arrive from Mundgod and would re-enact for the camera his arrival with the letter containing the list of candidates. The Dalai Lama would then perform further divination and complete the final process of identification. The name, however, and the fact that the child had been identified, would be made known only to the intimate circle of the Dalai Lama's advisers, to Chadrel Rinpoche and to me.

The Dalai Lama wanted the whole process filmed, with the exception of the private meditation and the divination by which the final choice would be made. The arrival of the messenger with the list, the proclamation of the child, the writing of a letter to Chadrel Rinpoche and the despatch of the letter back to Tibet – all were to be recorded so that, when the moment came, there would be no questioning the authenticity of the choice.

We talked on, discussing the risks involved. The biggest, and the one that preoccupied the Dalai Lama most, was to Chadrel Rinpoche.

'I am very worried,' said the Dalai Lama, 'about the Chinese reaction when they discover that there has been – shall we say – a subterfuge. They are bound to be angry. Chadrel Rinpoche says that he knows this and is prepared to risk his life. But this is a matter of great concern.'

I had a more mundane problem. Since I had known nothing of these dramatic developments when I had left London two days before, I had neither film crew nor camera. I was half-way up a mountain in northern India without the most elementary means of carrying out the proposition that had been put to me. I had two days to find a camera and crew.

I ran through the options with Tsering Tashi. There were film crews in Delhi, but not all were sufficiently skilled. And even if a good one could be found, there was no means of guaranteeing discretion. An Indian film crew would be unlikely to miss the significance of what was being enacted under their noses, and given the sensitivity of relations between India and China, there would be little incentive for them to maintain the length of silence that was going to be required. Then Tashi remembered the visitors who had preceded me that morning into the audience chamber: the Finnish film crew. We set out for the Hotel Tibet to find them.

Over lunch in the Hotel Tibet the next day I gently probed their purpose in India. They were, they said, making a religious film. Both were committed Buddhists and the highlight of their trip had been the audience they had just had with the Dalai Lama. Now they were planning to leave, to continue filming elsewhere in India.

'What if,' I suggested, 'you stayed a couple of days longer and had the opportunity to meet the Dalai Lama again?' I needed a crew unexpectedly, I said, for a sensitive interview. I could not, I said, explain, but if they were prepared to promise that they would not reveal what they saw and heard, they would have several opportunities to meet the Dalai Lama. I knew how extraordinary it must have sounded. But they took it solemnly, asking only for my assurance that nothing dishonourable was being asked of them. We agreed a price, and the next day we met in the gatehouse of the palace. There a monk sat quietly, in the waiting room, a thin middle-aged man with prominent ears. He glanced briefly in our direction, then fixed his gaze past us. I wondered if he was the one.

The Dalai Lama was cheerful as the morning's work got under-way. He has been filmed as much as anybody on earth and he happily co-operated with the camera's demands. In a small room next to the audience chamber, we recorded the arrival of what indeed turned out to be the nervous monk from the waiting room, his prostration before the Dalai Lama and the presentation of the holy texts. The monk settled on a low seat, and from the depth of his maroon robes he drew the package. The Dalai Lama opened it and photographs spilled on to the low table in front of him. He picked up one of them and looked at it for several minutes. It was my first sight of a photograph that was to become known around the world.

The play-acting over, we settled down to a formal interview.

'Who was the boy,' I asked, 'and how has he been identified?'

The Dalai Lama talked of the burden of trust that had lain upon him since the death of the Panchen Lama in 1989. It had always been like that, he said, but formerly it had been a burden shared by the Tibetan government. There was an element of personal obligation in this case, because the ninth Panchen Lama had played a key role in his own recognition. He had regularly consulted the Nechung and the Tsangba oracles and had learned that the child had been born, but until the beginning of 1994 neither oracle had said that it was the right time to identify him. Then, a few days previously, the list of names had arrived.

'I made a divination, immediately,' said the Dalai Lama. 'It pointed to one boy, a boy of six. When I looked at that boy's picture, I felt a warm feeling, which developed the more I looked at it. Then, two days ago, I tested, on Monday morning. I asked if I should make the decision today. The indication was no. I tested again, and it seemed that Wednesday was the right day – yesterday [25 January].

'So the first thing in the morning I meditated. It was a special meditation in which I remembered all the previous panchen lamas and all our important teachers. I needed to have a clear mind so I visualized the panchen lamas and the deity with which they have a special relationship. I meditated upon interdependent nature. Then, I made a divination and the name of the boy came. Then I repeated it and the name came again.

'Now,' he beamed, 'I feel relieved of a huge responsibility – one stage of the responsibility. But because of today's situation, the next question is, how should this true reincarnation be installed and have a proper education, proper care? The problem is how to resolve this –' he laughed – 'with our new masters. It's all very sensitive. So one worry is over, but another one begins.'

I looked at the photograph of the child. He stared at the camera, his head slightly tilted back, his lips parted. He seemed to be sitting in one of those large, heavy brown-leather armchairs that used to be the universal official furniture in China. He wore a dark blue shirt with an orange tunic over it. His eyes, widely spaced, betrayed nothing of whatever emotions he felt as that photograph was taken. It was a photograph that was to be reproduced thousands of times and come to adorn hundreds of private and public altars, the object of devotion of thousands of followers. He came from Nagchu, a remote district in central Tibet. He had been born in the year of the earth snake, 1989, 25 April. Gedhun Choekyi Nyima, almost six years old, the eleventh Panchen Lama.

At such a moment, his predecessors would have been prepared for a life of prayer and devotion. They would now be made ready to be installed in Tashilhunpo monastery and their families raised to positions of wealth and respect, part of the noble class. But that was in a Tibet that no longer existed. What did fate have in store for this child? Would he grow up a puppet of the Chinese or a patriotic Tibetan leader? Would he ever meet the Dalai Lama, his spiritual brother, who had just taken a step that would change this child's life for ever?

He had not figured high on the original list, according to the Tashilhunpo report. But when the search parties began to visit the boys they thought likely, he had made a deep impression. I thought of the elderly tantric master, Ngagchen Rinpoche, making his way to Nagchu.

'When they reached there,' said the Dalai Lama, 'this boy showed no excitement or fear. He greeted him as though he was an old friend. And when the lama asked him where he came from, the child replied, "I come from Tashilhunpo." When the monk came to leave, the boy asked to go with him. He was ready to abandon his own house.'

There was more, he explained. The monks had found special signs on the child's body. 'I don't know what the meaning of those marks is,' said the Dalai Lama. Was it, I wondered, the mark that their visions in the lake had told them would identify the child? The monks had understood from Lhamo Latso lake that they must look in the east. This part of Nagchu lay to the north-east of Tashilhunpo.

'And what happens now?' I asked.

'Now,' the Dalai Lama replied, 'I wait. Until the indication comes from inside Tibet, I cannot announce this. I must wait, probably two or three months. I have to wait for a signal from those who have taken this great risk. I have the responsibility of their lives.

'The Chinese government wants them to make a decision before March, within a month. Now they will know the true candidate and they are hoping the Chinese government will agree. After the child is installed, and I make my announcement, then, they say, there are ready for any punishment that might befall them. Any sacrifice.'

'Are you afraid something might go wrong with this?'

'Very possibly,' the Dalai Lama replied. 'For instance, if the Chinese know, if they refuse the child, then I don't know.'

That afternoon I talked to the monk who had carried the message. He was anxious as he told his story, and his responsibility was not yet over. Now he must return to Delhi where a second messenger was waiting to receive the Dalai Lama's letter and smuggle it back to Tibet. As he talked of his companion, the monk became agitated. 'It is extremely dangerous for him,' he said. 'He cannot come here because there are so many spies. It is all so dangerous.'

The next day, I said goodbye to my emergency Finnish film crew and impressed upon them again that they must not speak of what they had seen. I packed the tapes and prepared to leave. That afternoon I set off for Pathankot to take the train to Delhi. I had two travelling companions: Tsering Tashi and the messenger monk. In Delhi, the second messenger was waiting. He, too, was anxious, but also proud of the trust that had been placed in him.

As we all parted, two to return to Dharamsala, I to London, and the young messenger to make the hardest journey – to Nepal, then across the border at Dram and on to Shigatse – we wished each other luck, then took our leave. I felt that, despite their fears, my three companions were bright with expectation. I shared neither their nation's story nor their religion, but it was impossible not to be moved by the courage and faith that impelled them to take such risks. For them the importance of the choice of the Panchen Lama transcended the physical risk. If it could be accomplished, whatever lay in store, it was worth it. I returned home, heavy with the secret, and prepared to wait.

The next day, the messenger, too, left Delhi. It must have been a lonely journey. By bus to Kathmandu, then on, north, to the border. It was meant to take four days, but bad luck intervened. As the messenger reached Kathmandu, the weather worsened. A heavy snowfall closed the road across the border. A snowfall like that could lie for weeks, closing down the traffic on the only and vital road that led from Dram to Shigatse, and then to Lhasa.

In the summer months it's an easy road, much travelled by that new generation of Tibet adventurers, the backpackers who congregate in Lhasa's cheap restaurants, exchanging experiences and gossip. But in the winter the harsh climate turns it into a lottery. Now the dice had fallen badly. The messenger knew he could not wait. His precious letters were urgently needed. If he could not travel by car, then he would walk. It took the best part of five days. He finally arrived back in Shigatse on 10 February.

In Tashilhunpo, Chadrel was waiting, nervously trying to fend off the increasingly pressing demands of the government that a decision be made. As his emissary struggled through the snow, he prevaricated, hoping the response would reach him in time for an important meeting of the search committee that was scheduled for 24 January: on the agenda for that meeting was the shortlist that had to be drawn up from the list of twenty-eight names selected by the search parties.

According to a later Chinese account, there was an argument at this meeting. Chadrel had received no confirmation from the Dalai Lama that the child the Tashilhunpo group so strongly preferred was, indeed, the Panchen Lama. But, as he waited, he had to keep the path open for his candidate.

Others on the committee, however, argued that the Golden Urn should be used in the final stages of the search. By Tibetan tradition, it came into use only, as the Qianlong emperor had suggested, when there was a conflict that could not otherwise be resolved. Chadrel's strategy was, therefore, to avoid such a conflict.

The meeting was to draw up a shortlist of seven boys, and a second list of five others who might be investigated further. Despite the strong signs in favour of Choekyi Nyima that Chadrel now laid before his fellow committee members, the official account of the meeting claims that he failed to win majority backing for his candidate. Most of the committee, the account claims, were unwilling to include Choekyi Nyima on the shortlist. The highest position they would give him was on the supplementary list of five. According to later Chinese charges, Chadrel included the boy on the shortlist, nonetheless.

But including him on the shortlist did not solve the larger problem of the Golden Urn lottery. Chadrel cast around for further evidence in favour of Gedhun Choekyi Nyima – evidence that would make his case so strongly that a lottery could be avoided.

Once he received the Dalai Lama's reply confirming the choice, it became imperative to press Choekyi Nyima's claim. If a lottery was held, there was always the risk that the child Chadrel was now convinced was the true Panchen Lama might lose. Faced with that risk, Chadrel now appears to have resorted to a subterfuge. According to the official Chinese account, on 10 February Chadrel informed the authorities that he had carried out a divination. The method he had chosen was the same as that used by the Dalai

Lama two weeks earlier in his own process of recognition. Small balls made of kneaded *tsampa* are carefully weighed so that they are identical. Then a slip of paper on which the name of a candidate is written is introduced into each. Accompanied by prayer, the balls are placed in a bowl and the bowl is rotated until one jumps out. The process is often repeated, as it had been in the Dalai Lama's private quarters in Dharamsala, to confirm the choice.

Chadrel now claimed that he had performed this divination and that the name of Gedhun Choekyi Nyima had been clearly indicated. The Golden Urn, therefore, was not necessary.

Mystery still surrounds this divination: the Chinese government was later to accuse Chadrel of lying. He had performed the divination, they said, but not until 21 February, eleven days after he had reported to the authorities. Did Chadrel pass off the Dalai Lama's divination as his own? Whatever the truth, the committee, with its Chinese placeman Sengchen and the local party secretary Sandrup, did not accept it. They continued to argue that the process could be completed only with the Golden Urn.

As Chadrel prevaricated, the suspicions that had begun to surround him grew. By the end of February Chadrel was already slipping into a web from which he was to find no escape.

If he was aware of it, he did not betray his fears. He was still, he insisted, in charge of the search. Armed with the Dalai Lama's blessing, he knew, at least, what he had to do. Now it only remained to execute the last part of his plan. In March 1995 Chadrel Rinpoche set out for Beijing, accompanied, as usual, by his loyal secretary Champa Chung-la. He had business to attend to. The dispute about the late Panchen Lama's property had still, finally, to be settled. The items that the monastery wanted returned were still in the possession of Li Jie, in the Chinese capital, and as the end of the search approached, Chadrel knew that he had to win the argument. The final authority lay in distant Beijing, so there he must go to make his case. He left in early March 1995. It was the last time the monks of Tashilhunpo monastery were to see him.

Chapter Seventeen

✯

In Dharamsala, silence fell. The tenuous communication between the Dalai Lama and Shigatse had ceased. In January the Dalai Lama had contacted TC Wu and reminded him that he still had had no reply to his invitation to Chadrel to come to India. In March TC Wu visited Beijing. There had been, he discovered, and there would be, no reply. The Chinese government now denied that they had ever sent TC Wu to Dharamsala. The Dalai Lama went into retreat at Dehra Dun, and in India and Tibet attention turned to the preparations for the passing of the Tibetan New Year.

In Tibet this has become a time for remembering the uprising of 1959 and, sometimes, for renewed protest. In Dharamsala it is the moment in the year when the Dalai Lama makes his annual address, a speech in which he tries to renew the resolve of his community, despite the passage of each fruitless year.

On this occasion, many of his followers were waiting for news that he did have, but which he was unable to give them. Far to the south, in the heavy, tropical climate of Karnataka province, the exile monastery of Tashilhunpo had thought of little else since the death of the Panchen Lama in 1989. They had placed absolute trust in the omniscience of the Dalai Lama, and it was their guarantee that the child would be found. Their hope was that he would be brought to live in their monastery. They were not privy to the secrets of the search, but as the Tibetan New Year of 1996 approached, the small community could contemplate with satisfaction the progress of their most important project: the construction of a palace that might just become home to the eleventh Panchen Lama.

It was a massive undertaking for a community that could scarcely afford medicine and food for its monks. But when the Panchen Lama died the monastery felt its spiritual obligation to respond. In March 1990 a search committee was elected from among the delegates to attend a meeting in Delhi. It undertook to raise the funds for the construction of a home fit for the Panchen Lama. From

Delhi, the monastery's representatives continued to Dharamsala for an audience with the Dalai Lama. There, they also consulted the Tsangba oracle, who gave them the reassuring news that the Panchen Lama would definitely reincarnate, though perhaps not very soon. In preparation for that eventual, fateful day, fund-raising began. The monks undertook long journeys through Nepal, Kalimpong and Delhi, wherever there were patrons who might be inclined to donate. By 1995 they had raised 22 million rupees, around half of their goal. Construction had already begun on a site outside the monastery gates.

One of the fund-raisers showed me around the building, his mind saturated with the vision of what it was going to be. We clambered through the empty concrete shell, climbing over the builders' clutter. 'This is for His office, that's for His private secretary, that's a lavatory and that's His secretary's living room. We plan to build a wall here,' he said, 'and make a garden with flowers and fruits. A beautiful garden.' He gestured through the empty space of the windows.

'This will be a veranda where they can stroll in the shade. This is the cook's room, where he can take a rest. This is the cook's bedroom, for him and the kitchen attendants. This is a room for the Dalai Lama when he visits. That's the dining hall. Over there is clear water and we shall cover the garden so that Gyalwa Rinpoche [the Dalai Lama] can stroll in it. We are going to build two storeys. Two storeys is good, isn't it?'

I looked out over the lush, green countryside. A huge orange sun was just beginning to graze the horizon and the lengthening shadows painted indigo streaks on the verdant fields. The evening air was warm and crickets were chirruping in the trees. The scent of flowers mingled with the perfume of the incense from the two burners at the monastery gate. The sound of laughter came from behind the monastery wall as the child monks chased each other around the courtyard. In that magical few minutes before nightfall, it seemed like a little paradise, no bad place for a child to grow up, not least the next Panchen Lama, after the high pomp and tragedy of his last incarnation. But as the sun dipped below the distant hills of Karnataka, I knew it was all but impossible that their dream would come true.

The next day the monastery's elderly administrator, Thupten

Nyendak, a man with sharp cheekbones and sunken cheeks, which give an unnerving death's head quality to his face, unrolled for me a huge painting of Tashilhunpo monastery as it used to be. It was painted, he said, by a monk who had fled to India and who devoted the rest of his life to recording in this picture his recollection of a world he feared would vanish for all time. Laid out in minute detail were Thupten Nyendak's memories, too.

He jabbed at the painting, angrily, pointing out how much of the monastery had been destroyed. 'Before the Cultural Revolution,' said the old man, 'Tashilhunpo was perfectly preserved. After 1959 there were four thousand monks in the four colleges. Three of them have gone and the one that survived was only spared because the Chinese stationed soldiers in it and stored their food in the Great Prayer Hall. There isn't anything precious for them left to steal. There were many millions' worth of valuable treasures. They didn't even leave the wooden furniture.'

After the Panchen Rinpoche's petition, he said, the Chinese had retaliated by making the monastery a military camp. 'The monks were sent out for hard labour during the day and locked up at night. They had a big prison there. When I left Tashilhunpo there were four thousand monks, and when I returned there were just seven hundred. What happened to those three thousand monks? Where are they? Have they all died? Nobody knows.'

The search committee was composed of some senior monks from the monastery and their major sponsors. It was clear that there was little they could do to further the search itself. There was some formal communication with the monastery in Tibet, but they had no news of the process. In 1994 they had applied for permission to visit Tibet, but this had been refused. They were powerless and marginalized, yet they still held out hope that their place would, one day, be occupied. For them, it was almost unthinkable that the child would be brought up in occupied Tibet.

'We thought,' said a member of the search committee, 'that if the reincarnation was born in Tibet, it might be a good idea not to announce it, but to keep it secret and smuggle him out to India. If we are able to bring him to India, the reincarnation could receive his monk's initiation from Gyalwa Rinpoche and everything would be ideal.' As the building slowly took shape in the early months of

1995, the abbot of the exiles' Tashilhunpo decided to make the long journey to Dharamsala to pay his respects to the Dalai Lama and to ask about the progress of the search. In March of that year a small group, comprising the abbot and two members of the search committee, set out from Karnataka.

The progress of the search was also on the Dalai Lama's mind. Six weeks had passed since the messenger had been despatched and now there was silence. Chadrel was absent, away in Beijing, and even his monastery had not heard from him. Cut off in Dharamsala, the Dalai Lama fretted and doubts grew in his mind about the wisdom of Chadrel's plan. He had never lost the anxiety that it might put the abbot's life at risk, even if it were to work.

The relief he had experienced when he made his choice gave way, in the long silence that followed, to a nagging worry that something had gone wrong. Would it not perhaps be better to cut the process short, announce the choice and see what the consequences were? At least if the announcement came from Dharamsala, it would draw Chinese attention away from Chadrel's subterfuge. As the Dalai Lama wrestled with these doubts, the delegation from Tashilhunpo arrived.

The usual formalities over, the abbot reported to the Dalai Lama on the progress of their epic construction. Then he respectfully enquired of his spiritual leader what news there was of the boy for whom they all waited so impatiently. The Dalai Lama decided that he could allow them to labour no longer under the delusion that the boy would ever live in their palace. The choice, he told them, had been made. Furthermore, there would be no dashing rescue from Tibet, no return in triumph to India, bearing the prize. The boy would stay in Tibet, to be brought up in the monastery the abbot had fled in 1959.

It was hardly welcome news to the men from the south of India. Immediately they raised objections to the plan. It was too late to influence the choice, but they could – and did – argue strongly that it would not go down well in the exile community if the Chinese were allowed to proclaim their candidate before the Dalai Lama had pronounced. Whatever evidence was produced to support the Dalai Lama's claim to have made the choice first, there would always be those who doubted. They would, the abbot argued, begin to murmur. Could the Dalai Lama really afford to let it be thought that he was simply following the Chinese lead in this, the most critical of religious moments?

The anxieties they planted in the Dalai Lama's mind fed his growing unease. As April wore on and his efforts to contact the search committee in Tibet continued fruitlessly, an alternative plan began to take shape. By the end of April it had taken on a momentum of its own. He, the Dalai Lama, would make the announcement on the next auspicious date and appeal directly and publicly to the Chinese government to accept the choice.

Encouraged by his advisers, he began to see it as a gesture of conciliation: after all, the boy was in Tibet, under the control of the Chinese government, and the Dalai Lama would make no attempt to remove him. The boy's family were devout Buddhists, but they had never been in contact with Dharamsala so could not fall under suspicion of collaboration. And the choice was the same as the preferred candidate of the search committee in Tibet. What happier resolution, then, than that both sides agree?

Whatever the view in Dharamsala, it was hard to view the political conditions for agreement as other than extremely unpromising. In Beijing, the patriarch Deng Xiaoping was clinging tenaciously but increasingly implausibly to life. Around his diminishing figure those who hoped to inherit his supreme position were vying with each other to assume pleasing political stances. In the bankrupt ideology of Beijing there was little firm ground to stand on, but patriotism and the supremacy of the Han race were still certain bets. And the prime internal challenge to Han supremacy was in Tibet.

Since the Third Forum in July 1994 there had been a renewed crackdown on religious practice in Tibet. Party members who inclined towards Buddhist practice were told to stop, and for them, possession of photographs of the Dalai Lama became an offence. New restrictions had been placed on the numbers entering monasteries and nunneries, all aimed at stopping the growth of Buddhism. In October 1994 a visiting Swedish delegation had been told that 1,400 monasteries and 34,000 monks were considered sufficient and no further permission would be given for restoration, even when the money to fund the work had been collected from private sources.[1]

In August of that year teams of government officials had toured

Tibet to notify the monasteries of the new restrictions and to stress to the religious community that, while Buddhism was tolerated, allegiance to the Dalai Lama was not.

The message provoked resistance in several monasteries. In December fourteen monks from a small monastery near Lhasa were arrested after protesting against political interference in the monastery: officials had threatened to close it down if any of its monks showed support for Tibetan independence.[2] Tensions were still high as the New Year approached. By late February news of some twelve demonstrations had reached the outside world, most of them brief affairs staged by monks and nuns, which often consisted of little more than shouting independence slogans in a public place. Such gestures invariably ended in arrest. From mid January, special restrictions were in place in the Barkhor in Lhasa, the favourite site for protest, and by the end of the month 600 extra soldiers had been moved into the city and a group of top-level army officers were installed in the opulent grandeur of the Lhasa Holiday Inn.[3]

The nervousness of the security forces was related both to the imminent New Year celebrations and to a significant date that fell in September 1995 – the thirtieth anniversary of the founding of the Tibet Autonomous Region. It was a date that the Chinese government had resolved to commemorate with all the trappings of an important state occasion.

Large numbers of senior officials were due to come for the ceremonies in September, and the Chinese government was determined that nothing would be allowed to spoil the party. From the turn of the year, a virulent propaganda campaign was launched against the Dalai Lama.

That much was visible from Dharamsala. But there were other problems, hidden behind the curtain of silence that had fallen on the search for the Panchen Lama, that were even more serious: Chadrel was losing his struggle to retain control of the process. The monks of Tashilhunpo had heard nothing of him since his departure in early March for Beijing. He had gone to conclude the negotiations over the late Panchen Lama's property with the widow, Li Jie, and to argue his case against the lottery. On 4 March 1995 Chadrel Rinpoche attended the eighth National Political Consultative Committee's third meeting in Beijing. It lasted ten days. Later it was learned that, afterwards, Chadrel had been virtually confined to his quarters in Beijing.

As the weeks went by Chadrel argued desperately against the lottery. The choice was clear, he said, and most of the committee agreed. Chadrel may have had the support of those senior religious figures who maintained their allegiance to the Dalai Lama. But he had at least one implacable opponent on the committee, Sengchen Rinpoche.

Sengchen Rinpoche had little influence in the monastery itself since his marriage some years before meant that he lived in Lhasa. He was unpopular in Tashilhunpo, and when he had tried to argue the case for the Golden Urn to the monks there, they had given him a hostile reception. He chose to influence the search through the Chinese, and here he played a powerful hand. He appealed to the Chinese desire for absolute sovereignty over Tibet and reinforced it by invoking tradition. Just as the *amban* sent by the Qing emperors had supervised the final lottery in the past, he argued, so must the Chinese insist that the culmination of this process should be a lottery. In Beijing, it was an argument that was bound to succeed. For the Chinese government, Sengchen's opinions offered a possible alternative to Chadrel's, who was now proving, from their point of view, uncomfortably recalcitrant. If Chadrel did not come into line, he could be replaced.

Chadrel argued his case against Sengchen for months, but by early May it was clear that he would not prevail. Eleven members of the search committee who had been summoned to Beijing returned to Tibet. Chadrel packed up the property he had recovered and prepared to return himself. He had one last card to play. If there had to be a lottery, then he would have to ensure that the result was the correct one.

Meanwhile, the Dalai Lama continued his round of international engagements. In early May I went to meet him in Dortmund, Germany. On the VIP floor of the Römische Kaiser hotel, secure behind heavy bombproof doors, the Dalai Lama was relaxing between engagements, surrounded by the familiar figures of his personal bodyguards and attendants. He had discarded his usual Doc Martens for a pair of flip-flops and seemed in a decided frame of mind. The waiting, he announced, could go on no longer. Messages he had been expecting the previous months had not come, but he knew that Chadrel was still in Beijing and, frankly, he was worried.

'I told you that I had thought of an alternative to Chadrel's plan,' he continued. 'Since the search committee at Tashilhunpo in India has asked me for a decision, I shall respond. Chadrel Rinpoche can appeal directly to the Chinese, that since the Dalai Lama has announced the choice, they should confirm it. The boy is in the People's Republic of China and they have had no contact with the Dalai Lama, so there is no reason for them to refuse.'

I thought of the propaganda campaign that was currently raging against the Dalai Lama in China and Tibet. The effects of the Third Forum were still working through, and with each month that passed the line seemed to be hardening against him. On 10 March the *Tibet Daily* had published a lengthy personal attack on the Dalai Lama, accusing him of having lost his spiritual credentials. Such language had not been seen since the end of the Cultural Revolution and had sparked a number of rural protests in Tibet. Official government documents described the Dalai Lama and his officials as the 'head of a serpent' which must be chopped off. They accused him of blasphemy and of distorting Buddhism. Previous attacks had only criticized his political role. Now a new campaign was trying to discredit him as a religious figure. It accused him of forging Buddhist texts, altering the teachings and violating the principles of Buddhism. It seemed implausible that, in such a political climate, the Chinese would accept any suggestion that came from Dharamsala, let alone one of such import. Yet this was the premise on which the decision to announce the choice was being proposed. There was only one caveat.

'I want to know Chadrel Rinpoche's opinion,' the Dalai Lama said. 'If he agrees to the proposal, I feel the appropriate date is in ten days, 14 May. It is a very auspicious date religiously. A month ago I told the people at Tashilhunpo that I had decided but that I am waiting for a final reply from Chadrel Rinpoche. They are worried that if, after Peking's announcement, the Dalai Lama says that he agrees, it will look as though the Dalai Lama has been compelled to accept. It looks odd that I had decided and not announced it. If I choose first, then there is no personal risk to

Chadrel Rinpoche. It's just that he had to persuade them to accept it.'

'And if Chadrel Rinpoche says no?' I ventured.

'Then I will not announce it,' said the Dalai Lama. 'He is inside China. His opinion and his safety are very important.'

I spoke at length to one of the Dalai Lama's advisers, who laid out the thinking behind the decision. He was convinced that the Dalai Lama should make his announcement before the Chinese because the other option involved a deception that might provoke Chinese anger and leave the question festering. If it could be done now, the first hope was that the Chinese would accept it. If they did not, then after the death of Deng, which was now clearly not far off, any unpleasantness over the issue could be blamed on the old regime. A fresh start could be made in which the Panchen issue could be seen as a path to reconciliation.

It was a fine and optimistic theory, but I left with a powerful sense of apprehension. Even if the death of Deng did change the atmosphere in Beijing, the weaker leadership that seemed likely to follow Deng would have less freedom to pursue compromise than Deng himself. His successor was likely in the first instance to draw his legitimacy from the blessing of the patriarch and even if, eventually, the line changed, it could take years. What would happen in the mean time to the little boy in Nagchu? What would happen, indeed, to Chadrel Rinpoche?

There was one precedent that offered some slight hope: in the case of the Karmapa, the child was discovered in Tibet by two members of the search party who had submitted the child's name to Beijing for approval. Once that approval was assured, they had consulted the Dalai Lama. The Dalai Lama confirmed the child and made the announcement, before Beijing did. Perhaps Beijing had held back out of deference to religious sensibilities. If so, then just maybe, a prior announcement by the Dalai Lama would be better received by the Chinese than I feared.

Meanwhile, there was, I learned, another worry. In Chadrel's protracted absence, there had been consultations with other trusted figures. From one of them, a rumour had reached Dharamsala that a lottery was being prepared in Tashilhunpo monastery: it would be held very soon, the rumour went, and the results announced immediately. If the rumour was well founded, then the game had changed again. Not only might Beijing steal a march on the Dalai Lama, which would upset the exile community, but there was also at least a possibility that a child chosen by such a lottery might be the wrong child.

There was anxiety, too, about the date on which the Chinese would make the announcement. In Dharamsala it was feared that they would choose 23 May, the anniversary of the signing of the Seventeen-Point Agreement, a date that would stamp the choice with the political authority of the Chinese to the detriment of its religious significance. But the only way to prevent that was to announce first, and the only auspicious date available was the anniversary of the birth and enlightenment of the Buddha, the date of the next full moon, by the Tibetan calendar, 14 May.

It seemed imperative that, at the very least, Chadrel should be warned of what was about to happen. I knew that every effort was being made to contact him. If that was not possible, would the announcement go ahead as planned? And if Chadrel said no, what would happen next?

In the days that followed, efforts to contact Chadrel continued. After several fruitless attempts, a message was relayed to an associate, who, realizing its importance, promised to reach Chadrel by whatever means were possible. The announcement, he was warned, would be made on 14 May, if Chadrel did not forbid it.

In Dharamsala, they waited all week. The phones went down. A junior official was sent to Delhi to try to make a phone call, without success. Late in the morning of Saturday 13 May, the eve of the Buddha's birthday, the Dalai Lama turned to his final resource, the method he had used repeatedly when faced with an impossible decision: he cast a divination. Was it the moment, he asked, to announce the choice of the eleventh Panchen Lama? The answer came back. It was.

On the morning of Sunday 14 May the Dalai Lama got up early, as usual, and spent the first hours in prayer. The night before, a heavy full moon had bathed the mountain landscape of McLeod Ganj in a clear silver light. But the Dalai Lama, suffering the effects of a cold, was feeling feverish and short-tempered. It was going to be a demanding day. The sun was already up as he consulted his spiritual protector, the Nechung oracle, over the step he was about to take. Then he made his way through the early morning air to the hall of ceremonies in his hilltop compound. Waiting for him there was a hastily assembled collection of dignitaries in exile: luminaries of his cabinet, the medium of the state oracle and prominent lamas of the Gelug and Nyingmapa sects. Amchok Rinpoche, the acting head of Ganden monastery in the south of India, who had himself been recognized by the late Panchen Lama, was also there, as was the head of the search committee of the Tashilhunpo monastery in exile.

It was not a large crowd, but it included most of those whose opinion the Dalai Lama had to respect in the secular and religious balancing act that is his government in exile. At 8.30 a.m., seated cross-legged on his throne in the gilded hall, facing the rows of seated monks, he read a simple prayer that he had written for the occasion. He asked that Tibetans everywhere learn and recite it. It was a prayer for the long life of a six-year-old boy whose photograph was displayed to the Dalai Lama's right, a boy who, at that moment, was at home with his family in the sparsely populated region of Nagchu in Tibet. That was how the Tibetan community in exile, the Chinese government and the boy himself came, finally, to hear the news that Gedhun Choekyi Nyima had been chosen as the reincarnation of the Panchen Lama. For all of the major participants, the moment was to mark an irrevocable change of fortune.

The deep, melodic resonance of chanted prayers filled the hall. The boy's religious name, the Dalai Lama said, would be Tenzin Gedhun Yeshe Thrinley Phuntsog Pal Sangpo. As the ceremony continued, a hastily drafted press release was despatched from the department of information:

Today is the auspicious day when the Buddha first gave the Kalachakra teaching. The Kalachakra teachings have a special connection with the Panchen Lama. On this auspicious occasion, it is with great joy that I am able to proclaim the reincarnation of Panchen Rinpoche. I have recognized Gedhun Choekyi Nyima, born on 25 April 1989, whose father is Konchok Phuntsog, and mother Dechen Chodon, of Lhari district in Nagchu, Tibet, as the true reincarnation of Panchen Rinpoche.

The press release detailed the Dalai Lama's attempts to negotiate the process with the Chinese government, the succession of offers and messages that had received only one brief response. It mentioned, without naming him, TC Wu's visit the previous October and the reminders that had been sent in January. It did not mention two further messages, sent only the day before, both intended to warn the Chinese government that an announcement was imminent: the Dalai Lama's office had telephoned both TC Wu and Gyalo Thondup in Hong Kong, asking them to contact Beijing urgently to advise them of what was about to happen. The message, I confirmed later, had been passed to Beijing.

The ceremony in Dharamsala, so long awaited, was quickly over. The Dalai Lama retired to nurse his cold, and the select group who had witnessed the ceremony fanned out in the little town to spread the news. Fifty-year-old Amchok Rinpoche was almost skipping with delight as he left the assembly hall. He had had a close and personal bond with the late Panchen Lama: the Panchen had recognized him as the fourth Amchok Trulku, and despite having lived much of his life in exile, he had been invited to teach in the Panchen's school for reincarnates in Beijing in the eighties and had got to know him well. As he made his way down the hill, he was looking forward to renewing his friendship. 'I wonder,' he thought, 'if he will recognize me.' The last time the two men had parted, the Panchen Lama had predicted that they would meet again. 'You will come and work for me,' he had said. Now Amchok was convinced this prediction would come true.

The community in exile, with their unshakeable faith in the Dalai Lama, had no doubt, at first, about the wisdom of the announcement. Only a tiny circle had been privy to the long and complicated process that had led up to it. Those outside this innermost circle assumed that the Dalai Lama's announcement meant that the child's future was assured. A rumour began to circulate, both in exile and in Tibet, that the child was already out of Tibet. It was not true.

Within a few hours the news of the announcement was the lead item on the Reuters New Delhi wires and Voice of America was preparing to broadcast an audiotape of the Dalai Lama's specially written prayer into Tibet itself. The following day it would appear in newspapers around the world. The representative's office in

Delhi was besieged with calls from the news organizations who were picking up the story and trying to make sense of it.

There were some injudicious statements made as the over-stretched staff tried to flesh out the meagre bones of what they knew. 'The Dalai Lama had been in contact with the parents,' one newspaper reported the Delhi office as saying. That was, the Dalai Lama stressed in private, emphatically untrue.

The statement the Dalai Lama released had been carefully con-structed not to reveal Chadrel's proposition, though anyone who knew about it could see the outlines in what had been revealed. The die was now cast, and all the Dalai Lama could do was to hope that the consequences would be as his advisers had predicted. The official statements from Dharamsala stressed that this was not a provocative but a conciliatory gesture. In any case, it was a huge gamble, and I was anxious to see what its effect would be in Tibet.

I tried to telephone Lhasa but could reach nobody, so I decided to go there myself. A few days later I left London for Nepal. By then, the forty-eight-hour silence with which Beijing had greeted the Dalai Lama's announcement had been broken. In Kathmandu, I learned that the foreign ministry spokesman had given the official Chinese response. They would not accept the choice. The Dalai Lama's representative in Kathmandu was moni-toring the news. The Chinese Buddhist Association, he told me, had also refused to accept the boy. He was philosophical about the news.

'I think they were taken by surprise,' he said. 'It's a panic reaction. But they also know that without the Dalai Lama's approval, the Panchen won't be accepted. If you are going to Lhasa,' he said, 'would you mind taking some copies of His Holiness's announce-ment and the special prayer? People will want to pray for the child.'

By Saturday I was in Lhasa. I called a contact. He sounded nervous. 'This is a very bad time,' he said. It was six days after the announcement.

When we met, he was tense and anxious, and he had good reason to be. As we drove along a main street in Lhasa, a motorbike came up to the driver's side, keeping pace with the car. The motorcyclist, who was wearing dark glasses, pointedly stared inside, holding his position for nearly half a minute before dropping back.

In the back room of one of the many bad Chinese restaurants in Lhasa, we ordered some food, which neither of us touched, and talked. Chadrel had been in Chengdu, waiting for a plane to Lhasa, when the news had broken.

'They moved too soon,' he complained. 'We thought it was going to be the 15th. Chadrel Rinpoche had been warned and was trying to get a message to them to say they should not do it. But the messenger was still on his way when we heard that the announcement had been made. We thought it was to be the 15th, but it was the 14th.'

'It was the Tibetan calendar,' I said. 'But I thought they were not going to do it unless Chadrel Rinpoche agreed.'

'He did not agree,' he said. His face was a mixture of bewilderment and pain. I thought of all these people had done and the danger they were now in. They had all acted out of religious devotion and now, it seemed, it had all been in vain. Chadrel had been caught in Chengdu, on his way back to Tashilhunpo, by the announcement. With his secretary and his personal attendant, he had been detained.

'After the announcement, they kept Chadrel Rinpoche in Chengdu, almost incommunicado. Someone managed to see him and found that they were putting enormous pressure on him to denounce the Dalai Lama. They suspect him of collusion. They want to know how the Dalai Lama got the name. He has refused to denounce the Dalai Lama or to reject the choice. Tell the Dalai Lama that.'

The proprietor of the restaurant pushed aside the curtain and started to refill our tea glasses. Behind us a window gave on to a small courtyard. We talked in whispers. I had a copy of the Dalai Lama's statement and the prayer but now I wondered whether it was safe to hand them over.

'Do you want them?' I asked.

'Yes,' he replied.

I pictured his car being stopped after I had left him, the incriminating documents being found. Long prison sentences for trivial offences were common in Tibet.

'If you don't want to take them now,' I said, 'I can keep them . . .'

'No, I'll take them,' he insisted. I handed them over and they disappeared into his pocket.

'Why was Chadrel so long in Beijing?' I asked.

'It was partly an argument about property,' he said, 'but that was resolved. It was a question of getting Panchen Rinpoche's property back and they had come to an agreement with his widow. They had sent back most of the things they had asked for to Tashilhunpo.'

'So what was the hold-up?'

'It was over the choice. Everything had been going quite well, then a rinpoche got suspicious of Chadrel – a man who had his own candidate. He said that it shouldn't just be left to Chadrel and Tashilhunpo and there should be a ballot. There was a long argument about that and Chadrel Rinpoche tried to say that this was definitely the child and there was no need for a ballot. The rest of the group – eleven of them – came back to Tibet and the two of them stayed behind. They hadn't really won the argument but they were coming back with a plan: if they had to have a ballot, they were going to put just one name in. They were coming back to do this when the announcement came.

'This rinpoche,' he continued, 'he went to Tashilhunpo to try to talk to the monks, but they threw him out. Chadrel Rinpoche hasn't been tortured yet. He probably won't be, but his secretary is with him, a monk called Champa Chung-la. I am worried about him because he isn't well known. He is more vulnerable. They might torture him.'

A mass of rumours was loose in Lhasa. Among them were some more reliable fragments of news. I was told that the child had been taken away, with his father, Konchok Phuntsog, a doctor at the Lhari district hospital and his mother, Dechen Chodon, a nurse. His elder brother, who, it seemed, had been recognized as the reincarnation of the Drubshah lama of Drigung monastery in 1991, had also vanished. The little family had been seen, in the custody of the security forces, in Nagchu, then Golmud. One story said that the police had tried to separate the child from his parents, but all three had resisted. In Golmud, they were put on a plane, and there all trace of them had vanished.

The area around Choekyi Nyima's birthplace in Nagchu, which risked becoming a site of pilgrimage, was now heavily patrolled, and people were strongly discouraged from going there. The volume of anti-Dalai Lama propaganda was at full blast. Thus far, at least, the plan seemed to be going very badly.

We sat in front of our now cold food. My contact shook his head. 'Chadrel Rinpoche said that whatever happens to him, he will never renounce this child,' he repeated. 'He wants the Dalai Lama to know that. You must tell the Dalai Lama that Chadrel will never reject the child.'

Five days later, the young manager of a branch of the late Panchen Lama's Gyang-gyen corporation from Dram, near the Nepalese border, was arrested. It was later announced that he had confessed to taking a message from Chadrel to the Dalai Lama. Two years later, he was sentenced to a prison term of two years.

Chapter Eighteen

✳

At the end of 1994 Tashilhunpo monastery had been singled out for praise as a model of the new relationship between the atheist state and the religious community. In the commendatory document, the monastery was praised for its 'long history of holding high the banner of patriotism and displaying the patriotic spirit of the late panchen lamas. It has also done a lot of dual work to safeguard the unification of the motherland and to enhance the solidarity of the nationalities.' Chadrel himself, as abbot of this model monastery, had been given an award for his management.

In one sense, part of this commendation still remained true. In July 1979 the Panchen Lama has been asked by a foreign journalist whether his recognition would depend on Chinese government approval. 'The Chinese emperor in the past,' he had replied, 'could not decide on a living Buddha, but could only approve of the person who had been chosen.'[1] Chadrel had fought to uphold that historical position.

But now, Chadrel had been absent for months and the atmosphere in the monastery was one of apprehension. The Dalai Lama's announcement on 14 May was to bring Chadrel's years of careful manœuvring crashing about his ears. Within weeks the monastery would be under martial law and the Dalai Lama loyalists purged from its management committee.

Despite Chadrel's absence and the prolonged uncertainty that surrounded the search, few of Tashilhunpo's monks had wavered from their belief that the Dalai Lama must choose the incarnation. They knew that there was an argument, that Chadrel said there was only one possible child, and that Sengchen was arguing that there were three candidates of equal strength. On 6 May Sengchen had visited the monastery to try to persuade the monks there that the Golden Urn must be used to choose from among the three. He had been shouted down and forced to leave.

The announcement, when it came, hit the monastery with the force of an explosion.

Tsering was a monk there at the time. Now he is in exile and speaks in whispers, as though afraid that his voice might carry over the mountains and incriminate the family he left behind. He remembers the elation that swept through the monastery when the news broke. 'When the Precious Jewel announced the reincarnation, the great majority of the monks and the people welcomed it as a wish fulfilled and were very happy,' he said. 'Many people began to celebrate secretly.'

But the happiness was short-lived. Two days later, Beijing rejected the choice. The day after that the monastery's leaders were summoned to the offices of the Shigatse district administration. There they were told that they must read out a denunciation of the Dalai Lama's announcement, which had been written by local officials. They were filmed for the television news and the images added to the steadily increasing mass of propaganda.

The following day the United Front, religious affairs and public security bureaus organized a fifty-strong work team to take up residence in the monastery. The term sounds innocuous, but a work team is one of China's most useful tools of repression. It is composed of interrogators whose task is to expose dissent by relentless questioning and political pressure, eventually either forcing it into the open or enforcing compliance.

The work group included the Shigatse party secretary, Samdrup, and representatives of the religious affairs bureau backed up by members of the security forces. Their task was to break the loyalty of the monks to the Dalai Lama and to Chadrel Rinpoche and to force them to denounce the Dalai Lama's choice. Finally, the monks were to be made to 'demand' the use of the Golden Urn to choose another candidate.

The work team organized 'study groups' in the monastery. Tsering, along with his fellow monks, was forced to take part. From 2 to 3 June, there were more than twenty meetings. The government's documents were read to the monks again and again. The monks were told to think carefully, but were not allowed to discuss their thinking. After the meetings they were questioned individually. Their answers were remarkably consistent: apart from the known Chinese agents, they supported the Dalai Lama's choice and rejected the Golden Urn.

'In the study groups, the monks were not allowed to voice their own opinions but had to sit there to listen to them say that the announcement made by the Precious Jewel was invalid and that the Panchen Rinpoche's reincarnation could only be recognized by shaking the Golden Urn,' Tsering recalls. The study groups now came to dominate life in the monastery. The monks were told that any monk in possession of a photo of the new Panchen Lama or the long-life prayer for him would be executed.

'The monks were very depressed,' said Tsering. 'They had a lot to say, but they knew that one wrong word could land them in prison.' The absence of Chadrel Rinpoche added to their depression: they had had no news of him, but already there were rumours that he was under arrest. The rumours were true, but for months they were officially denied as the Chinese foreign ministry insisted that Chadrel was 'ill' and undergoing 'treatment'.

Tsering remembers particularly vividly a meeting on 4 June. All the monks had been ordered to attend. The doors were closed and guarded by security police. The monks listened to the now ritualized reading of the government's document. But when it finished, the deeply respected figure of Ngagchen Rinpoche rose to his feet and asked to address the monks. Silence fell. Ngagchen was the head of the tantric college and had been a key figure throughout the search. If he were now to recant, then the government would have scored an important victory.

But Ngagchen did not recant. He told his audience that he continued to support the Dalai Lama's choice. He would not accept the use of the Golden Urn. He had seen important visions in the lake, he said, and when he had visited Gedhun Choekyi Nyima, he had found on his wrists the marks of the handcuffs that had been used on the late Panchen Lama. There were other mysterious signs on the child's body, he said, that put the choice beyond all doubt.

'So we asked the central government not to hold a lottery,' Ngagchen continued, 'because we had found the reincarnation. All we needed to do was to ask His Holiness the Dalai Lama to recognize him. We asked the Chinese government this several times.' The listening monks began to applaud. 'So we expect

Chadrel Rinpoche to come to the monastery very soon.' There was a roar of agreement. The meeting was hastily called to a halt. After it disbanded, the monks discovered that during that time Chadrel Rinpoche's quarters had been searched.

On 10 June the monks' dance festival began, but the meetings continued. That day, there was a new element. Phuntsog read what all the monks recognized as a denunciation of Chadrel Rinpoche, though it did not yet refer to him by name.

Outside, in the city of Shigatse, extra troops had been drafted in to keep the peace while the process of forcing the monastery to comply continued. The sight of armed troops patrolling the streets had been relatively rare: Beijing latterly had preferred less visible methods of coercion. Now it again became a commonplace as trucks full of heavily armed soldiers in riot gear began regular patrols. From Lhasa, too, came reports of armed patrols; unauthorized meetings and discussion of the Panchen issue were banned. Reports of popular resistance began to filter out. Posters appeared denouncing Chinese interference in the process.

'It is only the leader of the Tibetans and the World Peace Maker, the Dalai Lama, who can recognize the reincarnation of the tenth Panchen Lama' read one which appeared on 21 May. 'No one will accept political pressure from those devils who regard religion as a poisonous weed and who consider lamas and monks as wolves.' It was signed 'The representatives of the Tibetan people'.

Another, written on 19 May, rejected the use of the Golden Urn. 'It clearly shows that the Chinese tell lies to the whole world about Tibetan history. It makes all the Tibetans burn with anger.'[2]

At Tashilhunpo the authorities were having limited success. Bilung Rinpoche, a senior monk, and four others had rejected the Dalai Lama's choice. But the majority were holding out. On the night of 21 June Tsering and a fellow monk could bear it no longer. They ran away from the monastery and set off for Lhasa. The next day they were arrested. They were held in prison in Lhasa for thirteen days in conditions of virtual starvation, then transferred to a prison in Shigatse. Days of violent interrogation followed. Finally, they were transferred again, this time to Nyari, the main prison in Shigatse.

During their absence, the pressure on the monastery had continued. On 9 July a party of senior officials from the TAR government arrived in Shigatse. It included Ragdi,[3] Gyaltsen Norbu, Lobsang Tenzin, and the old enemy of Chadrel and of the late Panchen Lama, Sengchen Lobsang Gyaltsen. On the morning of 10 July the group went to Tashilhunpo monastery and told the democratic management committee that they had proof of contact between Chadrel Rinpoche and the Dalai Lama. They invited the committee to discuss this revelation. Shocked and fearful, the committee members stayed silent.

The next day was the first day of one of the monastery's major annual festivals – Dzamling Chizang or Universal Offering, the three-day display of the huge *thangka* paintings of the past, present and future buddhas (the Dipankara, Sakyamuni and Maitreya buddhas). The paintings are hung on the wall built for that purpose above the monastery and the *thangkas* are so large that some fifty monks are needed to handle them. That morning, the painting of the past Buddha had been displayed for three and a half hours. The next day, it would be the turn of Sakyamuni, the present Buddha.

There was another event that morning of 11 July. Chadrel's secretary, Champa Chung-la, who had been brought to Shigatse two weeks earlier, was interrogated and asked to confess. How, his inquisitors wanted to know, had Chadrel collaborated with the Dalai Lama? How had he sent his letters, and had he sent any other documents? Handcuffed and dressed in layman's clothes, Champa Chung-la 'confessed' to the local officials and to the democratic management committee that there had been contact. But he insisted that Chadrel had had nothing to do with the whole affair and that he himself had done it all, without Chadrel's knowledge.

Clearly under duress, he also 'confessed' that the Dalai Lama's recognition of the reincarnation of Panchen Rinpoche was 'incorrect policy' and they should have obtained permission from central government first, before making the announcement themselves, in Tashilhunpo monastery. He spoke for nearly an hour, and as he spoke his confession subtly changed into an affirmation of the choice. 'I just wanted,' he said, 'to ensure that we found the right child.' But despite Champa Chung-la's sincerity, the Chinese authorities now felt that they had an important body of evidence. That same afternoon they called a mass meeting of the monks.

Phun-la, the vice-chairman of the Tashilhunpo democratic man-agement committee, Chadrel's deputy and head of the monastery's security, presided. The meeting was held in the large courtyard, just behind the main gate. The ground had been divided into sections and a place assigned to each monk. The monk-informers, touting the walkie-talkies that are the badge of collaboration, had arranged the seating according to what they knew of their fellow monks' political views. They tried to separate them into different groups, perhaps so that they would be able to identify and control the ones most likely to make trouble.

The monks arrived in a truculent mood. They refused to be divided up or to sit in assigned places 'like soldiers'. They sat where they chose, and when the three Party leaders arrived, the monks greeted them with boos and whistles. There was a television crew present, to record the meeting for propaganda purposes: under Chinese instruction the meeting would be broadcast as evidence of the rejection of the Dalai Lama's choice by the monks of the Panchen Lama's monastery. But the monks were not inclined to co-operate.

Phun-la warned them not to move or talk during the meeting, not to turn their heads from side to side or to go to the lavatory. Any movement, he warned, would be interpreted as support for Chadrel Rinpoche. It was the first clear signal of what was to come. The importance of the meeting was underlined by the presence not only of the local party officials but also of the top hierarchy of the TAR party – Ragdi, Gyaltsen Norbu and Sengchen Lobsang Gyaltsen.

Samdrup, the Shigatse party secretary, rose to speak. In his hand was a fifteen-page document that had been prepared by Gyaltsen Norbu. He began to read. It was a detailed denunciation of Chadrel: he was accused of violating the tradition of the Golden Urn and of appealing to the central government, over the heads of the TAR government, for permission to allow the Dalai Lama to take the decision concerning the reincarnation. The central government's leaders, Jiang Zemin, Li Ruihuan and the leaders of the TAR had asked him frequently to finish the search as soon as possible, but he had delayed it. He had collaborated with the Dalai Lama and written him ten letters. He had gone to Beijing without informing the local authorities – a marked lack of respect. In Beijing he did not follow the rules for the recognition and showed a lack of respect to local city officials in Beijing.

They also accused Chadrel of having his own monastery – Oed-chen (Great Ray) – and of having come to Shigatse to provoke 'splittism'. He had been appointed to his present position as abbot by the late Panchen Lama, but he had betrayed the People's Republic of China, which had trusted him, given him high status as an outstanding member of the patriotic circles and had made him a member of the Chinese People's Political Consultative Conference at national level and a vice-chairman of the CPPCC within the TAR. A house had been built for him and a car worth 200,000 yuan provided.

As Samdrup read the litany of Chadrel's offences, the monks talked, shouted and protested. Several times, he had to stop and call again for order. When he finished, the monks bellowed 'Long live Chadrel Rinpoche.'

The filming was abandoned and the official party retreated to their cars. Some monks spat at them. As the convoy moved towards the main gate it came under a shower of stones. One car stopped as a stone bounced off its roof. A nervous official got out, retrieved the offending article, wrapped it in a handkerchief and hastily took refuge again inside the vehicle.

The monks were in angry mood as they left the meeting. Tsering remembers their reaction. 'They said, what is the point of being a monk in this monastery, if we cannot have our Panchen Lama and if Chadrel Rinpoche is under arrest? What is the point, either, of taking part in religious ceremonies, like the one that was to begin the following day?' That night, security personnel moved into the monastery and it was closed to the outside world. The monastery, and the town of Shigatse, waited uneasily for the dawn.

The next day was Dzamling Chizang, 12 July. Early in the morning, a group of some thirty tourists were waiting inside the monastery gates for the ceremony of unrolling the *thangka* to begin. At 9.30 a.m. three trucks crammed with police in riot gear arrived at the monastery and the tourists were bundled out of the main gate. The foreigners were escorted to their hotels and were later prevented by soldiers at roadside checkpoints from re-entering the centre of the town, where the streets had been cordoned off.

The huge monastery gates had been shut behind the indignant

tourists and remained firmly closed. By this time nearly five hundred people had gathered outside the main gate. They had come to take part in the ceremony; now they were witnesses to the monastery's resistance. From behind the gates, they could hear the monks shouting slogans demanding that the Panchen Lama be allowed to live in his monastery. They called on the townspeople to come and join them in the monastery compound. Five women who tried to enter were taken away by security forces.

Tibetans, including thousands who had come from the country-side to celebrate the three-day festival, were stopped from per-forming the *korwa*, the ritual of walking around the outside of the monastery, a ceremony which is considered particularly auspicious on Dzamling Chizang. The circumambulation path winds through hills overlooking Tashilhunpo and provides a clear view into the walled courtyards of the monastery. Inside, the monastery was in a state of rebellion. The religious ceremony was cancelled. As security personnel came and went, the cries of the monks continued. They shouted to the crowd outside to come in; they called out that they were being kept prisoner; they called for the release of Chadrel. As the townspeople kept vigil outside the main gate, they were steadily filmed from the vantage point of the Fruit Hotel, opposite the gates.

As darkness fell on the night of 12 July a running battle developed between the security forces and the monks. Just after midnight armed police raided the monk's quarters and twenty-seven monks were beaten, handcuffed and loaded on to trucks. They were driven to Nyari prison, where Tsering and his fellow detainees witnessed what happened next.

'We were asleep, when we were woken by loud noises. We looked out of the window and we saw monks from our monastery being brought in,' he said. They counted twenty-one. 'They were in a terrible state. They were handcuffed, their clothes were torn and they were covered in blood.' The group included many senior monks and several who had been personally close to the Panchen Lama. One of them, the fifty-year-old Gyaltrul Rinpoche, was a former member of the monastery's management committee and had been badly beaten. Shepa Kalsang[4] was a senior monk and had been the tenth Panchen Lama's secretary. Ngodrup, known as Champon (dance-master) Ngodrup, had been responsible for the monastic dance rituals. Ngag-khang Tenzin was in charge of the tantric temple at Tashilhunpo. All of them had been beaten. One of them, Dorje Gyaltsen, from Shigatse, was so severely injured that he was hospitalized, along with Gyaltrul Rinpoche, shortly after his arrest and spent the next nineteen days in hospital. In prison, the beatings continued until the monks 'confessed' their errors.

The day after the mass arrests, the police toured the Shigatse hotels, ordering tourists out of town. The road south from Shigatse was crowded with tourist minibuses and lone travellers attempting to hitch a lift. They were told, unofficially, that the town had come under martial law. Tibetans were told they could neither enter nor leave Shigatse.

In the days that followed the arrests the remaining monks were divided into two groups and the study sessions continued with even greater intensity. One group was clearly regarded as less reliable than the other and was subjected to three study sessions a day until they repeated the official mantra – that the child the Dalai Lama had chosen was not the true Panchen Lama. For the older monks the whole process revived traumatic memories of their sufferings in the 'democratic reform' movement and the Cultural Revolution. Some prayed that they might die quickly. Others faced their ordeal with determination.

The campaign against Chadrel continued. He was denounced as a traitor to the 'motherland'. He was officially removed from his post as head of the monastery's management committee, and in his place was appointed a long-standing enemy, Lama Tsering, a man whom the monks had long regarded as a Chinese puppet and for whom they had scant respect. They quickly nicknamed him the white crow – a particularly pejorative equivalent of the black sheep. Sengchen was appointed head of the monastery, the position filled, until his death, by the man against whom Sengchen had borne his long grudge – the tenth Panchen Lama.

A week after the arrests, on 18 June, another mass meeting was called at which the monks were collectively charged on three counts: their failure to perform the religious ceremony, their acceptance of the Dalai Lama's choice, and the fighting between the monks and the security forces. They were all instructed to write 500 words of self-criticism in recognition of these serious errors. They were organized into groups of seven and forced to discuss the issue with each other. Four army trucks were kept in the monastery to be ready for use at any time. The next day, one of the monks committed suicide. Those monks who refused to co-operate were beaten.

The monastery's new authorities had been picked for their loyalty to the Chinese – especially Lama Tsering, who had always supported the use of the Golden Urn. He was an elderly monk whose attitudes were formed at the time of the dispute between the Dalai Lama and the Panchen Lama. He had not changed them since. Now he urged that the resisting monks be dealt with severely.

Of the new committee, only Ngagchen, the head of the tantric college, was trusted by the monks. This time, they said sadly, he had been used like a towel for the Chinese to wipe their dirty hands on.

There were other arrests, beyond the confines of Shigatse and the monastery, now under military occupation. Throughout Tibet, the campaign against the Dalai Lama's choice was in full swing. In Lhasa, in late May, all leading figures in the Tibetan government and the religious hierarchy had been required to take part in meetings denouncing the Dalai Lama's statement. An emergency three-day session of the CPPCC issued a statement on 24 May describing the Dalai Lama's announcement as 'illegal and invalid'. Similar denunciation meetings were staged in each work unit and at all levels of government.

But as the campaign continued, it became evident that the more pressure was applied, the more private resistance there was. In conversations with foreigners throughout 1995 Tibetans insisted that they would never accept a Panchen Lama other than the Dalai Lama's choice. And the more the rumours circulated about Chadrel Rinpoche's role in the affair, the more his stature grew in the eyes of his fellow countrymen. On television, reports of meetings from all over the country tried to give the impression of a nation indignant at the Dalai Lama's action. But these were clearly recognizable as ritual affairs to people who had suffered decades of forced public acceptance of doctrines they abhorred. In private, it was another matter.

Of Chadrel himself, there was no news. The question was frequently put to the foreign ministry spokesmen by foreign journalists in Beijing. It elicited the standard response: Chadrel was ill and undergoing medical treatment.

The whole of the religious sector in Tibet was now under pressure. Gyaltsen Norbu, the chairman of the TAR government, had announced a purge of monasteries and nunneries in June to counter the influence of 'splittists', standard terminology for those who are loyal to the Dalai Lama. 'We must counter the infiltration of *splittist* groups inside our borders, carry out an effective struggle against them and handle troublemakers in a firm, resolute and timely manner,' he said. 'We must deepen our struggle against *splittism*, comprehensively boost our struggle against infiltration.' He reminded Party members that they were not allowed to believe in religion and now he added a new prohibition: they must not send their children to schools under the control of what he called 'the Dalai Lama clique'. Anyone found with subversive publications or pictures, by which he now seemed to mean photographs of the Dalai Lama, would be dealt with in strict accordance to law.

Thus far, however, though the Dalai Lama's actions had provoked a virulent rejection by Beijing, the child himself had not been rejected. The government's difficulty was that, although they were free to accuse the Dalai Lama of meddling in Chinese politics and trying to promote Tibetan independence, they were not free to nominate another candidate as the true Panchen Lama. To do so would have destroyed the carefully maintained fiction of religious freedom.

Since the beginning of the process, the government's case was that it was the religious hierarchy of Tibet that was charged with the task of identifying the reincarnation. This was to be done within a set of rules laid down by the government, rules that they claimed were in accordance with historical tradition and religious practice. The most important and disputed rules were, of course, that the final choice be made through the Golden Urn and sanctioned by the government. These last two stages were essentially political, not religious mechanisms, largely superfluous from a Tibetan religious point of view, but vital for the Chinese claim to historic sovereignty over Tibet.

But now a child had been chosen and the religious establishment was in turmoil. One of the most trusted religious figures, asked to choose between his faith and his political loyalty, had opted for faith. How many others would do the same? To proceed with the original plan the Chinese required the co-operation of the religious hierarchy. It was they, after all, who were needed to satisfy the requirements of religious practice. But the hierarchy was split. Accustomed as they were to Chinese political oppression, they were still reluctant to violate their consciences publicly in such an important religious matter.

Chadrel still held the key to the process: if he could be coerced into recantation the process could be resumed, albeit in a more than slightly tarnished fashion. As late as 21 August a senior Party official told journalists that Chadrel was 'in hospital' and that he had been 'ill' since May. The official, a deputy director of the United Front, said, 'I can't say where he is but he is in good shape and his health conditions are getting better.' He was unable to say what illness Chadrel Rinpoche was supposed to have been suffering from and declined to say where the hospital was. Western diplomats who enquired were told that Chadrel had 'completed his education', a euphemism for interrogation, and that he would be continuing his work in the official search committee for the reincarnation of the Panchen Lama.

But despite the months of interrogation and coercion, Chadrel remained true to his last message to the Dalai Lama. He had sworn that he would never deny the choice of Gedhun Choekyi Nyima and he did not. With Chadrel continuing obdurate, the Chinese had been forced to change the Tashilhunpo leadership for one more compliant. But still, they required the co-operation of several other senior religious figures if the process was to gain any credibility.

Particularly important were those directly associated with the Panchen Lama: the abbot of Kumbum monastery, Agya Rinpoche, the abbot of Labrang Tashikyil in Gansu, Jamyang Shepa, and the celebrated Amdo lama, Gungthang Rinpoche. Agya is an agile and successful religious leader, but he is not a man to rush to collaborate in a crisis. Gungthang is perhaps the most famous living Buddhist teacher, but he had already refused to take the leading role in the recognition of the Panchen Lama. Neither of them would be easy to persuade.

In July the government published a revised set of rules on how to respect 'historical precedent' in the search. It contained some elements of the original agreement, negotiated in 1989. In that agreement Tashilhunpo monastery had essentially won the right to conduct the religious side of the search free of political interference in return for conceding that the search would be confined to the People's Republic of China and the final stage would include the lottery and government approval.

Now, however, there was a different emphasis. According to the new regulations, five principles were to govern the search. The rules now said that patriotism should be upheld; Tashilhunpo monastery should be responsible for the work; the results must be 'reported' to the central government for approval; and the child should be trained and formally installed in Tashilhunpo monastery. For the Chinese government, the fifth rule, the use of the Golden Urn, was non-negotiable.

But the long silence over the legitimacy of Gedhun Choekyi Nyima's claim left some room for negotiation. If the Golden Urn was to be used, which names would be in it? Could the government be persuaded to take its chances by including Gedhun Choekyi Nyima and risk having the Dalai Lama's choice vindicated, provided they had successfully enforced their political point over the procedure? If Gedhun Choekyi Nyima was to be included, perhaps the world of Tibetan Buddhism could be pacified. If not, then it would come down to force. It took nearly six months, from the Dalai Lama's announcement, for the Chinese government to feel confident that they had re-established enough control to proceed.

Chapter Nineteen

✲

The Jingxi guest-house lies in eastern Beijing. It is a large building, of no particular distinction, protected by a high wall and large iron gates, customarily guarded by soldiers of the People's Liberation Army, the hotel's proprietors. To get to the main door visitors have to cross a wide-open area with the permission and under the eye of the guards. It is favoured, for the ease with which it can be rendered secure, by the Chinese Communist Party, who frequently hold high-level meetings there.

But the meeting that opened in the Jingxi guest-house on 5 November 1995 was not, formally, a Party meeting, though several prestigious Party figures were to put in an appearance over the next few days. Gathered there, under compulsion, were seventy-five Tibetans of whom approximately half were senior lamas. They had been told in no uncertain terms that attendance was obligatory. No excuse, not even one of illness among this elderly group, would be accepted. On 4 November they had been ordered to set out from their respective dwellings and arrive by 8.40 the following day, in Beijing.

The group included the leaders of the state-sponsored Buddhist Association and Tibet's most prominent lamas. Beijing needed their acquiescence, if not co-operation, for the next stage of the plan which had formed, with uncharacteristic slowness, over the last six months. Attendance at the meeting, the monks were warned, would be a 'test of your nationalism and your political stand'.

Absent from the meeting was Ngabo Ngawang Jigme, for decades the most prominent figure in Sino-Tibetan relations. Ngabo had demonstrated himself unusually unreliable as far as the Chinese claim to the historic right to nominate Tibet's religious leaders was concerned. It was Ngabo who had surrendered Chamdo and negotiated the Seventeen-Point Agreement for the Peaceful Liberation of Tibet in 1951. He had been rewarded with high official posts. He had survived all the vicissitudes of mainland politics, including the Cultural Revolution, unscathed. His children were in prominent jobs in the Chinese bureaucracy.

But Ngabo had also allowed himself some rare moments of dissent. Some years earlier he had disputed the Chinese claim that the enthronement of the fourteenth Dalai Lama had taken place under the supervision of a senior Guomindang official, Wu Zhongxin. There was, the government claimed, a photograph to prove it. Ngabo had discovered that the photograph had been taken some days after the enthronement, when Wu Zhongxin had been granted the favour of an audience with the child Dalai Lama. He concluded the claim was unfounded.

Nor was Ngabo any more reliable on the subject of the Golden Urn. Beijing was arguing in November 1995 that in 1940, after the Dalai Lama had been chosen, the Tibetans had asked for permission from the then Chinese government to dispense with the Golden Urn lottery. But in 1985 Ngabo had gone to Nanjing to consult the state archives and had concluded that this claim was also false.

'We were there,' he said in a speech to officials and scholars at the China Tibetology Centre in Beijing in 1989. 'And there was no question of using the Golden Urn – we all know that. There is no question of the Guomindang representative being send for to attend the enthronement or that he gave permission to instal the fourteenth Dalai Lama without using the Golden Urn,' he concluded.[1] His audience agreed, but Ngabo knew he was offending the new orthodoxy. 'I told the Chinese I could never change my words no matter what way they find to say,' he said. As the Chinese opened the conference of lamas in Jingxi guest-house, Ngabo, it was clear, would not be an asset to the proceedings.

The staging of the meeting represented in effect a collapse in the usual Chinese attention to presentation in matters concerning the troublesome minority nationalities, now deemed officially to be part of the happy family of nations that comprised the People's Republic of China. Security was both tight and obvious. Even those Tibetan lamas who lived in Beijing, several of whom attempted in the course of the week-long meeting to offer presents to the senior figures incarcerated inside the Jingxi, were not given access. There was no attempt to disguise the fact that the Tibetans were under extreme pressure.

There was unusually little attempt, either, to maintain the

impression that the decision that was to emerge was to be freely arrived at. When the announcement came it was marked by official photographs published in the Chinese media showing the Tibetans standing obediently behind President Jiang Zemin and Liu Huaqing, the deputy head of the central military commission, portentously dressed in full uniform. And in a hint of the bureaucratic confusion that bedevilled the government's attempt to present the meeting as a continuation of the process begun in 1989, it was described in subsequent official documents as the third session of the 'Leading Group for Locating the Reincarnated Child of the Panchen Lama', a group which had, in fact, not existed before the crisis emerged in May 1995.

Until the Dalai Lama's announcement the search had been under the direction of the government and its religious affairs bureau and nationalities commission, the government bodies responsible for Buddhism and for Tibet. Now the Party at its highest level had taken over direct control. It was to be announced on 13 November that Jiang Zemin and Li Peng had been directly involved in the Panchen Lama issue for some time. Later that month the official press revealed that, within the TAR, direct control of the Panchen Lama issue had been taken over by the TAR party in April 1994, a year before the dispute became public.

Now, yet another set of rules was published. Throughout this tortured process, the Chinese had tried to ensure that the search would not escape from their control by publishing ever more detailed 'historic' rules. The final set, which contained fourteen separate steps, was little more than a list of reports that had to be submitted to the central government for approval.

The fact that the Jingxi guest-house meeting was taking place was an open secret in the Tibetan community in Beijing. But, characteristically, the first the general public heard about it was on the evening of 11 November, the day it concluded, when the Central Television evening news ran its first report. Inside the conference room the rows of monks, eyes downcast, were shown listening. The meeting had agreed, the report said, 'to confirm the three candidates for the Panchen Lama chosen by the Tashilhunpo monastery'.

Since the leadership of the monastery had been hand-picked by the Chinese for its willingness to embrace the Golden Urn, the lottery was now inevitable. It was all, according to the news, in line with historical precedent and religious ritual. Or, as the *Tibet Daily* had put it more directly on 1 November, in accordance with two guiding principles: in religion 'it is most important to obey religious rules and historical precedents. In politics one must uphold patriotism and the leadership of the Communist party.'

There was to be a lottery. It only remained to be seen whether, finally, the name of Gedhun Choekyi Nyima would be included, and whether a religious figure of sufficient stature could be persuaded to conduct the lottery.

The answer to the first question came in the Xinhua news agency report of the proceedings the following day. 'Senior lamas at Tashilhunpo monastery said that . . . they would not recognize the reincarnated boy for Panchen Lama chosen by the Dalai Lama.' They went on to accuse the Dalai Lama of using 'fraud' to select the child and said that the child failed 'to meet the conditions'. Li Ruihuan, a member of the Politburo standing committee, added his own charges: the Dalai Lama, he said, had added the child's name 'illegally' to the list of candidates after the closing date.

The rejection of Gedhun Choekyi Nyima left the government with the problem of what to do with their six-year-old prisoner. One senior lama who attended the meeting summed it up, with characteristic accuracy. There were three alternatives, he said. The government could kill him, banish him or imprison him without a trial.

There were clues, too, as to how eager the Chinese were to have done with this troublesome affair. The meeting had been told by no less a figure than the Party secretary Jiang Zemin that 'the search would be completed soon, if they make persistent efforts.' Li Ruihuan urged them to 'complete their work at an early date'.

Attention now shifted to the lottery itself. One measure of the complexities of presentation the lottery involved was the secret day-long rehearsal of the lottery that had been held in August in the Jokhang temple. On that occasion, it was conducted by Dedrul Rinpoche, a successor of a former regent and himself a former candidate for Dalai Lama. The ceremony was filmed by Chinese television crews, though the film was never shown. It was, perhaps, held in reserve in case of trouble at the real ceremony, which was now under urgent preparation and which was also to take place in the Jokhang temple.

Chinese propaganda, of course, insisted that the Golden Urn was an indispensable part of the process, sanctified by historical precedent. But history, in this case, had been shamelessly rewritten. In fact, the Golden Urn ceremony had only been held in the Jokhang temple in the case of some junior incarnations. The urn had been used to select dalai and panchen lamas five times between 1822 and 1888, but though the Qianlong emperor's original instructions had specified that the ceremony should be held before the great statue of Sakyamuni in the Jokhang temple, in fact it had been held in the Potala palace, the residence of the Dalai Lama. On those occasions, the winning lot had been drawn by the Chinese *amban*, using ivory chopsticks. Now, the Potala was empty but for armed guards and tourist groups, and there was no *amban*. The highest representative of the Chinese government in Tibet was the party secretary of the TAR, a Chinese. But given that this was a propaganda exercise to demonstrate religious 'freedom', to invite the party secretary to draw the winning lot would hardly do.

There were other difficulties: on the rare occasions when the urn had been used to settle a disputed claim, it had been incorporated into Tibetan divination ritual and preceded by six days of prayers. If Beijing wanted a ceremony in accordance with historical tradition, some hasty invention would be required.

After the decimation of the ranks of senior religious figures by exile and political repression, there had been only three lamas whose rank corresponded to the rules laid down for the use of the Golden Urn by the Qianlong emperor in 1792, Retring Rinpoche, Tsomonling Rinpoche and Phagpa-lha Gelek Namgyal. Retring Rinpoche was considered one of the highest-ranking lamas left in Central Tibet until his death in 1997, though he suffered from a mental illness as a result of prolonged ill treatment during the Cultural Revolution, when he was only sixteen years old. There are a number of possible reasons why he was not chosen – he had been married, and perhaps he was considered insufficiently learned to act as the child's tutor. He might also have refused.[2] Tsomonling Rinpoche, when last heard of in the sixties, had been working as a fisherman. Phagpa-lha Gelek Namgyal, whose son was a convicted murderer, was himself a womanizer and a gambler; unlikely, therefore, to carry much conviction as a knowledgeable religious practitioner.[3]

Just after midnight, in the chilly first moments of 29 November, Lhasa was plunged into a power cut. In the darkness, armed police were stationed on the roof of the Jokhang temple. An hour later, the rest of the company assembled in the dim interior: several hundred monks under duress, and government officials, tasked with upholding the authority of the state. The high rank of several, including Luo Gan, secretary-general of the state council, and the chairman of the TAR, Gyaltsen Norbu, who had been given the hastily invented title of 'special commissioner' for the event, was an indication, if it were needed, that the government attached great importance to the ceremony that was about to be staged.

Among the monks were the new leadership of Tashilhunpo and a man who had just been promoted to the post of Acting Ganden Tripa. The Ganden Tripa is the nominal head of the Gelugpa order, the highest post among the Gelugpa. The Ganden Tripa had fled into exile after the 1959 uprising, but in 1988 monks in Tibet elected a respected lama, Bomi Rinpoche, to the post of Acting Ganden Tripa. The election had provoked a stand-off with the Chinese, who had refused to acknowledge Bomi's title. The problem was not with Bomi personally, but with the fact that the word 'acting' implied deference to the Ganden Tripa in India, who was, from the Chinese government's point of view, a traitor and therefore a religious non-person.

Now, however, such quibbles had been set aside as the Chinese government wrestled with the problem of how to give their ceremony religious credibility. To allow Bomi Rinpoche to use his title would elevate his ecclesiastical prestige. Bomi Rinpoche was a respected scholar, and even without his overnight promotion, a man of high status. In the absence of a better alternative, he had been chosen to perform the ritual. It is unlikely that Bomi accepted willingly. Sources suggest that he saw it as an act of self-sacrifice. He knew that, eventually, somebody would be coerced into it and, as an elderly man, he preferred to bear the consequences of defying the Dalai Lama's wishes himself, rather than see a younger person suffer. Besides, he knew that if he agreed to perform the ceremony, he would be appointed the boy's teacher and would have the opportunity to exert an influence on the child.

The officials, all of them Party members and therefore atheists, emphasized their dominant role by taking their seats on chairs, rather than sitting, as the Tibetans did, cross-legged on the floor. They had not, as television audiences throughout Tibet were to notice later, troubled to remove their shoes, as tradition demanded. It was still only 2 a.m. when Luo Gan rose to his feet to read a state council document approving the three candidates whose names were placed in the urn. Gyaltsen Norbu then announced that the ceremony had begun.

The three ivory tallies inscribed with names were solemnly inspected by all the officials and by the parents of the three children. Ye Xiaowen, the director of the government's religious affairs bureau, pronounced them 'correct' and gave Lama Tsering, the new head of the Tashilhunpo democratic management committee, permission to wrap them in yellow silk and place them in the urn. Tsering shook the urn like an oversized cocktail-shaker and placed it before the statue of Sakyamuni. Bomi prostrated, then drew out a tally and handed it to the 'special commissioner', Gyaltsen Norbu, who read out the winning name. The officials burst into loud cheers.

The boy who had been chosen, no doubt coincidentally, bore the same name as the TAR chairman. The Chinese government had its Panchen Lama, or as the official media were to put it, with the atheist's sensitivity to religious sentiment, Gyaltsen Norbu had the 'lucky number'.

With unusual haste they proceeded immediately to the tonsure – the first step towards monkhood. The child was given the religious name Jetsun Lobsang Chamba Lhundrub Choekyi Gyalpo Pe Zangpo. Bomi Rinpoche was duly appointed to the key position of the child's teacher. To nobody's surprise, the state council approved the choice later in the day, a decision solemnly conveyed to the child that afternoon by Luo Gan. He passed on to the boy the congratulations of the Party leaders Jiang Zemin, Li Peng, Qiao Shi and Li Ruihuan.

The ceremony sealed the fate of two small children: Gedhun Choekyi Nyima, who would continue to be the object of devotion for all Tibetans who honoured the Dalai Lama and, as such, now in the tragic position of being condemned to permanent confinement; and Gyaltsen Norbu, a six-year-old child from the same region of Nagchu, the son of two Party members, now destined to be enthroned in Tashilhunpo monastery over the profound objections of the monks and of the majority of religious Tibetans. Neither child had chosen his fate and neither was to be envied.

The choice of Gyaltsen Norbu was convenient in a number of ways, which led to suspicions that perhaps his selection was not entirely a matter of luck. He was born on 13 February 1990, more than a year after the death of the tenth Panchen Lama. Choekyi Nyima was born in April 1989, and the Chinese were later to claim that even this date was false: he had been born before the death of the tenth Panchen Lama and his parents had lied about the date. After all, the government's case ran, a child born before the death could hardly be an authentic reincarnation, having failed to fulfil the regulations on the minimum number of days in *bardo*.[4]

It was, from the Tibetan point of view, a misguided argument. As the Panchen Lama himself had told a group of *trulkus* only a few days before his death, 'The seventh Dalai Lama was born before the death of the sixth Dalai Lama. From the point of view of our spiritual tradition, there is no need for a year to pass before the reincarnation is born. A realized being can manifest himself in many forms at the same time. He need not rely on the passage of his previous body's consciousness. Premature and belated birth of reincarnation is possible in Buddhism.'[5]

Gyaltsen Norbu was from Lhari, in Nagchu, the same area which had produced Choekyi Nyima. If the visions in the lake were reliable, therefore, both boys satisfied the requirement that they come from the north-east of the monastery. But unlike Choekyi Nyima's, Gyaltsen Norbu's parents were both members of the Communist party. Given the new strictures against Party members observing any religious belief, the recognition of their son as a reincarnate lama in any other circumstances would have landed the unfortunate couple in hot water. To date, however, their 'deviation' from this particular rule has gone unpunished.

In another departure from orthodoxy, the official press now set about publicizing the kind of miraculous evidence that had rarely graced the pages of any Communist party newspaper and would, in other circumstances, have merited the labels 'rumour-mongering' and 'feudal superstition'. The boy's birth, it now seemed, had been accompanied by a series of remarkable events. The people who came to see the boy 'beamed with happiness' and they commented in private that the child 'might be the incarnation of a god'. Several months after his birth a bird with the beautiful wings of a peacock was observed – no doubt to the astonishment of any watching ornithologists in the chilly regions of Nagchu – flying around the house for several days and nights. Finally this exotic avian visitor nested on the roof that now sheltered the infant Gyaltsen Norbu.

At the tender age of eight months, according to the official press, another sign was observed by the child's mother: the sacred letter *Ah* appeared on his tongue – an alarming development for a member of the Party. Perhaps inspired by this manifestation, the child's mother dreamt that one of Tibet's most honoured guardian deities, Palden Lhamo, was cradling the boy in her arms.

In Dharamsala, the Dalai Lama issued a statement describing the Chinese action as 'unfortunate'. Since his own choice had been made in full accordance with religious tradition, he said, it could not be changed. 'At this moment,' he added, 'the safety of Gedhun Choekyi Nyima and his proper religious training is of particular concern to me. He has not been seen in public for some months and is reported to be in detention somewhere in Peking. I therefore appeal to all governments, religious and human rights organizations for their intervention to ensure the safety and freedom of the young Panchen Lama.'

A few hours later Beijing issued a long attack on the Dalai Lama's six-year-old nominee. The boy, it said, had 'once drowned a dog'. His parents were 'notorious for speculation, deceit and scrambling for fame and profit', and the family's attempt to 'cheat the Buddha would not be allowed by all ordinary pious Tibetans'. In case ordinary pious Tibetans themselves took a different view, possession of photographs of the child, and of the Dalai Lama, had been banned. A foreign ministry spokesman then insisted that the child had suffered no ill effects or problems as a result of his recognition by the Dalai Lama. He declined, however, to give any assurances about the boy's welfare or his whereabouts.

The next day Chadrel Rinpoche was named publicly for the first time by the Chinese authorities as a collaborator in the Dalai Lama's plot to split the country through the choice of the new

Panchen Lama. The campaign that now began marked a further escalation of a dispute that, until this moment, had been, at heart, about China's struggle to demonstrate the legitimacy of her occupation of Tibet by insisting on the fiction that China had always chosen Tibet's religious leaders. That right had been asserted by force and Chadrel, whose absence was, until that day, explained by his mysterious 'illness', had lost his long battle to uphold his religious conscience. Now his 'illness' was forgotten as the campaign to vilify him not just as a man who had made mistakes but as a criminal began.

This was the first public campaign against a senior Tibetan figure, let alone a religious leader, since at least 1980.[6] The Chinese attempted rapidly to correct the damage caused in the international media by the denunciation of Chadrel Rinpoche, and a statement was given in the next foreign affairs press conference.

In the week following the lottery, a series of background statements by senior figures were published, outlining the government's steadily hardening position on the role of religion in the People's Republic. On 24 November Phagpa-lha Gelek Namgyal, the senior, though not widely respected, religious figure and chairman of the TAR branch of the Chinese People's Political Consultative Conference, had told 'upper strata' Tibetans that in the coming campaign they would be judged by their performance in criticizing the Dalai Lama:

The struggle to expose and criticize the Dalai [sic] is a serious political struggle. Chinese People's Political Consultative Conference (CPPCC) at all levels in Tibet must follow the instructions of the Party Central Committee and the Regional Party Committee and boldly call on and organize CPPCC members relentlessly to expose and criticize the Dalai's schemes and crimes of splitting the motherland. All CPPCC members should participate in condemning the Dalai both orally and in writing. No matter what their rank, they must maintain a firm, clear stand. That is because their stand regarding the issue of exposing and criticizing the Dalai is a major political question that serves as the main basis for determining whether the political orientation, stand and viewpoint of CPPCC cadres, particularly high-ranking cadres, including CPPCC members, is correct; whether cadres can distinguish between right and wrong; and whether their political acumen is strong or weak. At the same time it also serves as the main basis for determining whether patriots are worthy of the name. The people will judge your practical performance in this serious political struggle; they will judge whether you side with the party and the people and play a positive role in matters of great importance at a critical juncture.

The speech was delivered to the members of the CPPCC, a committee on which all Tibet's major lamas set. The government was now demanding that all of Tibet's religious leaders repudiate the Dalai Lama. There could be no more divided loyalties. They would be required, specifically, to condemn the Dalai Lama's 'crimes' of undermining the search for the Panchen Lama and to criticize Chadrel, who had 'colluded'. They would be asked, too, to negate the Dalai Lama's choice and to affirm the necessity of the Golden Urn lottery and the government's rules.

Gedhun Choekyi Nyima and Chadrel Rinpoche were now to be publicly vilified by the official media and became the subjects of criticism sessions throughout the TAR. The Chinese had their Panchen Lama. Now they were determined to stamp out any loyalty to the rival candidate. The Panchen Lama dispute had thus been transformed from a crisis of sovereignty to a nation-wide loyalty test.[7] It was a test in which the official aim now became to remove the influence of the Dalai Lama from religious as well as from political life – to eliminate him not only as a focus for nationalist sentiment but also, implausibly, as a religious leader.

Phagpa-lha's speech carried a warning about what would happen to the practice of Buddhism if these instructions were not heeded:

The Dalai's [sic] behaviour has not only run counter to the fundamental interests of the people of the whole country, including the people of Tibet, but also runs counter to the dignified and deeply felt religious rituals of Buddhism. If his words are followed, Tibetan Buddhism will be led on to a path of going against the interests of the people and the laws of the country, thereby endangering its due position and future in Chinese society. Therefore, what the Dalai has done is not for love of Tibet and love of religion as he has advertised; but, on the contrary, is an out-and-out calamity for Tibet and religion. Only by adopting a clear-cut stand in waging a struggle against the Dalai clique to wipe out his influence totally can Tibet enjoy long-term stability and can Tibetan Buddhism establish a normal religious order in a better way.

In the language of the campaign the Dalai Lama was described as 'the biggest obstacle to the establishment of a normal order for Tibetan Buddhism', and Chadrel Rinpoche and his supporters became 'the scum of Buddhism'. On 11 December the government announced that the Dalai Lama was 'no longer a religious leader'.

Tibet's monks and nuns had been faced with a stark choice: if their religious communities were to survive, they must repudiate the man who most felt to be their spiritual superior. Nor was that all. Under new guidelines on the role of religion, the Chinese government announced that, henceforth, patriotism would be the first condition by which any religion would be judged. This, they elevated to the status of universal truth:

In the history of China and in all the countries of the world that value their own independence and dignity, religious belief and patriotism have always been unified. A qualified religious believer should, first of all, be a patriot. Any legitimate religion invariably makes patriotism the primary requirement for believers. One can talk about love of religion only if one is a patriot. A person who is unpatriotic and has even rebelled against the country not only cannot be forgiven by the country but also cannot be tolerated by religion.

A week after the Golden Urn ceremony, the child, Gyaltsen Norbu, was enthroned at a heavily guarded and much publicized ceremony in Tashilhunpo monastery. Extra troops were drafted in to line the streets of Shigatse and to ensure the safety of the presiding Chinese official, the state councillor Li Tieying. Shortly after the ceremony, the boy was flown to Beijing. There he was filmed, exchanging *khatas* with a beaming Jiang Zemin.

The item was broadcast on Central Television's news programmes, as a final declaration of the success of the government's strategy. But the limits of that success became apparent when the boy was not returned to Tashilhunpo monastery. Instead, he was installed in the villa in Huairou county, on the outskirts of Beijing, which had belonged to Chen Xitong, the former Party secretary of Beijing who had fallen into disgrace in a corruption scandal.

The villa is now guarded by the People's Armed Police. It is a comfortable prison: it lies in a walled compound surrounded by wooded hills. Inside is a traditional courtyard house, an open-air swimming pool and an office building. But it is an odd choice for a child whose destiny was to be a religious leader in Tibet and it was one that the authorities seemed reluctant to acknowledge. Officially a spokesman for the Tibet Autonomous Region said he had no knowledge of the boy's whereabouts. The religious affairs bureau in Beijing said the same.[8] Were the authorities afraid for the safety of the child whom they now hoped would fulfil the hopes that his predecessor had disappointed and become the puppet leader of Tibet? Or was the confinement to remove him from the influence of the Tashilhunpo monks who might talk to him of the Dalai Lama?

In the outside world, there was a wave of protest at the Chinese actions. In Delhi, exiled Tibetans staged a protest meeting on 2 December, accompanied by hunger strikes and prayer meetings throughout the exile community. The French, Australian and European parliaments passed resolutions of condemnation, as did the US Senate. Such protests were unacceptable, said the Chinese government. The selection of the Panchen Lama was an 'internal affair'.

Chapter Twenty

✶

The abrupt disappearance of Gedhun Choekyi Nyima that May morning in 1995 dashed many hopes and left countless Tibetans bereft of the expectations that the recognition of the eleventh Panchen Lama had briefly inspired. And of all those Tibetans who felt deeply involved in the search for the boy, few could have been more disappointed than the little community of Tashilhunpo in exile. In early March of 1996, as I made my way back to the monastery, the reverse they had suffered seemed particularly cruel.

I passed through the lush elegance of Bangalore, with its flower stalls and its tropical scents, and down that long road through the gentle green landscape of Karnataka. As I arrived, the whitewashed walls and incense-burners of Tashilhunpo were washed in the faint apricot tint of the warm morning light. There was always something touching about this fragile community: the old men nursing their memories of the great monastery in which they had spent their youth, having pieced it together in paintings and rituals re-enacted in exile; the young men struggling to observe the monastery's discipline and to raise the money they needed to give their traditions a future. This time it was more poignant than ever: the monks were preparing for a symbolic enthronement of the missing child.

The palace they had hoped would house him was now nearly complete. The windows boasted freshly installed glass, the surrounding wall was built and the gardens were being planted. It was modest by the standards of old Tibet but it was a monument to the devotion and sacrifice of the monks. In the adjacent monastery, chairs and tables were being delivered for the ceremony which would take place two days later, timed to coincide with the anniversary in the Tibetan calendar of the day the tenth Panchen Lama had died.

I awoke the next day to the sound of the monks at early prayers. In the tropical morning the surrounding hills were still shrouded

in mist. As the day wore on the monastery came alive with preparations: coloured lights were strung from the balconies; and from
the kitchens on the floor below my room came the sound of
chopping and conversation as the Tibetans from the nearby settlements prepared the feast. Heaps of chopped garlic, carrots, cabbages and onions grew steadily bigger, and inside the kitchen, the
young monk in charge of the cooking was already bathed in sweat.
In the main courtyard bare-armed monks drove posts into the hard
ground with sledgehammers, erecting a frame for a huge blue and
white awning, which was already laid out. As the awning was
hauled into place over the frame, child monks swung from the
ropes like chattering monkeys.

At dawn on the day of the ceremony the monastery woke to the
deep notes of a long horn blown from the roof-top, and I could
hear the slap of sandalled feet as the sleepy monks ran to the main
temple. By seven o'clock the courtyard had filled up: old Khampa
men, veterans of the 1959 uprising, their long plaits now white but
still adorned with red tassels, sat next to elderly wives in long skirts
and striped aprons; in the rows behind, children in baseball caps
and jogging suits, little girls in traditional dress, local dignitaries
from the community decked out in their best clothes.

At 8 a.m. the ceremony began. The courtyard congregation
gathered around the flag-pole and each took a handful of *tsampa*.
As the monks intoned a prayer, the *tsampa* was thrown in the air.
The cloud of barley flour scattered, then rained down on the crowd.
Laughing, they brushed it off each other's hair and shoulders.

At the palace, the procession was assembled: the aged acting
abbot, a monk carrying a many-tiered and fringed yellow silk
parasol, others with drums and cymbals – all lined up to honour
the photograph of the missing boy. It was the same photograph
that I had first seen in a litter of snapshots on the Dalai Lama's
table that momentous day nine months earlier. Now it had been
enlarged into a ceremonial portrait, heavily framed and embellished
with painted robes.

Bearing the image shoulder-high, the monks walked in procession
from the palace, across the courtyard and into the temple, through
the ranks of believers, who bowed deeply as they passed. The
picture was placed reverently on the throne, beside a small pile of
neatly folded robes which had been made for the boy who would

never come. There it sat, flanked by photographs of the ninth and tenth panchen lamas, all three victims in their different ways of their country's troubled and ambiguous relations with China.

The congregation of monks and dignitaries took their seats on cushions flanking the aisle, and as the discipline master patrolled with a long, smoking incense stick which filled the air with fragrance, the deep voice of the chant-master struck up the prayer and was answered by the low melodious chorus of the monks. As the ceremony progressed, the faithful lined up to lay their offerings, one by one, before the photograph. Soon the image of the absent boy seemed to float in a sea of white silk *khatas*. By the time it was over, the boy's face was almost obscured, cocooned in these tangible manifestations of his followers' devotion.

As this distant exile community enthroned his image, the fate of Gedhun Choekyi Nyima himself remained a secret that the Chinese government was determined to preserve against all enquiries. Back in November 1995, when Tibet's religious élite was coralled in the Jingxi guest-house and obliged to reject the Dalai Lama's choice, the consequences for Gedhun Choekyi Nyima had been in the thoughts of many. However much the Chinese government would insist that another boy was the true incarnation, the fact that the Dalai Lama had named Choekyi Nyima ensured that his followers would always revere the boy. To allow him to return home to become the focus of that devotion was unthinkable.

Of the three options that one of the lamas present at the Jingxi guest-house had produced – killing, banishing or imprisoning the boy – the second would, of course, have delighted the Tibetan exiles. But the Chinese were not inclined to gratify the wishes of the Dalai Lama or his followers. The Dalai Lama, indeed, appealed to Beijing to permit the boy to leave and expressed his concern for the child's safety. The Chinese responded with prevarication and contradictory statements.

At first, the Chinese authorities pretended to have no knowledge of his whereabouts. In November 1995 a foreign ministry spokesman told journalists that 'Chinese officials have no idea of the whereabouts of the soul boy [sic] designated by the Dalai Lama.' In March the following year, Ragdi, the chairman of the Standing Committee of the TAR and, as deputy Party secretary, the region's highest-ranking Tibetan, claimed that the boy was 'with his family, happy and contented'. Ragdi gave his assurance that 'From now on, the government will send him to school and he will grow up like other Tibetan children,' and described reports that the boy had been detained as 'a sheer groundless fabrication. How can a little boy as young as Choekyi Nyima commit any crime and be imprisoned?' he asked, disingenuously.

It was not until May 1996 that the government acknowledged that they had, indeed, detained Gedhun Choekyi Nyima. It had been necessary, they said, for his own safety. The admission came during a session of the United Nations Committee for the Rights of the Child in Geneva. The committee was charged with assessing whether China had complied with its legal obligations under the Convention for the Rights of the Child, which China had ratified in 1991.

China's ambassador to the UN in Geneva, Wu Jianmin, was questioned closely by the committee. He was not, according to the committee vice-chairman, Thomas Hammarberg, very positive on the prospects of a peaceful solution to the Panchen Lama dispute, but the committee did force an acknowledgement from the ambassador that the Chinese government had him in their custody. He had, Ambassador Wu told the committee, been put 'under the protection of the government at the request of his parents'. The Chinese government, he claimed, considered the boy was at risk from 'kidnapping' by 'Tibetan separatists'. The ambassador declined to reveal where the boy was being held and a request that the committee be permitted to send a representative to visit him met with no response.

Two years later, in 1998, in a rare press interview, the veteran Ngabo Ngawang Jigme told the *South China Morning Post*'s correspondent, Jasper Becker, that he believed Gedhun Choekyi Nyima was living in the province of Gansu. The Chinese government has never permitted independent verification of the child's whereabouts or his well-being.

Beijing's Panchen Lama, Gyaltsen Norbu, had no more freedom of movement than Choekyi Nyima did, but as the Chinese invoked their propaganda to reinforce his credentials as the true incarnation, he did enjoy higher visibility. He was frequently featured in television reports that gave glowing accounts of his scholastic progress, his love for the 'motherland' and the devotion of his followers. His precise whereabouts, however, were almost as uncertain as those of Gedhun Choekyi Nyima.

After the lottery, in December, Gyaltsen Norbu had been taken, briefly, to Tashilhunpo monastery but had then been removed to Beijing, prompting speculation that the monks of Tashilhunpo were still unwilling to accept this candidate, who had been forced upon them. Then, as Ambassador Wu was giving his evidence in Geneva, nine months after the monks' protests and the mass arrests that had followed the Dalai Lama's announcement, China's official news agency reported that the boy had been returned to Tashilhunpo monastery.

The boy's visit to the monastery was made the occasion for more official celebration of his status and a reminder of the significance of his selection by the Chinese government: a nine-foot-long plaque bearing the legend 'Safeguard the Country and Benefit the People' in President Jiang Zemin's handwriting, was solemnly unveiled in a ceremony which figured prominently on the national news bulletin. Xinhua news agency reported that Gyaltsen Norbu 'thanked the president from the bottom of his heart'. The plaque, a present from this leading Communist, who was forbidden, by the Party rules, to hold any religious belief, was hung over the entrance to the monastery's main temple. To complete this surreal episode Xinhua's report continued, 'Tibetans sang and danced hand-in-hand in the courtyard to express their heartfelt gratitude for the care for Tibetan Buddhism from [sic] the central government and the Communist party.' The message to Tibetans was unmistakable: the religious sector was never to forget that it was permitted to exist only on sufferance and only to the extent that it acknowledged Chinese political supremacy over Tibet.

The following month, on 1 June 1996, the anniversary of the birth of the Buddha, a year after the Dalai Lama's announcement, there was further official publicity: Gyaltsen Norbu was to take his initial religious vows in a three-hour ceremony pointedly attended by senior government officials. The ritual afforded another opportunity to insist on the legitimacy of a child who was proving to be a worthy object of official attention. He was, it was reported, extraordinarily 'cute and smart'. Sengchen, now secure in his position as honorary director of the democratic management committee of the monastery, reiterated his determination to bring up the eleventh Panchen Lama as 'a great religious leader . . . devoted to Buddhism and the cause of safeguarding the country and benefiting the people'.

Despite these highly publicized celebrations of the milestones in Gyaltsen Norbu's career as the Chinese Panchen Lama, Sengchen's plans for the boy still did not seem to include permitting him to live in the monastery on a permanent basis, as tradition dictated that he should. Shortly after his initiation, according to Ngabo Ngawang Jigme, Gyaltsen Norbu was returned to his villa in Huairou, in the suburbs of Beijing.

In all these ceremonies, the presence of Party and government figures was a reminder of the real situation of the monasteries in the wake of the Panchen Lama dispute. They were the target of a campaign launched by the government which aimed to reduce the importance of religion in Tibetan life and to remind believers that religious practice would be permitted only to those who demonstrated their 'patriotism' – in other words, who rejected not only the political but also the religious role of the Dalai Lama.

A week after Gyaltsen Norbu's initiation into monkhood, the campaign intensified. An article was published in the *Tibet Daily* that called for a reduction in religious belief and asserted, in a troubling echo of a creed that had been all but forgotten in the rest of China since the death of Chairman Mao, that 'class struggle' was still a key factor in Tibetan affairs. Religion, the article said, was deceitful, backward and poisonous and, it warned, the monasteries had been allowed to grow in size and influence because many officials were not sensitive to the dangers that religion posed. In other words, even within the Party and government structures, Tibetans could not be relied upon to maintain the official policy of atheism. The task now was to re-establish the Party's creed internally and to strengthen the government's control of the potentially rebellious religious sector.

To do that, Beijing had to renew its efforts to weaken the influence of the Dalai Lama. New rules prohibited the display of the Dalai Lama's photograph, and the government ordered all such images to be removed from the public areas of Tibet's monasteries and from temples. It was a prohibition that caused deep distress in Tibet and provoked outrage in the main Gelugpa monasteries. The strength of the continuing loyalty to the Dalai Lama can be gauged by what happened in the key Gelugpa monastery of Ganden, near Lhasa, in May 1996 when the government attempted to enforce the ban.

The trouble began on 6 May when Party officials arrived at the monastery to try to remove all photographs of the Dalai Lama. The monks resisted, verbally at first, then physically. The security forces were summoned, and in the ensuing fighting, three monks were shot and wounded and sixty-one were arrested. Three days later, a further twenty-five monks were arrested at the monastery while one of the wounded, Kelsang Nyendrak, was reported to have died of his wounds.

A month later, according to the reports of court proceedings in Lhasa, fourteen of the Ganden monks, described in the official report as 'criminals from Ganden monastery', were found guilty of 'inciting monks to shout reactionary slogans, organizing illegal demonstrations, smashing up a police sub-station, beating up state functionaries, stubbornly following the Dalai clique, [and] vainly attempting to smash up the motherland'.

Their cases were dealt with under the rapid judicial procedures introduced as part of a major crackdown on law and order known as the 'Strike Hard' campaign. The campaign was a national one and, in the rest of China, it was concentrated on criminal activity. In Tibet, however, it also served as a cover for the repression that accompanied the attempt to bring the monasteries under control. The sentences the monks received were not published, but according to the reports, the Lhasa Intermediate People's Court 'adjusted major elements of the trial procedure and brought this case to a rapid conclusion, dealing a ruthless blow to the rampant arrogance of the splittists'.[1]

After more than three decades of trying to solve the problem of governing Tibet, and having failed to eradicate Buddhism, the Chinese government was trying, once again, to create a religious sector in Tibet that would not nurture nationalist sentiments or become the motor of political protest. The size of the religious sector was to be reduced: strict quotas were announced on the number of monks and nuns permitted in the monasteries and enforced by expulsion of any who exceeded that number. The construction of new monasteries was also to be controlled and those religious establishments that remained in business were told that they had to 'adapt to the socialist system', in other words, to obey the Communist party.

The new rules were widely resisted. The government's work teams began to visit monasteries to confiscate the highly prized photographs of the Dalai Lama and to demand guarantees from monastic leaders that they would ensure their monks and nuns took no part in any future demonstrations or protests. As they did so, reports proliferated of incidents in monasteries all over the country.

Outside the monasteries, too, there was trouble: in January 1996 a bomb exploded outside the house of the man who was widely regarded as the villain of the Panchen Lama story, Sengchen Rinpoche. Sengchen himself was not injured, but that bomb was followed on 18 March 1996 by another explosion outside the Party headquarters in Lhasa.

These were not the first bombs in Lhasa: the previous July, a Chinese monument in Lhasa had been damaged, and several more devices had been planted in and around the Tibetan capital in August and September, as the government was preparing to mark the thirtieth anniversary of the founding of the Tibet Autonomous Region. But the targets chosen were generally symbolic. The choice first of Sengchen's house and then of the Party headquarters as targets were much more direct acts of confrontation and indicated the strength of feeling that the Panchen Lama affair had provoked.

No Tibetan group claimed responsibility for any of these attacks, but the Chinese authorities continued to rail at the 'Dalai clique' whom they blamed for the 'sabotage'. At the same time, it was clear that the Chinese would not entirely rely even on the Tibetan security forces to be free of ambivalent feelings about this latest campaign. They were warned to guard against 'political, ideological and cultural infiltration of the Dalai Lama clique'.

Altogether, the Strike Hard campaign in 1996 led to the arrest and trial of 1,293 people in the TAR, of whom 1,173 were tried for 'severely threatening public order'. The same year, ninety-seven people were charged with state security offences and twenty-nine were executed.[2]

In tandem with its campaign to suppress devotion to the Dalai Lama, the government set about reinforcing the credentials of the two young incarnations whom they regarded as under Chinese control, no doubt in the hope that Tibetan Buddhist believers would transfer their allegiance to these relatively safe lamas. One, of course, was the young Gyaltsen Norbu. As the Dalai Lama's photographs were steadily stripped from religious institutions, a substitute was offered. In January of the following year the photograph of Gyaltsen Norbu was released, with great official fanfare, in a religious ceremony that marked the anniversary of his enthronement. Unlike the Dalai Lama's image, the new photograph of Gyaltsen Norbu, the *Tibet Daily* instructed, was 'suitable' to be shown at sites of public events and in people's homes.

Gyaltsen Norbu, the message read, was the real thing. The Dalai Lama, on the other hand, was described in ever more intemperate language as a 'fake' religious leader whose influence must be eliminated. In a meeting on legal work that year officials were told that the 'splittist' activities of the 'Dalai Lama clique' were a major cause of damage to social stability and the biggest impediment to the development and reform of Tibet. At the same meeting, the regional deputy Communist party secretary Guo Jinlong urged the police to strike harder at those Tibetans who continued to want independence. Stability in the TAR, he said, depended on official efforts to expose the Dalai Lama's 'pretence of being a religious leader so that all the masses and monks and nuns in the region are clear that the Dalai [Lama] is a political subversive and a religious sham . . . a traitor to the motherland, the scum of the people [and] the chief criminal of religion'. Patriotic instruction in the monasteries, he said, must be intensified.[3]

The second young lama whom Beijing was intent on promoting as a substitute for the Dalai Lama was the then eleven-year-old Karmapa. The Karmapa, who had been officially recognized by the Chinese government in 1991, was living in his historic monastery of Tsurphu, a remote and beautiful spot thirty miles north-west of Lhasa. There, he received the devotion of his followers every day.

The Karmapa had already been celebrated in Chinese official media as an example of a patriotic religious leader. In 1994 he had been invited to Beijing as a guest of honour during the National Day celebrations and in October 1995 his monastery was declared outstandingly patriotic and law-abiding by the Lhasa authorities.

At the same time as their Panchen Lama was promoted to

Gelugpa followers, the Chinese and Tibetan press began to attack the position of the Dalai Lama as the supreme religious symbol of Tibetan Buddhism. Articles were published attacking the idea that the Dalai Lama represented all schools of Tibetan Buddhism as opposed to just his own sect, the Gelugpa.

If this was an official attempt to inflame factional rivalry between the four schools of Tibetan Buddhism, it appears to have enjoyed mixed success. According to reports from Tibet, it was not only in the Gelugpa monasteries that the removal of the Dalai Lama's photograph provoked an angry response. In January 1995 the monks of the Kagyupa monastery of Yamure, ninety-nine kilometres north-east of Lhasa, unexpectedly staged their own pro-independence demonstration in reaction to the enforced removal of the photograph, a protest that reportedly led to a raid on the monastery by over a hundred troops. The same month, three monks from a Kagyupa monastery near Katsel, a village sixty-five kilometres north-east of Lhasa, were arrested after pro-independence posters appeared and 'subversive' literature was found in the monastery. In February that year, seven monks from the Kagyupa monastery of Taglung, sixty-five kilometres north of Lhasa, were also arrested. Even closer to home, five monks from the Karmapa's own seat at Tsurphu fled the monastery, having been accused of putting up dissident posters. After their departure, letters were discovered which accused the Chinese authorities of taking advantage of the Karmapa and expressed their rejection of the anti-Dalai Lama campaign.[4]

It was not only inside Tibet, however, that the Dalai Lama's religious status came under attack. He also had a number of serious difficulties in the exile world, which began, for the first time, to threaten to tarnish his image.

As far as the outside world was concerned, the trouble came to light through the activities of a Gelugpa dissident, Geshe Kelsang, who had left India to live in the UK. After a controversial passage he gained control of a spiritual centre in Cumbria in the north of England, from where he launched a campaign that appeared to be aimed at destroying the reputation and authority of the Dalai Lama.

The substance of the campaign was the right to worship a particular deity called Dorje Shugden. Dorje Shugden was a popular deity for many Tibetans. He had the reputation of being able to impart enormous good fortune to his devotees but also of being extremely vindictive and jealous. One of the Dalai Lama's tutors had encouraged the Dalai Lama himself to worship Dorje Shugden, but the Dalai Lama had decided, as a result of several dreams, that the deity was harmful. He gave up the practice himself, then banned it in all institutions that were connected with his person. This included Gelugpa monasteries and, of course, the government in exile.

There was some resistance to this edict in the monasteries in India, but the most visible and virulent campaign against it was conducted in exile on the direction of the Cumbrian centre. From Cumbria came a stream of anti-Dalai Lama invective which accused him of violating the religious freedoms of Dorje Shugden followers. It was a damaging charge against a man who had spent forty years pleading his country and his religion's case.

The origins of the Dorje Shugden dispute lie deep in Gelugpa politics and the controversy is too complicated to explore here. But the significance of it pertains to sectarianism in Tibetan Buddhism: the defenders of Dorje Shugden are characterized as Gelugpa fundamentalists who regard the Dalai Lama's association with other Buddhist sects – an association greatly strengthened in exile – as a betrayal of the Gelugpa. By insisting on worshipping the deity, they attack the Dalai Lama's authority as a true Gelugpa leader.

It was a controversy that the Chinese, of course, were happy to publicize inside Tibet, and although no direct connection between the Dorje Shugden campaign and the Chinese government can be proved, there is no doubt that it served Beijing's purposes well. In February 1997, for instance, the magazine *China's Tibet* published a two-page article in which the Dalai Lama was ridiculed as a 'self-styled believer in religious freedom' and attacked for his rejection of what the author described as an 'innocent guardian of Tibetan Buddhist doctrine'. The Dalai Lama had, the article claimed, 'declared a virtual war against a holy spirit of the Gelug sect'.

The vigour with which the Chinese attempted to eradicate the Dalai Lama's influence in the wake of the Panchen Lama affair can be explained, in part, by the government's fury at the role that

Chadrel Rinpoche had played in the search. For Beijing, Chadrel had appeared to be a model religious leader: he was strict with any Tashilhunpo monks who transgressed the rigid disciplinary code of the monastery – a code which had, of course, included strictures on political activity. He had been well rewarded in material terms and had been trusted as a model of the acceptable face of the kind of Buddhism the Chinese wished to foster. The government needed some functioning monasteries to display to the outside world as evidence of China's official claim to promote religious freedoms. Ideally, they would have enough monks and sufficient ritual to serve as an exotic tourist attraction, yet they would be loyal to the government and the Party and their leaders would enforce the prohibition on political dissent.

Chadrel had seemed an ideal figure in this scheme. The discovery that, in this crisis of conscience, Chadrel had risked everything to honour his religious faith was a shock to the government. They could draw only one conclusion from the affair: as long as the Dalai Lama lived and was revered as the supreme incarnate lama, no Buddhist practitioner, however compliant he seemed, could entirely be trusted.

Chadrel himself has not been seen since his arrest at Chengdu airport in May 1995. For months his disappearance had been explained as an illness, though the Chinese spokesmen who were repeatedly questioned about Chadrel's fate were curiously unable to be specific about the exact nature of the affliction from which he was supposed to be suffering. He had been criticized in the course of the suppression of the Tashilhunpo revolt, but it was not until the Jingxi guest-house meeting in November 1995 that the full fury of the government case against Chadrel Rinpoche was revealed.

In a long official denunciation Chadrel was accused of a treasonable conspiracy. Later, he was named as the target of a campaign to raise awareness of and to criticize what was officially described as a 'new and dangerous type of enemy' – one who is clever enough to disguise his disaffection.

It was not until the summer of 1997 that there was hard news of Chadrel's fate. He had been found guilty, an official announcement said, in April 1997 at a trial in Shigatse on charges of 'leaking state secrets' and 'splitting the country'. He had been sentenced to six years in prison and three further years' deprivation of political rights. His secretary, Champa Chung-la, was also convicted on the same charges and sentenced to four years' imprisonment and two years' deprivation of political rights. The third detainee, Samdrup, a 30-year-old former employee of the Gyang-gyen corporation, received a two-year prison sentence. Samdrup has since been released. Chadrel Rinpoche was recently reported to be in isolation and on hunger strike in Sichuan's number 3 prison.

The trial of the three men was held in secret, according to the official explanation, because the charges against two of the defendants involved 'state secrets'. They had been convicted under Article 92 of the Criminal Law, which deals with 'plots to subvert the government and dismember the State'. The nature of the 'state secrets' was not explained. Under Chinese law, defendants accused of 'conspiring to split the country', as Amnesty International swiftly pointed out, are supposed to be tried in public.

Ngabo Ngawang Jigme, who had survived this, as he had all previous crises, unscathed, gave the *South China Morning Post* his own version of Chadrel's conduct. 'I had talked to Chadrel Rinpoche and asked him to write a letter to the Dalai Lama to choose his own candidate,' he said, 'and that he could have that boy and the others registered as candidates when lots were drawn in the Jokhang temple. But the Dalai Lama suddenly announced that the candidate he chose is the true incarnation.'

Chadrel's mistake, he said, had been to exchange secret letters with the Dalai Lama and to ask the Dalai Lama to announce the selection. 'He must be under arrest now,' he added, 'but I don't know where he is. Chadrel made serious mistakes on this issue. If he had only written letters telling the Dalai Lama to select the boy as a candidate it would have been O K.'

The record hardly supports Ngabo's faith. Even before the crisis of the Golden Urn lottery Chinese attitudes to the Dalai Lama had visibly hardened. Besides, though this was, for the Buddhist believers, a dispute over which boy was the true incarnation of the Panchen Lama, on the political level this was a battle over authority and legitimacy. Ngabo's proposal would, at best, have offered the Dalai Lama a one-third chance of including his candidate in a lottery conducted under conditions that he could not control. In return for this doubtful privilege, he would have had to make the fatal concession of handing over to the Chinese the right to authenticate the choice.

There were several reasons why the Dalai Lama would have found such a proposition unacceptable. It ignored the undisputed historical fact that the Golden Urn had been presented with the express purpose of resolving the selection in cases where there was a genuine doubt. On this occasion both the Dalai Lama and Chadrel were convinced they had found the right candidate. Besides, when it came to the Jingxi guest-house meeting, Gedhun Choekyi Nyima was ruled out of the lottery there on the grounds that he 'had not fulfilled the criteria'. Given the political tensions in 1995, there is no guarantee that the government would ever have agreed to the inclusion of a candidate known to be supported by the Dalai Lama.

Despite the highly visible and damaging confrontation with Tibet's religious community, Beijing seemed satisfied that it had come out on top in the Panchen Lama dispute. In November 1997 Tibet's party secretary Chen Kuiyuan told the monks of Tashilhunpo monastery that, 'Finding the new Panchen Lama was a great victory for us in opposing the political conspiracy of the Dalai Lama to split our nation. Now that we have cleared up the small number of splittists,' he told them, 'you must all hold high the banner of patriotism and unity.'[5]

But a few months later another incident, little publicized in the West but potentially a serious embarrassment for China, provided further evidence that the Chinese candidate has won little acceptance in Tibet. Fearful, apparently, that the boy would never be safe living in his own monastery of Tashilhunpo, the Chinese government ordered the abbot of Kumbum monastery in Qinghai, the subtle and diplomatic Agya Rinpoche, to make a permanent home for the boy at the monastery, where the Chinese could point to his pursuit of the religious life as evidence that all had turned out well. Agya refused, and when Chinese pressure grew insistent, he left the country, the second of Beijing's apparently compliant senior Buddhist figures to abandon everything rather than collaborate over the Panchen Lama dispute.

Argya's defection was only to be upstaged by another that was even more dramatic. In the summer of 1999, the seventeenth Karmapa was taken to Tashilhunpo monastery to pay his respects to Gyaltsen Norbu, then on his heavily guarded visit to Tibet. It may have proved the last straw for the Karmapa. In late December, the Karmapa, by then fourteen years old and a strapping six feet tall, announced that he was going into retreat. On 26 December, he climbed out of his bedroom window and ran to a waiting car. With his elder sister, a Buddhist nun and three attendants, he fled towards the border with Nepal. Eight days later, after crossing the Himalayas—and the border—on foot in the depths of winter, the Karmapa and his little party arrived in Dharamsala.

"You must be very tired," said the Dalai Lama when he greeted his unannounced guest.

"I am," replied the Karmapa.

The Karmapa's flight caused a worldwide sensation. The Chinese government at first denied that he had fled, but it soon became evident that the Karmapa wished to stay in India. It was an embarrassing humiliation for Beijing.

I saw the Dalai Lama again, several times, and we discussed the sad end of a story that had begun with such high hopes. He was grieved by the outcome and worried about the little Panchen Lama. He felt the Chinese were capable of anything, even of doing him physical harm. And even if the boy was not in physical danger, he pointed out, he was certainly being deprived of the religious education that he needed to assume his proper place in the chain of belief. I asked the Dalai Lama if he now regretted making the announcement which had precipitated the final crisis.

'No,' he replied, 'no regrets. I waited several months after finalizing my choice, trying to communicate with the Chinese. Then I conducted my own religious investigation as to whether I should make the announcement, and it was positive. So I have no regrets.' Months later, when I again broached the subject with the Dalai Lama, he briefly revealed how much personal anguish the whole affair, with its harsh consequences for Chadrel Rinpoche and the other Tibetans who had tried to follow their spiritual conscience, had cost him.

'I feel,' he said, 'that I committed the crime here, and they took the punishment there.'

I asked him if he would have delayed the announcement if his advisers inside Tibet had asked him to – as, indeed, I had discovered they had wished him to do.

'Yes,' said the Dalai Lama, 'because they are the ones who are living that difficult situation.'

That moment had passed. There was no point in reflecting on how it might have turned out, if Chadrel had been able to carry through his last attempt to influence events.

'Now,' the Dalai Lama resumed, 'my main concern is whether the Panchen Lama's life is safe. Even if he isn't physically harmed, I am anxious because in Communist countries, they sometimes put prisoners in a psychiatric hospital and use medication to make them dull, to make them lose interest in life.'

There was another wider consequence of the search for the Panchen Lama – the future of the institution of the Dalai Lama. The fourteenth Dalai Lama had played a difficult and complicated role for his people, acting as the focus of their memories and their hopes. Without him and the world-wide respect and attention he brings to the fate of his people, the Chinese ambition to obliterate the memory of a separate Tibet would undoubtedly be easier.

When the fourteenth Dalai Lama dies, the question will be who, in this now fragmented political and religious world, will have the authority to identify his successor. Had the eleventh Panchen Lama been identified without dispute and entered religious life unchallenged, then his voice would have carried the authority of continuity and universal respect. Now, that hope is gone. The Dalai Lama's choice, Gedhun Choekyi Nyima, may never emerge from the shadows of his confinement. A boy identified by the Chinese Panchen Lama would carry no weight with the exile Tibetans or their religious institutions. What future is there, then, for the supreme Tibetan institution, the Dalai Lama?

The present Dalai Lama has often said that he might be the last of the line, a prediction that seems, if anything, to have been strengthened by the Panchen Lama dispute. I asked him why he foresaw the end of the institution.

'I don't think it matters whether the institution of the Dalai Lama stays or not,' he replied, 'it's up to the Tibetan people. If in twenty years' time they feel it is irrelevant, then there will be no more dalai lamas.' He beamed, and continued, 'Sometimes I think this present stupid Dalai Lama, this Buddhist monk, may not be the best, but he's not the worst either. I think it might be better to make a dignified farewell in case some other Dalai Lama comes along and disgraces himself.' He burst out laughing, then resumed. 'But if there is another Dalai Lama, I have made it clear that the next reincarnation will certainly appear outside Chinese control.'

If that were to happen, though, without the authority of the Panchen Lama to settle any potential dispute, how would the next Dalai Lama be identified?

The Panchen Lama, he agreed, would normally have an important say in the identification of the next incarnation of the Dalai Lama. 'But under the present circumstances, without free will and freedom of spiritual practice,' he added, 'it's very difficult.'

As he looked at the photograph of Gedhun Choekyi Nyima, I asked him what he imagined the child was feeling. He sighed. 'I don't know. As a human being, he will feel frustration and fear, and I think he will have a lot of questions. When I look at his photograph, I feel very sorry that he should have become a political prisoner through no fault of his own. I think every human being has a responsibility to do something.'

The freedom of Gedhun Choekyi Nyima has now joined the list of causes for which Tibetan exiles and their supporters campaign. But while supporters around the world gear up for repeated petitions, postcards and letter-writing campaigns on behalf of the child they call the world's 'youngest political prisoner', the Dalai Lama remains, at one level, serene. If the child is the correct choice, as he believes him to be, then he remains the Panchen Lama, whatever happens.

Others were less sanguine. I asked a well-informed Tibetan in Beijing what he thought the Chinese would do with the child.

'If I were them,' he replied, 'I would bring him up stupid.'

Appendix:
The Panchen Lama's Petition

✿

The Panchen Lama's petition provides an extraordinary and detailed critique of the 'mistakes' of the Chinese Communist Party in central Tibet, Amdo and Kham and gives clear warning of further disasters to follow if the Party does not change its approach. While the Panchen Lama is careful to emphasize his loyalty to the Party's principles and leadership, at the same time he offers a detailed analysis of the shortcomings of the Party machine. Throughout the text he points to the wide gap that exists between the Party's stated aims and its practice. For instance, in central Tibet, he writes, the 'pacification' that followed the rebellion of 1959 had been indiscriminate and unfair. Those who surrendered had 'suffered violent struggle sessions, arrests and imprisonment' and there had been no effort to distinguish between ringleaders and those who had been deceived or coerced into rebellion. The rebellion, he pointed out, had been unnecessarily prolonged as a result.

On agricultural reform in central Tibet, the Panchen Lama pointed out that successive campaigns had been marred by arbitrary behaviour. Innocent people had been falsely charged with crimes that cadres had fabricated. 'If I give as an example,' he wrote, 'the fabrications directed against myself and other individuals who, despite being well known as patriots and progressives, have still been regarded as reactionaries, then there is no need even to mention what other people have had to put up with.'

Land distribution, too, had been carried out unfairly and many households had had their land wrongly confiscated. The categorization of people according to their class background – a critical procedure for the people involved – had also been indiscriminate and, he wrote, 'cadres' have acted rashly and, not caring whether punishment is correct or not, have . . . branded as feudal lords or their associates the vast majority of those who in the past served as village heads, township leaders or served in temples,' despite their widely varying circumstances.

In the notorious struggle sessions, cadres had failed to get the political message across to the people and had recruited large numbers of poor-quality activists. People did not understand the political theory because there were no documents in Tibetan and the cadres were too lazy to make themselves understood. Untrained activists were encouraged to be violent and were rewarded with the confiscated possessions of their victims. Some activists, he said, were themselves criminals who were trying to conceal either the wrong class background or past crimes by their activism.

Many innocent people had been beaten in 'struggle sessions'. If they had committed no crimes, the Panchen Lama wrote, they, too, were falsely accused. Allegations of crime were not investigated in struggle sessions because the purpose of the exercise was to incite the mob to attack the victim. Many people died in the course of such sessions, and many innocent people had fled the country and others committed suicide as a result of them.

The Party's excessive grain confiscations, the Panchen Lama pointed out, had led to starvation in central Tibet for the first time in its history:

This is a grave matter and totally unnecessary. Although Tibet was in the past a society under the barbarous rule of feudalism, grain was never this scarce. This was especially due to the wide influence of Buddhism, which ensured that everyone, no matter if they were noble or humble, had the good custom of aiding the poor. People could live by begging for food, and it wasn't possible for someone to starve to death. We have never heard of such an occurrence.

On the conditions in labour camps, he complained that there were too many prisoners and only a few jailers treated them according to the law. The rest subjected the prisoners to a range of abuses and ill treatment. The Panchen Lama complained that officials paid

[N]o attention to the lives or the health of the prisoners and intimidate them or beat them without reason. The prisoners are intentionally moved back and forth, from high altitude to low altitude and from warm areas to cold areas, so that they cannot acclimatize. They are inadequately housed and fed and required to perform backbreaking labour, their health deteriorates . . . and a large number die. Many prisoners appear to have been executed and many have been jailed with no effort made to establish their guilt or innocence.

On the sufferings of the religious sector, the Panchen Lama described what he called 'an insane and violent opposition to [religion]':

Those people who openly express their religious beliefs are labelled as superstitious and accused of disliking revolution. They suffer unbearable attacks and struggle sessions . . . When lamas are asked if they will return to secular life, if they wish to continue to serve as lamas, they are told, 'You still haven't eradicated your superstitions through education.' They then undergo violent struggle. Under these conditions, unless they are extremely strong-minded, they cannot possibly admit that they want to serve as lamas. Thus, even those lamas who are sixty or seventy years old ask to be allowed to return to secular life. These individuals have no way of establishing a family or of engaging in production, nor do they really wish to leave the monastery in which they have spent most of their lives.

This is all common knowledge. The fact that these people have to return home is evidence of the serious problem that they find it impossible to stay in the monasteries. In some monasteries the work teams draw up a list of lamas who are to return to secular life. Even more serious than this is that they have the lamas stand on one side, and the Buddhist nuns on the other, and they are then forced to select someone from the other side.

This is totally at odds with the law, which guarantees citizens' rights and the equal rights of men and women, and which does not permit any interference in these matters. In remote mountain monasteries there are many people who devote their whole lives to self-cultivation. They are devout religious disciples, who have no interest in affairs of the world. Because the revolutionary cause is a thing of human society, very few of them welcome it, or have any enthusiasm for it . . . However, the cadres believe that they are incorrigibly obstinate and reactionary, and many of these religious disciples have been put under surveillance or imprisoned . . .

Innumerable Buddhist figures, sutras and pagodas have been burnt to the ground, thrown into rivers, demolished or melted. There has been

307

reckless and frenzied destruction of temples, *mani* walls and pagodas. Many ornamental Buddhist figures have been stolen, along with many other valuable items. Those institutions purchasing non-ferrous metals have paid no attention as to the metal's origins and this attitude has encouraged the destruction of Buddhist figures, pagodas and other objects that contain these metals, with the result that temples look as if they have been hit by artillery shells during wartime.

In addition, there have been quite open insults against the religion. For instance Tibetan Buddhist classics have been used as material for compost and very many painted Buddhist images and classics have been used for manufacturing shoes ... There have been actions committed that even a lunatic would find difficulty doing. People at all levels of Tibetan society are shocked and their state of mind is extremely unsettled and dejected ...

Before democratic reform in Tibet, there were over 2,500 large, medium and small temples, but after democratic reform, only seventy were left by the government, a reduction of more than 97 per cent. Because there is no one resident in the majority of temples, there is no one to take care of the monasteries' shrine room and monks' lodgings. Massive damage has been inflicted by man or nature resulting in the temples being in a condition of collapse or near-collapse.

In the past, the total number of monks and nuns totalled more than 110,000. Of these, possibly 10,000 fled abroad, leaving a remainder of 100,000. After the completion of democratic reform, there were around seven thousand remaining in the monasteries, a reduction of 93 per cent.

Apart from in the Tashilhunpo monastery, which is an exception, the quality of the remainder of monks and nuns is generally low. As I described above, the religious intellectuals and spiritual masters who carry out religious work were attacked to such an extent during the democratic reform period they couldn't live in peace, and so now they do not live in the temples, or only a very few of them do. In actual fact, the temples have already lost their purpose and significance as religious institutions.

As far as Tibetan language and culture was concerned, the Panchen Lama complained that Tibetans were forbidden to wear their traditional dress and that misguided efforts at language reform had resulted in changes to the written language that had rendered it incomprehensible to Tibetans outside central Tibet:

[A]rrogant individuals with only poor ability in Tibetan, together with those who fawn on them, have ranted and raved, calling 'incorrect', and 'imperfect', the commonly used written language and the studies by scholars throughout history who have studied the Tibetan writing systems . . . In addition, the central government has adopted the dialect of Tibetan spoken in Lhasa as the standard for Tibet, but has allowed into the written language various speech sounds that are not in accordance with the standard dialect. Therefore, people who speak Lhasa dialect can understand but others cannot. In addition, secretaries and teachers of the Tibetan language in areas such as Qinghai, Gansu, Sichuan and Yunnan all use their respective dialects as the means of spoken communication and these dialects have to some extent entered the written language. This means that people who can speak those dialects can understand what has been written, but anybody else will not be able to understand completely the meaning of what has been written. Thus the unity of the Tibetan written language has been lost.

If the language, clothes, ornaments and customs of a nationality disappear within a short period of time, then that nationality also disappears with it, or changes into a different nationality.

The most shocking passages in the petition describes the abuses and starvation that the Panchen Lama had discovered in the area the Tibetans call Amdo, including the Panchen Lama's home province of Qinghai and the neighbouring province of Gansu. Immediately after the revolution of 1949, he said, conditions improved in the area, but then, he complained, as a result of the Chinese reforms, there were several rebellions. After the rebellions, he said, 'the majority of men were imprisoned.'

Then, when the People's Communes were established, 'the population was deprived even of its everyday possessions, production targets were set unrealistically high and, when they were not met, disaster followed.' The Panchen blamed the cadres 'who regard themselves as perfect with not a single fault' for the disaster. They had, he said, 'become lords sitting on the necks of the people'. The cadres did not understand agricultural and pastoral production. 'They are greedy and covetous, coercing and ordering the people to rise early and go to sleep later in order to participate in labour. Meetings are crammed into the period when the people are not labouring,' he complained.

As the Great Leap Forward began, the Panchen Lama complained, local officials competed with each other to report larger and larger harvests, which meant that the government claimed ever increasing amounts of grain at a time when yields were actually falling:

As regards production targets, the higher authorities, out of their desire to increase production, increased the production targets to unattainable levels, with no thought being paid to the actual productive capacity of grass roots production lines, or to the feelings of the majority of the masses regarding production. If people in authority at the lower levels say that there is no way that these targets can be achieved, then they are labelled as conservative elements, sticking to old ways, who have not liberated their thinking. They are told they do not acknowledge objective laws, that they are unscientific and unwilling to make the Great Leap Forward and so are struggled against ... The Great Leap Forward is written and talked about, but it is not necessarily true in practice. Also, during the past few years, agricultural and pastoral production has been hit by many disasters, both natural and manmade, so it is difficult to come close to the production targets boasted of by the cadres. Many cadres are afraid that they will be punished if it is discovered that what has been produced falls far short of their boasts, so they claim in their reports that: 'We have already exceeded the production targets set by the higher authorities. They have been successfully achieved.' The higher authorities do not investigate these statements and thinking themselves clever, they pretend they know what they don't and pile praise upon those who speak pretty lies. This causes the practice of boasts and exaggeration to increase on a large scale.

As the cadres reported ever-increasing yields, the Panchen Lama discovered, the rations of the peasants had been steadily cut:

Working people say that one person gets a monthly grain ration of only 10 jin [1 jin = ½ kg], but there are people in some areas that don't even get that much. After the communal canteens were set up, the masses were forced to go, whether they agreed or not, and so the people didn't even know if that amount of grain ration was sufficient or not. Because of the extremely small grain rations, there has not been enough food to sustain life, and the people started to starve. Therefore dregs of fat and wheat husks that were previously used for cattle fodder became the people's food, even though there are virtually no nutrients in it. The people running the canteens, in order to make the people's food heavier with the purpose of relieving hunger for a day, gather up much that is virtually inedible – all kinds of grasses, and even such inedible things as tree bark, leaves, grass seeds and roots. After processing, they mix them with the small amount of grain to turn it into gruel like pig feed and give it to the people to eat. But even this is in limited amounts, and does not satisfy hunger.

The people cannot resist this cruel torment, and the health of the masses is getting weaker day by day. In some areas a percentage of people have been dying in large numbers, catching a common cold or other very minor infections. In some other areas, many people have starved to death because their grain supply has been cut off. In some areas, there have been cases of whole households starving to death. The mortality rate is critical. This is all because there is insufficient food and so people have died, and in fact everyone is starving.

Notes

✣

CHAPTER TWO

1. Frank Moraes, *Revolt in Tibet*, p. 35
2. Li Tieh-tseng, *Tibet: today and yesterday*, p. 10
3. Charles Bell, *Tibet, Past and Present*, p. 24
4. Ibid., p. 30
5. C. R. Bawden, *The Modern History of Mongolia*, pp. 29ff.
6. Joseph Head and S. L. Cranston, *Reincarnation, an East-West Anthology*, Julian Press, New York, 1961, p. 42
7. *Gallic War*, book 4, ch. 13, quoted ibid.
8. Ya Hanzhang, *Biographies of the Dalai Lamas*
9. Bawden, op. cit.
10. Ibid.
11. Ya Hanzhang, op. cit.
12. Melvyn C. Goldstein, *A History of Modern Tibet, 1913–1951: the demise of the Lamaist state*
13. Literally, 'the Palace of Happiness', a college within Drepung monastery which was the seat of government in the seventeenth century. The term continued to be used for the government of Tibet until the Chinese invasion.

CHAPTER THREE

1. K. Dhondup, *Songs of the Sixth Dalai Lama*

CHAPTER FOUR

1. Parshotam Mehra, *Tibetan Polity, 1904–37: the conflict between the 13th Dalai Lama and the 9th Panchen Lama*, p. 3
2. Ya Hanzhang, *Biographies of the Tibetan Spiritual Leaders: Panchen Erdenis*
3. Ibid.

4. The numeration of the panchen lamas is in itself contentious. According to the scholar Hugh Richardson (*Tibet and Its History*, p. 55), the Tibetans consider the ninth Panchen to be the sixth in succession from Lobsang Choekyi Gyaltsen, the teacher on whom the fifth Dalai Lama first bestowed the title. The higher numbering is the result of calculating that two abbots of Tashilhunpo before Lobsang Choekyi Gyaltsen and one of Tsongkhapa's disciples were all earlier incarnations of the Panchen Lama. Richardson argues that Tibetan records show that none of these persons was considered in his lifetime to be an incarnation of any holy person. For many Tibetans, therefore, the Panchen Lama who died in 1989 was the seventh, not the tenth, and the larger number is considered a Chinese aberration. However, for the sake of simplicity, I have adopted the practice of numbering Lobsang Choekyi the fourth in the line and subsequent incarnations accordingly. The higher numeration was also preferred by the Panchen Lama's *labrang*, though not by Lhasa.

5. Ya Hanzhang, *Panchen Erdenis*, op. cit.

6. HH Dalai Lama, *Freedom in Exile*

CHAPTER FIVE

1. Clements R. Markham (ed.), *Narratives of the Mission of George Bogle to Tibet and of the Journey of Thomas Manning to Lhasa*

2. Ibid.

3. Ya Hanzhang, *Panchen Erdenis*, op. cit.

4. Ibid.

5. Li, op. cit.

6. Charles Bell, *Portrait of the Dalai Lama*

7. John Snelling, *Buddhism in Russia, the story of Agvan Dorzhiev, Lhasa's emissary to the Tsar*, p. 11

8. Ibid., p. 133

9. Imperial decree, February 1910, trans. Teichman (1922:16–17 from *Government Gazette*)

10. Bell, op. cit., p. 132

11. Richardson, op. cit., p. 125

12. Mehra, op. cit., p. 43

13. Goldstein, op. cit.

CHAPTER SIX

1. Snelling, op. cit.
2. Ibid.
3. Bawden, op. cit., p. 270
4. Ibid., p. 317
5. Testament of the 13th Dalai Lama, quoted in Goldstein, op. cit.
6. Mehra, op. cit.

CHAPTER SEVEN

1. Peter Fleming, *News from Tartary, a journey from Peking to Kashmir*
2. Jampal Gyatso, *Banshen Dashi (Great Master Panchen)*. Professor Jampal Gyatso's memoir of the tenth Panchen Lama was published in Chinese in 1989. It is one of the most complete accounts available of the life of the tenth Panchen Lama, but it was later withdrawn from circulation. I have used both the original Chinese and an unpublished English translation, by kind permission of the translator, Rachel Schlesinger.
3. Ibid.
4. Ibid.
5. Ibid.
6. Ibid.
7. Khamtroul Rinpoche, interview with author, Dharamsala, 1994

CHAPTER EIGHT

1. Ya Hanzhang, *Panchen Erdenis*, op. cit., p. 310
2. Gyatso, op. cit.
3. Ibid.
4. Quoted in Goldstein, op. cit.
5. Francis Watson, *The Frontiers of China*, Chatto and Windus, London 1966, p. 54
6. Heather Stoddard, 'Tibetan Publications and National Identity', in *Resistance and Reform in Tibet*, R. Barnett and S. Akiner (eds.)
7. Ya Hanzhang, *Panchen Erdenis*, op. cit.

CHAPTER NINE

1. 22 April Conference on the Establishment of the Preparatory Committee of the TAR opened in Lhasa. Chen Yi said: 'According to the constitution, all nationalities in our country will make their way into a socialist society through different channels. It is inevitable for each nationality to undergo necessary internal reforms if it wants to stamp out its backwardness and go for political, economic and cultural development . . . The Communist Party of China and the central People's government believe that only when the leaders and people of Tibet unanimously request and decide to reform can reforms be carried out in Tibet; no other nationality can possibly carry it out on their behalf.' Quoted in Gyatso, op. cit., p. 90
2. Ibid., p. 132
3. Ibid., p. 119
4. HH Dalai Lama, *My Land and My People*
5. Gyatso, op. cit.
6. Ibid.
7. Ibid.
8. HH Dalai Lama, *Freedom in Exile*, op. cit.
9. Gyatso, op. cit.
10. Ibid.
11. For a longer exposition of the Panchen Lama's attitudes, see the Panchen Lama's 70,000-character petition.
12. Sonam Topgyal, 'Panchen Lama: a patriot despite Chinese manipulation', *Tibetan Bulletin*, Mar–Apr 1992
13. Gyatso, op. cit.

CHAPTER TEN

1. A reliquary or stupa.
2. Gyatso, op. cit.
3. The Panchen Lama's petition. A summary of the contents of the Panchen Lama's petition can be found in the appendix to this book. The complete text has been published by the Tibet Information Network under the title *A Poisoned Arrow*.
4. Ibid.
5. Ibid.
6. Ibid.

7. Gyatso, op. cit.
8. Ibid.
9. Ibid. Jasper Becker describes a similar, or possibly another version, of the same incident involving 5,000 young people from Henan province sent to nearby Tongren county. *Hungry Ghosts*, pp. 167–8
10. Interview with the author, Dharamsala, 1994
11. Gyatso, op. cit.
12. Ibid.
13. Panchen Lama's petition, op. cit.

CHAPTER ELEVEN

1. Panchen Lama's address to the TAR Standing Committee Meeting of the National People's Congress, Beijing, 28 March 1987. Full text published in *The Panchen Lama Speaks* by the Department of Information and International Relations, Dharamsala, November 1991

CHAPTER TWELVE

1. Ronald Schwartz, 'Resistance and Reform in Tibet 1987–1990', in Barnett and Akiner, op. cit.
2. Ibid.

CHAPTER THIRTEEN

1. Reported in *The Times*, 11 March 1989
2. *Ta Kung Pao*, 26 January 1989. Full text appeared in *Summary of World Broadcasts*, 15 February 1989
3. *The Times*, 26 January 1989, quoting a report in the *China Daily*
4. Interview with the author, 1994
5. Ibid.
6. *Hong Kong Standard*, 5 February 1989
7. *Economist*, vol. 310, issue 7588, 4 February 1989
8. Xinhua news agency, 29 January 1989
9. *China Daily*, 5 February 1989
10. *South China Morning Post*, 16 February 1989
11. Ibid.
12. Author's interview with exiled monk, 1995

CHAPTER FOURTEEN

1. TIN, 17 August 1990
2. *Guardian*, interview with Agya Rinpoche, December 1990
3. Xinhua news agency, 26 September 1992
4. TIN, 19 July 1990
5. Robert Barnett, 'Cutting off the Serpent's Head', report for TIN, March 1996
6. Ibid.
7. Ibid.

CHAPTER FIFTEEN

1. *Dorje*, the emblem of the indestructible reality of buddhahood, is a sceptre-like object that is held in the hand while a ritual bell is held in the left.
2. TIN new update, 14 March 1995

CHAPTER SEVENTEEN

1. TIN background briefing no. 25
2. Ibid.
3. TIN news update, 7 April 1995

CHAPTER EIGHTEEN

1. *Tibetan Bulletin*, Jan–Feb 1996
2. TIN Update, 11 June 1995
3. *Rag sdig*, Chinese: Raidi
4. Also named Thubten Kalsang

CHAPTER NINETEEN

1. TIN report, 21 September 1995
2. TIN report, 4 August 1997
3. TIN report, 12 November 1995
4. *Bardo* (in Sanskrit *antarabhava*) is the interval between death and rebirth

5. Panchen Lama's last speech, translated by TIN, document no. 15 (VN)
6. TIN Update, 11 August 1995
7. TIN report, 'Anti-Abbot Campaign Begins', 11 August 1995
8. *South China Morning Post*, 5 January 1996

CHAPTER TWENTY

1. TIN Update, 22 June 1997
2. Amnesty International Report, 27 May 1997
3. *Tibet Daily*, reported by Reuter, 27 January 1997
4. TIN Update, 7 April 1995
5. *South China Morning Post*, 15 November 1997

Suggested Further Reading

✺

Avedon, John F. (1984): *In Exile from the Land of Snows*, Michael Joseph, London

Barnett, Robert and Akiner, Shirin (eds.) (1994): *Resistance and Reform in Tibet*. 1st edn. Hurst and Company, London

Bass, Catriona (1992): *Inside the Treasure House, a time in Tibet*. 3rd edn. Abacus, London

Bawden, C. R. (1968): *The Modern History of Mongolia*. 1st edn. Weidenfeld and Nicolson, London

Becker, Jasper (1996): *Hungry Ghosts*. 1st edn. Vol. 1. John Murray, London

Bell, Charles (1946): *Portrait of the Dalai Lama*. 1st edn. Collins, London

Bell, Charles (1992): *Tibet Past and Present*. Reprint. Asian Educational Services, New Delhi

Bharati, Agehanando (1974): *Fictitious Tibet, the origin and persistence of Rampaism*. *Tibet Journal*

Bishop, Peter (1993): *Dreams of Power, Tibetan Buddhism and the Western Imagination*. Athlone Press, London

Byron, Robert (1933): *First Russia then Tibet*. 1st edn. Macmillan and Co., London

Craig, Mary (1992): *Tears of Blood, a cry for Tibet*. 3rd edn. Indus, New Delhi

Dalai Lama (1962): *My Land and My People*. 1st edn. Weidenfeld and Nicolson, London

Dalai Lama (1990): *Freedom in Exile*. 1st edn. Hodder and Stoughton, London

Dalai Lama (1991): *Freedom in Exile*. 2nd edn. Rupa Paperback, New Delhi

David-Neel, Alexandra (1991): *My Journey to Lhasa*. 3rd edn. Time Books International, New Delhi

Dhondup, K. (1981): *Songs of the Sixth Dalai Lama*. 2nd edn. Library of Tibetan Works and Archives, Dharamsala

Dhondup, K. (1986): *The Water Bird and Other Years, a history of the*

13th Dalai Lama and after. 1st edn. Rangwang Publishers, New Delhi

Fleming, Peter (1936): *News from Tartary.* Jonathan Cape, London

Ford, Robert (1958): *Captured in Tibet.* Pan Books, London

Franke, H. (1981): *Tibetans in Yuan China.* In *China under Mongol Rule* (ed. Langlois)

French, Patrick (1994): *Younghusband, the last great imperial adventurer.* 1st edn. HarperCollins, London

Gernet, Jacques (1959): *Daily Life in China on the Eve of the Mongol Invasion.* Stanford University Press, Stanford

Ginsburgs, George and Mathos, Michael (1964): *Communist China and Tibet.* The Hague

Goldstein, Melvyn C. (1989): *A History of Modern Tibet 1913–1951.* University of California Press, Berkeley, California

Grunfeld, Tom (1987): *The Making of Modern Tibet.* Zed Press, London

Gyatso, Jampal (1990): *Banshen Dashi (Great Master Panchen).* Dongfang Chubanshe, Beijing

Gyatso, Palden (with Tsering Shakya) (1997): *Fire under the Snow.* Harvill, London

Harrer, Heinrich (1955): *Seven Years in Tibet.* 2nd edn. Reprint Society, London

Haslund, Henning (1935): *Men and Gods in Mongolia.* Kegan, Paul, Trench, Trubner and Co., London

Heberer, Thomas (1981): *China and Its National Minorities, Autonomy or Assimilation.* 1st edn. Vol. 1. M. E. Sharpe, New York

International Commission of Jurists (1960): *Tibet and the People's Republic of China.* Geneva

Kelly, Petra K., Bastian, Gerd and Aiello, Pat (eds.) (1991): *The Anguish of Tibet.* 1st edn. Parallax Press, Berkeley, California

Lamb, Alastair (1960): *Britain and Chinese Central Asia.* 1st edn. Routledge and Kegan Paul, London

Lamb, Alastair (1989): *Tibet, China and India 1914–1950.* 1st edn. Roxford Books, Hertingfordbury

Langlois, J. D. (ed.) (1981): *China under Mongol Rule.* Princeton, New York

Levenson, Claude B. (1988): *The Dalai Lama, a biography.* 1st edn. Unwin Hyman, London

Li, Tieh-tseng (1960): *Tibet: today and yesterday.* Bookman Associates, New York

Mackerras, Colin (1994): *China's Minorities, Integration and Modernisation in the Twentieth Century*. 1st edn. Vol. 1. Oxford University Press, Hong Kong

Maillart, Ella K. (1937): *Forbidden Journey, from Peking to Kashmir*. William Heinemann, London

Markham, Clements R. (ed.) (1989): *Narratives of the Mission of George Bogle to Tibet and of the journey of Thomas Manning to Lhasa*. 3rd edn. Cosmo Publishing, New Delhi

McKay, Alex (1997): *Tibet and the British Raj*. Curzon Press, Richmond

Mehra, Parshotam (1969): *The Younghusband Expedition, an interpretation*. 1st edn. Asia Publishing House, London

Mehra, Parshotam (1976): *Tibetan Polity, 1904–37: the conflict between the 13th Dalai Lama and the 9th Panchen*. 1st edn. Otto Harrassowitz, Weisbaden

Michael, F. (1982): *Rule by Incarnation: Tibetan Buddhism and its role in society and state*. Boulder, Colorado

Moraes, Frank (1960): *Revolt in Tibet*. 1st edn. Macmillan, New York

Morgan, David (1986): *The Mongols*. 1st edn. Blackwell, Oxford

Norbu, Dawa (1987): *Red Star over Tibet*. Sterling Publishers, New Delhi

Norbu, Jamyang (1986): *Warriors of Tibet 1986*. Wisdom Publications, London

Norbu, Thubten Jigme and Harrer, Heinrich (1961): *Tibet is My Country*. 1st edn. Readers Union Rupert Hart-Davis, London

Norbu, Thubten Jigme and Turnbull, Colin (1976): *Tibet*. 3rd edn. Penguin Books, London

Panchen Lama (1997): *A Poisoned Arrow, the secret report of the 10th Panchen Lama*. 1st edn. Tibet Information Network, London

Richardson, Hugh (1962): *Tibet and Its History*. Oxford University Press, Oxford

Rockhill, W. (1910): *The Dalai Lamas of Lhasa and Their Relations with the Manchu Emperors of China 1644–1908*. T'oung Pao X1

Roerich, Nicholas (1997): *Shambhala*. Reprinted. Aravali Books International, New Delhi

Schwartz, Ronald D. (1994): *Circle of Protest, political ritual in the Tibetan uprising*. 1st edn. Hurst, London

Shakabpa, W. D. (1984): *Tibet, a political history*. 3rd edn. Potala Publications, New York

Shakya, Tsering (1998): *The Dragon in the Land of Snows*. 1st edn. Pimlico, London

Snelling, John (1993): *Buddhism in Russia, the story of Agvan Dorzhiev, Lhasa's emissary to the Tsar*. 1st edn. Element, Longmead, Shaftesbury, Dorset

Teichman, Sir Eric (1922): *Travels of a Consular Officer in Eastern Tibet*. Cambridge University Press, Cambridge

Thomas Jr, Lowell (1960): *The Silent War in Tibet*. 1st edn. Secker and Warburg, London

Van Walt van Praag, Michael C. (1987): *The Status of Tibet, history, rights and prospects in international law*. 1st edn. Westview Press, Boulder, Colorado

Verrier, Anthony (1991): *Francis Younghusband and the Great Game*. Jonathan Cape, London

Waddell, L. (1905): *Lhasa and Its Mysteries*. John Murray, London

Waddell, L. (1972): *Tibetan Buddhism*. Dover Publications, New York

Wang, Furen and Suo, Wenqing (1984): *Highlights of Tibetan History*. 1st edn. New World Press, Beijing

Winnington, Alan (1957): *Tibet*. Lawrence and Wishart, London

Ya, Hanzhang (1991): *Biographies of the Dalai Lamas*. 1st edn. Foreign Languages Press, Beijing

Ya, Hanzhang (1994): *Biographies of the Tibetan Spiritual Leaders, Panchen Erdenis*. Paperback edn. Foreign Languages Press, Beijing

Index

✧

Principle figures have been indexed chronologically for the convenience of the reader.